History of Middlesex County, New Jersey, 1664-1920

John P. b. 1867 Wall, Harold E. Pickersgill

HISTORY

OF

MIDDLESEX COUNTY

NEW JERSEY

1664—1920

UNDER THE ASSOCIATE EDITORSHIP

of

JOHN P WALL AND HAROLD E PICKERSGILL

ASSISTED BY AN

ABLE CORPS OF LOCAL HISTORIANS

HISTORICAL —BIOGRAPHICAL

VOLUME III

1921

LEWIS HISTORICAL PUBLISHING COMPANY, INC

NEW YORK AND CHICAGO

BIOGRAPHICAL

D.C.Chase

BIOGRAPHICAL

PETER FRANCIS DALY, the County Judge of the county of Middlesex, has been one of the foremost and most forceful leaders in the civic, professional and governmental life of this historic county since his very early manhood, and his prestige with its people generally and their esteem and affection for him have constantly grown stronger and deeper with the years. First elevated to this position of large responsibility as well as power by Governor Woodrow Wilson in April, 1911, he was reappointed by Governor James F. Fielder in 1916, and again in 1921 by Governor Edward I. Edwards—three terms in succession, a record in this respect unprecedented in the history of the office, in this county at least.

He was born in New York City on May 19, 1867, son of Timothy Edward and Catharine (O'Grady) Daly, natives of the County Galway, Ireland. The family moved to New Brunswick when he was seven years of age, and there he has since resided. He attended St. Peter's Parochial School and later the Livingston Avenue High School. At the age of seventeen he entered the law office of Senator James H. Van Cleef, and in November, 1888, was admitted to the New Jersey bar, being then in his twenty-first year. Soon afterward he became a partner in the law firm of Van Cleef, Daly & Woodbridge, the other members being Senator Van Cleef, and the Hon. Freeman Woodbridge, now judge of the District Court of the city of New Brunswick. This partnership continued for three years, and since then he has continued the general practice of his profession alone.

During the first ten years of Judge Daly in the general practice of the law, he was engaged in most of the important criminal cases tried in Middlesex county, but since has given his attention almost entirely to the practice of the other branches of the law. Because of his nineteen years experience in the surrogate's office and ten years as judge of the Orphans' Court, he is recognized by the profession as a specialist in matters of probate law and procedure. He has also had an unusually wide experience and practice in municipal law. He was county counsel for four years from May, 1899, and was the attorney who directed the incorporations of the boroughs of South River, Roosevelt and Spotswood, and has been the counsel for those municipalities as well as for the townships of Piscataway, Raritan, Monroe, East Brunswick and Sayreville, and the borough of Helmetta. Since its organization in 1895, he has been counsel to the Workingmen's Building and Loan Association of New Brunswick, New Jersey, one of the most progressive and substantial corporations of the kind in the State.

Judge Daly's first elective public office was that of alderman of the Sixth Ward of New Brunswick. The vote for him in the ward where he had lived since childhood was three hundred above the next highest candidate on his ticket. During his term of two years on the board of aldermen 1894 to 1896, he was its leader and the chairman of the finance committee This period included what was called the "great refunding year," the most important epoch in the financial history of the city up to that time He was also chairman of the sewerage committee and in that position he established the beginning of a general sewerage system in his own ward—the Sixth, personally securing the right of way for the trunk line over private properties, more than a mile in length, and without a cent's cost to the city Because of the increase of other public and professional duties he could not accept a reelection, though the same was assured to him without opposition.

He was deputy-surrogate of the county of Middlesex during the two terms of the Honorable Leonard Furman as surrogate from 1892 to 1902, and succeeded him through election to the office of surrogate He was elected twice, and at his election in 1902 he ran nine hundred votes ahead of his ticket and at his reelection in 1907 he was eighteen hundred votes ahead of his ticket There was over a year and a half of his second term left when he was made county judge by Governor Wilson

During the period of the World-wide War, Peter Francis Daly, through the profoundly efficient discharge of the broad and varied duties of his high official county position—made abnormally onerous and exacting by the extraordinary conditions of the times, through his distinctive genius in the work of organizing popular movements, his tireless energy, his stirring eloquence and his strong hold upon the imagination and good will of the people and their admiration for the intensity and zeal of his Americanism, was indisputably the most outstanding leader and chief spokesman of America's cause in this county of one hundred and sixty-eight thousand people and which embraces within its confines so many different racial strains

Judge Daly was chairman of the county legal advisory board, with former Senator Theodore Strong and Judge Freeman Woodbridge as associate members This board, under authority of the United States government, had the general supervision and direction of the Selective Service Law as well as many other serious duties confidentially as well as publicly assigned to them He organized the Patriotic Force of the city of New Brunswick, composed of five representatives from each of one hundred and twenty-six distinct organizations of the county seat and its immediate vicinity, representative of all that went to make up the civic, religious social fraternal, industrial, professional, educational, mercantile and financial life of the territory and making a powerful unity and cohesion of every element of the community He was active in the executive work and direction of all the Liberty Loan Drives and of the campaigns of the Red Cross, Y. M C A. and Salvation Army, and was chairman of the Knights of Columbus War Drive and treasurer of the Jewish Relief War Drive and a director of the United War Drive

Judge Daly is a Democrat, and for twenty years before he went on the bench was second to none in his constant, prominent and arduous activities and labors in the organization, councils and leadership of the party, and throughout all that time was recognizedly its leading advocate on the public platform For a number of years he was chairman of the Middlesex County Democratic Executive Committee

Upon the organization of the present Middlesex County Bar Association, Judge Daly was unanimously elected its first president, and has since actively continued his membership therein he is also a member of the American Bar Association He was the founder and first grand knight of New Brunswick Council of the Knights of Columbus, and is a charter member and past exalted ruler of the New Brunswick Lodge of Elks and is a member of the Royal Arcanum For a number of years he was an officer of the University Extension Society of Rutgers College, and is on the executive committee of the Dante Society of the city of New Brunswick His clubs are the Union New Brunswick Country Club, also the East Jersey Club of Perth Amboy and the old Colony of New York City, of which latter he is a director He is a member of St Peter's Roman Catholic Church

After ten years' service on the bench, the reappointment of Judge Daly was generally and earnestly urged from every section of the county and by people in every walk in life and Governor Edwards made the reappointment and it was unanimously confirmed by the Senate A splendid tribute to the judge was the petition of the lawyers advocating his reappointment, and a most remarkable tribute it was, as well, from the fact that it was signed by every practicing lawyer in the whole county, save two or three This petition, the work of the lawyers themselves and done entirely upon their own initiative and because of their admiration. esteem and affection for the man and their desire for an impartial able and exalted administration of law and justice, not only faithfully expressed their own estimate but that of the people generally of Judge Daly as a man, a citizen and a jurist It was as follows

The members of the Bar of Middlesex county are interested in seeing the judicial affairs of our county administered in a capable, dignified and honest manner, and because of this do most respectfully petition your Excellency to reappoint as County Judge of the County of Middlesex the Honorable Peter Francis Daly, who has for ten years most signally honored that position

The reasons moving us to urge this appointment are During the ten years that Judge Daly has acted as County Judge he has shown an extraordinary keen grasp of the legal questions that were involved in the administration of the probate law, the criminal law and the many and varied duties imposed upon him as such Judge he has been fair and just in his determination of all matters brought before him and his decisions have been rendered conscientiously with regard only for right and justice Never during that time has the least hint of bias or prejudice, affecting his public acts been breathed His industry is meeting the great volume of work that has come before him has been unflagging and the public's business has been handled by him with skill and dispatch

On many occasions he has been singularly distinguished by the Justices of the Supreme Court to preside over important cases in other counties and his work in such counties as well as in his own county whenever taken up for review by higher courts has been uniformly approved

Just fearless and capable as Peter Francis Daly has been as the Judge he has always been a man of large and generous heart desirous of blending mercy with justice in every justifiable case and ever ready to lend a sympathetic ear to worthy petitions for clemency addressed to him He has treated the bar and litigants with consideration and courtesy and both on the bench and as a citizen he has taken an active honorable and leading part in every movement, having for its end the relief of suffering the inculcation of patriotism and the advancement of Americanization His time and talents have been at the service of the people of the State at all the charitable, educational and patriotic organizations who both before, during and after the War have been of such great service to our country

We feel that the record of this faithful conscientious and able Judge, who has so richly earned the esteem confidence and affection of the people of this county, entitles him to reappointment, and are glad of this opportunity to express to Your Excellency our approbation of him and of his work and our earnest hope that you will reappoint him to this high office in which he has so eminently distinguished himself and which he is so particularly fitted to fill by temperament, training, experience, knowledge, heart and rare good judgment

Judge Daly married, September 25, 1893, at the Church of the Sacred Heart, New Brunswick, Mary Rose Mansfield daughter of William and Margaret (Fitzgerald) Mansfield, her father a member of the firm of Harding & Mansfield wholesale and retail shoe dealers Mrs Daly died January 13, 1917 Judge and Mrs Daly had one daughter Margaret Mansfield, who married William Thornton Campbell, of New Brunswick, June 5, 1920

GOVERNOR JOSEPH BLOOMFIELD, fourth governor of New Jersey under Revolutionary and State governments, traced his descent from Henry Bloomfield, of Woodbridge, Suffolkshire, England, who fled from England in Cromwell's time and came to Newburyport, Massachusetts, in 1632 The line is traced from the founder through his son Thomas of whom further

(II) Thomas Bloomfield, son of Henry Bloomfield, came from England with his father, and accompanied by his sons: John, Thomas (2), of whom further, Nathaniel, Ezekiel, and a daughter, Mary They also settled in Newburyport, Massachusetts

(III) Thomas (2) Bloomfield, son of Thomas (1) Bloomfield, married, about 1640, Mary ———, and their children, born in Newburyport, Massachusetts, were Mary, Sarah, John, Thomas (3), Nathaniel, Ezekiel of whom further, Rebecca, Ruth, and Timothy

Sir George Carteret was appointed governor of New Jersey, and he deputized his brother Philip acting governor to go to New Jersey and represent him Philip Carteret settled at Perth Amboy, and made that the seat of his government To induce settlers from New England, he sent agents to invite them, and in consequence several persons came from Newburyport and settled in the township, later called Woodbridge for that of the town in England Among those who came to Woodbridge township, now in Middlesex county, New Jersey, were Thomas Bloomfield William Bloomfield, and five others, who came and patented many acres of farm land, in December, 1669 Thomas Bloomfield was a freeholder in 1670; represented Woodbridge in Colonial Assembly in 1670 and was a magistrate in 1675-80

(IV) Ezekiel Bloomfield, son of Thomas (2) and Mary Bloomfield, was born in Newburyport, Massachusetts, in 1653, died in Woodbridge township, Middlesex county, New Jersey, in February, 1702 He was a deputy in 1686-87 He married Hope Randolph, and they were the parents of. Timothy, Ezekiel (2), Rebecca, Joseph, of further mention; Jeremiah, and Nathaniel

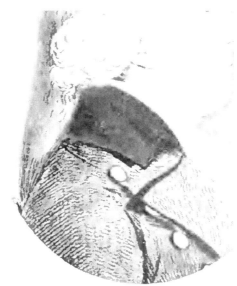

JOSEPH BLOOMFIELD ESQ.
Governor of New Jersey

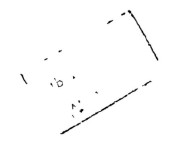

(V) Joseph Bloomfield son of Ezekiel and Hope (Randolph) Bloomfield, was born in Woodbridge township, Middlesex county, New Jersey,
he married Alice Dunham   Joseph Bloomfield held important town
offices, and was a man of influence.

(VI) **Dr Moses Bloomfield**, son of Joseph and Alice (Dunham)
Bloomfield, married Sarah Ogden, and they were the parents of four
children Governor Joseph of whom further, Dr Samuel, Nancy, who
married Dr Wall, and Hannah, who married General Giles

(VII) Governor Joseph Bloomfield, son of Dr Moses and Sarah
(Ogden) Bloomfield, was born in Woodbridge, New Jersey, October
18, 1750 He married (first) Mary McIlvaine, (second) Isabell Ramsey
There were no children of these two marriages   Governor Bloomfield
died at Burlington, New Jersey, October 3, 1823 The following head
stone marks his grave in St Mary's Churchyard, Burlington, New Jersey
(2171 headstone)

> In memory of Joseph Bloomfield, a soldier of the Revolution,
> late Governor of New Jersey and general in the Army of the United
> States He ceased a life of Probity, Benevolence and Public Useful-
> ness, October 3, 1823, in the 70th year of his age

In the register of St Mary's Church is the entry, "October 5, buried
General Joseph Bloomfield"

In youth he attended Dr Enoch Green's School in Deerfield, Cumberland county, New Jersey, and after finishing his school years, began
the study of law under Cortland Skinner, a former attorney-general
of New Jersey He was licensed to practice law in 1775, and in that
year located at Bridgeton, New Jersey, and began practice One of his
first cases was as one of counsel retained by the defendants in a suit
brought by the owners of a cargo of tea which was taken from a vessel
at Greenwich, New Jersey, November 22, 1775, and stored there On
the night of the day named, forty men took possession of that tea and
set fire to it   That "Tea Party" antedated the Boston "Tea Party"
twenty-four days

Joseph Bloomfield was commissioned captain of militia by the Pro-
vincial Congress of New Jersey in 1775, and in 1776 that commission
was confirmed by the Continental Congress and made to apply to the
New Jersey Line Third Battalion, First Establishment One hundred
men were recruited in two weeks by Captain Bloomfield and Lieutenant
Elmer, and in the spring, Captain Bloomfield was on duty in the Mohawk
Valley, New York They built Fort Peyton at Herkimer, New York,
named after a colonel of their regiment The following November he
was with his troops at Ticonderoga and there was named judge advocate of the army of the North He was stricken with illness, and on
Christmas Day, 1776, started for home At the organization of General
Maxwell's brigade, February 1, 1777, Joseph Bloomfield was made
captain of the Seventh Company, Third Battalion On September 11,
1777, the "Jersey Line" opened the battle of Brandywine and there Captain Bloomfield was wounded Maxwell's brigade wintered at Valley
Forge, and when Philadelphia was evacuated by the British, June 18,

1778, he was detached from the main army and with the militia ordered to harass Clinton's forces On June 28, 1778, the "Jersey Line" joined the left wing of the army and Maxwell's brigade fought at Monmouth Captain Bloomfield remained in active field service until 1778, when he became clerk of the New Jersey Assembly In 1783 he succeeded William Patterson as attorney-general, serving until 1788.

Captain Bloomfield moved to Burlington after resigning from the army, and that town was henceforth his home. In 1791 his name heads the list of principal practitioners before the Supreme Court, asking the Court to vacate the order compelling the wearing of "bands and gowns," the Court complied In 1792 he was presidential elector for George Washington and John Quincy Adams In 1794, as brigadier-general of militia, he was sent to Pennsylvania to quell the "Whiskey Insurrection " In 1802 he was made chancellor, and at his first Court of Chancery he asked that he be not addressed as ' Excellency " In 1795-1800 he was mayor of Burlington, and in 1801 was appointed governor of New Jersey In the fall of 1801 the Legislature for the first time was Democratic and at a joint meeting, held October 31st Joseph Bloomfield was elected governor, receiving thirty votes against twenty cast for Richard Stockton In 1802 there was no choice for governor, but in 1803 Joseph Bloomfield was elected, was again reëlected and held the office until 1812, serving the State as governor eleven years, Governor Livingston's term only exceeding that of Governor Bloomfield

In 1812 Governor Bloomfield was appointed by President Madison a brigadier-general, with the rank of general in the army to invade Canada He was at Sacket Harbor, New York, with his brigade in the spring of 1813, and later was assigned to the command of the Philadelphia Military District, there remaining until honorably discharged, June 15, 1815 He served as Congressman from New Jersey, 1817-21, being chairman of the committee on Revolutionary Pensions, and introduced and forced to passage bills granting pensions to veteran soldiers of the Revolution and Revolutionary widows

The historian says of General Bloomfield "He was undoubtedly a man of considerable ability, of unquestioned probity, and great benevolence and took a very active interest in public affairs not only of those relating to the politics of the country, but in many benevolent associations He was always a prominent citizen in whatever community he lived, and his influence has ever been lifted for the right "

Governor Bloomfield was president of the Society of the Cincinnati, and for many years president of the New Jersey Society for the Abolition of Slavery the object of the society being to protect slaves from abuse and to assist them to obtain their liberty by legal proceedings Bloomfield, New Jersey, was named in his honor, and he was recognized as a man of ability and worth He was elected a trustee of Princeton College in 1793 Governor Bloomfield's last public service was as Congressman He was elected by the Democrats in 1816, and retired March 4, 1821 He died about two years later He was deputy grand master of the Masons of New Jersey in 1795-96-97-98, and grand master in 1799-1800

WILLIAM BLOOMFIELD, father of Charles A. Bloomfield, of Metuchen, New Jersey, is a son of Smith Bloomfield, and a collateral relative of Governor Joseph Bloomfield William Bloomfield was born in New York City, February 8, 1808, and there died at his residence, No 28 Dominick street, January 23, 1879, in his seventy-first year His father, Smith Bloomfield, was a builder of New York City, and gave his son the best school advantages William Bloomfield graduated with distinction from Rutgers College, and soon after began the study of law with Judge John L Mason, a former judge of the Superior Court In 1832 he was admitted to the New York bar, and in 1838 entered into a partnership with Thomas McElrath and Charles P Daly, he the youngest member of the firm of McElrath, Bloomfield & Daly That firm engaged in lucrative practice until 1841, when Thomas McElrath withdrew, and with Horace Greeley he published the daily New York "Tribune," under the firm name of Greeley & McElrath It was Mr McElrath's judicious management, and his business sagacity, upholding Mr Greeley's editorial genius, that placed that journal on its foundation of prosperity Charles P Daly was the junior member of the firm, although but twenty-eight years of age and in law practice but five years, in 1844 he was appointed judge of the Court of Common Pleas. Judge Daly held that office by appointment, then by election, until compelled to retire under the age limit of the law Such were the two law partners of William Bloomfield, and to neither was he inferior After Judge Daly's retirement from the firm in 1844 to go on the bench, Mr Bloomfield assumed the entire burden of practice, and for thirty-five years conducted a very large law business in the city of New York His great reputation was made as chamber counsel, he rarely appearing in the public courts He was learned in the law, skilled in its application, wise in counsel, but far too modest and unassuming for a public advocate Yet he was a powerful pleader and debater, his arguments in chambers carrying great weight His well-stored, logical mind went quickly to the kernel of a question, and his opinions on any question of law, particularly the law of real estate, was confidently relied upon His high reputation brought him many difficult and intricate cases, and his judgments were so clear and convincing, and so in accord with the highest law, that they were almost always confirmed by the courts when any litigant rashly appeared

Judge Bloomfield's clients relied upon him absolutely, he was a most valuable citizen and a lawyer who combined the highest integrity and the most delicate sense of honor with the greatest sagacity in all legal matters

William Bloomfield married, May 24, 1834, Catherine Van Mater Croes, daughter of the Rev John Croes, of Christ Church, of New Brunswick, New Jersey, and granddaughter of the Rt Rev John Croes, first Protestant Episcopal Bishop of the State of New Jersey To William and Catherine Van M (Croes) Bloomfield seven children were born 1 Smith, deceased, a well known lawyer and a member of the Board of Education of New York City 2 John Croes, who fought in the Civil War and became a lieutenant-colonel through promotion in the different grades from that of a private he died in Akron Ohio, in his seventy-first year 3 Eleanor Van Mater, died unmarried 4 William (2) died young 5 Thomas Blanch an eminent physician at the time of his death, who lived at Saybrook, Connecticut 6 Jessie, unmarried, died at the age of seventy years 7 Charles A, of further mention in the following sketch Judge Bloomfield was buried from old St John's Church in Varick street of which he was an active member and long-time vestryman

---

CHARLES A. BLOOMFIELD, like his eminent father, William Bloomfield (q v), the well known New York attorney, was also destined for the law and was in practice for a time, but he had little liking for his profession and he abandoned practice organized The Bloomfield Clay Company and has been a leading figure in the clay and ceramic business for many years He is now a resident of the town of Metuchen, in Middlesex county New Jersey his home a historic homestead that has been in the family since his first ancestor came from Massachusetts in 1639 and bought it from the Indians

Charles A Bloomfield is a collateral relative of General Joseph Bloomfield, who was governor of New Jersey for eleven years, and the grand master of New Jersey Grand Lodge, Free and Accepted Masons, in 1799 and 1800 Another monument to the family name is found in Bloomfield, formerly a suburb of Newark, New Jersey, named after Governor Bloomfield, a deeply religious man, who assisted in the building of the old Bloomfield church The home in which Mr Bloomfield resides at Metuchen is a rare old building, his library is trimmed and decorated with the finest black walnut, hewn from a tree that grew on the old farm a hundred and eighty-seven years ago During the World War, 1917-18, he kept "open house" for the officers on duty at the Raritan arsenal, only a short distance away, standing on land taken over by the government, a part of which was formerly owned by Mr Bloomfield

Charles A Bloomfield was born in New York City, February 25, 1849 the son of William and Catherine Van M (Croes) Bloomfield (q v), grandson of Smith Bloomfield a well known builder of New York City, and great-grandson of Dr Samuel Bloomfield of the seventh American generation He began his education under private teaching, and when about ten years of age became a pupil at Summit Academy, Summit, New Jersey remaining there until 1863 He was next a pupil at Dr Hunter's old No 35 Public School, Thirteenth street and Sixth avenue, said to have been the best school in New York City in its time From that school he passed to the Free Academy, afterward known as the College of the City of New York, there remaining until 1867. He began the study of law under his father, formerly a member of the firm of McElrath, Bloomfield & Daly, and one of the distinguished lawyers of New York City, but after five years which to him were exceedingly distasteful, he left the law and entered business life, and so continues, although more than forty years have since elapsed.

Mr Bloomfield entered the clay business, near the family home at Metuchen, and organized The Bloomfield Clay Company to work the clay beds or mines that the company owned on Raritan Ridge He has been connected with clay manufacturing until the present time, and is one of the most prominent men in the State He was president of the National Brick Manufacturers' Association in 1912 and 1913, and has held a similar position with the New Jersey Clay Workers' Association. He has taken a deep interest in ceramics, and was the founder of the Department of Ceramics in the State Agricultural College at New Brunswick which is part of Rutgers College He is a veteran of the old New York Seventh Regiment, National Guard, and was once president of the Masonic Veterans' Association of the Grand Lodge of New Jersey

There is no better known man in the clay and ceramic industry, and the Bloomfield name is equally well known in the Masonic order On May 12, 1921, Charles A Bloomfield celebrated the fiftieth anniversary of his Masonic birthday, having been made a Mason on that date, in 1871, in Belleville Lodge, No 108, Free and Accepted Masons, Belleville, New Jersey, later taking a demit to help form Mount Zion Lodge, Free and Accepted Masons, when Metuchen became his home The members of Mount Zion Lodge, together with a number of distinguished guests from the Grand Lodge of New Jersey, gave him a banquet in celebration of his fiftieth anniversary as a Mason on this occasion At a previous session of the Grand Lodge of the State of New Jersey Free and Accepted Masons, Mr Bloomfield presented to that lodge a commission borne by his distinguished relative, General Joseph Bloomfield, a former grand master of the State (1799-1800), and governor of the State of New Jersey for eleven years, his the longest term any governor of New Jersey ever served, excepting that of Governor Livingston's.

Charles A Bloomfield is a member of the Grand Lodge being past master of Mount Zion Lodge, No. 135, Free and Accepted Masons, of Metuchen, New Jersey, is a member of Jerusalem Chapter, No 8, Royal Arch Masons, New York City, Temple Commandery, No 18, Knights Templar of New Brunswick New Jersey, is a thirty-second degree Mason, being a member of the Scottish Rite Valley of New Jersey, Jersey City and a member of Salaam Temple, Ancient Arabic Order Nobles of the Mystic Shrine, of Newark, New Jersey He was one of the originators of the St John Guild of New York, and for many years its financial secretary.

Charles A Bloomfield married, January 20, 1874 in old St John's Episcopal Church, New York City, Mary Andrews daughter of George F and Mary (Holbert) Andrews, of Orange county, New York where these two families were among the best known people To Mr and Mrs Bloomfield two children were born 1 Eleanor Andrews, who resides unmarried at the homestead at Metuchen 2 Howard Weston a graduate of the City College of New York, and a post-graduate of the Department of Ceramics of Rutgers College, he married Anita I Lundy, of Metuchen and they have three children Eleanor V M, Howard L, and Harold R

DANIEL COY CHASE—Prior to 1785, Joseph Chase came from England to New England, locating at Fall River, Massachusetts, where his son, Stephen Chase was born in 1785. Stephen Chase served in the American army during the War of 1812, and settled at Broadalbin, Fulton county, New York. There a son Holden T. Chase, was born, in 1812, and he married Phoebe Coy, they the parents of Daniel Coy Chase, the principal character in this review.

Daniel Coy Chase was born in Broadalbin, Fulton county, New York, May 4, 1850, and was educated in the public schools there. Later he came to New York City, where he was a student at Paine's Business College. He began his long successful career in marine affairs October 16, 1864, as night watchman of steamboats at the Delaware & Raritan Canal terminal at the foot of Morton street, New York City. He quickly rose in rank with this company which was then the Camden & Amboy railroad, but soon afterward became a part of the Pennsylvania railroad system. On October 1, 1866 he was made assistant towing agent at New York City during the open months of navigation, and in the winter months served as freight clerk at New York City and assistant train despatcher at Jersey City. He was again promoted October 1, 1874, to the post of towing agent at New York City, where he also acted as chief master and pilot of steamboats. In 1875 he was made general agent of the Pennsylvania railroad's New York-Albany and New Brunswick towing lines. Again on September 1, 1880, he was promoted to the position of superintendent of steam towing for the Pennsylvania railroad, a position he held for a number of years. From March 1, 1902, to December 1, 1905, he also held the position of terminal and shipping agent at South Amboy, and in 1906 he was made superintendent of the lighterage department of the company's business. After the railroads passed under Federal control in 1917, Mr. Chase was advanced to a higher position his title being consulting superintendent, and he acted in an advisory capacity on many of the most important maritime and railroad affairs in this section of the country.

On all matters pertaining to lighterage business of the harbor and its relation to admiralty law, he is an authority, his long connection with such work having compelled him to study the subject from every angle. Harbor, pilot and tow boat laws and duties are all familiar subjects. He has been called on many times by the National and State governments, as well as by other large bodies, to render decisions in such matters. It was partially through his efforts that Congress appropriated large sums of money for much needed improvement of the navigable channels in New Jersey and New York harbors. Mr. Chase has invented and patented many devices and attachments used in tugs and barges, and originated the duplex system used by the towing department. Besides these he was the first to designate the system of painting steamboat stacks with designs to describe their ownership. The keystone on the Pennsylvania Railroad boats is a design originated by Mr. Chase, and many other companies have followed this custom.

In April, 1889, Captain Chase was appointed by Governor Robert S

D.C.Chase

Green a member of the Board of Commissioners of Pilotage for the State of New Jersey, a post he ably filled until his retirement in 1906. In 1894 he was chosen president of the board For upwards of fifty years Captain Chase was an active pilot master and engineer on local and coastwise waters, having a license for such duties should occasion arise.

Other interests have claimed him outside his railroad duties; for years he was president of the South Amboy Lumber and Builders' Supply Company , for a long time he was a director of the Maple Realty Company , and vice-president of the First National Bank of South Amboy He was one of the organizers and the first president of the Raritan River Railroad Company, and for years was a member of its board of directors. He organized the Perth Amboy Dry Dock of Perth Amboy, and was its first president Later he organized the Raritan Dry Dock Company, and likewise was its first president, being president of both these companies at the same time

A Democrat in politics, Captain Chase has held many offices of public trust He was at one time chosen freeholder of Middlesex county, and in 1884 he was elected State Senator from this county While Senator he drafted, introduced and pressed to passage the bill creating the borough of South Amboy in 1887 that borough, in appreciation of his work elected him for five successive terms as mayor In 1894 he was the choice of his party in the New Jersey Third Congressional District, but declined the nomination for Congressman Mr Chase is a member of the Railroad Club; the Traffic Club; the Maritime Exchange of New York, the National Board of Steam Navigation, and a member of the legislative and executive committees He has been for years chairman of the legislative committee of the New Jersey-New York State Chamber of Commerce, and has performed notable service in securing legislation of benefit to those interested in anchorage and navigable waterways' questions He is a long time president of the Board of Health of South Amboy in addition to his other local activities also president of the local Chamber of Commerce For several years he was president of the Maritime Reporter Publishing Company of New York City, publishers of the well known "Maritime Reporter"

In the Masonic order, Captain Chase is a past master of St Stephen's Lodge, No 63. Free and Accepted Masons, of South Amboy, a companion of the Royal Arch Masons; a Knight Templar, and a noble of Salaam Temple. Ancient Arabic Order Nobles of the Mystic Shrine He is also a member of the Order of United American Mechanics, the Improved Order of Red Men, Pennsylvania Railroad Benevolent Society, Telegraphers' Benevolent Association, Young Men's Christian Association; various automobile clubs, trustee and deacon of the Baptist church of South Amboy and a member of Chase Lodge, Independent Order of Foresters, which was named in his honor

Such in brief has been the career of a man now retired to the privacy of his beautiful home in South Amboy, and a man of extraordinary keenness of mind and good health for one of his years He numbers among his friends everyone who knows him in the community in which he lives, and all over the State and country men of influence and wealth claim his friendship A leader among men, he has not sought his own ends, but all organizations and enterprises with which he has been connected have been benefited, strengthened and advanced through his connection with them Besides his leadership in many things, he has appeared upon many platforms, and has won more than local fame as a speaker It can be truly said that Captain Chase is a citizen of the first rank, and his home town gladly claims him, Middlesex county is well represented by his presence, and New Jersey is benefited by such citizenship

---

M. IRVING DEMAREST —The family of Demarest, so influential in New Jersey, descends from Jean Des Marets, a French Huguenot, who with his family fled from France and sought refuge in Holland, settling at Middelburg, on the Island of Walcheren, in Zealand His son, David Demarest, as the name became in this country, came to New Amsterdam on the ship "Bontecou" (Spotted Cow), April 16, 1663, and finally settled on the tract which he bought in Bergen county, on the Hackensack river, known as the French patent, where he hoped to establish a colony of French refugees That land was originally bought from the Indians in 1677 but owing to the fact that it lay partly in New York and partly in New Jersey, David Demarest found difficulty in procuring a valid title, and it is said that before he did come into peaceful and undisputed possession he paid for his land four times the original purchase price He moved with several other Huguenot families to the tract in 1686, and there died, in 1693 He married, at Middelburg, Island of Walcheren, Zealand, Marie Sohier, and they were the parents of two sons: David and Samuel, both of whom married From David and Marie Demarest sprang the numerous ancient and honorable Demarest families

M Irving Demarest, of Woodbridge, New Jersey, is a son of William H and Agnes (Van Derveer) Demarest, his mother of equally ancient and honorable family William H. Demarest was born in Woodbridge, and there died, in 1903, after a long and useful life He was for many years and until his death engaged in the coal business which he founded and which after his passing was sold to Thomas F Dunigan. Mr Demarest was active in town affairs, and was one of the organizers of the First Congregational Church of Woodbridge, and from its organization, in 1876, until his passing, in 1903, was a member of its board of trustees

M Irving Demarest was born in Woodbridge, Middlesex county, New Jersey, July 23, 1876 and there attended the public schools until he was sixteen years of age He then became associated with his father in the coal business, continuing with him for two years, 1892-94, then formed a connection with E J Gillis & Company, dealers in teas and coffees, at No 245 Washington street, New York City, as traveling salesman He traveled for that company for two years, then in 1896 entered the employ of Gorham L Boynton, a contractor of Sewaren, New Jersey Mr Boynton was also the agent for the owners of the Sewaren

Irving Demarest.

Morgan F. Larson

tract, and when in 1899 he retired from the business, Mr Demarest succeeded him and still fills the position In 1907 he began taking contracts
for road building and has since built roads all over the State of New
Jersey He is still active in the contracting field, and in that field has
gained high reputation He is vice-president of the First National Bank
of Woodbridge, and a man universally respected and esteemed.

In 1903 Mr Demarest was elected clerk of Woodbridge township,
serving three years In 1906 he was appointed clerk of the Middlesex
county Board of Chosen Freeholders, holding that position four years
He is a member of the Masonic order, holding the thirty-second degree
of the Ancient Accepted Scottish Rite, is a noble of the Mystic Shrine,
a member of the Perth Amboy Lodge, Benevolent and Protective Order
of Elks, the Independent Order of Odd Fellows, and the Royal Arcanum He is a member of the First Congregational Church of Woodbridge, a society his father aided in organizing in the year his son was
born, 1876

Mr Demarest married, in Sewaren, New Jersey, June 25, 1901,
Elizabeth B Voorhees, of ancient New Jersey family, daughter of J Van
Cleef and Isabel (Voorhees) Voorhees Mr and Mrs Demarest are the
parents of a son, Irving Voorhees Demarest, born May 1, 1904, now a
student at Blair Academy, Blairstown, New Jersey The family home
is in Sewaren, New Jersey.

MORGAN FOSTER LARSON, a well known civil engineer of
Perth Amboy, New Jersey, in spite of his years, has already earned a
distinction in his particular line of work which might be the envy of a
much older man. His efforts have been so discerningly directed along
well defined lines that his may already be called a successful life in the
true sense of the word

Peter Larson, father of Morgan F Larson, was born in Denmark,
July 4, 1849, and came to this country at the age of twenty-two years,
settling in Perth Amboy, New Jersey, where he has ever since resided
and where he is the owner of a blacksmith shop and wagon factory
located on Prospect street He is a staunch Republican in politics,
and takes a keen and lively interest in the principles of his party He
married Regina Knudsen, a native of Denmark, having been born there
October 31, 1848, she came to Perth Amboy when a young woman and
has since resided in this city. Mr and Mrs Larson are the parents of
five children · George T, born August 6, 1878, a member of the city fire
department of Perth Amboy, is married, and has four children; Louisa,
born April 11, 1880, wife of Thomas Jensen, and has one child, Morgan
Foster, of further mention, Peter, born October 3, 1884, a blacksmith
by trade, is married and has one child, Edward, died in infancy

Morgan Foster Larson was born in Perth Amboy, June 15, 1882, a
son of Peter and Regina (Knudsen) Larson He received his preliminary education in the local public schools, later matriculating in Cooper
Union University, from which he was graduated B C in 1907, and
immediately established himself as an engineer in his native city, receiv-

ing that same year the appointment of county engineer, which position he held for three years. In 1911, he received his degree of Civil Engineer, and the year previous he formed a partnership with Alvin B. Fox and this still exists under the name of Larson & Fox. In 1917, Mr. Larson was appointed city engineer of Perth Amboy, and township engineer of Woodbridge, which offices he still holds.

A Republican in politics, he is peculiarly popular in the organization and has for the past four years been president of the Perth Amboy Republican Club. He has ever identified himself with the interests of the community in which he resides, and his executive ability is well recognized, in consequence of which he is a director of the Perth Amboy Trust Company and also director and one of the organizers of the Perth Amboy Building and Loan Association. In religion he is a Lutheran and a member of Grace Lutheran Church. He is prominent in many of the fraternal organizations being a member of Lodge No. 61, Free and Accepted Masons, the Independent Order of Odd Fellows, and the Benevolent and Protective Order of Elks, Lodge No. 784.

Mr. Larson married, January 7, 1914, Jennie Brogger, a daughter of L. C. N. and Karen (Larson) Brogger. Mr. and Mrs. Larson have no children.

No citizen of the community is more highly respected than he, his fellow-citizens recognizing his merit and rejoicing in his advancement and the honors which he has attained. Honorable in business, loyal in citizenship, charitable in thought, kindly in action, true to every trust confided to his care, his life is worthy of emulation, and gives promise of future success.

CHARLES R. SIMMEN, son of Theodore and Marie (Lecker) Simmen, was born in Hoboken, New Jersey, November 12, 1881, but two years later his parents moved to Perth Amboy, where Theodore Simmen engaged first in the pottery business, but later was engaged in the management of a bakery.

Charles R. Simmen was educated in Perth Amboy public schools. Since leaving school he has been principally employed as a baker, having been taught that trade by his father. He continued with his father so long as the latter was in the business, then joined forces with his brother, and with him is now associated in the Simmen's Model Bakery, at Perth Amboy.

Mr. Simmen is a member of the Improved Order of Red Men and the Benevolent and Protective Order of Elks, being past sachem of the former and at present (1921) exalted ruler of the latter. He is a Republican in politics.

Mr. Simmen married, at Perth Amboy, New Jersey, in June, 1907, Ella Hughes, daughter of Henry and Mary (Ryan) Hughes, of Perth Amboy. Mr. and Mrs. Simmen are the parents of two daughters, Marie and Eugenia. The family home is at No. 122 Lewis street, Perth Amboy, New Jersey.

LOUIS A. VOORHEES—The surname Voorhees is of early Dutch origin and traces to an ancestor known as Albert of Voorhees, who resided before (voor) the village of Hees, in the Province of Drenthe, Holland

(I) The American progenitor of this branch is Steven Coerte Van Voorhees, who emigrated from "before the village of Hees," Holland, in April, 1660, in the ship "Bontekoe" (spotted cow), whose captain was Pieter Lucassen He purchased, November 29, 1660, from Cornelius Dircksen Hoogland nine morgens of cornland, seven morgens of woodland, ten morgens of plainland and five morgens of salt meadow in Flatlands, Long Island, for three thousand guilders, also the house and houseplot lying in the village of "Amesfoort en Bergen" (Flatlands), with the brewery and all the brewery apparatus, kettle house and casks, with the appurtenances He had seven children

(II) Lucas Stevense Van Voorhees son of Steven Coerte Van Voorhees, was born at Flatlands, Long Island, and married Catherine Hansen Van Noortstrand They had seven children

(III) Jan Lucasse Van Voorhees, son of Lucas Stevense and Catherine Hansen (Van Noortstrand) Van Voorhees, married Mayke R Schenck, and removed in 1717 to Six Mile Run, Somerset county, New Jersey

(IV) Isaac Voorhees, son of Jan Lucasse and Mayke R (Schenck) Van Voorhees, married Helena, daughter of Derrick Barkaloo, and resided in the vicinity of New Brunswick

(V) David Voorhees, son of Isaac and Helena (Barkaloo) Voorhees married Eve Oakey, and resided in New Brunswick They had seven children Mr Voorhees participated in the Revolutionary War, and in 1781 was a lieutenant of the New Jersey Militia

(VI) Ira Condict Voorhees, son of David and Eve (Oakey) Voorhees, married Ann Rolfe Holbert and they had three children

(VII) Charles Holbert Voorhees, son of Ira Condict and Ann Rolfe (Holbert) Voorhees, and father of Louis A Voorhees, was a physician for many years in New Brunswick, New Jersey, and also served as county physician During the Civil War, he took an active part in the medical corps He married Charlotte Bournonville, and to them were born four children Ira Condict (2), a resident of New Brunswick, Vanderbilt Spader, a resident of New Brunswick, Anthony Bournonville, of Belmar, New Jersey, and Louis A, of further mention

(VIII) Louis A Voorhees, son of Charles Holbert and Charlotte (Bournonville) Voorhees, was born March 6, 1865, in the old homestead in which he now resides at No 111 Carroll place, New Brunswick, New Jersey His education was obtained at the private school of Miss Ten-Broeck Rutgers College Grammar School, from which he was graduated in 1881 and Rutgers College, where he obtained the degree of Bachelor of Arts in 1885, and Master of Arts in 1888 In 1885, after completing his studies, he secured a position as assistant chemist with the New Jersey Agricultural Experiment Station, subsequently being promoted to chief chemist in 1895, which office he held for ten

years   As such, he prepared many of the bulletins that went out from
that office for the instruction and edification of the agricultural communities   At present (1920), he is chemist in the Department of Health
of the city of New Brunswick   In 1899 he formed an association in
company with E N Bedford and George Kuhn, which instigated the
plan of purchasing what had been the Remsen Avenue Baptist Church
and converting it into the Masonic Temple of New Brunswick, of which
association he became its first secretary and is still holding that office

Mr Voorhees has delved deep into the technicalities and intricacies
of his profession, and, in consequence, is a member of many of its leading societies, among them being   The American Chemical Society,
the American Electro-Chemical Society, the American Association for
the Advancement of Science, the New Jersey Chemical Society, and
the Society of Chemical Industry, of London, England   He is also
prominent in Masonic circles, being past master of Union Lodge, No
19, Free and Accepted Masons, formerly high priest of Scott Chapter,
No 4 Royal Arch Masons, past thrice illustrious master of Scott Council, No 1, Royal and Select Masters, a member of Temple Commandery,
No 18 Knights Templar, New Jersey Consistory, Ancient Accepted
Scottish Rite, and Mecca Temple, Ancient Arabic Order Nobles of the
Mystic Shrine   He is also affiliated with the Benevolent and Protective
Order of Elks, New Brunswick Lodge, No 324, and is a member of the
Sons of the American Revolution   His clubs are   The Chemist Club,
of New York City   the Middlesex Automobile Club, of which he is
secretary ; the New Jersey Automobile and Motor Club of Newark;
and he also holds the office of secretary of the State Automobile Association known as the Associated Automobile Clubs of New Jersey   He is a
member of Phi Beta Kappa fraternity, and Delta Upsilon

On October 24, 1900, Mr Voorhees was united in marriage with
May Wilcox daughter of Theodore and Annie (Stroud) Wilcox, of
New Brunswick   Mr and Mrs Voorhees have no children

FRANK NEER—For many years Frank Neer was a well known
figure in the social, business and political circles of Perth Amboy, New
Jersey   The Neers were an old and highly respected family in Holland, and came to this country in the very early history of the American
colonies

Mr Neer's father was Charles Neer   He was a farmer by occupation, and owned a considerable acreage in Summit Schoharie county,
New York   He married Levantia Schermerhorn, who died in Summit
They were the parents of five children, of whom Harmon is now living
at Binghamton, New York, and Emily, widow of David Houck, is also
a resident of Binghamton

Frank Neer, son of Charles and Levantia (Schermerhorn) Neer, was
born March 18, 1852 in Summit, Schoharie county, New York   It was
there that he received his early education, which was completed with
a course at the Charlotteville, New York, Academy   Upon leaving
school, the young man assisted his father on the farm, but feeling that

Amos Wheatley.

he could win more from life by branching out upon some line of individual effort, he at length decided to leave home He came to Perth Amboy, New Jersey, in 1876, and from that time until his death, was actively identified with the life of that city He began as yard master in the Lehigh Valley Railroad yards, in which position he remained for about ten years His tastes, however, were along a different line, and in 1887 he made the start that was to mean definite achievement At this time he established, at No 100 Smith street, a stationery store, which is still a feature of the business district of Perth Amboy, having been conducted for this very considerable period of time, at the same address For a time Mr Neer operated the store adjoining, at No 98 Smith street, as a confectionery store, but discontinued this, and devoted all his time to the stationery and book business

Mr Neer not only dealt in books, he loved them His recreation was closely akin to his occupation He spent the greater part of his leisure time at home with the choicest volumes of history and fiction, which his broad acquaintance with the world of books placed in his hands He was a discriminating and careful reader, and a deep thinker

In political affiliation he was a Republican of the old school, and while never seeking political preferment, served for some years as a member of the Board of Assessors His interests reached out in many directions He was a member of the Royal Arcanum, and also of the East Jersey Club He was a member of the Methodist Episcopal church, and for many years served on the board of trustees

Mr Neer married, in 1875, at Waverly, New York, Mary E, daughter of John and Eliza (Durland) Ball They were descendants of early New England settlers, and both father and mother are now buried at Waverly The father was a Baptist minister Frank and Mary E (Ball) Neer were the parents of two children Carolyn, who died in Perth Amboy, December 24, 1915, and Anne English

Mr Neer died October 27, 1917 and since that time, the business, to which he had so long devoted his constant attention, has been conducted by his daughter, Anne E Neer

---

AMOS WHEATLEY.—Since 1906 Mr Wheatley has been a resident of New Brunswick, New Jersey, a silversmith, conducting a prosperous business He is of English birth and parentage, and from early boyhood has made his own way in the world, beginning when a boy of eleven years He has always been a worker and has always set high standards for himself in everything he has done He bears honorable reputation among business men, and in his residence borough, Highland Park, has gained public support for borough office

Amos Wheatley, son of Isaac and Mary (Crowder) Wheatley, was born in Fulford near York, Yorkshire, England, his father now deceased His youth was spent in Lancashire, England, his education being obtained in Fallowfield British school, Fallowfield near Manchester, and later for two years he attended night sessions of the Manchester Technical School At the age of eleven years he graduated from Fallowfield

school and that year began working in an attorney's office on Cross
street, Manchester, but a few months later became office boy for two
Danish gentlemen. His next position was taken a few months later
with the shipping and warehouse business of Fraser Brothers, Limited,
of Prince street, Manchester. He spent two years with that firm,
then began learning the trade of engraver, continuing until his full
years of apprenticeship were accomplished Coming out a finished
workman, Mr Wheatley at once established in business in Manchester,
England, continuing until his departure for Canada to manage a factory Two years later he came to the United States and has been in
business for himself until the present (1921), being now located at
No 83 Albany street, New Brunswick, New Jersey He is connected
with the National Bank of New Jersey and the Middlesex Title and
Trust Company In 1919 Mr Wheatley was an independent candidate
for councilman of Highland Park borough and was elected to serve
three years He is a member of Union Lodge, Free and Accepted
Masons past president of the Sons of St George, member of Friendship
Lodge, No 30 Knights of Pythias Craftsman's Club Tall Cedars of
Lebanon, and of the First Baptist Church of New Brunswick

Mr Wheatley married, in Memorial Congregational Church Chorl-
toncum-Hardy, near Manchester, England, June 1, 1899, Mary A
Wright Mr and Mrs Wheatley are the parents of seven children
1 Frank, born February 22, 1900 2 Elizabeth Mary, born July 31 1901,
died October 2, 1918 3 James W, born July 16 1903 4 Nora, born
November 23, 1905, died November 6, 1913 5 Amos, born October 5,
1910 6 Kathleen, born February 28, 1913 7 Marguerite, born March
6, 1916

ROBERT WOOD JOHNSON—Among the younger generation
of enterprising citizens of this community no name stands out more
prominently than that of Robert Wood Johnson, mayor of Highland
Park, New Jersey Not only has he taken a public-spirited interest in
municipal concerns, but also the industrial life of the place has claimed
a large share of his time since 1910

Mr Johnson was born April 4, 1892, the son of Robert W and
Evangeline (Armstrong) Johnson He received his education in Rutgers Preparatory School and Lawrenceville School In 1910, when the
business of life commenced for the young man he became an active
member of the firms of Johnson & Johnson, the Brunswick Refrigerating
Company, the Chicopee Manufacturing Corporation, and the Neverslip
Manufacturing Company. He is general superintendent of all operations
of the Johnson & Johnson concern, and second vice-president and director
of the other concerns mentioned

Mr Johnson entered political life in 1917, when for three consecutive
years he served his community as councilman, and in recognition of
his capable and disinterested service he was elected mayor of Highland
Park in 1919 He affiliates with the Ancient Free and Accepted Masons
and the Benevolent and Protective Order of Elks He also holds mem-

John Paulus

bership in the New Brunswick Board of Trade, the New York Yacht Club, the New Brunswick Country Club, the Union Club, the East Jersey Club, and the Baltusrol Country Club. In religion he is an Episcopalian and attends the church of this denomination at New Brunswick.

Robert Wood Johnson has made his own way and has attained to his present position both in the business and political life of the community by force of the characteristics which have best fitted him to hold it. Such a man is destined, as a matter of course, to still further advancement, the past being ample promise for the future. He has become very much interested in the Middlesex General Hospital, and is vice-president and chairman of its executive committee, and is generally interested in philanthropic organizations.

On October 18, 1917, Mayor Johnson was united in marriage at New Brunswick with Elizabeth Dixon Ross, daughter of Millard F. and Mary (Dixon) Ross, and to them has been born one child, Robert Wood, Jr., October 9, 1920.

JOHN PAULUS—Providing for the daily needs of the people, and doing this ordinary work in an extraordinary way, is a career worthy of the highest endeavor and deserving of the highest honor. John Paulus, of New Brunswick, New Jersey, conducts one of the cleanest and most sanitary milk depots in the State.

Mr. Paulus was born in New Brunswick, New Jersey, January 18, 1883, a son of John and Christina (Kealman) Paulus, both parents having been born in Germany. John Paulus, Sr., came to America fifty-four years ago, a young man, alone and friendless. Locating immediately in New Brunswick, he established the business which the younger man is now carrying on and conducted it until his death, July 1, 1901. His wife, who is seventy-eight years of age, is now living with this son. They were the parents of six children: Adam, a well known cigar maker of New Brunswick; William, deceased; Joseph, deceased; Minnie, also deceased; Margaret, the wife of Herman Hauer, of New Brunswick, and John.

John Paulus received his education in the public schools of New Brunswick, and at the early age of eight years spent his time outside of school hours assisting his father in the milk business, which was then located on Comstock street. After leaving school the young man worked in various factories here in this city until he was eighteen years of age. Then his father died, and the son took over the business thus left without a head. He has developed it in a remarkable manner, broadening its scope and improving the conditions of handling the work. In 1909, he removed to the present commodious and up-to-date quarters, where every kind of modern equipment was installed to perfect the methods of caring for and delivering the product. This plant, located at Nos. 189 to 193 New street, is a model of cleanliness and sanitary perfection. It is the largest milk business in Middlesex county, employing twenty-two men, and keeping ten wagons and three motor delivery machines constantly busy   All milk handled is a local product of Somerset and Middlesex counties

Mr Paulus is widely connected, fraternally, and in many ways prominent in the life of the city   He is a member of Union Lodge, No 19, Free and Accepted Masons, Scott Chapter, No 4, Royal Arch Masons, Scott Council, No 1, Royal and Select Masters; Temple Commandery, No 18, Knights Templar, Salaam Temple, Ancient Arabic Order Nobles of the Mystic Shrine   New Brunswick Forest No 12 Tall Cedars of Lebanon, New Brunswick Lodge, No 6, and Middlesex Encampment No 43, Independent Order of Odd Fellows, Friendship Lodge, No 30, Knights of Pythias, Ahander Tribe, No 182, Improved Order of Red Men; New Brunswick Lodge, No 324, Benevolent and Protective Order of Elks   Board of Trade, of New Brunswick, Turn Verein and Aurora Singing societies   In periods of relaxation, Mr Paulus turns to those pursuits which carry him outside of the conventionalities of the city, particularly enjoying hunting and fishing

Mr Paulus married (first) Minnie White, who died August 19, 1918, and their children are as follows   John E, born November 28, 1903, Chester W, born March 3, 1905, Helen M, born October 7 1906, and Reinhold M, born May 19, 1911   Mr Paulus married (second) April 16, 1919, Anna Bindseil, daughter of Henry and Louise (Hannaman) Bindseil   The family attend the Reformed church.

JOHN DAWSON —In Woodbury, Connecticut, and Metuchen, New Jersey, John Dawson engaged in mercantile life, and as a dry goods merchant was very successful accumulating a fortune which enabled him to retire prior to his passing away, although he continued in business until a short time before his death   He was born in the eastern part of New York State, the son of Hugh and Nancy (Pearsall) Dawson his father also a native of that State   He was a man of public spirit, interested in town affairs, and a devout Christian   Mr and Mrs Hugh Dawson were the parents of ten children, this review following the career of their son John Dawson of Metuchen, New Jersey

John Dawson was born April 1 1833, and died in Metuchen New Jersey, December 7, 1907   He was educated in the public district schools, and grew to manhood at the home farm, but when seeking a life occupation, chose the career of a merchant, for which he prepared through a series of clerkships in dry goods and general stores in different localities about the east   Finally he opened a dry goods store in Woodbury, Connecticut, which he operated successfully until his removal to Metuchen, New Jersey, where he continued his successful career as a dry goods merchant for many years   He was a man of character, and his life abounded in good deeds   He was a member of the Dutch Reformed Church, a Republican in politics, and was affiliated with Metuchen Lodge, Free and Accepted Masons   He was highly regarded by his brethren of the church and fraternity, while as business man and citizen his life was beyond reproach

Mr Dawson married, October 22, 1888, in Metuchen, New Jersey, Julia M Thomas, born September 25, 1843, in Metuchen, daughter of David Graham and Anna Elizabeth (Ross) Thomas In 1880 Mr Dawson erected a dwelling at No 352 Le Grand avenue, Metuchen, and there Mrs Julia M Dawson yet resides Her home is one of the largest residences of the town, but the memories of former years endears it to her and there she remains surrounded by the many mementos of other days

---

PHILIP HERMAN BRUSKIN —Since coming to New Brunswick, New Jersey, in 1910, Mr Bruskin has been closely identified with the affairs of the community He was born in Newark, New Jersey, April 30, 1889, the son of Abraham and Fanny (Rosenbaum) Bruskin, both natives of Russia, and now residents of Nutley, New Jersey Abraham Bruskin has conducted a large department store there for many years To Mr and Mrs Bruskin were born the following children Benjamin, who served in the United States army during the World War; Theodore, also enlisted in the United States army; Julius, enlisted during the World War and was killed in action at Belleau Woods, June 5, 1917, at the age of seventeen; Philip Herman, of further mention; Oscar, Lawrence

The elementary education of Philip Herman Bruskin was obtained in the schools of West Orange, New Jersey, and after graduating from the high school there, in 1905, he entered Coleman's Business College, completing his studies there in one year, after which he began the study of law and continued this for three years or until 1910, when he came to New Brunswick and established himself in the shoe business, eight years later, having decided to enter the real estate and insurance business, he opened his present office, which is at No 86 Church street Possessing all the qualities of a wise and successful executant, he has been sought for and has accepted many offices of trust, among them being Secretary of the Lucas Realty Company, director of the A S Marcus Hebrew School, organizer and now secretary of the Welfare Building and Loan Association Mr Bruskin has been president of the Young Men's Hebrew Association since 1917, and it is through his efforts that the handsome new home of the organization was built He is also district department president of the Middlesex, Hunterdon and Somerset counties' Federation of the Young Men's Hebrew Association and the Young Women's Hebrew Association of New Jersey, and is also a member of the Loyal Order of Moose He is vice-president of the New Brunswick Real Estate Board, and chairman of the Fire Insurance division of the Real Estate Board, a member of the Board of Trade, and of Anshe Emeth Reformed Jewish Temple Mr Bruskin affiliates with the Benevolent and Protective Order of Elks, and with the Independent Order of Brith Abraham of which he is the treasurer Mr Bruskin served in Company H, National Guard, Fifth Regiment of New Jersey, for three years, after which he was honorably discharged During the World War he acted as secretary of the World War Welcome Home Organization of New Brunswick His hobby is baseball and football and while in high school he played on both teams

On September 1, 1912, Philip Herman Bruskin was united in marriage with Rose I Tapper, daughter of Samuel and Mary Tapper, the latter residing in Los Angeles California Mr and Mrs Bruskin are the parents of three children Ruth D , born in August, 1913 , Charlotte E , born in July, 1915 Harold M born in February, 1917

A man gifted in manner, and enterprising in business, Mr Bruskin is personally liked most by those who know him best He is a man of quiet force, the force that accomplishes large results with but little friction, the force that counts in the upbuilding of any community

---

JAMES PALMER PRALL, since 1887 a resident of Woodbridge, New Jersey, has converted the rich clay lands he owns into a merchantable product and has long been a miner and shipper of clay used in manufacturing fire brick, plain brick and other clay products, which demand the finer clays with which Middlesex county abounds He is a son of Cornelius and Eliza (Howell) Prall, and a grandson of Isaac and Mary Prall, founders of the family in Middlesex county, New Jersey, who long owned and cultivated the homestead in Woodbridge township, Middlesex county, they coming from Staten Island Isaac Prall died December 29 1849, and his wife April 15, 1844

Cornelius Prall, son of Isaac and Mary Prall, was born at the homestead, February 19, 1809, was a farmer all his life, and died March 25, 1887 He married, November 6, 1833, Eliza Howell, born December 15, 1812 died March 14, 1876 daughter of Henry and Catherine Howell Cornelius and Eliza (Howell) Prall were the parents of five children Margaret S born October 7, 1836, married October 25 1877, Rev Joseph N McNulty, pastor of the First Presbyterian Church, of Woodbridge. Isaac born September 11, 1841, died January 4 1896, James P , of further mention; Mary E L , born September 17, 1847, died April 5, 1878, Walter P , born February 22 1850, married Anna L Spaulding

James Palmer Prall was born at the homestead in Woodbridge township Middlesex county, New Jersey September 3 1843, and at the old farm spent the first forty-four years of his life He was educated in Woodbridge schools, and Fort Edward Collegiate Institute, and until reaching legal age was his father's farm assistant He then began farming on his own account but did not leave the homestead until 1887, when he located in the town of Woodbridge, where he still resides (1920) He has long been engaged in developing the clay beds which he owns, mining the clay and shipping same to manufacturers of clay products in many localities

Mr Prall is a Republican and has served his township as freeholder and commissioner of appeals, he is an elder of the First Presbyterian Church, having long served in that office as trustee and treasurer His life has been one of success as a business man, and he is held in high regard by his fellowmen

Mr Prall married, May 10, 1883, Emily Cutter, born May 31, 1852, daughter of Hampton and Mary Ross (Crane) Cutter, of Woodbridge

and Cranford, New Jersey   Hampton Cutter, a farmer engaged in clay mining in 1850, was a pioneer in the business in which he engaged until his death, when he was succeeded by his son, William H Cutter, and he by his son, Hampton (2) Cutter, the present head of the business Mr and Mrs Prall are the parents of two children. William Henry, born August 14, 1887, now a member of the Woodbridge Ceramic Corporation, he married Edith Grace Hasbrook, and they have a daughter, Dorothy C, and a son, Robert H   2 Mary Ross, born May 5, 1893, married Arthur Randolph Lee, and they have four children George A, James P, Margaret, and Emily H   Mr and Mrs Prall are members of the Presbyterian church, the family home is at No 164 Greene street, Woodbridge

---

EUGENE JOHN MULLEN —The father of Eugene J. Mullen, Owen Mullen, was born in Ireland, came to the United States as a boy and located in Perth Amboy, where he conducted a successful shoe business for forty years   He married in Perth Amboy, Catherine Foley, who long survived him dying in Perth Amboy in 1911, aged eighty-four years   They were the parents of three children Mary, now the widow of Dennis Whalen, of Perth Amboy; Eugene John, of further mention, Catherine, widow of William Clapsadell, of Perth Amboy

Eugene John Mullen was born in Perth Amboy, New Jersey, October 1, 1869 and there attended public schools until aged fifteen   He then entered the employ of the Perth Amboy Terra Cotta Company, continuing with that corporation for fifteen years   The following two years were spent with the C Pardee Works, and in 1907 he established his present undertaking business at No 190 New Brunswick avenue, Perth Amboy Four years later, in 1911, he moved to No 251 Madison avenue, where he continues well established in public regard as a business man and citizen   Mr Mullen is a Democrat in politics, and in 1914 was elected coroner of Middlesex county   For twenty-five years, he has been a member of Protection Hook and Ladder Company, and during 1907 and 1908 he was chief of the Perth Amboy Volunteer Fire Department   He is a member of St Mary's Roman Catholic Church, and the Knights of Columbus   He is a motoring enthusiast, and a patron of out-of-doors sports, particularly baseball

Mr Mullen married, in Perth Amboy, June 5, 1902, Helen Cecelia Gibbons, born in Jersey City, New Jersey, daughter of John Leo and Catherine (Burk) Gibbons, her father born in Liverpool, England, her mother in Jersey City, and both now reside in Perth Amboy   Mr and Mrs Mullen are the parents of two children Eugene J, Jr, born July 11, 1906, Eileen, born August 3, 1910

ALFRED WARFFUELL REEVE, of New Brunswick, New Jersey, is one of the leading pharmacists of this city and has built his success on the sure foundation of expert efficiency in his line, which involves more closely than any other branch of mercantile enterprise the life and well-being of the public

The Reeve family was among the early settlers of New Jersey, Joseph Reeve, the founder of this family in America coming from England, in 1664 and settling in Burlington county. Always active in constructive lines of endeavor the family has been prominent to the present time. Mr. Reeve's grandfather was a contractor and builder.

Elwood Joseph Reeve, father of Alfred W. Reeve, was born in Woodstown, New Jersey, February 11, 1852, and is now a resident of New Brunswick and still actively engaged in contracting and building. He married Caroline Harris Warfuell, who died on January 20, 1909, at the age of fifty-five years. They were the parents of four children: Leslie, who died in infancy; Alfred W., of whom further; Prentice C., now a resident of Trenton New Jersey, superintendent of power for the Pennsylvania Railroad shops and instructor in electricity at the Trenton School of Industrial Art, and Ethan C., a resident of Jersey City, and assistant manager of the Newark office of the Venestra Metal Sash Company.

Alfred Warffuell Reeve was born in Bridgeton New Jersey, on May 2, 1875. His parents removing to Port Norris, and some years later from there to Sea Isle City the boy's education was gained in the public schools of these two towns. He continued his school attendance until sixteen years old, but from the age of ten earned his own clothes and spending money doing the many little odd jobs which can be found by a boy of energy and spirit. Upon leaving school he became a mail carrier in Sea Isle City. His ambitions however placed this work in the category of the stepping-stone. In 1896 he began the study of pharmacy and received his degree of Doctor of Pharmacy in 1902. He then entered this field without delay.

Mr. Reeve's first position was that of manager of the drug store in the Albion Hotel, at Oil City, Pennsylvania, but remained for only a short time then came to Jersey City, also for a short time. On May 4 1903, he came to New Brunswick, where he has since been identified with the drug trade. On March 18, 1906, he bought the present business, located at No. 229 George street, and has conducted it continuously since that date. His success has been such as was due a man of skill along technical lines and practical business ability. He stands high in the trade and is considered a leader in the business world of New Brunswick. He is president of the Sanitary Autokone Company, of New Brunswick, incorporated in 1919 and one of the founders.

Mr. Reeve is prominent in Masonic circles. He is past master of Palestine Lodge, No. 111, Free and Accepted Masons is high priest of Scott Chapter No. 4 Royal Arch Masons, and past commander of Temple Commandery, Knights Templar. He is also a member of Salaam Temple Ancient Arabic Order Nobles of the Mystic Shrine of Newark, and the Independent Order of Odd Fellows Lodge No. 6 of New Brunswick. Mr. Reeve is a member of the Board of Trade of New Brunswick, he is an active and influential member of the Young Men's Christian Association and he holds the honor of membership in the National Geographical Society. His personal tastes take him into the great out-doors for relaxation, being fond of all sports. The family are members of the First Reformed Church of New Brunswick, and interested in all its social and benevolent activities

On October 27, 1906, Mr Reeve married in New Brunswick, Elizabeth H Hubbard daughter of John V and Hattie S (Oram) Hubbard, of this city, Mr Hubbard now being a retired merchant   Mr and Mrs Reeve have three children, all living   Edith W, born on September 5, 1907, Alfred W, Jr, born on June 19, 1911, and Elizabeth born on June 2, 1912   The family home is at No 229 George street, which he purchased in 1908

CHARLES SCHONCEIT, one of the prominent and influential business men of Perth Amboy, has since 1910 been engaged in the real estate and insurance business, with offices in the Raritan building

Meyer Schonceit, father of Charles Schonceit, was born in New York City   He was a meat merchant for many years and is now deceased   He married Rebecca Weinstein, who resides in New York City   To Mr and Mrs Schonceit were born six children   Isaac deceased, Charles, mentioned below, Herbert, sales manager for the tobacco industry, New York City, Elsie, wife of Sydney Richmond, of Rochester New York, Edward salesman for a tobacco manufacturing business, New York City, Lewis, engaged in a theatrical enterprise

Charles Schonceit was born in New York City, March 10, 1885, and received his elementary education in the public schools of his native place   After graduating from the Morris High School, he entered Wood's Business College, from which he was graduated in 1905, and then came immediately to Perth Amboy where he secured the position of manager for the Pearlman Jewelry Store, acting in that capacity until Mr Pearlman retired from business   In 1910 he established himself in his present line of business, real estate and insurance in the Raritan building   Mr Schonceit is also president of the National Investment Company of Perth Amboy   In politics Mr Schonceit is an Independent, but has not identified himself with any political party, preferring to remain free from all partisan influences in the exercises of his judgment on political issues   He affiliates with Mystic Lodge, No 21 Free and Accepted Masons, and is a member of the Jewish Synagogue Beth Mordacai

On June 26, 1910, Mr Schonceit was united in marriage with Bessie Elizabeth Levy, a daughter of Harry and Dinah Levy, of New York City   Mr and Mrs Schonceit are the parents of one child, Inez Hope, born October 10, 1914   The family home is at No 101 Brighton avenue, Perth Amboy New Jersey

FREDERICK JEROME POTTER, for the first nineteen years of his life, resided in his native Connecticut, then came to New Jersey, locating in New Brunswick, which has since been his home   He is of English ancestry, and a son of Orrin Jerome Potter, born in Plymouth, Connecticut, who died in 1898 at the age of sixty-seven years, a contractor He married Mary Matilda Hudson who died in Plymouth, Connecticut, aged forty-one years, and they were the parents of seven children Edwin, Lillian, Wilbur, Estelle, Frederick J, Lucina, and Archibald

Frederick Jerome Potter was born in Plainville Connecticut, March 24, 1867, and there obtained his education In 1886 he located in New Brunswick New Jersey, and entered the employ of Loyal T Ives a manufacturer of needles, and for twenty-one years remained with him He then established in business for himself as Fred J Potter & Company, manufacturers of spring beard needles, quills, sinkers, jacks, etc The first plant a small one was occupied until 1915, when the present plant at Somerset and Bethany streets, New Brunswick, was occupied, one hundred and fifty men now being employed in the business which began with a force of five men

An energetic, efficient business man, Mr Potter has fairly won the success he has attained, and in all things has proved himself a man of strong character His business is his chief concern, but he takes deep interest in outside affairs, catering to his love of the out-of-doors by frequent indulgence in hunting, fishing, and the game of golf He is a member of the Congregational church the New Brunswick Young Men's Christian Association and the New Brunswick Country Club

Mr Potter married in New Brunswick New Jersey in 1889 Mary Jane Matthews, daughter of James and Julia Matthews, of New Brunswick, her parents both now deceased Mr and Mrs Potter are the parents of seven children 1 Frederick Jerome (2), born November 7, 1890 in New Brunswick New Jersey, now associated in business with his father as office manager of the Fred J Potter Company, he married November 3, 1915 Nellie Gisburne Clark, of Perth Amboy New Jersey, children Marjorie Imogene and Frederick Jerome (3). 2 James Harold, superintendent of the Fred J Potter Company 3 Lucina M a teacher in the public schools 4 Willard F a foreman with the Fred J Potter Company 5 Anita M, deceased 6 Raymond A a student at Rutgers College class of 1922 7 Edgar, a student at Rutgers College, class of 1924

A business is indeed fortunate that can attract to itself such loyal family cooperation as has the Fred J Potter Company, officered and conducted in its executive recording and making departments by father and sons The history of the company is one of progress and prosperity, a fact that may be justly attributed to its able management

---

WILLIAM HENRY GRISWOLD, who for the past eighteen years has been superintendent of the New Jersey Terra Cotta Company's Works at Perth Amboy, has been numbered among the prominent citizens of the community He is active in the philanthropic and religious work of his adopted city, and all that makes for civic betterment finds in him a warm supporter

James P Griswold, father of William Henry Griswold, was born in Enfield, Connecticut, and died in Longmeadow, Massachusetts at the

age of seventy-two years   During the latter years of his life he had
acquired fame as an agriculturist   He married Emiline C Chilson, a
native of Springfield, Massachusetts, and she died in Longmeadow at
the age of eighty-one   Mr and Mrs Griswold were the parents of
seven children   John M, an accountant at Matawan, New Jersey;
Lucy J, widow of the late D T Smith of Springfield, Massachusetts;
James, deceased, Edward, deceased; Emerson, an inspector for Smith
& Wesson at Springfield, Massachusetts, William Henry, of further
mention   Herbert T, who resides in California

William Henry Griswold was born July 26, 1865, in Longmeadow,
Massachusetts, the son of James P and Emiline C (Chilson) Griswold
He received his preliminary education in the public schools of Springfield
and later attended Eastman's Business College in Poughkeepsie, New
York, from which he was graduated in 1883   His initiation into business
life took place in a general store at East Berlin, Connecticut where he
remained for four years   He was then successively employed by the
P & F Corbin Company of New Britain, Connecticut, and the New
York City Corset Company, remaining with the latter concern for a
number of years, this concern finally being succeeded by the A H
Senior Corset Company, of which Mr Griswold was a member for several years   Finally withdrawing from this company, he associated
himself with the New Jersey Terra Cotta Company and was employed in
the New York office, which is located in the Singer building, until May 1,
1902, when he was made superintendent of the works of this organization in Perth Amboy, New Jersey, which position he holds at the present
time   The success of this business is owing in a large measure to the
tireless energy, practical mind and sound judgment of Mr Griswold
The business capacity which he developed early in life proved to be of
a superior order, and he displays a broad grasp of affairs combined with
his exceptional knowledge of men   To his associates he shows a genial,
kindly nature which has ever made their business relations most enjoyable, while his uniform justice and consideration toward his subordi-
nates is worthy of praise

All movements tending toward civic betterment and municipal reform
have received from Mr Griswold active interest and hearty cooperation
In politics he affiliates with the Republican party   A man of action
rather than words, he demonstrates his public spirit by actual achievements that advance the welfare of the community   A man of great
aggressiveness, he is manager of the Perth Amboy Savings Institution,
and for the past three years has been president of the Sinking Fund
Commission   Mr Griswold attends the Presbyterian church of Perth
Amboy and has been on its board of trustees for several years   His
hobby is automobiling and what little time he can spare from his ever
increasing business activities he devotes to his particular enjoyment

On October 27, 1886, Mr Griswold married Isabella L Belden,
daughter of the late Edwin Belden of East Berlin, Connecticut and
they are the parents of four children   James Edwin, born September
18, 1887, now in the insurance business in Claypool Arizona, William

H , died in infancy, Ruth E , formerly a Red Cross nurse now wife of Captain G L Harker, of the United States Medical Corps, Lloyd C , born January 5, 1896, is now in Perth Amboy, having recently received his honorable discharge from the United States navy

Mr Griswold is a man whose business capacity is of the highest order, and being honorable in purpose and fearless in conduct has stood for many years as one of her most prominent citizens, using his talents and his opportunities to the utmost in every work which he undertakes and is an inspiration to all who know him

HARRY F BELDON —Since 1914 New Brunswick New Jersey, has numbered among her representative business men no abler nor more progressive citizen than Harry F Beldon distributor for the Cadillac automobile, at No 413-415 Raritan avenue In every thing pertaining to the welfare of the community, he takes a keen interest and is ever ready to give substantial aid to the furtherance of all good measures

Harry F Beldon was born November 15, 1881, at Flemington New Jersey the son of Heber C and Margaret (Van Deveer) Beldon Heber C Beldon was sheriff of Hunterdon county, New Jersey, at the time of his death, which occurred in 1883 The education of Harry F Beldon was obtained in the schools of Flemington until 1894 when he entered Reading Academy where he remained for four years, when the business of life began for the boy His first employment was in a chainless bicycle shop at Newark New Jersey, but he resigned in 1901 to establish himself in the automobile business, in which he continued for the next six years, selling out at the end of this time to become manager for the J M Quimby Company, automobile chassis department for the Simplex and Isotta Franchino machines In 1914 he came to New Brunswick and located at No 146 Church street, having the local agency for Cadillac automobiles On December 1, 1920, he moved his business to his new plant at Nos 413-415 Raritan avenue, where Cadillac owners will find a modern and fully equipped plant, able to care for their every want

Mr Beldon is a member of the Board of Trade, the Union Club of New Brunswick, the Automobile Club of America the Young Men's Christian Association, and is a director of the Rotary Club In religion he is a Presbyterian

On June 24 1920, Mr Beldon was united in marriage with Viola Theodore The success of Harry F Beldon has been in every sense of the word self-made—the result of his own untiring effort and his own unfailing belief in his confidence to succeed, and within the short space of four years that he has been located in New Brunswick, he has risen to a place of prominence in business circles which might well be the envy of a much older man

OLE N. OLESEN, JR., who holds a prominent place among the citizens of Perth Amboy is a funeral director with an undertaking establishment at No 43 Smith street, that city He is also engaged in

Charles A. Olivier, Sr.

the real estate and insurance business at this same location, and is recognized as a successful business man in his particular line of work

Ole N Olesen, father of Ole N Olesen, Jr, was born in Denmark, January 16, 1850, and emigrated to this country when a boy, coming direct to Perth Amboy, where he has ever since resided   He married Meta Nelson, who was born in Denmark, and died in Perth Amboy in 1887   Mr and Mrs Olesen were the parents of three children   Ole N, mentioned below, Meta, a school teacher in Jersey City, Laura, wife of Viggo O Peterson, of Perth Amboy

Ole N Olesen, Jr, was born in Perth Amboy, New Jersey December 6 1883   He received his education in the schools of his native city, and then worked for his father in the latter's livery stable for about ten years   In 1904 having decided to become an undertaker he associated himself with Mr Fox, a local funeral director, and while here gained a thorough knowledge of the profession   In 1913 he established himself in this business, and two years later, June 1, 1915, he formed a partnership with J Alfred Compton under the firm name of Olesen & Compton, real estate and insurance, which existed for four years, when in 1919 this business was taken over by Mr Olesen and the name changed to Ole N Olesen   Mr Olesen is affiliated with the Knights of Pythias, the Danish Brotherhood, and Improved Order of Red Men   His club is the Raritan Yacht   In religion he is a Presbyterian, and his means is generously contributed to the church and its benevolences   He is ever ready to lend his aid and influence to any good cause, and in a progressive, public-spirited way continues the friend of every movement looking toward uplift and improvement

On June 21, 1914, Mr Olesen was united in marriage with Irene Marjorie Owens, a daughter of the late John Mitchell and Katherine (Gurry) Owens   Mr and Mrs Olesen have no children

---

CHARLES AUGUSTUS OLIVER, SR—Holding positions of trust in his home town for thirty-four years, giving satisfaction to the public, Charles Augustus Oliver, Sr, has a fine record of service well rendered in New Brunswick

Born in that city, September 8, 1843, he is the son of Francis Manly Oliver, a native of New York City, where he learned the trade of cabinet making, following it until the outbreak of the War of the Rebellion, when he enlisted in the Twenty-eighth Regiment, New Jersey Volunteers   He was killed at the battle of Fredericksburg   His widow, Jennette (Wells) Oliver, survived him for a number of years, dying at the age of eighty years in New Brunswick   She was born in Patchogue, Long Island   Francis Manly and Jennette (Wells) Oliver had ten children, of whom three only are now living   1 Charles Augustus, of further mention   2 Amanda, the widow of William Talmadge, of Brooklyn, New York   3 Eveline also a widow, residing in Brooklyn

Attending the public schools in New Brunswick in his boyhood the boy, Charles Augustus early in life entered into business   Obtaining employment in a butcher shop he learned the trade and continued it

until 1861, when the Civil War started, and he enlisted as a private in
Company I, Eleventh Regiment, New Jersey Infantry He remained
in the army until the close of the war in 1865 having been promoted
five times during the four years His record is a fine one of bravery
in the twenty-seven battles in which he engaged. In the "Battle of
the Wilderness" he was so severely wounded that he was confined in
the hospital for many months and at Fredericksburg where his father
lost his life, the son was badly wounded Just before the surrender of
General Lee, Mr Oliver's commanding officer sent him an order to be
careful of the ammunition, an order which he still has in his possession
When the war was over it was as Captain Oliver that he returned to his
home

In 1870 Captain Oliver was elected to his first political office, that
of chief of police, and he held it for ten years He was a member of
the Board of Aldermen for twenty years from the Third Ward of New
Brunswick, and was commissioner of public improvements for four
years his public service covering a period of thirty-four years After
giving up politics Mr Oliver became engaged in detective work and has
followed it for several years Mr Oliver is a member of that honorable
body of men, the Grand Army of the Republic, also of the Methodist
church of New Brunswick

In New Brunswick September 8, 1870, Charles Augustus Oliver
and Sarah Aletta Boudinot were married She was born in the West,
the daughter of William B and Mary (Taylor) Boudinot, both of whom
died in New Brunswick Mr and Mrs Oliver had three children 1
William T who died in infancy 2 Charles Augustus, Jr, born October
27, 1877, residing in Milltown New Jersey 3 Harry Van Cleave, born
June 1, 1879 a contractor, living in New Brunswick Mr and Mrs
Oliver reside at No 138 Livingston avenue New Brunswick

HANS CHRISTIAN SMITH, JR, well known among the business
men of Perth Amboy, is a general roofing contractor at Nos 123-125
Madison avenue

Hans Christian Smith, father of Hans C Smith, Jr, was born in
Denmark, May 1, 1854, and came to the United States when a young
man Upon landing in this country he decided to locate in Perth Amboy,
New Jersey, and it was here that he worked at his trade of carpentering
until he retired from active business life He married Andrea Hanson
a native of Denmark, who died in Perth Amboy, March 29 1897, at
the age of forty-seven years Mr and Mrs Smith were the parents of
two children: Andrew M, a plumbing contractor, located on Hall
avenue Hans C, mentioned below

Hans Christian Smith Jr, was born in Perth Amboy, New Jersey,
September 10, 1881 He attended a private school of his native place
until he was fourteen years of age when he discontinued his studies,
desiring to learn the butcher's trade, at which he worked for seven
years at the end of which time he drove a truck for the New Jersey
Terra Cotta Company in New York City for two years, and then started

his present business, that of general roofing contractor, locating first on Hall avenue, and removing to his present location, Nos 123-125 Madison avenue, July 29, 1919 Mr Smith is affiliated with the Independent Order of Odd Fellows and the Benevolent and Protective Order of Elks He holds membership in the Raritan Yacht Club and is an ardent lover of all outdoor sports When he was twenty years of age he won as a bicycle racer the amateur championship of the South at Jacksonville, Florida His hobby is bowling

On October 3, 1903, Mr Smith was united in marriage with Elisa Schroeder, a daughter of Peter and Christine (Tidea) Schroeder, of Perth Amboy Mr and Mrs Smith are the parents of two children Peter Andrew, born September 10, 1904, Andrea Catherine, born February 21, 1907. The family attend the English Lutheran church of Perth Amboy

The success that Mr Smith has attained is the result of his own unaided efforts, for throughout his career he has ever been animated by the spirit of progress, always seeking to make the most of every opportunity, and such a record is certainly worthy of recognition in a work of this sort

---

ELWOOD ECCLESTON WALLER—A newly established business firm in New Brunswick is that of Elwood E Waller & Son dealers in automobiles, and agents for particular makes of high-grade motor vehicles The senior member is Elwood Eccleston Waller, a resident of Dunellen, New Jersey, having his home at No 331 Dunellen avenue

Mr Waller's ancestors came from Ireland, the original emigrant being his grandfather, William Waller, who with his wife came from Ireland about the middle of the last century and locating in Brooklyn brought up his children there. One of them, William Edgar Waller, born in Brooklyn later became a resident of Rutherford, New Jersey, where he conducted a drygoods business for many years, so engaged at the time of his death He married Emma Daisy Eccleston born in Brooklyn, and since her husband died she has resided in Newark, New Jersey Mr and Mrs William Edgar Waller became the parents of eight children Daisy, William E Elizabeth deceased, Lillian, Violet, deceased; Florence, Olive, and Elwood Eccleston, of whom further

The education of Elwood Eccleston Waller was acquired in the public schools of Arlington, New Jersey, and in Rutherford, continuing it until he had reached the age of seventeen, when he entered business life His first position was in a real estate office, where he remained for a short time only, leaving it to enter a feed store This, too, was given up and Mr Waller became engaged in gas construction work in various cities of New York and New Jersey This in turn he gave up, he and his brother William E, starting an automobile business in Rutherford which they continued for three years Following this he went to Plainfield and was there connected with Lang's garage for a period of about ten years Then he opened a garage in Dunellen, remaining there for five years, relinquishing that business to enter into a larger concern at No 72 Albany street, New Brunswick, with his son, Elwood E, Jr During the last two years Mr Waller has been a councilman of Dunellen, a position he now holds

Mr Waller is fond of outdoor sports, living in the open as much as possible, he finds his greatest pleasure in duck hunting and fishing, and is also a most enthusiastic baseball fan He enters into the social life of the community, and is also a member of the lodge of Free Masons Mr Waller and his family attend the Episcopal church

In Brooklyn, New York, Elwood Eccleston Waller was united in marriage with Francina Claire Shaughnessy, born in New York City, she was the daughter of Mr and Mrs James Shaughnessy, residents of New York, both now deceased Mr and Mrs Elwood Eccleston Waller have two children Elwood Eccleston, Jr whose sketch follows, and Eunice Claire, born November 1, 1900 a graduate of the grammar school of Dunellen Both children, being unmarried reside at home with their parents, at No 331 Dunellen avenue Dunellen New Jersey

---

ELWOOD ECCLESTON WALLER, JR, the junior partner in the automobile business at No 72 Albany street New Brunswick New Jersey, is the son of the founder of the firm of Elwood E Waller & Son Much of the early life of the young man was spent in Rutherford, New Jersey, where he was born, March 8, 1896 He attended the public schools of that town, afterward going to Suffern, New York where he again became a pupil in the public school After a time, his family moving to Dunellen, New Jersey to make their home, the young man entered the high school of Plainfield and had partially finished the course when he left to start upon a business career His first venture was as runner for the Plainfield Trust Company From time to time Mr Waller was promoted during his three years' stay in the bank until, when he resigned from his position, he held the office of assistant receiving teller He was next employed by Busk & Daniels, importers and exporters, No 301 Produce Exchange New York City remaining with them for five months At this time the United States became involved in the World War, and Mr Waller immediately volunteered his war record being one which he and his family have every reason to be very proud of

On Friday, April 13, 1917, Elwood Eccleston Waller, Jr, enlisted with Troop D New Jersey Cavalry of Plainfield later being transferred to the 112th Heavy Field Artillery, and again transferred to the 104th Regiment of Military Police, 29th Division After being sent to France, Mr Waller was almost continuously on the fighting line, he was engaged in the defense of the Alsace sector and was in the reserve at Verdun At the terrible Meuse-Argonne defensive he was engaged from October 8 to October 29, 1918, serving actively in seven different battles of the long siege of Meuse-Argonne Mr Waller has been recommended for the Distinguished Service Cross, under date of October 23, 1918, and awarded a citation for bravery in the battle of Etrave Ridge Though under fire for such long periods and in the worst engagements of the war, Mr Waller escaped without being wounded and was never taken prisoner He received his discharge June 3, 1919 After his return from France and following his discharge, the new firm of Elwood E Waller & Son was formed and the young soldier has again taken up business life

Mr. Waller is a member of Dunellen Post, No 119, of the American Legion, and of the Patriotic Order Sons of America, of Dunellen He also is connected with a Greek letter fraternity, Chi Upsilon, its headquarters being in Plainfield Though the family of Mr Waller all attend the Episcopal church and he also is a member of it, he is at present greatly interested in the Presbyterian church of Dunellen

---

RICHARD CASPER STEPHENSON.—In business circles, civic work, or in club life, Richard Casper Stephenson is equally well known and popular For most of his life he has been a resident of South Amboy, New Jersey, and his interests and pleasures are centered in that locality

Born in West Philadelphia, Pennsylvania, October 21, 1870, he came to South Amboy when a child with his parents, Abraham Wilson and Sarah Elizabeth Stephenson The former was born in Pennsylvania, but in his later life lived in South Amboy, where he died at the age of sixty-seven years His business was that of car inspector in his early life he served in the Civil War as a private Mrs. Sarah Elizabeth Stephenson died in South Amboy when seventy-one years old

The education of Richard Casper Stephenson was acquired in the public schools of South Amboy, later taking private lessons from a tutor After reaching young manhood he became interested in several forms of business life and is now actively engaged in banking affairs In 1888 he entered the employ of the First National Bank of South Amboy, later becoming a director of same, and since January, 1902 has been cashier Mr Stephenson is also a director of and treasurer in the South Amboy Lumber and Supply Company. In addition to these daily occupations he is vice-president of the Star Building and Loan Association of South Amboy, and is one of the Sinking Fund commissioners of the city

Some years ago Mr Stephenson was an enthusiastic yachtsman, but latterly, being greatly occupied in business, he has only indulged in his favorite diversion occasionally, whenever opportunity offers He is, however, deeply interested in all fraternal matters, being a Free Mason in high standing, a member of and past master in St. Stephen's Lodge, No 63, Free and Accepted Masons and of Amboy Chapter No 41, Royal Arch Masons, he is also a Knight Templar, connected with Temple Commandery, No 18, and is a noble of Salaam Temple, Ancient Arabic Order Nobles of the Mystic Shrine, of Newark, New Jersey. Mr Stephenson is a member of Good Samaritan Lodge, No 52, Knights of Pythias, and of the Pennsylvania Railroad branch of the Young Men's Christian Association He is one of the trustees of the South Amboy Hospital Association, and a worker in the Chamber of Commerce and one of the directors

In club circles Mr Stephenson is equally to the fore, he is a member of the Ashler Club of Washington, D C, also of the Middlesex Automobile Club of New Brunswick, and of the South Amboy Yacht Club. Mr Stephenson and his family are prominently engaged in the work of the First Methodist Episcopal Church of South Amboy

On March 20 1895, in South Amboy, Richard Casper Stephenson was united in marriage with Georgianna Emmons, daughter of George N and Sarah Emmons, residents of South Amboy Mr and Mrs Richard Casper Stephenson have two children Harold Francis, born February 17, 1898, married Hazel M Mason, and Mildred Emmons, born May 26, 1904 The family home is at No. 248 David street

---

JOHN JAMES MONIGAN, numbered among the influential citizens of New Brunswick, New Jersey, is the owner and manager of a drug store at No 376 George street Since coming to this community, in 1898, Mr Monigan has identified himself with the leading business interests of New Brunswick and is ever a zealous advocate and supporter of her most vital and essential interests

John J Monigan, father of John James Monigan, was born in Baltimore, Maryland, and died there in 1890 at the age of forty-eight years He was a civil engineer for many years He married Anne Otis, who still survives him To Mr and Mrs Monighan was born one child, John James, of further mention

John James Monigan was born in Baltimore, Maryland, June 7, 1889, and was brought by his parents to Cortland, New York, when he was but five years of age Here he attended the public schools, graduating from the Cortland High School, after which he attended the State Normal School On May 1, 1895 having decided to become a pharmacist, he commenced to study with this end in view, and four years later became a registered pharmacist in the State of New York, subsequently securing a position with Fitz Boynton & Company, and later with William Rust & Sons, of New Brunswick, where he remained until 1906, when he established himself in the drug business at his present location

Mr Monigan affiliates with the Knights of Columbus, is a member of the New Brunswick Board of Trade, the Rotary Club, and the New Brunswick Country Club He is also a member of the New Jersey Pharmaceutical Association and the National Druggists' Association

On June 27, 1906 Mr Monigan was united in marriage with Agnes R McCormick a native of New Brunswick and the daughter of Bartholomew and Catherine (Houghton) McCormick, both deceased Mr. and Mrs Monigan are the parents of two children Louis C and John J Monigan

---

HAMPTON CUTTER—Woodbridge New Jersey, has long been the home of the Cutter family, Richard Cutter coming from New England to Woodbridge, Middlesex county, in 1709 in company with John Pike He built what is believed to have been the first mill in the township, locating it on Woodbridge creek at what was later the Cutter and Prall dock Richard Cutter was a son of William and Rebecca (Rolfe) Cutter, grandson of Richard and Elizabeth Cutter, he the brother of William Cutter, and son of Samuel and Elizabeth Cutter. Richard and William Cutter with their widowed mother came to New England about 1640 Richard Cutter, of the third generation, and the founder of the Woodbridge branch, married and had fourteen children, and was succeeded by his son, Richard Cutter, who married, August 20, 1706, Mary Pike, and they were the parents of Deacon William Cutter, who married Mary Kent Kelsey Cutter, of the sixth generation, son of Deacon William and Mary (Kent) Cutter, married Hannah Marsh, and they were the parents of a large family, including a son, William Cutter, born October 6, 1778, died February 8, 1838 He married Sarah, daughter of Ephraim Harriot, of Woodbridge; she was born December 7, 1783 and died March 14, 1840 They were the parents of a large family including a son Hampton, of further mention

Hampton Cutter was born in Woodbridge, New Jersey December 25, 1811, fifth child of William and Sarah (Harriot) Cutter He died in Woodbridge, February 22, 1882 He grew up at the homestead, obtained a good public school education, and until 1836 remained at home and cultivated the farm In the year named he married and began the cultivation of his own farm. In 1846, a large deposit of a high grade of fire clay, also pottery clay, was discovered on his farm, which is used in ore for pottery, ornamental tile, terra cotta, electric and sanitary ware, also fire brick, and is used in carborundum Mr Cutter supplied these clays to the fire brick manufacturers of his section and shipped heavily to points of fire brick manufacture as far away as Portland Maine and Cleveland, Ohio, especially to the potteries of East Liverpool, Ohio, Sebring Ohio, Trenton, New Jersey, and many other plants also the terra cotta plants throughout the East As his sons reached manhood they were admitted to the firm of Hampton Cutter & Sons, and that house became one of importance in the clay industry The sons were Josiah C and William Henry

A man of strong character and deep convictions, Hampton Cutter not only was a factor of strength in the business world, but in public life also left a lasting impression He was a justice of the peace for fifteen years, and the record reads that in that then very important office his "even handed justice won golden opinions from all sorts of people" He served the county of Middlesex on the Board of Freeholders and his township as committeeman He was well qualified for leadership, and his unswerving Democracy was a tower of strength to his party In religious faith he was a Presbyterian, and for about a quarter of a century he was one of the trustees of the Presbyterian church in Woodbridge, he during seven of those years being a member of the board In addition to his private enterprise, farming, and Hampton Cutter & Sons, he was a director of the Rahway National Bank and the owner of valuable real estate He was a man whose daily life inspired confidence and respect, and he closed his long and useful life honored and trusted by all who knew him

Hampton Cutter married, January 26, 1836, Mary Ross Crane, born in Craneville (now Cranford), New Jersey, daughter of Josiah Crane They were the parents of four children Josiah Crane, who died aged forty-one, William Henry, of further mention Sarah Anna married Freeman Rowland, Emily, married James P Prall

William Henry Cutter was born in Woodbridge, New Jersey, June 22, 1840, and died September 24, 1918 He was educated in the public schools and upon leaving school became associated with his father and elder brother in the firm, Hampton Cutter & Sons dealers in fire and potteries clay mined from the farm at Woodbridge owned by Hampton Cutter. This business a most profitable one, was continued by the father and sons jointly but death removed the founder and elder brother and William Henry Cutter was left with the entire management of the business which he still further developed He worked over eighty acres of clay beds from which several different kinds of merchantable clay was mined and from which fire brick tile, terra cotta drain pipe and potters clay were manufactured the clay shipped by Cutter & Sons going to all parts of the country to be converted into manufactured products The clay beds were operated throughout the entire year and formed an important addition to the industrial importance of the town Like his honored father, William H Cutter was progressive and public-spirited and deeply interested in the welfare of the community In politics he was independent, and in religious faith a Presbyterian serving the Woodbridge church as trustee. He was very charitable and proud of his clean record, honest in all his dealings to the extreme, and was one of the county's noblemen

He married Sarah R Barron, daughter of Samuel and Eliza A (Jacques) Barron, of Woodbridge The old homestead situated just south of Woodbridge, is a landmark, erected about 1840 This was their home for a time, but in 1870 Mr Cutter erected a suitable house on Green street, Woodbridge which was ever afterward the family home Mr and Mrs Cutter were the parents of two children, Hampton (2) of further mention, and Laura L

Hampton Cutter (2) was educated in private schools, attending the Pingree Preparatory School of Elizabeth graduating in the class of 1890, and the Packard Commercial School of New York City graduating in the year 1891 He immediately engaged in business with his father this connection being uninterrupted until the death of his father, when he succeeded to the business, being now the sole owner, and he continues to operate the original clay mines on an extensive scale, using the latest improved methods He is a director in the Alpine Cemetery Association, served on the Board of Education for over six years is president of the board of the Barron Library Association, and is a member of the board of trustees of the Presbyterian church

---

LUKE D LINDLEY—Since the inception of his business career, Mr Lindley was connected with but one particular line of industry the meat packing business and in this he met with phenomenal success

William H Cutter

Luke D Lindley was born February 10, 1871, at New Brunswick, New Jersey, and died October 18, 1920, the son of Samuel S and Mary E Lindley Samuel S Lindley was a jeweler by trade, but for the past twenty years has been retired from active business life. A young man at the outbreak of the Civil War, heartily in sympathy with the cause of the Union and fired with the patriotism which swept the North at the news of the firing on Fort Sumter, he enlisted with the 11th New Jersey Volunteers subsequently being promoted to the rank of sergeant With his regiment he participated in many of the most stirring engagements of the war, and during the battle of Chancellorsville was severely wounded

The education of Luke D Lindley was obtained in the public schools of his native place, and upon graduating from the New Brunswick High School, in 1892, he matriculated at Rutgers College, where he was a special student in the class of 1896 Immediately upon finishing his educational career, he entered into business life as bookkeeper for G V Bartlett & Company a slaughtering and hog-shipping concern at Jersey City Here he devoted all his available time to this work and by this untiring devotion steadily gained in advancement until November, 1914, when he was able to purchase a half-interest in the concern In October, 1918, he bought out the remainder of the business, the firm then becoming known as the Luke D Lindley Packing Company The enterprise steadily and consistently grew to its present large proportions, turning over more than a half million dollars annually, due in a large measure to the capable management of its executive head

A man true to his friendships, honest and impeccable in all the relations of life, Mr Lindley was highly respected and honored in New Brunswick He was a member of the New York Produce Exchange, the Alumni Association of Rutgers College, and the Young Men's Christian Association at New Brunswick In religion he was a Presbyterian and attended the First Church of that denomination

On June 12 1906, Luke D Lindley was united in marriage with Mary Ethel Franken daughter of John and Ida M. (Martin) Franken, of Prattsville Greene county New York No children were born to Mr and Mrs Lindley A man of dynamic and tireless energy, he gave the best that was in him to his business, and his success was essentially the result of hard toil, indomitable will power, and an unconquerable belief in his own ability

---

LEROY JEROME BERGEN —Thirteen generations of Bergens have lived in Chautauqua county, New York, counting the first comers from Holland down to the youngest of the present generations The original home was New Amsterdam (now New York), but the overflow into New Jersey was early and constant The early settlers gave name to the localities, and Bergen county, Bergen Hill, Bergen village, and Bergenfield show how Hudson county, New Jersey, attracted the Bergens and how well they were appreciated

Leroy Jerome Bergen is of the Middlesex county branch, his father

Addison Bergen, born on a farm on the outskirts of Cranbury, but now living in South Amboy, New Jersey, engaged in the real estate business Addison Bergen married Cecilia Ada Roll, born in Perth Amboy in 1856, died in South Amboy January 12, 1915 They were the parents of four children Leroy Jerome, of further mention, Albert R, a lumber dealer of South Amboy, Clymenda May, wife of Robert Greenleaf, of South Amboy, Ada Dorothy, a teacher in Trenton, New Jersey, public schools

Leroy Jerome Bergen was born in South Amboy, New Jersey, December 29, 1888, and there attended public schools until reaching the age of seventeen, graduating from the high school in 1905 He then spent a summer in the employ of Donnell & Miller, lumber dealers, but in the fall of 1905 he entered the Coleman Business College at Newark, where he finished the course and then returned to business life On July 1, 1919 he became a member of the corporation, Miller Bergen & Welsh, dealers in lumber, millwork and masons' supplies, located at Broadway and First street, South Amboy, New Jersey. The officers of the company are as follows A J Miller, president, O. W Welsh, vice-president, L J Bergen secretary and treasurer

During the World War period, 1917-18, Mr. Bergen was in the service, serving at Camp Dix and on local draft board duty He is a Presbyterian in religious preference, a member of the Young Men's Christian Association, and the American Legion He is fond of out-of-door sports, particularly power boating He has won honorable place in the business life of his community, and is one of the young business men of South Amboy whose career has been most creditable

---

HENRY CHRISTIAN AXEN—From the time he left school in 1907 until the present, Henry C Axen has been connected with the printing business in Perth Amboy, and since 1912 has been proprietor of his own shop, The Axen Press, No 145 Fayette street He is a son of John Henry Axen, born in Flensborg, Denmark who married Annie Christine Sorensen, born in Denmark, and he came to the United States with his wife and three children settling in Perth Amboy, where he died March 13, 1913, aged sixty-one years His wife died December 13, 1912, aged fifty-six They were the parents of the following children, the youngest born in the United States· 1 John Peter a painter of Perth Amboy 2 Mary married Alfred P Thompson a chemist of Perth Amboy, they are the parents of eight children 3 Carolina Serena, married Jens Olson an employee of the Lehigh Valley Railroad, they are the parents of five children 4 Henry C, of further mention

Henry C Axen, youngest and only American born child of John Henry and Annie Christine (Sorensen) Axen, was born in Perth Amboy, New Jersey. September 27 1883 He attended the public schools until he graduated from the grammar grades then began learning the printer's trade in the office of the 'Evening News" He served a full term of apprenticeship at his trade and continued with the "News" until 1912, when he established the Axen Press, a modern print shop at No 174

New Brunswick avenue, moving later to No 145 Fayette street His job printing shop is well patronized and is a well known Perth Amboy institution Mr. Axen is a Republican in politics, and for the past three years (1918-1920), has been president of the Fourth Ward Republican Club As a boy he was fond of bicycle racing, and at the age of sixteen won his novice race He attended meets at the nearby towns and met with a fair amount of success in carrying away winners' prizes His favored recreation now is automobiling He is a member of the Free and Accepted Masons, Improved Order of Red Men, Independent Order of Odd Fellows, Benevolent and Protective Order of Elks, Owls, D B S Haymakers, Perth Amboy Typographical Union, No 658 and Western Improvement Association

Mr Axen married (first) in New York City, February 22, 1906, Minnie K Swendsen, who died in 1914, leaving four children Mary Elizabeth, born September 15, 1907, Clara Henrietta, born April 11, 1909, Anita Christina, born March 15, 1911, John Henry, born November 7, 1914 He married (second) Meta Marie Sandholdt, born in Woodbridge, New Jersey, her parents Jens and Mary Sandholdt, now residing in Perth Amboy One child was born of this marriage, Myrtle Meta, born September 29, 1920

PETER HARRY STOVER HENDRICKS—Well known in the administration circles of New Brunswick, Peter Harry Stover Hendricks, postmaster, has lived most of his life in this community which he is serving He was born in Neshanic, New Jersey, November 30, 1872 His parents were John and Cornelia (Bennett) Hendricks John Hendricks was born in New Brunswick, and died here, March 30, 1918 He was a brick mason here for many years He and his wife had eight children John, deceased Louis, deceased, Katherine, deceased, Mary, deceased, formerly the wife of George McMullin· Emma Loblein, deceased, William H, brick mason of New Brunswick Peter Harry Stover, of further mention, Cora May, wife of William H. Colburn

Peter Harry Stover Hendricks was brought by his parents to New Brunswick, New Jersey, when he was an infant, and here he attended school until he was fourteen years of age, when he entered upon his business career, securing a position as office boy with the Norfolk & New Brunswick Hosiery Company Later he served an apprenticeship to the mason's trade and was associated with his father for twenty-five years in this particular occupation A Democrat in politics, Mr Hendricks has always taken an active part in the affairs of the organization In 1910 he was elected a member of the Board of Freeholders and resigned in 1913, when he received his appointment as postmaster of New Brunswick, a post which he is still (1920) filling with untiring faithfulness and devotion to duty which are characteristic of the man He occupies a high place in the opinion of those who know him, a place which he has won by his own energy and upright character He fraternizes with the Benevolent and Protective Order of Elks, and with the Senior Order of United American Mechanics Mr Hendricks also holds membership in the Union Club of New Brunswick

On April 11, 1902, Mr. Hendricks was united in marriage with Fay Farmer, daughter of John V and Mary Farmer Her father owns a farm just outside of New Brunswick To Mr and Mrs Hendricks have been born two children Eldon L, born January 6, 1904, Robert Ross, born March 30, 1911

LOUIS YALE SOSIN, independent candidate for the office of county clerk for Middlesex county, New Jersey, a member of the famous 'Lightning" or 78th Division, with which he saw active service in France during the closing campaigns of the World War, and one of the prominent among the younger attorneys of Perth Amboy, is a native of New York City, born July 23, 1891

Mr Sosin is a son of Jacob and Rachel (Sosin) Sosin, the former named having been born in Bohemia, where he spent the first years of his childhood Bohemia, it will be remembered, is the home of the Czecho-Slovaks who did such heroic service for the allied cause, and which has now won its independence from Hapsburg rule and the Austrian Empire, so that it has something of poetic justice in that the descendant of one of its sons should have played his part, though in the armies of a new world, to secure its hard won freedom The elder Mr Sosin came to the United States with his parents while a young man and located in New York City, where he became engaged in a mercantile line of business and prospered He later came to Perth Amboy, New Jersey, and here established himself in the crockery and glass business in which he continues active at the present time He married, in New York City, Rachel Sosin, a distant cousin, and they were the parents of four children, as follows Louis Yale, Jennie, now the wife of Herman Sloan, a druggist of Perth Amboy, Maxwell, now a law student in Perth Amboy, and Sadie, who attends the Perth Amboy High School

Until he had reached the age of ten years, Louis Yale Sosin lived in his native city of New York, but in 1901 came to Perth Amboy with his parents and has ever since made this place his home He attended the local public schools, and although the educational advantages to be had therein were somewhat meagre in comparison to what they are today, yet he was of an ambitious nature, and took advantage of every opportunity to the full He was a student in the local schools at the time of the opening of the Public Library, and was one of the first to avail himself of the extended field of study and reading that it offered to the community After passing through the grammar grades, Mr Sosin entered the High School, where he remained four years and was graduated with the class of 1909 Ambitious of a professional career, the young man determined to take up the law and with this end in view matriculated in the New York University Law School He also attended the Law School of Columbia University, and at these two institutions pursued his studies to such good purpose that in 1915 he was admitted to the New Jersey bar He had already, however, gained considerable experience in the practical side of legal work, having served while a

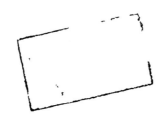

Norman H. Smith.

student for three years in the office of Joseph E Stricker, public prosecutor so that he was far from unknown when he finally established himself in Perth Amboy as an attorney   This he did in association with
City Solicitor Francis P Coan of South Amboy, and it was not long
before his really unusual abilities as a lawyer, coupled to an engaging
personality and a character that imposed trust upon all who came in
contact with him, brought him to a position among the leading members
of the Middlesex county bar   He speedily made his personality felt in
his home community, and gained for himself many warm friends, not
only there but throughout the State, who are now enthusiastically sup-
porting him in his candidacy   Mr Sosin's war record is a fine one and
has added greatly to his reputation and popularity in Middlesex county
In February, 1918, he enlisted in the 311th Regiment of Infantry, which
became a part of the 78th Division, known as the "Lightning" Division,
and after less than three months training in this country was sent to
France   He saw much of the most bitter fighting in which the American
troops took part and was present in the St Mihiel and Argonne-Meuse
battles, it being his fortune to ' go over the top" no less than four times
It was also his most extraordinarily good fortune, considering the fact
that his regiment lost about two-thirds of its effectives in the last of
these actions, to come through unhurt, although he had many hair-
breadth escapes   Since the signing of the armistice, Mr. Sosin has given
much of his time to educational work among the foreign elements in
his regiment   He is a figure in fraternal circles in Perth Amboy, and is
a member of the Masonic order, having attained the thirty-second degree
He is affiliated with Prudence Lodge, No 204, Ancient Free and Accepted Masons, Amboy Chapter, Royal Arch Masons, Jersey City
Council, Royal and Select Masters, ——— Temple, Ancient Arabic
Order Nobles of the Mystic Shrine and New Jersey Consistory, Sovereign Princes of the Royal Secret   He is also a member of the Order
of the Sons of Zion, and Perth Amboy Lodge, No 784, Benevolent and
Protective Order of Elks   He was one of the principal organizers of
Perth Amboy Post, No 45, American Legion, and has since held the
office of treasurer, he is also vice-commander of the post, and vice-com-
mander of the Middlesex County American Legion executive committee
He attends the Bnei Zion Temple in Perth Amboy.

NORMAN HARRISON SMITH—Among those New Brunswick
business men who are actively influential in the community is Norman
Harrison Smith, who has for the past ten years since coming here been
interested in everything that pertains to the welfare and development
of New Brunswick   Mr Smith is descended from ancestors in the
Colonial and Revolutionary periods of our history and is conspicuously
identified with the developments of the most vital interests of the State
of New Jersey
    Harvey Isaac Smith, father of Norman Harrison Smith, was born in
Jersey City and died there in March, 1889, at the age of twenty-nine
years   He was a member of a branch of the Smith family who have

resided in New Jersey for many generations He married Clara Tetlow, who now resides in Dunellen, New Jersey Mrs Smith's father and her uncle, Henry Tetlow, were prominent manufacturers of soaps and perfumes in Philadelphia, and descend from one, ——— Tetlow, who came to this country from England in the middle of the seventeenth century Mr and Mrs Smith were the parents of two children Maude May, wife of John B Buckalew, of Dunellen, New Jersey, and Norman Harrison, of further mention

Norman Harrison Smith was born in Jersey City, New Jersey, June 28, 1888, and came with his mother to New Brunswick, New Jersey, when he was but two years of age Here he attended the local public schools and after his third year in the New Brunswick High School, he entered Coleman's Business College, at Newark, New Jersey, from which he was graduated in 1904 He then secured a position as bookkeeper with the Beckwith-Chandler Company of Newark, but resigned after two years to accept a position with J H Dunham & Company, of New York City. Two years later, he left this concern to go with the Crandell & Godley Company as salesman, and remained with this firm until 1910, when he came to New Brunswick and established the Williamson Garage Company with Walter Williamson as a partner This association continued until September, 1911, when Mr Smith disposed of his interests and established a new business under the name of Garside & Smith, Walter L Garside having become a partner in the enterprise Five years later, Mr Smith absorbed the whole business, and on January 1, 1920, moved to his present location, No 68 French street New Brunswick having erected suitable quarters covering a space of 50x110 feet, his enterprise being known as the American Auto Company It has been due to his own efforts that his business has grown to its present extensive proportions, and he is looked upon by his associates and fellow-citizens as a most capable business man He handles the Buick, Dodge, Studebaker and Jordan pleasure cars, and the Brockway and Day-Elder trucks, as well as a full line of accessories, and also conducts a service station for the repairing of the cars handled by the concern

Mr Smith has always taken an active interest in educational matters, and is chairman of the committee on instruction and discipline of the Highland Park Board of Education He is a member of St James' Methodist Episcopal Church, and also is prominent in the local fraternal organizations He has taken his thirty-second degree in Freemasonry, affiliating with Union Lodge, No 19, Free and Accepted Masons Scott Chapter No 4, Royal Arch Masons, Scott Council, No 1, Royal and Select Mastors· Temple Commandery, No 18, Knights Templar Salaam Temple, Ancient Arabic Order Nobles of the Mystic Shrine, Newark, New Jersey He is now (1920), junior warden of Union Lodge, and also junior warden of Temple Commandery He is a member and past grand of the Independent Order of Odd Fellows, a member of the Junior Order of United American Mechanics, and the Benevolent and Protective Order of Elks He also holds membership in the Craftsmen's Club, the Middlesex Automobile Club, and the New Brunswick Boat Club, a trustee of same, and is vice-president of the Knights of King Arthur Club. Mr. Smith is treasurer of the New Brunswick Motor Trade Association. In politics he is a Republican, being a member of the Highland Park Republican Club, and one of the active workers of his party.

On June 2, 1909, Mr. Smith was united in marriage with Hazel A. Swenarton, a daughter of Thomas H. and Adele (Stivers) Swenarton. Mr. and Mrs. Smith are the parents of three children: Norman Russell, born March 12, 1911 Spencer Hazelton, born December 3, 1913; Thomas Harvey, born February 28, 1915. Mr. Smith has a beautiful home in Highland Park, at No. 9 Grant avenue.

JOHN BAYARD KIRKPATRICK—The name of Kirkpatrick has been prominently identified with the insurance business in New Brunswick, New Jersey, for a great many years, but together in this business both Mr. Kirkpatrick and his father have been influential citizens, giving to the welfare of the community the interest demanded of every good citizen.

John Bayard Kirkpatrick, father of the subject of this review, was born in Washington, D. C., in 1857 and died September 6, 1912, at New Brunswick, in his sixty-seventh year. He founded the John Bayard Kirkpatrick Insurance Agency and conducted it for forty-nine years previous to his death. Being ever prominent in the city's affairs, he was city treasurer for many years. He married Mary Elizabeth Phillips, a native of Riverdale, New York, she is still living and resides in New Brunswick, New Jersey. To Mr. and Mrs. Kirkpatrick were born four children. Mary Jane Bayard, wife of Abram Van Ness Baldwin. Laura Boardman, John Bayard mentioned below, and Andrew.

John Bayard (2) Kirkpatrick, son of John Bayard (1) and Mary E. (Phillips) Kirkpatrick, was born in New Brunswick, New Jersey, February 23, 1887. His elementary education was obtained by private tutor, after which he entered Rutgers Preparatory School, from which he was graduated in 1896 subsequently matriculating at Rutgers College, from which he graduated in 1900, having completed the prescribed four years' course. In 1912 when his father's death occurred Mr. Kirkpatrick entered the insurance business which his father had established and has continued in it ever since at the present location No. 393 George street. On October 1, 1912, the business was incorporated under the name of the J. Bayard Kirkpatrick Company, J. Bayard Kirkpatrick, president, Mary E. Kirkpatrick, vice-president, Andrew Kirkpatrick, secretary and treasurer, for the purpose of handling real estate and insurance. He is also treasurer and a director of the Second Merchants' Building and Loan Association.

Mr. Kirkpatrick has taken considerable interest in military affairs, and for fifteen years was a member of the National Guard, eight years a member of Essex Troop, of Newark, N. J., and for seven years was connected with Company H, 2nd New Jersey Infantry National Guard, of New Brunswick, holding the commission of first lieutenant, from which he went into World War as first lieutenant and in May was promoted to captain, he served from March 31, 1917, until December 31, 1918 when he was honorably discharged from the service He is an attendant of the Second Reformed Church of New Brunswick, and a member of the Delta Phi fraternity.

On June 15, 1912, Mr Kirkpatrick was united in marriage with Bessie Madeline Fisher, daughter of Charles and Ella Fisher, of New Brunswick, New Jersey They are the parents of one child, Mary Elizabeth Bayard Kirkpatrick, born October 27, 1918 The family home is at No 15 Cleveland avenue.

ARTHUR ERSKINE GRAHAM, who for some years has been prominently connected with the general life of Perth Amboy, New Jersey as a business man and man of affairs, is a member of an old and distinguished Scottish family, this branch of which was founded in the United States by his grandfather, James Graham, who came here from Scotland and located in Woodbridge, New Jersey

Mr Graham's parents were John Henry and Anna Marion (Brown) Graham, old and highly respected residents of Perth Amboy, now both deceased John Henry Graham was born in Woodbridge, in the year 1847, and as a young man went to Tottenville, Staten Island where he resided for a time He later removed to Pleasant Plains, New York, and from there came to Perth Amboy, New Jersey, in 1896 He was the proprietor of two successful bakeries here and also taught vocal music in the local public schools, remaining active until his death, October 29 1914 His wife, who was a Miss Brown of Manasquan, New Jersey, died at Perth Amboy July 1, 1907, at the age of sixty-four They were the parents of four children, as follows George, who died at Pleasant Plains at the age of twenty-one years Lillian May, who now makes her home in Perth Amboy James William, died February 11, 1919, at the age of thirty-eight and left two children, Marian and Natalie, and Arthur Erskine

The birth of Arthur Erskine Graham occurred in Tottenville, Staten Island June 5, 1882, but he was yet an infant when his parents removed to Pleasant Plains and it was with that place that his earliest associations were formed He attended school there until his fifteenth year, when he came to Perth Amboy, where he has made his home ever since He continued to attend the grammar schools of this city until he was sixteen years of age, when he gave up his studies and secured a position as a stenographer in the office of the vice-president of the Lehigh Valley Railroad in New York City There he remained for five years, learning much about business methods and gaining in experience, and then gave up his position to take one with the National Fire Proofing Company of Perth Amboy, one of the largest industrial concerns in the region Until quite recently Mr Graham has continued a valuable employee of this company, his association with it continuing over a period of some seventeen years, but in the meantime he also took an active part in local public affairs until at the present time he is devoting all his time and attention to the discharge of his official duties For eight months, in 1919, he served as secretary of the local draft board under Mayor Ten Brook. From January, 1919, for one year he was secretary to former Mayor Dorsey, who is mentioned at length in this work, and on January 1, 1920, was appointed city clerk of Perth Amboy by the Board of Aldermen for a three-year term He is now engaged in filling that responsible post, displaying an efficiency and disinterestedness that have already won the approval of all classes of his fellow-citizens Mr Graham is a member of the Raritan Yacht Club of Perth Amboy, serving for eleven years as its secretary, and is now on its board of governors He is devotedly attached to all forms of out-door sports and takes particular pleasure in baseball and automobiling In his religious belief Mr Graham is a Presbyterian and attends the First Presbyterian Church of Perth Amboy, of which he is a trustee

Arthur Erskine Graham was united in marriage, October 5, 1903, in Perth Amboy, with Ada Tyrell, a native of this place, born July 5, 1882, a daughter of James and Mary (Martin) Tyrell, both deceased Mr. Tyrell was for many years the owner of a large livery stable in Perth Amboy, was a leading figure in banking and financial circles and took a prominent part in the development of the volunteer fire department

ALEXANDER MERCHANT was born in Glasgow, Scotland, January 7, 1872, the son of Alexander and Barbara (Findlay) Merchant Alexander Merchant, Sr, was a purser on the National Line, sailing between Liverpool and New York City for many years He died in Glasgow, in 1877, at the age of thirty-three years

Alexander Merchant was brought by his parents to this country when he was very young and upon landing in New York went immediately to Long Island City, where the lad received his education In 1888, at the age of sixteen years, he came to New Brunswick, New Jersey, and secured a position with D D Williamson, an architect, where he remained for five years, subsequently going to New York City, where he continued in this line for twelve years In 1906 he returned to New Brunswick, and established himself at his present location, No 363 George street He has been very successful from the very outset in this enterprise and is eminently respected for the unimpeachable integrity of all his dealings He specializes in school buildings, but also handles all kinds of work in his line of business, the New Brunswick High School being one of his pieces of work

Alexander Merchant is one of the foremost citizens of New Brunswick, always a leader in movements which have for their end the advancement of civic conditions A Republican in political affiliations, he is a keen student of all issues and has taken a keen and active interest in the affairs of the local organizations, having served on the Highland Park Council for many years, and also on its Board of Education Mr Merchant is a director of the Highland Park Building and Loan Association, also the Young Men's Building and Loan Association He is affiliated with Palestine Lodge, No 111 Free and Accepted Masons, and New Brunswick Lodge, No 324, Benevolent and Protective Order of Elks He also holds membership in the New Brunswick Club and the New Brunswick Boat Club His hobby is tennis Mr Merchant and his family are members of the Highland Park Reformed Church

On June 24, 1896, Mr Merchant was united in marriage with Margaret Beaton Henderson, of New Brunswick, daughter of William and Agnes (Thomson) Henderson, both deceased. Mr. and Mrs Merchant are the parents of one child William Alexander Merchant, born August 17, 1898, he enlisted in the United States army during the World War and was assigned to the 504th Motor Truck Company, stationed at Charleston, South Carolina, and received his honorable discharge in June, 1919, he is a student at Syracuse University, a member of the class of 1923

WILLIAM SCHLESINGER, numbered among the prominent business men of New Brunswick New Jersey, is the owner and manager of the Schlesinger coal and grain business Since 1890 Mr Schlesinger has been a resident of this community and none of her vital interests lack his influential and public-spirited support

Henry Schlesinger, father of the subject of this review, was born in Austria, in 1826, and died in Brooklyn, New York For many years he was a shoe dealer in New York City He married Sophia Frend, also a native of Austria, and to them were born eight children, of whom three are still living William of further mention Frank in the cigar business at No 90 Church street, New Brunswick; Frederick H , in the employ of the Texas Company, at Hamburg, Germany

William Schlesinger was born in Detroit, Michigan, August 14 1860, and was brought to New York City by his parents when very young, and here in the public schools of the city, obtained his education after which he attended New York University Until 1890 Mr Schlesinger was in the cigar manufacturing business in New York City then came to this community and was employed by the Charles C. Davis Cigar Company until 1908 when he engaged in the cigar manufacturing business on his own account until 1910, at which time he purchased the Henry H Banker coal and grain business which he is conducting at the present time, his success being due to his untiring energy and firm belief in his own ability

In politics he is a Republican and takes an active part in the affairs of the local organizations having been a member of the Water Commission and of the County Board of Taxation serving as president of both and a member of the Board of Trade He affiliates with National Lodge, No 209 Free and Accepted Masons of New York City, a past master of same and with New Brunswick Lodge No 324 Benevolent and Protective Order of Elks a past exalted ruler He is a prominent member of the congregation, Anshe Emeth Synagogue, of New Brunswick, also former president of that organization

On February 22, 1900, Mr Schlesinger was united in marriage with Rae Wolfson, a native of New Brunswick, and the daughter of Aaron and Augusta Wolfson, both deceased Mr and Mrs Schlesinger are the parents of two children. Gertrude, born in October, 1903, and William Henry, born May 10, 1905

ARTHUR STERN, the active head of one of Perth Amboy's most important business establishments, is in the prime of life and full of the vital energy which is so large a factor in business confidence, and he is a part of the city's prosperity

Simon Stern, his father, coming to this country as a boy from his native city of Berlin, Germany, went direct to St Joseph, Missouri There he grew up, putting his natural business ability to excellent account in the clothing business, which he followed for thirty-five years He was very successful and retired from active business twelve years before his death, devoting his time after his retirement, to charity He married Henrietta Hart, who was born in Cincinnati, Ohio She died in St Joseph, in 1910, at the age of sixty-four years They were the parents of six children, all of whom are now living Bertha, wife of Julius Rosenblatt, Arthur, of whom extended mention follows, Stella, now a widow, residing in Kansas City, Florence, who also lives in Kansas City, Sidney, a resident of Los Angeles, California and Maurice, of St Joseph

Arthur Stern was born in St Joseph, Missouri, March 1, 1873 He received his early education at the excellent public schools of that city, supplementing this preparatory study with a course at the Wentworth Military Academy, at Lexington, Missouri After this three years' course he returned to St Joseph, and opened a furniture store under the name of the People's Furniture Company He was successful from the start, but after four years there, he decided to remove to a larger city He went to St Louis and opened a store in the same line of business, remaining there twelve years, with most satisfactory results At the end of that period various considerations induced him to come East, and he bought out the business which he now conducts in Perth Amboy Under his management the business has fully doubled its capacity, and the store has become one of the show places of the town

While his mercantile interests almost completely absorb his time, Mr Stern is not wholly a man of business His chief delight is getting into the great out-door world, motoring hunting, or fishing, and he is a member of the Raritan Yacht Club He is also a member of the Benevolent and Protective Order of Elks

Mr Stern married in El Paso, Texas, on June 19, 1903, Belle daughter of Thomas and Margaret Ogden She was born in Salt Lake City, Utah Her father is now a resident of Traverse City, Michigan, her mother died in 1913 Mr and Mrs Stern are the parents of two children, both living Irma Ogden, born June 6, 1904; and Arthur H, born October 16, 1906

WILLIAM GORDON HOWELL, who occupies the highest position of trust in the gift of the city of New Brunswick New Jersey, descended from an old New Jersey family, of English origin, and himself long active in the manufacturing interests of the State. Mr Howell represents the solid citizenship which is the basis of all progress

Mr Howell's father, George Wilson Howell, was a native of New Brunswick, New Jersey, and died here at the age of seventy-eight years, in 1913 He was superintendent of the Janeway & Carpender Wall Paper plant for many years, having become associated with this firm at its organization, and remaining with them until his death He was widely celebrated in fraternal circles as one of the most loyal Masons in the State of New Jersey, and one of the best posted men in the Masonic fraternity on the subject of Masonry, having advanced to the thirty-third degree He was a member of Union Lodge, Scott Chapter, No 4, Temple Commandery, Mecca Temple, Ancient Arabic Order Nobles of the Mystic Shrine His advice was frequently sought in this connection, and his decisions were considered final George Wilson Howell married Priscilla Van Deventer, who was born in South River, a locality known in recent years as Van Deventer Station from the prominence of this family They were the parents of eight children, the three now living being Charles, Alice and William Gordon, all living in the family homestead on the corner of George street and Remsen avenue

William Gordon Howell was born in New Brunswick, New Jersey He received his education in the public schools of the city At the age of nineteen years he entered the business in which his father was engaged filling the position of wall paper designer for a period of twenty-five years the greater part of that time with the Janeway-Carpender Company, but for a time connected with New York City concerns In 1908. Mr Howell was elected assessor of the city of New Brunswick, in which office he served the people with the same capability which he had always put into his business interests, holding this office for six years At the end of that period he succeeded to his present office, that of city treasurer He entered upon the duties of this office, July 15, 1919, and is serving the interests of the public with rare judgment In addition to his duties in this connection, Mr Howell holds the office of custodian of school funds, to which he was elected for a term of four years He is secretary of the Building and Loan Association which has offices in the National Bank Building, and during the World War was fuel administrator for this district Mr Howell spends little time in recreation, being devoted to his many interests of a business nature, but finds his favorite relaxation in fishing and home gardening He is single He is a member of Christ Episcopal Church

---

ALVIN BARTHOLDI FOX, one of the busiest men in Perth Amboy, a member of the firm of Larson & Fox, civil engineers and also secretary and treasurer of the Union Garage Company of Perth Amboy, has from the inception of his business career, been identified with local industrial

interests, making his way to the position of prominence which he holds today Mr Fox, in addition to his prominent connection with the business life of the city, is officially and influentially associated with the various other elements of her life as a municipality

Frederick F Fox, father of Alvin Bartholdi Fox, was born in New York City, June 2, 1842 During the Civil War from 1861-1865, he was a member of Hawkin's Zouaves, Company C, Ninth New York Regiment, and, consequently, saw much active service. At the age of thirty-seven he came to Perth Amboy, New Jersey, and here was engaged in the undertaking, real estate and insurance business up to the time of his death, which occurred May 15, 1914 Mr Fox married Maria L Bohr, a native of Clarkstown, Rockland county, New York, where she was born September 11, 1851, at the present time she resides at Perth Amboy Mr and Mrs Fox were the parents of two children Caroline M , wife of Matthew D Sherrill, of Irvington, and Alvin B , subject of this review

Alvin Bartholdi Fox was born in Perth Amboy, New Jersey, October 29 1886, the son of Frederick F and Maria L. (Bohr) Fox He was educated in the public schools of his native city, and Rutgers College, from which institution he was graduated in 1908, and received his degree of Civil Engineer in 1912 Immediately after leaving college he entered the employ of Mogan Larson, civil engineer, and at the same time took a night course at the Brooklyn Polytechnic School It was with Mr Larson that he received his business initiation and it was here that he exhibited his ability and developed those executive talents which enabled him to gain the success which he has since attained Perhaps the truth of this statement is best attested by the fact that in 1910 he was received into partnership forming the firm of Larson & Fox The success which uniformly attends the company is due in large measure to the mingled aggressiveness and conservatism always exercised by Mr Fox In 1912, the same year that he received his degree of Civil Engineer. he was appointed county engineer of Middlesex county, and also resident engineer of the New Jersey State Highway Department, which latter office he held for a period of one year On January 1, of the year 1920, he was made borough engineer of Spotswood, Middlesex county, New Jersey

In 1918 he assisted in the organization of the Union Garage Company of Perth Amboy, New Jersey, and since May, 1918, he has been secretary, treasurer and general manager of the organization The same year that he became associated with this company, he served on the commission to suggest a revision of the motor vehicle laws which pertained to automobile trucks That the Union Garage Company has prospered during the past two years is largely due to Mr Fox. who has displayed a keen interest in its welfare from the beginning and has viewed its increasing success with no little satisfaction

In politics Mr Fox is a Democrat, and is a member of the Perth Amboy Democratic Club He is also a member of the United Business Men's Association, the Chamber of Commerce and the Perth Amboy

Automobile Dealers' Association, associate member of the American Society of Civil Engineers, and is treasurer of the County Engineers' Association of the State of New Jersey His clubs are the East Jersey, and the Raritan Yacht In religion, Mr Fox is a Baptist

Mr Fox married, in Matawan, New Jersey, July 15, 1912 Marjorie M Brown, daughter of Harry A Brown, a shoe manufacturer of New Oxford Pennsylvania Mr and Mrs Fox are the parents of three children Frederick F., born July 3, 1916, Jean M., born March 1, 1918, Ruth E, born November 5, 1919

Alvin Bartholdi Fox is one of those substantial and aggressive business men who constitute the bulwark of a city's development, and he stands as an able exponent of the spirit of the age in his efforts to advance progress and improvement His business transactions are conducted in accordance with the highest principles, and he fulfills to the letter every trust committed to him

---

ARTHUR HOWARD DUNHAM is among the successful men of Perth Amboy, New Jersey, where he conducts a large business in real estate, and occupies a prominent place Mr Dunham is a native of Woodbridge township, and a member of an ancient New Jersey family which was founded here in early Colonial days and has ever since maintained a high place in the esteem of their fellow-citizens

Hezekiah Dunham, father of Arthur Howard Dunham, was born in Woodbridge, New Jersey, April 10, 1843, and died there October 8, 1908 He followed the trade of mason for a number of years He married Louisa Murdock, who was born in New York City, and died in Perth Amboy, October 11, 1910, at the age of seventy-seven years Mr and Mrs Dunham were the parents of seven children Charles, Mulford, deceased, William, Harriett, wife of Bruce L Drummond, Della, wife of Theodore Aschenberg, George, and Arthur Howard, of further mention

Arthur Howard Dunham was born in Woodbridge New Jersey, March 28, 1879, and attended the grammar schools of his native place, after which he took a course with the Scranton Correspondence School He then served an apprenticeship to the mason's trade, and subsequently became foreman for the National Fireproofing Company at Woodbridge, with whom he remained five years In 1905 he established himself in the contracting business in Woodbridge, and four years later moved to Perth Amboy, where he has since been engaged in the real estate business He has been highly successful in this venture, and within a short period of eleven years has risen to a place of prominence in business circles In 1920-21, he erected seventy-five houses in Woodbridge New Jersey, representing a sum of over $395,000 Unswerving honesty and fairness has won for him his success, which is in every sense of the word self-made—the result of his own indefatigable effort and his own unfailing belief in his ability to succeed In politics, Mr Dunham is a Republican and takes a keen interest in the activities of the organization He is a member of the Bricklayers' and Plasterers' Union No 27 In religion he is a Methodist

On March 5, 1902, Mr Dunham was united in marriage with Margaret Sofield, of Perth Amboy Her father was a native of Perth Amboy, and died there, February 11, 1916, at the age of sixty-eight He was a ticket agent for the Pennsylvania Railroad for many years previous to his death Mr and Mrs Dunham are the parents of three children Byron, born June 10, 1904, A Gordon, born March 6, 1906, Malcomb born June 27, 1909

PERCY LYLE VAN NUIS was born in New Brunswick, New Jersey, March 17, 1882, the son of Lyle and Emma (Snedeker) Van Nuis Lyle Van Nuis was at the time of his death in 1914, cashier of the National Bank of New Jersey, at New Brunswick Percy Lyle Van Nuis, since reaching young manhood, has identified himself with every movement pertaining to the welfare and advancement of the community

Percy L Van Nuis obtained his preliminary education in private and public schools of his native place, and upon graduating from the New Brunswick High School in 1899, matriculated at Rutgers College from which he was graduated in 1903, after having completed a four years' course of thorough training That same year he entered the employ of the Western Electric Company and remained for five years, and in 1908 he entered the Nevership Manufacturing Company Ten years later he resigned and became identified with the Cronk Manufacturing Company, the Highland Park Building Company, and the Highland Park Lumber Company, in whose employ he has since continued, proving himself to be most efficient, and holding the office of treasurer and director in same

In politics, Mr Van Nuis is a Republican, and although he has not sought public office he nevertheless always interests himself in public affairs, and holds decided views upon all questions which come before the public for discussion He is affiliated with the Delta Upsilon fraternity of Rutgers College, and was treasurer of the Rutgers Chapter from 1911 until 1918 While in college, he was active in all athletics and for four years was a member of the track and relay teams captain of both teams in the senior year He attends the First Dutch Reformed Church of New Brunswick, and also holds membership in the Rutgers and Country clubs of New Brunswick and is a member and director of the Young Men's Christian Association Mr Van Nuis is unmarried

---

JOHN BANKER —As a business man, owner of a line of busses operating in New Brunswick and vicinity, John Banker and his son, William J Banker, Jr , are well known in this section of the State of New Jersey In social life and fraternity affairs Mr Banker takes an active part and lends his influence to all movements that tend to uplift and advance the standard of right living

John Banker was born in New Brunswick, New Jersey, May 2, 1869, a son of Frederick William and Elizabeth Clara (Lewis) Banker, natives of Germany. Frederick W. Banker was reared and educated in his native land, coming to the United States at the age of twenty. He located in New Brunswick, New Jersey, and later engaged in the grocery business, success attending his efforts. He died in New Brunswick, in 1892, aged fifty-four years, survived by his wife, whose death occurred in New Brunswick, August 5, 1916, aged seventy-six years. They were the parents of seven children, John Banker, of this review, being the only one now living.

John Banker attended the school in the vicinity of his home in New Brunswick, completing his studies at the age of fifteen years. He then entered his father's grocery store, located at No. 143 Throop avenue, known as F. W. Banker, grocer, and remained as his assistant for several years. His father's health then began to fail, and for a period of six years the son conducted the grocery business at the same address on his own account. He then entered the employ of Mr. Fleischmann, of compressed yeast fame, with whom he remained three years, and for the following eight years served in the capacity of assistant superintendent of the New Jersey State Reformatory. This brought him up to March, 1919, when he established the business he is now engaged in, transportation, the running of busses being a large feature of the work, the plant located at Nos. 3-5 Schuyler street, New Brunswick, his son, William James Banker, known as William J. Banker, Jr., who is associated with him, serving as president of the Gray Bus Line, Inc. During the years 1895-96-97-98, Mr. Banker represented the Second Ward of New Brunswick as alderman, and in 1898 was chief of the Volunteer Fire Department, reëlected in 1899. He is a member of the German Lutheran church, the Free and Accepted Masons, in which he attained the thirty-second degree, the Improved Order of Red Men, the Benevolent and Protective Order of Elks, the Junior Order of United American Mechanics, the Senior Order of United American Mechanics, and the Red Cross.

Mr. Banker married, in New Brunswick, March 9, 1888, Lizzie C. Colton, born in New Brunswick, daughter of Thomas and Mary (Van de Water) Colton, the former named deceased, the latter named a resident of New Brunswick. Two children were born to Mr. and Mrs. Banker, namely: 1. William James, above referred to, born December 4, 1888, married Laura Hunter, a native of Canada, no children. 2. Sophia Florence, who became the wife of Fred Hamer, of New Brunswick.

DAVID J. WILLIAMS, owner and manager of the monumental works at No. 311 New Brunswick avenue, Perth Amboy, has been identified with the business life of this community since coming here in 1900, and in all that makes for the betterment of the city he is an earnest worker.

John R. Williams, father of David J. Williams, is a native of Lemont, Pennsylvania and now lives there retired, having been a shoe manu-

Edward W. Space.

facturer for many years   He married Sarah Z. Young, now deceased,
and to them have been born ten children   George a teacher of Lemont,
Pennsylvania , Edward, a farmer of Lemont   David J , mentioned below
Frank S , a stone cutter in Perth Amboy , Nelson W , a resident of
Lemont , Zepora M , deceased , Martin W , a resident of Lemont   Moses,
deceased , Isadora, wife of George Fike, of Lemont, Pennsylvania ,
Sarah E , deceased

David J Williams was born in Lemont, Pennsylvania, December 25,
1872, the son of John R and Sarah Z (Young) Williams   He obtained
his education in the public schools of his native place, and then learned
the trade of marble cutting   In 1900 he came to Perth Amboy and
established monumental works on South Second street, where he
remained for eight years, at the end of which time he moved to his
present location, No 311 New Brunswick avenue   The enterprise
which he started in a small way has consistently grown and developed
until it is now one of the largest and most successful of its kind in the
county, and is the result of determination perseverance and strict attention to business duties   Mr Williams is prominent in the fraternal
life of the city and affiliates with Huguenot Lodge, No 381, Free and
Accepted Masons, the Junior Order of United American Mechanics,
the Woodmen of the World, Camp 31 and the American Order of United
Workmen, Great Kills   His hobby is hunting and he devotes a portion
of what little time he can take from his ever increasing business duties
to this particular pastime

On June 28, 1896, Mr Williams married (first) Alene M Petersen,
daughter of Frederick and Emma Petersen of Tottenville, Staten Island,
New York   To Mr and Mrs Williams were born three children   Helen
E , June 4, 1899, Kenneth D April 24 1905 , D Leonard July 23 1906
Mrs Williams passed away in 1909   Mr Williams married (second)
June 2, 1912 Marie A Neilsen they have no issue

EDWARD WELLS SPACE—In the early part of the nineteenth
century, about 1816, the Space family emigrated from Germany to the
United States and located upon a farm in Tompkins county, New York
One of the descendants of this original settler, George A Space, came
to New Jersey in 1850 and located in New Brunswick, where one of
his children, George Noble Space, was born, July 17, 1852, and lived
there all his life   He learned the machinist trade, which he followed for
many years.   He married Elizabeth Bell, also a native of New Brunswick, where she still lives   They had six children   1 George A , a
machinist, who died in New Brunswick, June 14, 1894   2 Edward
Wells, of whom further   3 William Arthur, deceased   4 Charles A
garage keeper   5 Jennie May, wife of Albert Sevenair, a resident of
Teaneck, New Jersey   6 Ruth Evelyn who married Walter E Pierson
and resides in New Brunswick

The second son of this family, Edward Wells Space, was born in New
Brunswick, October 11, 1877   His birthplace has always been his home,
and here he attended the public schools until, at the age of thirteen,

he left to become an apprentice in the machinist's trade   For the next
eighteen years, Mr Space was in the employ of the John Waldron
Company, machinists, and following this he worked for one year with
the Simplex Auto Company   On April 1, 1913, Mr. Space bought out
the business and so successful has this investment proved to be that
on September 1, 1920, he purchased the property upon which his garage
is located, at No 256 George street

While Mr Space has been employed almost all his life, he has
devoted some of his time to travel, this being his special form of relaxation   His wanderings have taken him over the entire United States,
and in the spring of 1920 he had just finished a tour through a large
portion of South America

That Mr Space is interested in fraternal matters is evidenced by
his membership in the Junior Order of United American Mechanics
in the Young Men's Christian Association, and in the Benevolent and
Protective Order of Elks, he being a past exalted ruler of New Brunswick Lodge, No 324   Mr Space and his family all attend the Methodist
church there

On February 16, 1920, in New Brunswick, Edward Wells Space
married Jane M Edmonds, born in that city the daughter of William
E and Elizabeth L (Smith) Edmonds   Mr Edmonds died in New
Brunswick, May 5, 1920   Mrs Edmonds is still living in New Brunswick

---

JAMES ALFRED COMPTON —Upon leaving educational halls in
1910 Mr Compton entered the insurance business, being employed first
by the firm of Frasers Brothers   then entered the insurance business
for himself, representing the Travelers' Insurance Company of
Perth Amboy, New Jersey, and has since continued in that line most
successfully   his line of life and accident insurance being supplemented
by all kinds of casualty and surety insurance written by responsible
companies   He is a son of James Lewis Compton, also born in Perth
Amboy, former mayor of the city, and a lifelong resident, his death
occurring in 1903   his business, real estate dealing   James L Compton
married Emma De Bow, born in South River, Middlesex county, New
Jersey, who survives a resident of Perth Amboy   They were the parents
of five children: Sophia Brown, married, September 12, 1900, Francis
Luis Mora, now a well known artist of New York City, former resident
of Perth Amboy, Lola residing in Perth Amboy, New Jersey, James
A , of further mention Lewis, and William Arnold, the two last named
are naval veterans of the great World War and now proprietors of the
Ford Agency at Summit, New Jersey

James A Compton was born in Perth Amboy, New Jersey, February
3, 1889, and there attended the public schools   He completed his studies
in Phillips Academy, Exeter New Hampshire, and immediately after
graduation, class of 1910, he returned to Perth Amboy and has for the
past decade been interested in the insurance business   He represents
the Travelers' Life Insurance Company of Hartford as his principal
company, specializing in life insurance, but also writing accident, fire

casualty and surety insurance. Mr Compton is a Democrat in politics, a member of the Benevolent and Protective Order of Elks, Raritan Yacht Club, and of the Presbyterian church. In recreation his hobby is yachting and his craft the "Natirar," is well known on Raritan bay. He is a successful young business man, managing a constantly growing business.

THOMAS FRANCIS DUNIGAN.—In the business and banking circles of Woodbridge, New Jersey, the name of Dunigan is a prominent one.

Thomas Francis Dunigan was born in Woodbridge New Jersey, May 1, 1847, and is a son of Bernard and Julia (Ryan) Dunigan, both parents having been born in Ireland. They became acquainted in Woodbridge, and were married there.

As a boy, Thomas F. Dunigan attended the public and parochial schools of this town, then completed his education at St John's Academy, at Fordham, New York. He started in business with his father, who was a prosperous contractor, having interests also in clay. Later the young man became associated with the Ostrander Fire Brick Company, at Fords, New Jersey, where he remained for some years. Thereafter, Mr Dunigan was with Henry A. Maurer, at Maurer, New Jersey, interested along similar lines. He is now in business for himself in Woodbridge, retailing coal and wood, and doing an extensive business throughout this section in builders' supplies. He has become a power in the construction world of Middlesex county.

Mr Dunigan is also influential in other interests. He is a director and vice-president of the First National Bank of Woodbridge, and was at one time town committeeman and freeholder. In political affiliation he is a Democrat. Mr Dunigan is a member of the New Brunswick Lodge, No 324, Benevolent and Protective Order of Elks.

Mr Dunigan married, in Woodbridge, Jane M. Finn, of that place, and they have four children. Florence, now the wife of James T. Dunn of Brooklyn, New York, George F, Jane M, now the wife of Edmund A Hays, a prominent attorney of Highland Park, New Jersey, and Anna B, who resides at home.

WALTER B FLAVELL.—The Flavell family is an English one, the father and grandfather of Walter B Flavell having come to this country a short time before his birth. The grandfather, Thomas Flavell, left England in 1870, and located in New Brunswick, where he became a farmer, continuing as such until his death in 1911, at the age of eighty-eight years. His son, Walter Flavell, was born in London, England, in 1853. After arriving in the United States, he entered the employ of Janeway & Carpender manufacturers of wall paper, as clerk in their shipping department. He died in New Brunswick, June 10 1907. His wife, Mary Jane (Bloomer) Flavell, was a native of Scotland, born in Glasgow, in 1858. Her death occurred in New Brunswick in 1884. They had six children Walter B of whom further, Lucy E, Harry N Charles W, Mary J, and Thomas P

Walter B Flavell eldest child of Walter and Mary J (Bloomer) Flavell, was born in New Brunswick, New Jersey, September 5, 1877 He acquired an education in the public schools of that city and later attended Wilson's Business College, following this by a course of training in accounting at the New York School of Accounting Some years ago, Mr Flavell became connected with the Janeway & Carpender Wall Paper Manufacturing Company, first as a traveling salesman and later was added the duties of manager of their advertising department which is his business at the present time (1921)

Mr Flavell is exceedingly fond of outdoor exercise, particularly motoring and boating the latter being a favorite pastime of the residents of the city on the banks of the Raritan He is also devoted to music, it being a hobby with him During his service in the Spanish-American War, Mr Flavell was in the department of field music He served with the Third Regiment, New Jersey Volunteer Infantry, during the period of that conflict In Freemasonry, Mr Flavell is very active, he is a member of Palestine Lodge No 111, Scott Chapter, No 4, Royal Arch Masons, is a Knight Templar, connected with Commandery No 11, and also is a member of Salaam Temple, Ancient Arabic Order Nobles of the Mystic Shrine, of Newark, New Jersey. Mr. Flavell is greatly interested in the work of the Young Men's Christian Association of which he is a member, and also of the Craftsmen's Club, of New Brunswick, and the New Brunswick Rotary Club

On July 16, 1902, Walter B. Flavell was united in marriage with Grace M Van Liew, born in New Brunswick the daughter of Henry and Ellen Van Liew, residents of that city Mr and Mrs Flavell reside at No 207 Lawrence avenue, in the Highland Park section of New Brunswick They are members of Christ Protestant Episcopal Church

---

CHRISTIAN JOHNSON is among the younger men who have established themselves as significant factors in the business life of Perth Amboy

His father, Benjamin Johnson was born in Sweden, and came to this country, bringing all the sturdy traditions of his race and a great ambition for the future He began his life in the new country at Oxford Furnace New Jersey securing employment in the mills there He was a faithful worker honest and industrious but his high hopes of the life that was to be so bright were brought to naught by his untimely death when his youngest child was a year and a half old His wife, Annie Mary (Madson) Johnson, was born in Denmark They were the parents of six children, four of whom are living James, Charles F, Alfred B and Christian whose name heads this review

Christian Johnson, familiarly known by his business associates as "Chris" was born in Oxford Furnace, Warren county New Jersey. Here he lived until he was ten years of age, receiving his early education in the public schools He then removed with his mother to Perth Amboy, where he continued his school attendance up to the seventh grade At the age of fourteen years he left school and went out into the world to take care of himself. He became connected with a sewing machine store and began life as salesman and collector. This was a position of considerable responsibility for his years, but he proved himself worthy of his trust, and made the experience his preparation for the time when he should strike out in business for himself. He remained in this store for six or seven years, and by thrift and economy managed to lay up a little capital. In February, 1912, he started in business for himself, choosing the line of taxi service. Time proved the young man well justified in his choice. The rapid development of the automobile from a plaything to an eminently practical servant had opened an avenue of business which demanded men of sound common sense and solid business ability. Mr. Johnson was not slow in perceiving the possibilities in connection with his start. From time to time, as he saw opportunity, he branched out into various lines of automobile accessories and supplies and now conducts one of the most complete establishments of its kind, where the motorist can have practically every need supplied.

Mr. Johnson spent nine months in the service of the government during the late World War acting in the capacity of foreman in the repair shops on the proving grounds at Aberdeen, Maryland. Later, and also at Aberdeen, he was inspector of cars, and in full charge of motorcycles there. He has made a place for himself in the city of Perth Amboy that many young men might envy. He is a member of the Junior Order of United American Mechanics, and of the American Legion. He is an attendant of the Presbyterian church.

Mr. Johnson married, September 14, 1920, Anna A. Bachman, of Perth Amboy, New Jersey, daughter of Daniel and Anna A. Bachman, of Perth Amboy.

ALFRED THOMPSON KERR—For more than a decade Alfred Thompson Kerr has been prominently before the public in various ways, holding several different offices in South Amboy. In 1908 he was elected tax collector, and in 1909 to the Board of Freeholders of the county, serving in this capacity for eight years. In 1916 Mr. Kerr was chosen to fill the chair of chief executive of the city at a time when the office of mayor was an unusually trying one, it being during the period of the World War and also when the terrible explosion at the Morgan Works occurred, at which so many families were made homeless. The present water works system and the new high school were both started during Mr. Kerr's administration.

Though of Scotch ancestry Alfred Thompson Kerr was born in the United States, at Bordentown, New Jersey, June 24, 1864, the son of Thomas Kerr, a native of Edinburgh, Scotland. Thomas Kerr came to this country when fourteen years old and landed at Newburyport, Massachusetts, then came to New York City, later removing to Bordentown. In 1873 he came to South Amboy and lived there for more than forty years, his death occurring in that city, in September 1906, at the age of eighty-nine years. His occupation was that of master mechanic for the Pennsylvania Railroad, he being the oldest on the system at the time

when he was retired from active service on a pension   He married Mary
McLeay, also a native of Edinburgh, Scotland   She died in South Amboy, August 16, 1892   Mr and Mrs Thomas Kerr had a family of
thirteen children, but of this number only four are now living, as follows
1   Mary J, living in Trenton, New Jersey   2   Emma, wife of Peter A
Stults, of No 212 Second street, South Amboy   3.   Robert, residing in
South Amboy.   4   Alfred Thompson of whom further

During his early childhood, Alfred Thompson Kerr lived in the city
of his birth, attending the public school in Bordentown, but when eight
years old his parents came to South Amboy and he entered the public
school here, continuing until eighteen years old, then, going to Trenton,
he attended "The Model School" for three years, graduating from it in
1887

The first position young Mr Kerr held was in the freight office of
the Pennsylvania Railroad in South Amboy and in a short time he was
promoted to the position of assistant shop clerk on the Amboy division
His next position was as assistant coal premium clerk of the United
Railroads of New Jersey   His health failing, Mr Kerr was compelled
to give up his occupation to seek one in the open air and he became a
fireman on a locomotive on the Pennsylvania Railroad, continuing it for
nine years   In 1899 Mr Kerr went into his present business, a dealer
in paints, oils glass, etc   his store located at the corner of First and
Stockton streets, South Amboy   It is a well-established business, and
for the past twenty-two years Mr Kerr has been located at the original
stand   In addition to this he is secretary and treasurer of the R U Rue
Company, Inc, dealers in clay and sand, their headquarters being on
Main street, South Amboy

Alfred Thompson Kerr is a most enthusiastic musician that being
his particular form of recreation, he having been president of the Musi
cians' Union of Perth Amboy at three different times   He is also a
prominent figure in fraternal circles, being a member of the local lodge
of Free and Accepted Masons, the Tall Cedars of Lebanon, the Knights
of Pythias, the Loyal Order of Moose, and the Benevolent and Protective Order of Elks   Mr Kerr is also affiliated with the Brotherhood of
Locomotive Firemen and Engineers, and was the first master of Lodge
No 484 of that association   Mr Kerr is active in the work of the South
Amboy Memorial Hospital being president of the board of managers
of that institution   He is a member of the Protestant Episcopal church

On July 21, 1890, in South Amboy Alfred Thompson Kerr was united
in marriage with Carrie Straub, born in South Amboy, the daughter of
Gottlieb Straub, the dean of the butcher's business in South Amboy
where he is still actively engaged at the age of seventy-seven years   Mr
and Mrs Alfred Thompson Kerr have one child, Antoinette S. now the
wife of James Gordon, of South Amboy

ASHER K FLEMING —The Fleming family has figured prominently in the life and affairs of Middlesex county for two centuries   The
family traces its origin to several immigrant ancestors who originally

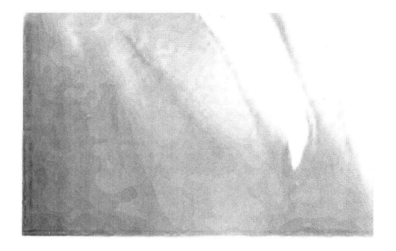

settled in Delaware, later pushing West into Ohio, where all were killed by the Indians with the exception of Jordan Fleming, then an infant. He was later found and raised by a family in Delaware, but at the age of fifteen ran away from his benefactors, boarded a canal boat and landed at New Brunswick, thus establishing the Fleming family in this county.

Asher K. Fleming was born at New Brunswick, New Jersey, July 9, 1890, the son of John Kesby Fleming, an electrician of New Brunswick, and his wife Mary Emma (De Hart) Fleming. He received his education in the public schools of his native place and at the American Technical Society schools, where he took a course in electrical engineering. After graduating, his first position was with the Bosch-Rushmore Company as experimental engineer, later becoming chief automotive electrical engineer for the Simplex Automobile Company, and the Wright-Martin Aircraft Corporation. In 1914 he established himself in business as an automotive electrical engineer, with offices on Jersey avenue, which he conducted in connection with his other duties, and in 1918 he established laboratories at No. 41 Albany street, New Brunswick. He has been highly successful in this venture and within a short period has risen to a place of prominence in business circles. His success is in every sense of the word selfmade, the result of his own indefatigable effort. He was one of the pioneers in the perfecting of electric lighting of automobiles.

Mr. Fleming is affiliated with the Benevolent and Protective Order of Elks, New Brunswick Lodge, No. 354, the Junior Order of United American Mechanics, and also holds membership in the Society of Automotive Engineers, and the American Institute of Electrical Engineers. During the World War, Mr. Fleming perfected and installed the high tension electrical ignition system as used on the famous Hispano-Suiza airplane motors, which motors propelled the fastest planes on the battle fields of France.

Mr. Fleming is a lover of all outdoor sports, especially fishing and hunting, and is a member of the New Brunswick Sportsmen's Association. In religion he is a Methodist and attends the First Church of that denomination.

On February 4, 1914, Asher K. Fleming was united in marriage with Nellie L. Creager. Mr. Fleming has made his own way and has attained to his present position in the business world by force of his ability, which has fitted him to hold it. Such a man is destined as a matter of course to still further advancement. His residence is at No. 291 Powers street.

HENRY SYLVESTER HULSE, JR—The excellent school system of Perth Amboy is the pride of the city. In this organized preparation of the children and youth of the city for their future usefulness, Henry Sylvester Hulse, Jr. bears a significant part.

The founder of the Hulse family in America was one of the early settlers of Long Island, and came from Holland, where the name is a well known and honored one. Mr. Hulse's grandfather Sylvester Hulse, is still living at the age of ninety years, in Port Jefferson Long Island.

Henry Sylvester Hulse, Sr , is a dairy farmer in that vicinity He married Melissa Barton

Henry Sylvester Hulse, Jr , was born in Astoria, New York, May 28, 1880 He received his early education in the Port Jefferson Union School, where he completed the course in 1897 He then attended the Jamaica State Normal School from which he was graduated in 1904 He then entered New York University and was graduated in 1909 Mr Hulse came to Perth Amboy, New Jersey, in 1906, as principal of School No 2 Since 1909 he has filled a more important position, that of principal of the Grammar and Manual Training schools of the city He is very enthusiastic about his work, and believes deeply in the importance of manual training to the thousands of children who can never expect to receive higher education

Outside his strictly professional work Mr Hulse is interested in other activities for the young people of the city He is director of the Junior Red Cross chairman of the Troop Organization Committee of the Boy Scouts of America, and chairman of the Fourth Red Cross Roll Call He is a private in the State Militia Reserve, and did active service at the time of the Morgan explosion and also during the influenza epidemic He is a member of Suffolk Lodge, No 60, Ancient Free and Accepted Masons, of Port Jefferson, New York, and of Lodge No 785, Independent Order of Odd Fellows, Phillipstown, New York Mr Hulse finds his tastes leading him into the great out-of-door world whenever opportunity offers He is very fond of all out-door sports, and takes particular delight in gardening

Mr Hulse married, December 24, 1908, in the Church of St Mary's in the Highlands, Cold Spring, New York Marie Edna Haight, daughter of Cyrus J and Elizabeth (Traver) Haight She was born in Phillips-town, Putnam county, New York Her parents are now deceased Mr and Mrs Hulse have two children Barton Traver, born August 21, 1910, and Irene Elizabeth, born September 8, 1911 The family are attendants upon the services of the Episcopal church and active in all its work

INGVARD GREISEN —Behind the work of the laborer's hand is the creation of the designer's mind Thus the completed structure which stands the pride of any city means far more than the laying of one stone upon another. In Perth Amboy, New Jersey, Ingvard Greisen is one of the men whose work lives in the form which he designs

Mr Greisen's father, Hans Greisen, has for many years been engaged in construction work in Perth Amboy He came from Denmark about thirty-six years ago, located in Perth Amboy and has been a building contractor ever since His wife Marie was also born in Denmark, and they are the parents of two sons, Ingvard and Sophus

Ingvard Greisen was born in Perth Amboy, February 15 1889 He received his early education in the public schools of this city, being grad-uated from the high school in 1907 The same year he entered the Pratt Institute, Brooklyn, New York, from which he was graduated in

1910 He is rapidly winning his way to success as an architect He has worked at the building game since childhood, having always followed his father's work with the keenest interest Spending the greater part of his leisure time throughout his boyhood about whatever piece of construction his father had in hand, the older man taught his son all the ins and outs of the contracting business This was a wonderfully practical foundation for his training along the special line chosen Now for the past eight years Mr. Greisen has been actively practicing his profession, first under the firm name of Goldberger & Greisen, and now under his own name His present office is conveniently located at No 320 Raritan building Mr Greisen is a member of the Ancient Free and Accepted Masons, Benevolent and Protective Order of Elks, and the Dana Relief Association He is greatly interested in water sports, and a member of the Raritan Yacht Club. He finds his most enjoyable recreation in volley ball at the Young Men's Christian Association

Mr Greisen married April 13 1914 Signa Nelson, and they have two children Agneta, born May 13, 1916, and Kenneth, born January 20 1918 The family are members of St Stephen's Lutheran Church

---

WILLIAM EDMUND WOODRUFF—Born in New Brunswick, February 8, 1884. William Edmund Woodruff is the son of Hiram Wilson Woodruff of Stelton New Jersey, and his wife, Mary E (Gilhand) Woodruff, now deceased William Edmund Woodruff has two sisters and one brother Addie, the wife of Weldon Weidner of Boston Massachusetts, Hiram Wilson, Jr, who resides at East Millstone, New Jersey, and Margaret A, the wife of William MacMillan of Easton, Pennsylvania

William Edmund Woodruff attended the village school at Middlebush for some time, and later at Three Mile Run This was followed by a course in business training at Wilson's Commercial School at No 380 George street, New Brunswick

On February 15 1905 Mr Woodruff entered the employ of the National Bank of New Jersey, his first position being that of check clerk After two and a half years at this work, he was promoted to the desk of passbook clerk, later was advanced to bookkeeper, and then to teller of the bank In 1918 he became chief clerk, a position he holds at the present time

To be in the open and to be engaged in out-of-doors sports is Mr Woodruff's favorite pastime He is a member of the Sportsmen's Association of New Brunswick, the New Brunswick Country Club the Young Men's Christian Association, and the Junior Order of United American Mechanics Automobiling is his hobby and almost daily he may be seen enjoying this form of exercise He attends the Livingston Avenue Baptist Church

William Edmund Woodruff was married to Helen M Whitfield, November 3, 1909, her death occurring November 8, 1918 She was the daughter of Jacob H and Julia A Whitfield, both now living in New Brunswick Mr and Mrs Woodruff had no children

CHARLES WESTON BARNEKOW—When a young man of twenty-one, Baron Kiell Volmer Barnekow left his native Sweden and found a new home in Boston Massachusetts He was an educated young man of artistic talent and later became professor of music and painting in the famous Emma Willard School in Troy New York During his stay in that city, his home was at Watervliet, nearby, he later residing in Albany, then in Newburgh, New York He died in Newburgh, at the age of seventy-nine years and is buried in Albany Professor Barnekow married Sarah Jane Bunker, who died in Albany at the early age of twenty-seven leaving two children Charles Weston, of further mention and a daughter who died in childhood Professor Barnekow was a man of culture, ranking high as an artist, and was widely known when in his prime

Charles Weston Barnekow was born in Watervliet New York, November 2 1855 but soon afterward the family moved to Albany, going thence to Newburgh, New York, in 1861 where the lad was educated and grew to manhood He was employed in a drug store during his youth but at the age of twenty-two he started in business for himself as a retail hatter and shoe dealer Later he returned to the drug business, entering the employ of Dr Wiggins, in Newburgh, there remaining until 1892, when he located in Perth Amboy, New Jersey There he engaged in the drug business, first as Keasbey & Company, later as Keasbey & Barnekow, so continuing until September, 1904, when the present firm, Barnekow & Petz, was formed Their store is located at No 335 State street, a location that has long been occupied by a drug store in fact the pioneer drug store of the city was located there Mr Barnekow is a Republican in politics, and has represented his ward as alderman He is a member of the Masonic order the Knights of Pythias the Young Men's Christian Association Chamber of Commerce, Raritan Yacht Club and is devoted to all out-of-door athletic sports In religious faith he is a Presbyterian belonging to the First Church of Perth Amboy

Mr Barnekow married, at Cobleskill, New York, April 30, 1878, Emma Vansteenburgh born in Hudson, New York daughter of Matthew and Harriet (Smith) Vansteenburgh Mr and Mrs Barnekow are the parents of a son, Charles Weston Jr, born September 20, 1885, now in charge of the polychrome department of the Atlantic Terra Cotta Company

---

HOWARD WARREN KINSEY—One of the oldest established business houses of Perth Amboy New Jersey, dealing in coal, and known under the title of Kinsey Brothers, was founded in the early nineties by Henry Warren Kinsey father of Howard Warren Kinsey The latter succeeded his father in the management of this business and continued to conduct it until it was sold to the Lake Coal Company

Henry Warren Kinsey the founder of this business, was born in Woodbridge New Jersey He retired from active business and now lives at No 367 New Brunswick avenue Perth Amboy He married Ettie Hope who was born in this county and died in Perth Amboy,

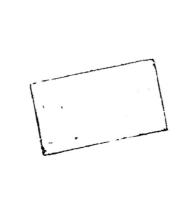

Raymond P. Wilson.

New Jersey, in 1905 They were the parents of six children, of whom three are still living Howard Warren whose name heads this review, Edward H, who is engaged as clerk in the postal service, and Fannie wife of George Therkelson, a piano dealer All are residents of Perth Amboy

Howard Warren Kinsey was born in Woodbridge, October 1, 1889 He received his education in the public schools of Perth Amboy, leaving school at the age of fourteen, he took charge of a team and drove one of his father's coal wagons This he continued to do for eight years, then entered the office as bookkeeper The firm was then known as Kinsey Brothers, and was located at No 367 New Brunswick avenue The business constantly grew and developed, and on September 17, 1917, was sold to the Lake Coal Company He then became manager for the Convery Coal Company, which position he has continued to fill ever since, and is demonstrating his executive ability in this business, which at the present time is a difficult one to handle The firm does considerable wholesale business, and handles wood in large quantities as well as coal Mr Kinsey is a Republican by political affiliation, and his tastes are those of the out-door man—hunting, fishing, gardening, automobiling—all these, in turn, claim him when the arduous duties of the office leave him free

Mr Kinsey married, June 18, 1902, in Perth Amboy, Bertha May Wolney, who was born in Woodbridge Both her parents died when she was a child Mr and Mrs Kinsey have two children Evelyn May, born November 2, 1905; and Arthur Warren, born June 18, 1906 These are the only grandchildren in the Kinsey family

Mr Kinsey and his wife are both members of the Baptist church

---

RAYMOND PERCY WILSON—Among the men rapidly coming to the front as civil engineers is the one whose name stands at the head of this article Mr Wilson, who is a resident of New Brunswick, is not only an active business man, but an energetic citizen, keenly interested in everything pertaining to the welfare and progress of his home community

Charles Edgar Wilson, father of Raymond Percy Wilson, was born April 29, 1854, in East Millstone, New Jersey, where he has for many years conducted a general grocery business He married Sarah Elizabeth Palmer, daughter of B D and Margaret (White) Palmer, the former a minister of the Methodist Episcopal church.

Raymond Percy Wilson, son of Charles Edgar and Sarah Elizabeth (Palmer) Wilson, was born September 29, 1886, in East Millstone, New Jersey, where he received his early education in local schools Later he entered the New Brunswick High School, graduating in 1903, and then matriculated in Rutgers College where he graduated in 1907 with the degree of Civil Engineer In association with the late Josiah Tice, Mr Wilson entered upon the practice of his profession in New Brunswick, meeting almost from the outset with merited recognition In 1917 he went into business for himself, and is now in possession of a lucrative practice, his office being situated at No 46 Paterson street The professional standing already attained by Mr Wilson gives abundant assurance that he has a future before him Politically Mr Wilson is a Republican, but his devotion to his profession precludes active participation in public affairs In his few hours of leisure he engages in various forms of outside work, which with characteristic energy he regards as recreation During the World War he served in the militia reserve and played an active part in a number of war activities The fraternal associations of Mr Wilson include membership in the Junior Order of United American Mechanics the Improved Order of Red Men, and the Chi Phi college fraternity He and his family are members of the First Presbyterian Church

Mr Wilson married, October 9, 1912, in New Brunswick, Lillian M. Morrison, born in that city, daughter of James A and Rebecca (MacCowan) Morrison, who still reside there The following children have been born to Mr and Mrs Wilson Jean M born May 25, 1914 died March 3 1915, Janice Elizabeth, born January 6, 1916, and Raymond Merrill, born December 23 1919

MAXWELL LOGAN—As owner of the Middlesex Press and the "Woodbridge Independent," a newspaper of the township of Woodbridge, Maxwell Logan has during his long residence in this community been closely identified with her leading interests and is always numbered among her foremost citizens

Maxwell Logan was born in Brooklyn, New York June 13 1894, the son of Percival Willoughby and Matilda Catherine (Platt) Logan. When but a small boy he was brought by his parents to Woodbridge, New Jersey, and there attended the grammar and high schools from which latter institution he was graduated, in June, 1913 In 1912 one year before finishing his high school course, he became interested in printing and, in consequence, set up a small printing press, doing church printing and also printing the high school publication, "The Dial" Immediately following his school career, he went to Brackenridge, Pennsylvania, to work for the Allegheny Steel Company, but returned to Woodbridge after a few months and resumed printing, removing to No 7 Green street which is a Revolutionary landmark of the town January 1, 1918, Mr Logan bought out the equipment of the Woodbridge Printery and together with his own business moved to his present location, No 23 Green street, and until April, 1919 printed the "Woodbridge Leader" In March, 1919, he began the publication of the "Woodbridge Independent" Three months later he purchased "The Mosquito," a weekly newspaper, which was published by H E Pickersgill, in Perth Amboy, and on August 1 he moved the paper to Woodbridge and it became incorporated with the "Woodbridge Independent" into the "Woodbridge Independent and the Mosquito" Now he ably conducts this business maintaining it on a firm basis enlarging its facilities and extending its scope, and has conclusively proven his possession of a marked executive ability

In all matters relative to the welfare of the community, Mr Logan ever manifests a deep and sincere interest, aiding to the utmost of his power any movements which tend to further public progress and good government   He adheres to the Republican party, but office seeking is foreign to his nature and he prefers, moreover, to concentrate his energies on the faithful discharge of his various trusts and responsibilities   In religion he is a Presbyterian, and attends the Presbyterian church at Woodbridge   Mr Logan is unmarried

EDWARD E CLARK.—The name of Mr Clark can properly be mentioned among those whose energy, business tact and public enterprise have made them important factors in the development and improvement of Sayreville, New Jersey, located on the Raritan river, noted for its manufactures of brick, soda water and cigars   His effort has not been in the field of finance, nor in the promotion of great schemes employing vast capital, but it has been in the walks of ordinary business, and by faithfully performing the duties of every-day life he has won for himself the respect and esteem of those with whom he is brought in contact

Edward E Clark was born in Englishtown, New Jersey, December 16, 1882, son of Owen and Catherine (Kelly) Clark   He acquired a practical education by attendance at St Mary's School, Sayreville, and he began his active career in the grocery business, continuing along that line until January 1, 1917, meeting with the success which attends well directed effort   He erected the Union Hotel at Sayreville, in the year 1917, of which he is still the proprietor, being well qualified for that line of work, possessing the power to correctly judge human nature, a social, genial disposition, and a sincere desire to please   Everything possible is done for the comfort and convenience as well as the pleasure of his guests, and in consequence the house is receiving a very liberal patronage   In 1913 Mr Clark added to his business pursuits that of real estate, in which he is engaged at the present time (1920) and from the conduct of which he derives a profitable income, real estate during the past few years changing hands constantly owing to the scarcity of houses for the accommodation of the people in the great cities and their environs   Mr Clark gives his political allegiance to the Democratic party, and was elected on that ticket to serve in public office, having been township committeeman from 1913 to 1920, treasurer of the township and school funds from 1913 to 1915, and was chairman of the township committee for three years   On May 21, 1918, he was compelled to close his business on account of the Raritan Arsenal being within the three-mile limit   He then went to work for the Morgan plant, remaining six months   He then returned to the real estate business, in which he still continues   He was one of the committee who erected the monument in memory of the boys who went over seas   This was done without any cost to the borough, through the kindness of the Sayre & Fisher Company, who donated the land and the material, and the mechanics gave their services free of charge   In 1919 he was the one who was instrumental in having a bill passed through the Legislature making Sayreville a borough   He is a member of New Brunswick Lodge, No 324, Benevolent and Protective Order of Elks; Foresters of America· Improved Order of Red Men and the Arion Singing Club

Mr Clark married, September 26, 1917, the ceremony taking place in the Church of Our Lady of Victories at Sayreville New Jersey, Florence Meyer, born in Sayreville May 14 1890, daughter of Ignatz and Augusta (Gunkel) Meyer   One child has been born to Mr and Mrs Clark, namely, La Vern Marie born July 12, 1918   Mr and Mrs Clark are attendants of the Church of Our Lady of Victories

---

RAYMOND PIUS WHITE—Though not a native of New Brunswick Raymond Pius White has been a resident of that city all his life having been brought there by his parents while still a very young child, and has always been closely identified with many of the activities of the city   At the present time (1921) he is in the employ of W E Mount as an automobile salesman

John J White, father of Raymond Pius White, is a railroad detective, residing in New Brunswick, where he was born and where he has lived for the greater part of his life   He married Mary Magdalena Phillips, who was born in Newark, New Jersey, but died in New Brunswick   John J White and his wife were the parents of two children: Raymond Pius, of whom further, and John Edward, also living in the city on the Raritan

Raymond Pius White was born in Rocky Hill, Connecticut, August 21, 1894   During his infancy his father and mother removed to Newark but their stay there was of short duration as they soon went to New Brunswick, where they made their permanent home   Here the boy was educated, attending St Peter's Parochial School and later taking a course at the New Brunswick Business College   Afterward in 1910 he entered the employ of Johnson & Johnson, the well known manufacturers of medical and hospital supplies, remaining with them until August 13, 1920

During this time Mr White entered the army serving in the World War for more than two years   On September 21, 1917, he was sent to Camp Dix, remaining there until June, 1918, when he was transferred to Camp Lee   His stay at this point was very short, as he left in a few months to go to Camp McClellan, Alabama, in September, 1918, where he became sergeant of infantry, First Provisional Company, 98th Division, and from which post he was discharged, December 9, 1919   Sergeant White is now county commander of the American Legion of Middlesex county   and a member of the executive committee of the Department of New Jersey, American Legion   He is also a representative of the State Bonus Commission for the distribution of the State bonus given to the ex-service men of the World War in the Third Congressional District of New Jersey

In all affairs pertaining to the Roman Catholic church, of which Mr White is a devoted adherent, he is among the foremost workers   He is an attendant of St Paul's Roman Catholic Church of Highland Park He is a member of the Knights of Columbus, and of the National Executive Committee of the Catholic Young Men's Union He represents Middlesex county on the State Executive Board of the Federation of Catholic Societies

Mr White is very popular among the lovers of athletic sports and is connected with several societies organized for the promotion and welfare of athletics He is one of the board of managers of the Amateur Athletic Union of the United States of America Metropolitan Association, in 1916 and 1917 Mr White was president of the Knights of St Peter, a young men's athletic organization of New Brunswick Mr White is also a member of the Order of Red Men, a benevolent and fraternal organization

---

GEORGE ERNEST GILLIS, prominent in the direction of the great Roessler & Hasslacher Chemical Company of Perth Amboy, in which he holds the position of supply and traffic manager, and a well known figure in the business circles of the city, is a member of an old British family, the founder of which, in America, came from England to Prince Edward Island, Canada, at an early date He is a son of Alexander and Anna (Ellis) Gillis, both natives of Canada, who came when young to the United States, making their home in various places, including Perth Amboy and finally at Providence, Rhode Island, where their deaths occurred respectively, July 30, 1919, at the age of sixty-eight, and February, 1918, at the age of sixty-six The elder Mr Gillis was a shipbuilder by occupation most of his life, and for a number of years followed that profession at Perth Amboy They were the parents of ten children as follows Two children, who died in infancy, Clifford now engaged in business as an industrial chemist at Fords, New Jersey, Laura, who became the wife of William Lydard of Hartford Connecticut, Victor Herbert, now residing at Tottenville, New York, where he represents the Roessler & Hasslacher Chemical Company, Chester Arthur, who is engaged in business as a traveling agent, and makes his home in Philadelphia, George Ernest, whose career forms the subject matter of this sketch Helen, who became the wife of Samuel Simpson of Providence, Rhode Island, William Ellis, an educator, who makes his home in Stonington, Connecticut, and is vice-principal of the Stonington High School, Louis, deceased

George Ernest Gillis was born in Perth Amboy, New Jersey, April 18, 1889 during his parents residence there, and passed his childhood in that city He attended the local public schools until he had reached the age of fifteen years when, being anxious to begin his business career, he left school and secured employment in the Art Glass Works of his native city He remained with that concern only one year, however, and then, on April 11, 1908, entered the employ of the Roessler & Hasslacher Chemical Company, thus commencing an association which has continued uninterruptedly ever since He was first given work to do in the laboratory where he did so well as to attract the attention of his superiors, and put himself in line for promotion   Three years after coming with this concern he was made assistant purchasing agent, a position that he held for five years, when he was advanced to that of traffic manager   Shortly afterwards, another department was placed in his charge and he was given his present title of supply and traffic manager   The duties of this responsible office he discharges with skill and efficiency, and has made himself one of the most valued members of the staff of this large concern, one of the largest, if not the largest of its kind in the United States   Mr Gillis has also interested himself in the general life of the city, and is a member of a number of clubs there including the Chemical Club and the Raritan Yacht Club both of Perth Amboy   He is keenly interested in all manner of out-door pastimes and sports, especially boating and automobiling, and up to about six years ago took part frequently in motor boat races, notably those covering great distances, such as five hundred miles or more   He is a Presbyterian in his religious belief and attends church of that denomination at Perth Amboy

George Ernest Gillis was united in marriage, March 2 1910 in New York City, with May Carney, a native of Monmouth county, New Jersey, and a daughter of Richard and Sarah Carney of that city the former now deceased   Three children have been born to Mr and Mrs Gillis as follows George, born December 20, 1912, Richard Ernest, born September 15, 1914, and Francis, born May 15, 1916

HENRY RUTGERS BALDWIN MEYERS —The advance in sanitary precaution, safety appliance and working condition is nowhere more marked than in the corporate industries that were formerly most indifferent   The establishing of welfare departments in mills and factories has called into being a new profession, and as welfare manager Mr Meyers, of Milltown, New Jersey, is now devoting his talents that had formerly been devoted to pedagogy with marked success   His present engagement is with the Michelin Tire Company and his work has borne abundant fruit   He is a son of Marion H and Elizabeth (Bessonnett) Meyers, his father a journalist

Henry R B Meyers was born in New Brunswick, New Jersey, October 29, 1886, and there completed public school courses of study of grade and high   He was also a student in Rutgers College Summer Schools and pursued special courses in oratory and public speaking under private instructors   For fifteen years Mr Meyers was supervising principal of schools, and in 1919 became employment and welfare manager for the Michelin Tire Company, of Milltown, New Jersey   He is a director of Milltown Building and Loan Association and interested in other community activities   In fraternal relation, Mr Meyers is affiliated with Palestine Lodge, No 111 Free and Accepted Masons Improved Order of Red Men (past great guard of forest, and past sachem), Patriotic Order Sons of America (past president), Daughters of Pocahontas, the Order of United American Mechanics, and the Junior Order of

Wm. Edw. Gorrow.

United American Mechanics   In religious faith he is connected with Milltown Methodist Episcopal Church

Mr Meyers married, November 25, 1908, Gulielma Clark, daughter of Francis Asbury and Sarah Clark   Mr and Mrs Meyers are the parents of a daughter, Marguerite Elizabeth, born November 9, 1912, and a son, Henry R B, Jr, born April 25, 1918, deceased

---

WILLIAM EDWARD GOWEN—Although having been established in the undertaking business on his own account but a short time, William Edward Gowen has already proven that his venture is a success, due in a large part to the thorough knowledge that he obtained along this particular line before starting out for himself

Henry Harper Gowen, father of William Edward Gowen, was born in New Brunswick New Jersey, February 9, 1851, and for many years previous to his retirement from business life was engaged in the rubber trade   He now resides in Arlington, New Jersey   He married Elizabeth Steinart, of New Brunswick, and to them have been born five children, as follows Freeman, deceased , Isaac, deceased , Antoinette, who married Allan Peluso, of New Brunswick , William Edward, of further mention , Samuel Long, a mechanical electrician of New Brunswick

William Edward Gowen was born February 8, 1888, in New Brunswick   He obtained his education in the public schools of his native place, but at the age of fourteen years left school and served an apprenticeship at the blacksmith's trade, later enlisting in the United States army, first in the infantry, but later transferring to the cavalry   After serving one term in this capacity he returned to New Brunswick and for a short time resumed his former trade   In the meantime, however, he had become interested in the undertaking business, and with a keen desire to ultimately establish himself as a funeral director he secured a position with William J McDede and later with A J Martin, both undertakers in New Brunswick   He remained with Mr Martin for ten years, during which time he gained a thorough practical knowledge of the undertaking business, and on October 15, 1920, opened parlors on his own account at No 99 French street, New Brunswick, which have since continued to be his headquarters

On May 26, 1908 William Edward Gowen was united in marriage with Helen Stangler, a native of Germany, and the daughter of Charles and Theresa Stangler, who for several years have resided in Philadelphia   Mr and Mrs Gowen are the parents of two children Helen Anna, born March 3, 1909 , Gizzella, born October 30, 1911   The family attend the Fourth Reformed Church of New Brunswick

---

GEORGE F REYNOLDS, one of the most prominent business men and merchants of Perth Amboy, Middlesex county, New Jersey, and the proprietor of the large mercantile establishment at No 136 Smith street, in that city, is a native of New Brunswick, New Jersey, a son of Charles and Mary (Nevins) Reynolds, old and highly respected residents of that place. Charles Reynolds was born in County Leitrim, Ireland

in the year 1814, and came to the United States when but seven years
of age in company with three brothers and one sister The family located
in New York City for a time, but not long afterward removed to New
Brunswick, New Jersey, and Charles was bound out to a farmer at
Millstone, where he worked for a time His extraordinary ambition
caused him to walk daily the twenty-four miles to and from Millstone
and New Brunswick so that he might learn the trade of tailor's cutter, a
craft which he followed for some years Finally, by dint of industry
and economy, he saved up enough capital to engage in business on his
own account and he set up an establishment as a clothing merchant at
New Brunswick, conducting the same successfully for about thirty-five
years His death occurred at New Brunswick, January 28, 1901, at the
venerable age of eighty-seven years His wife still survives him They
were the parents of five children as follows Walter C, who now resides
at New Brunswick, and is occupied as a machinist, John F, of Trenton,
New Jersey, where he works as a tailor's cutter, George F, with whom
we are here especially concerned, Howard A, who studied law and is
now a practicing attorney at New Brunswick, a daughter who died
in early infancy

George F Reynolds, third son of Charles and Mary (Nevius) Reynolds, was born April 11, 1865, in New Brunswick, New Jersey He
attended for a time the public schools of that town, later studied at the
Rutgers Preparatory School, and upon completing the course there
secured a clerical position with the local establishment of John Lambert
He there remained for two years or until Mr Lambert sold out his
business, and then found employment with the firm of Myer Brothers
in the same city, where he continued for the following seven years
During that time the superintendent of the firm was Charles Hess, with
whom he developed a warm friendship, so that when that gentleman
severed his connection with Meyer Brothers and removed to Perth
Amboy to open a dry goods store, Mr Reynolds came with him, and
for the following seven years was employed by Mr Hess When the
latter disposed of his business to Crosby & Hill, of Wilmington, Delaware, Mr Reynolds, having laid aside a small sum of money, found
himself in a position to engage in business for himself Accordingly
he established himself in the dry goods business on State street in a
store 18x65 feet, this enterprise meeting with success from the outset
and it soon became a flourishing concern He continued on State street
until about 1903, and then removed to his present store at No 136
Smith street, where he has remained continuously up to the present
time Mr Reynolds' business ability, combined with his well known
and unimpeachable integrity, has given him a most enviable reputation in
the region, and he is now at the head of one of the largest and best
known enterprises of its kind hereabouts He has not, however, confined
himself entirely to the development of his private concern, but has
become prominent in the general business and financial life of the community, and is now associated with a number of important banking institutions in the locality He is a director of both the Perth Amboy
Trust Company and the City National Bank, and is also affiliated with a

George F. Reynolds

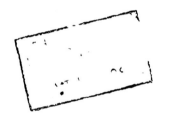

number of fraternal orders and clubs here, among which should be mentioned the Benevolent and Protective Order of Elks, the Knights of Columbus, the Woodmen of the World, the East Jersey Club, the Raritan Yacht Club, and the Hydewood Golf Club of North Plainfield, New Jersey He has been active in local politics in Perth Amboy as an Independent, and for two years has held the office of president of the local Board of Health As will be seen from the clubs of which Mr Reynolds is a member, he is extremely fond of all sorts of out-door sports and pastimes, and he takes an especial interest in automobiling In his religious belief, Mr Reynolds is a Roman Catholic and attends the Church of St Joseph's, North Plainfield, where he now resides

George F Reynolds was united in marriage, July 5, 1891, with Cora M Williamson, of New Brunswick, New Jersey, a daughter of William and Adeline (Allen) Williamson, of that city, now both deceased Mr and Mrs Reynolds are the parents of one child, Charles Hess, born September 22, 1903, now a student at Carlton Academy Summit, New Jersey

RAMON MONTALVO, JR—On the site where once stood the famous old Mansion House in New Brunswick, New Jersey, there now stands a new building devoted to music in its various forms, the name of this attractive structure being "The Temple of Music" It is located at Nos 101-105 Albany street

The proprietor of this new enterprise is Ramon Montalvo, Jr, a native of New Brunswick, where he was born August 22, 1881. His parents are Ramon and Mary Montalvo, the former a retired business man of New Brunswick Ramon, Jr, has always resided in the city of his birth and there he received his education, attending the public schools, his graduation from the high school taking place with the class of 1899

A year later, 1900, Mr Montalvo opened an agency for talking machines, at No 341 George street, gradually introducing other musical features, and eventually developing a large trade He started with a very small capital, but in the years that followed he made good and, purchasing the property at Nos 101-105 Albany street, he erected his own building which he now occupies, and named it the "Temple of Music" It is 90x150 feet, including salesrooms, and is devoted to the interests of music It has been carefully planned, combining harmony and attractiveness with its main idea Just inside the entrance at the right are hundreds of sheet music files, and beyond these are to be found enclosed offices, modernly equipped, for the convenience of the officials and clerks, at the left a staircase leads to Mr Montalvo's private office The architectural work was designed by Alexander Merchant, and well illustrates his fine ability and excellent taste. There are salesrooms especially fitted up for the displaying of pianos and piano players, talking machines and their accessories, and the children's room, which is furnished in kindergarten style, with its miniature talking machine, and records especially suitable for the kiddies, is an attractive feature

Another attractive feature of this establishment is the five period rooms, each fitted up in the style of a different period—Adam Colonial Gothic, Pompeian, and Modern—and each having a talking machine installed whose lines follow those of the particular period represented In addition to all this, there is the auditorium 40x30 feet, which is reached by a wide, winding stairway leading from the front or main salesroom This is a well-planned theatre with 550 comfortable seats, a curtained stage at the end, and every detail as may be found in the highest class theatres and is so planned, that when occasion demands, it can be transformed into a ballroom A model repair room is also to be found in one part of the building, which enables Mr Montalvo to do extensive repair work on the premises This new establishment represents an achievement that places Mr Montalvo in the foremost ranks of New Brunswick business men

In all progressive societies having the advancement of New Brunswick as their object. Mr Montalvo takes an active interest, one of them being the Rotary Club of which he is the president at the present time, he is also president of the Retail Merchants Division of the New Brunswick Board of Trade, he is a director of the Middlesex County Building and Loan Association, and a member of the Scientific Society of Rutgers College One of Mr Montalvo's especial interests is the Young Men's Christian Association, having given evidence of this in many ways His chief recreation is any form of out-of-doors sport and in pursuance of it, is an active member of the Manasquan River Yacht Club

In fraternal circles Mr Montalvo is equally active, being connected with the local lodge of the Benevolent and Protective Order of Elks, No 324 in the Masonic world he is very greatly interested, being a member of Palestine Lodge. Free and Accepted Masons, No 111, and of Scott Chapter, Royal Arch Masons, No 4, also of Temple Commandery, No 18, Knights Templar Mr Montalvo is a Shriner, attached to Salaam Temple, Ancient Arabic Order Nobles of the Mystic Shrine; and in addition to these, he is a past grand Tall Cedar of New Brunswick Forest, No 12, Tall Cedars of Lebanon

Ramon Montalvo was joined in matrimony with Gertrude Lieberum, daughter of Charles and Gertrude Lieberum, January 1. 1905, in New Brunswick They have one child, Helen Marguerite, born December 25, 1905 Mr and Mrs Montalvo reside at No. 203 Lawrence avenue, Highland Park, New Brunswick. They are members of Christ Protestant Episcopal Church of that city.

GEORGE RAYMOND CARMICHAEL—All honorable success is based upon a definite aim in life and the persistency of purpose which enables one to persevere in a given course regardless of difficulties, obstacles and discouragements There are many self-made men whose life record proves this fact and among this number is George Raymond Carmichael

Mr Carmichael was born in Wellsburg, West Virginia, March 27, 1887, the son of Thomas Ward and Gertrude Elizabeth (Henke) Carmichael Thomas W Carmichael is a prominent citizen in Wellsburg, where he resides, being cashier of the First National Bank there and president of the Board of Trade

George Raymond Carmichael received his education in the public schools of his native place, and after graduating from the Wellsburg High School he entered upon his business career with a borrowed capital of $500 The steam vulcanizing business in which he has been engaged since the inception of his business career has steadily and consistently grown until today it represents a twenty thousand dollar a year enterprise, and Mr Carmichael has invested ten thousand dollars alone in fixtures and machinery Although Mr Carmichael has always maintained a deep interest in public issues, he is independent of party restriction when casting his vote During the years 1904 to 1908 he belonged to the National Guard of West Virginia, being a member of Company C, First Regiment, but never saw any active service except camp life and the rifle range

On February 3, 1916, George Raymond Carmichael was united in marriage with Edna Christie daughter of Jacob and Mary Eliza (Roark) Christie of Perth Amboy, New Jersey Mr and Mrs. Carmichael are the parents of two children· George Nichols, born May 28, 1917, Wilbur Leroy, born April 3, 1919

Mr Carmichael's life has been one of service, and he has prospered in business He has always been found among the loyal supporters of all progressive movements for his community's welfare, and when opportunity has offered has been ready to aid those less favored than he From unfavorable circumstances he has won success and standing, and is one of the respected business men of Perth Amboy, New Jersey, a product of democratic institutions

RAYMOND ROBBINS ANDERSON, purchasing agent of the Roessler & Hasslacher Chemical Company of Perth Amboy, New Jersey and a well known figure in the business world of this region, is a member of an old New Jersey family which has resided in the State from pre-Revolutionary times His great-great-grandfather, George Anderson, was one of the earliest settlers of Hamilton Square, New Jersey, and was engaged in business there when New Jersey was yet a colony He took part in the Revolution, and through him the present Mr. Anderson is eligible for membership in the Society of the Sons of the Revolution.

A great-grandson of this George Anderson was Henry Franklin Anderson, father of Raymond R Anderson, who was born in Flemington, Hunterdon county, New Jersey, in the year 1852, and died in 1911, at the age of fifty-nine years In early life he followed the trades of carpenter and mechanic, but later became the possessor of a fine farm, where he carried on general agricultural operations and made something of a specialty of dairying He married Frances H Mershon, of Trenton who survives him and continues to make her home in Hamilton Square the old family residence of the Andersons Mr and Mrs Anderson were the parents of three children, as follows Florence, who became the wife of Thomas Watson, of Hamilton Square, Raymond Robbins, whose career is the subject of this sketch, and Chester Franklin, a farmer by occupation who resides in Hamilton Square

Raymond Robbins Anderson was born in Hamilton Square, Mercer county, New Jersey, August 29, 1887 and passed his childhood there He attended the local public schools for his general education, and later entered the Rider Moore & Stewart Business College in Trenton, New Jersey, where he took a commercial course He was graduated from the latter institution with the class of 1905, and immediately afterwards secured a clerical position with the firm of Thomas Maddock's Sons, dealers in pottery in Trenton He remained with that concern for some twelve years and there became familiar with business methods making himself valuable to his employers but at the close of that period left them in order to accept a position with the great Roessler & Hasslacher Chemical Company of Perth Amboy He entered the employ of the latter concern as assistant purchasing agent, and displayed such efficiency in the post that one year later he was advanced to the office of purchasing agent which he continues to hold at the present time In politics Mr Anderson is an independent Republican and has always shown a keen and intelligent interest in local affairs and a public-spirited willingness to take part in all movements undertaken for the advancement of the public interest He served for three years in Company D, Second Regiment, New Jersey National Guard, and is a member of various fraternities and clubs, among which should be mentioned the Independent Order of Odd Fellows, the Junior Order of United American Mechanics, the Chemical Club of Perth Amboy, and is a charter member of the board of governors of the last named organization In his religious belief he is a Presbyterian and attends the First Presbyterian Church in Perth Amboy

Raymond Robbins Anderson was united in marriage, October 12, 1915 at Ewing, New Jersey, a small town in the vicinity of Trenton, with Edith Eloise Vernam, a daughter of Sanford J and Ada (Maguire) Vernam, old and highly respected residents of that place

---

LOUIS POSNER, numbered among the successful merchants of New Brunswick, New Jersey, is the proprietor of a store at No 55 Church street Since 1877 he has been engaged entirely in mercantile business, his life having been an active, busy one, although ample in its rewards, all richly deserved

Isaac Posner, father of Louis Posner, was born in Germany, and died in New Brunswick New Jersey November 10 1900 at the age of sixty-nine years He came to this country in 1848 with his parents and located in New York City, where he remained until 1872 when he came to New Brunswick and established himself in business as a dry goods merchant at No 55 Church street, where he continued for the remainder of his lifetime, and at the time of his demise the enterprise which he had started on a small scale had proven highly successful He married Bertha Vogel, a native of Germany, she died April, 1918, at

Conrad Scholz

the age of seventy-seven years   They were the parents of eleven children, of whom there are but five living, Martha, a resident of New Haven, Connecticut, Stella who resides at New Rochelle; David, who is associated with Louis in business, Camilla, a resident of New Brunswick, Louis, of further mention

Louis Posner was born May 30, 1860, in New York City, where he attended the local public schools until he had reached the age of fourteen years when he left school and became assistant bookkeeper for his father   Here he remained until 1877, when he went to Cohoes, New York, and established himself in the dry goods business, which he continued for four years, selling out at the end of that time in order to return to New Brunswick and associate himself with his father in the latter's business.   In 1882, the business had increased to such an extent that it was necessary to enlarge their building and they purchased the store next door, making over the two stores into one large one   Here they continued successfully until the elder man's death in 1900, when Louis and his brother David took over the management of the enterprise   As an able organizer and executive, Louis Posner, keenly alert to every changing phase in the business, has ever been an active factor in its development and growth   The welfare and advancement of New Brunswick are always in his heart, and although he has never consented to hold office he has always identified himself with notable movements which have for their aim the betterment of civic conditions   He is affiliated with the Benevolent and Protective Order of Elks and the Young Men's Hebrew Association.   He attends the Jewish Synagogue of New Brunswick   Mr Posner is unmarried

---

CONRAD SEBOLT, in 1896, at the age of seventeen years, entered his father's business and assumed the entire control of it, owing to the elder man's sudden death at that time   This contracting trucking business which was founded by Mr Sebolt, Sr, had grown extensively by this time, and it was quite a responsibility for Conrad Sebolt who at that time was little more than a boy, but being a tireless worker and determined to do his part he has now attained the position of a successful business man

John Sebolt, father of Conrad Sebolt, was born at Milltown, New Jersey, and was killed there in 1896 at the age of forty-eight years, his death occurring while he was riding on a flat car loaded with wire   He married Catherine Wallace, a native of New Brunswick, who still survives him   To Mr and Mrs Sebolt were born fourteen children, of which number five are now living   Adeline widow of Garrett Selover, William, a farmer in New Brunswick, Conrad, of further mention, Katherine, wife of Edwin Hornbey, Ruth, wife of Harry D Shea

Conrad Sebolt was born October 24, 1879, in New Brunswick New Jersey   He obtained his education in the public schools of his native place graduating from the New Brunswick High School in 1896, subsequently assuming the responsibility of his father's established business which was first located on George road   In 1910 Mr Sebolt removed to Nos 16-18 Richmond street and here he has since continued in the general contracting and trucking business He also deals in sand, gravel, stone and cinder, and his storehouses are located at Nos 235-239 Burnett street He is a member of the Board of Trade

On April 9, 1902 Conrad Sebolt was united in marriage with Nellie Rolfe, daughter of Edgar C Rolfe, a lumberman of New Brunswick, and his wife, Mary (Ferguson) Rolfe Mr and Mrs Sebolt are the parents of one child, Conrad, Jr, born April 9, 1903 The family attend the Fourth Reformed Church in New Brunswick

---

JOHN WILLIAM KELLY is known and respected as one of the public-spirited and representative men of Perth Amboy and has been a resident of this city all his life He takes an abiding and practical interest in all that concerns the welfare of the community, and as president of the firm of Kelly & McAlinden, holds a prominent place in the business circles of the city

Edward Michael Kelly, father of John William Kelly, was born in Perth Amboy, in 1848, and died here, May 9, 1919 His entire business life was spent in his native city, he being the founder of the E M Kelly Realty Company, and also president of the Kelly & McAlinden Company. In addition to exceptional business talents, Mr Kelly possessed resolute industry, purity of purpose, and integrity of conduct, and on these foundation stones the fair structure of his success was reared Never did he allow questionable methods to enter into any transactions to which he was a party, and as a citizen with exalted ideas of good government he stood in the front rank A vigilant and attentive observer of men and measures his opinions were recognized as sound and his views as broad, and his ideas therefore carried weight among those with whom he discussed public problems In politics he was a Democrat He served as president of the School Board for a number of years Mr Kelly married Ellen A Doyle, a native of Perth Amboy, now living near Bound Brook Middlesex county, New Jersey, at the age of seventy-three years Mr and Mrs Kelly were the parents of nine children Edward Michael, deceased, Mary E, deceased, Michael A, deceased, Julia L, a resident of Bound Brook, New Jersey, Helen A ; John William, of further mention, James E, resides at Bound Brook, New Jersey, Loretta C wife of William J Martin, of Bound Brook, Joseph A, of Perth Amboy Mr Kelly used his talents and his opportunities to the utmost in every work which he undertook, fulfilling to the letter every trust committed to him, and was generous in his feelings and conduct toward all He made for himself a record of noteworthy achievement and public-spirited service, and his name is inscribed in the annals of his city

John William Kelly, son of Edward Michael and Ellen A (Doyle) Kelly, was born May 19, 1882, in Perth Amboy, New Jersey After graduating from St Mary's Parochial School, he spent three years in the local high school supplementing this with a course in Wood's Business College, Newark, from which he was graduated in 1901 He then accepted a position as clerk with the Kelly & McAlinden Company, of which his father was the president, and in June, 1919, upon the death of the latter, John William Kelly succeeded his father and became the president, which position he still holds at the present time, and which office he fills in the same able manner as did his father. The thorough business qualifications of Mr Kelly are in great demand, and his public-spirit has led him to accept of such trusts. He is a director of the Middlesex County Bank, and also director of the Smith Street Improvement Company. Mr Kelly, like his father, is a strong Democrat in political faith, and has played a decidedly prominent part in the public life of the city of Perth Amboy, having served two terms or four years as alderman on the Democratic ticket. He affiliates with the Knights of Columbus and is past grand knight of the organization. In religion he is a Roman Catholic and is a member of St Mary's Roman Catholic Church. He has always been a lover of out-door sports and when a boy was captain of the Crescent baseball team, and a great lover of bicycling, and took part in many bicycle races.

Mr Kelly was united in marriage, November 9, 1909, with Margaret J Noone, a native of Scranton, Pennsylvania and the daughter of the late Timothy and Katherine Noone. Mr and Mrs Kelly have one child, Katherine, born December 12, 1910.

CHESTER WALKER WOOD —Of Massachusetts Colonial family, Mr Wood spent his youth in his native Massachusetts, the town of Mendon his birthplace, and also that of his father, William Perry Wood, a farmer and lumberman. The family moved to Upton, Massachusetts, in 1874, and there William P Wood died aged over seventy. His wife, Adeline Stoddard (Walker) Wood, died in Upton at about the same age. They were the parents of four children: Perry, Chester Walker, Benjamin Claflin, and Mary Josephine, the latter deceased. This review follows the fortunes of the second son, Chester W Wood, who for thirty-one years 1890-1921 has been connected with the great Chicago dressed meat house, Swift & Company, and for twenty-four years has been manager of the New Brunswick branch of Swift & Company.

Chester Walker Wood was born August 16, 1869, and in 1874 his parents moved from Mendon to Upton where the lad was educated in the public schools. After graduation from high school in 1886 he became his father's assistant on the farm and in his lumbering business, remaining as such until he began his long connection with the dressed meat industry. His first position was at Jamaica Plains, and in 1890 he entered the employ of Swift & Company in New York City. He was with that company in New York City, Trenton, New Jersey, and Bridgeton, New Jersey, from 1894 until 1896, coming in that year to New Brunswick as manager, a position he has most ably filled during the entire twenty-four years which have since intervened. Mr. Wood has entered heartily into the life of his adopted city, he is interested in its real estate activities, is a charter member of the Board of Trade, and has served on its official board. He is a member of Palestine Lodge, No 111, Free and

Accepted Masons, Scott Chapter, No 4, Royal Arch Masons, Temple Commandery, No 19, Knights Templar, and Mecca Temple, Ancient Arabic Order Nobles of the Mystic Shrine He is a member of the Odd Fellow lodge, also encampment, Young Men's Christian Association, and is a popular member of the Union Club He is an attendant of the Baptist church, and holds all out-of-door sports in high regard, but is particularly fond of swimming

Mr. Wood married, in Trenton, New Jersey, June 1, 1891, Emma Frances Klemmer, born in Trenton, New Jersey, where both her parents died Mr and Mrs Wood are the parents of two children Lillian Frances, born December 8, 1893, and Walker K, born May 10, 1897, married May Elizabeth Van de Watering

---

JACOB HALL WHITFIELD, present comptroller of the city of New Brunswick, was brought to that city in 1866 by his parents, Samuel and Mary (Hall) Whitfield both of English birth Samuel Whitfield was a tanner of leather, a trade he followed in New Brunswick until his death They had but the one child, Jacob H, born in New London, Connecticut, December 31, 1865, he a babe in arms when the family first came to New Brunswick

Jacob Hall Whitfield completed grammar school courses of study in 1880, then entered the employ of the Consolidated Fruit Jar Company in the machine shop, continuing with that corporation for fifteen years He then, with two partners, organized the Phoenix Metal Company, a concern which one year later was sold to the American Can Company Mr Whitfield, after the sale of his company, entered the employ of the purchasing company, remaining with that company for five years He was superintendent of the New Brunswick Water Department during the next four years, then and for five years was superintendent of the Brass Goods Manufacturing Company, Brooklyn, New York, but retained his New Brunswick residence

During one year of the World War period he was associated with the American Can Company, manufacturing war goods for the government, then until the close of the war, was with the Wright Martin Aircraft Corporation On July 15, 1919 he entered upon the duties of his present position, comptroller of the city That is not, however, his first public position Mr Whitfield having served as alderman in 1892-96, and represented New Brunswick in the New Jersey House of Assembly in 1896 He is a strong and capable man, held in the highest esteem wherever well known He is a member of Union Lodge, No 19 Free and Accepted Masons, Scott Council, Royal and Select Masters, and Salaam Temple, Ancient Arabic Order Nobles of the Mystic Shrine, the Benevolent and Protective Order of Elks, and the Baptist church

Mr Whitfield married, in New Brunswick April 2, 1885, Julia A Kemp, born in New Brunswick, daughter of Thomas Kemp, deceased Mr and Mrs Whitfield are the parents of three children William H, born April 2, 1886 now a clerk in the New Brunswick Water Department, Mary C, born September 29, 1887, wife of Harvey L Hullfish, of New Brunswick. Helen W, born September 29, 1889, died November 11, 1918

GEORGE HILTON COATES, master mechanic for the American Smelting and Refining Company, is a man still in the prime of life, whose history thus far has been full of interesting activities

His father, George Coates, was born in Brompton, Yorkshire, England, and was also a master mechanic in his day He died in Kansas City, Missouri, in 1906 He married Mary Hodgson, born in Willington, England, who now lives in Los Angeles, California, spending the winters in Phoenix, Arizona They were the parents of eleven children, of whom two died in infancy Those now living are George Hilton, whose name heads this review, Thomas, David, Sarah, Lilly, William, Charles, Bertha, and Henry, all living in America

George Hilton Coates was born in Willington, England, July 26, 1865 There he attended school until eighteen years of age, being a graduate of the High School in the class of 1879 Being interested in the line of work which his father had always followed, and naturally of a mechanical bent, he learned the machinist's trade He worked at the machinist's trade both in England and America In 1881 the young man came to America, going to Pueblo, Colorado, where he entered the employ of the Colorado Coal and Iron Company He remained with these people for six years on the same basis as at the start, then became foreman of one of their shops Later he went to work for the Denver & Rio Grande Railroad, at Pueblo, as assistant foreman of water service Still later he became associated with the Guggenheim Smelting Company, of Pueblo In 1896 he came to Perth Amboy, New Jersey, as foreman in the mechanical department, which became the American Smelting and Refining Company With this firm Mr Coates has remained since, and has been master mechanic for the past twenty years In the social and fraternal life of the city, Mr Coates has wide and varied connections He was master of Raritan Lodge, No 61, Free and Accepted Masons, 1907 and 1908, was high priest of the Royal Arch Masons in 1912 He is a member of the Order of the Eastern Star, of which he was worthy patron from 1912 to 1920 He is a thirty-second degree Mason, holding membership in the Valley of Jersey City, also a noble of Salaam Temple, Ancient Arabic Order Nobles of the Mystic Shrine He is also a member of the Raritan and Craftsmen's clubs

Mr Coates married, December 24, 1900, in Pueblo, Colorado, Henrietta Wilson, daughter of Henry R and Mary (Coates) Wilson Mrs Coates was born in West Hartlepool, England, but was reared in Scotland Her father died in Scotland, but her mother died in Pueblo, Colorado Mrs Coates is very prominent in the social and welfare work of Perth Amboy She organized Raritan Chapter, No 58, Order of the Eastern Star, and was its first worthy matron from 1912 to 1914, and worthy district deputy of the Eighth District of New Jersey 1921 She was a charter member of the Red Cross and was on the executive staff during the war Mr and Mrs Coates are the parents of two children, both living: George Bradfield, born April 3, 1902, and Lawrence Hilton, born May 11, 1906 The elder son, George B, enlisted in the regular army, 64th Infantry, and was later commissioned lieutenant and saw active service in France He married Eva Hoyt Reynolds, of New Brunswick The family are members of St Peter's Episcopal Church

ASHER FITZ RANDOLPH —The Fitz Randolphs were concerned in the early settlement of Woodbridge, New Jersey, and there Asher Fitz Randolph was born, as was his father, Everts Fitz Randolph, who at the time of his passing, October 10, 1901, was connected with a New York City drug house

Asher Fitz Randolph was born in Woodbridge, New Jersey, November 11, 1888 He was educated in Woodbridge, finishing as president of the high school graduating class of 1906 He began his business career with the Delaware, Lackawanna & Western Railroad, as a clerk in the auditor's department, but the following year, 1907, he entered the employ of J G Hilliard, insurance broker, No 45 Pine street, New York City, remaining with them nearly two years His next position was with Starkweather & Shepley, New York City, his next with Arbuckle Brothers, No. 71 Water street, New York City, in their insurance department He is yet with the last-named company, holding a responsible position

During the World War, 1917-18, he was a member of Company A, Woodbridge Battalion, of the New Jersey Militia Reserves He was on duty at the time of the great explosion at Morgan, New Jersey, being then sergeant of the company Later he was promoted to the rank of first lieutenant, and was holding that rank when mustered out of the service He is a member of Anchor Council, No 40, Junior Order of United American Mechanics, and an elder of the First Presbyterian Church of Woodbridge

Asher Fitz Randolph married, in Woodbridge, September 10, 1915, Anna M Pfeiffer, daughter of John Pfeiffer, who was born in Woodbridge township The family home is at No 198 Rahway avenue, Woodbridge, New Jersey

JAMES HENRY MAHER —Successful in the business he chose when a young man, and master of its every detail, Mr Maher may be properly classed among the leading funeral directors of New Brunswick A graduate in embalming, he is familiar with all processes, ancient and modern, used in the undertaking business and may be classed as an expert He is a son of Edward Maher, born in Ireland, who came to the United States with his mother when a lad of sixteen, and finally became a farmer of East Millstone, New Jersey, where he died, November 10 1890, at the age of fifty-two Edward Maher married Honora Dwyer, born in Ireland, who was brought to East Millstone, New Jersey, when a girl, she died in Brooklyn, New York, April 13, 1914, aged sixty-two years They were the parents of eleven children Mary, wife

of T J Ahern, of Bath Beach, New York, Katherine, wife of J O'Rourke, of Brooklyn, New York, Richard, of Baltimore, Maryland, Thomas F, of Brooklyn, New York James Henry, of further mention, Edward, of Brooklyn, New York, John, of Chicago, Illinois, William, of New Brunswick, Joseph, of Brooklyn, New York, George, died in infancy, Philip, of New York City

James Henry Maher, fifth child of Edward and Honora (Dwyer) Maher, was born at the home farm in Somerset county, New Jersey, and attended the East Millstone schools He spent the first nineteen years of his life at the farm, then began contracting on his own account, succeeding very well He continued in the contracting business five years, then sold his team and outfit and entered the employ of W J McDede, an undertaker at No 23 Easton avenue In 1903 he left New Brunswick and went to New York City, there pursuing a course at Raynard College of Embalming, finishing with graduation in 1904 The next ten years he spent with the Merritt & Campbell Undertaking Company, of New York City, but in 1914 he resigned, came to New Brunswick and bought the undertaking business of his old employer, W J McDede, and still continues the establishment at No 23 Easton avenue As a funeral director Mr Maher has with dignity and consideration so conducted himself as to be considered more in the light of a friend, and has won public confidence in a degree most unusual He is a member of St Peter's Roman Catholic Church the Knights of Columbus, and the Benevolent and Protective Order of Elks He is fond of out-of-door sports, particularly automobiling, and spends many vacation hours in that way

Mr Maher married, in Elizabeth New Jersey, April 25, 1906 Katherine G Ahern, born in Elizabeth, October 15, 1892, died October 21, 1919, daughter of James and Maria Ahern, both deceased, James Ahern dying in Elizabeth, in 1911, his wife in New Brunswick, in 1916 Mr and Mrs Maher are the parents of two children Anna, born November 20, 1908, and James, born August 5, 1913

KLEIN BROTHERS—The capable, successful and even the most prominent men are not always those who start out with the ambition to achieve something especially great and famous, but often they are the men who at the very outset of life place just valuation upon integrity, honor, industry and determination With these qualities only as a capital, the Klein brothers entered into the hotel business, and together they have made the name of Klein prominent in business circles in New Brunswick, New Jersey

Henry George Klein son of Martin and Anna Maria (Krollman) Klein, was born in New Brunswick, New Jersey, September 12, 1866 Martin Klein settled in New Brunswick in 1842, next door to the present Hotel Klein, and engaged in the hotel business, which he followed through life His place was a recruiting station during the Civil War, and was headquarters for the New Brunswick Artillery Company, he holding the commission of second lieutenant He established the first brewery in this section in 1861 and sold the first glass of beer in New Brunswick His family was the sixth German family to locate in New Brunswick Besides the brewery business, he was also engaged in the wholesale grocery business Martin Klein married (first) Elizabeth Krollman, who bore him four sons Alois, Martin, George and John Martin and John served in the Civil War He married (second) Anna Maria Krollman, by whom he had four children Henry George, of further mention, Kate, deceased; Joseph, deceased, and Peter Frank, of further mention

Henry George Klein obtained his education in Sts John's and Peter's Parochial schools and in the public schools of New Brunswick, after which he entered upon his business career In 1912, together with his brother, Peter Frank Klein, they established themselves in the hotel business, and this partnership has continued to the present time, they having conducted successfully for many years the Hotel Klein, which was the outgrowth of the Raritan House, established by Martin Klein in 1872 Henry G Klein holds a prominent place in the local fraternal organizations of the community, being affiliated with the Benevolent and Protective Order of Elks and the Fraternal Order of Eagles In religion he is a Roman Catholic and attends the Church of St John the Baptist

On January 11, 1891, Mr Klein married Kate W Mauer, daughter of Anton and Wilhelmina Mauer, and they are the parents of one child, Anna M, born October 18, 1891.

Peter Frank Klein, third son of Martin and Anna Maria (Krollman) Klein, was born in New Brunswick, New Jersey, May 13 1875 He secured his education in the parochial and public schools of his native place, and upon completing his education entered upon his business career, and since boyhood, as has been previously mentioned, he has been engaged in the hotel business, meeting with the success which is the ultimate result of good executive ability He is affiliated with New Brunswick Lodge, No 324, Benevolent and Protective Order of Elks In religion he is a Roman Catholic and attends the Church of St John the Baptist Mr Klein is unmarried

---

JACOB SYLVESTER KARKUS, although not a native of Perth Amboy, has resided here most of his life and is today recognized as one of the promising young representatives of the legal fraternity, due to his ability, both natural and acquired

Meyer Karkus, father of Jacob Sylvester Karkus, was born in Russia and came to the United States when a young man It is interesting to note here that while on the boat he met and later married in New York Golda Miller, who too, had left Russia for the purpose of making her home in this country Mr Karkus with his wife made his home in Brooklyn for a while, later moving to a farm in Franklin Park, Middlesex county, New Jersey, and still later removing to Perth Amboy, where he and his family now reside and where Mr Karkus is a successful real estate broker Mr and Mrs Karkus are the parents of nine

children, all of whom are still living Bessie, wife of Alexander Kosene,
of Perth Amboy, Dora, wife of Benjamin Goldberger, Kate, a teacher
in the public schools of Perth Amboy; Jacob Sylvester, of further mention, Louis, assists his brother Jacob S as secretary, Bernard, associated with Mack International Truck Company, of Newark, New Jersey,
Ezra, a student of the New Jersey Law School; Monroe, attends City
College of the City of New York, Irwin, a grammar school student

Jacob Sylvester Karkus was born in Brooklyn, New York, April 27,
1893, and when he was eight years old moved with his parents to Franklin Park, Middlesex county, New Jersey, where he attended the public
schools for two years, at the end of which time he continued to pursue
his studies in Perth Amboy, New Jersey, where the family then removed,
graduating from the local grammar school in 1908 After spending one
year at the high school, he accepted a position as stenographer in New
York City, and here the ambition of the young man is clearly shown
in the fact that during these three years that he was thus employed he
was pursuing a course of study evenings to meet the requirements of
the New Jersey State Board of Education and reading on his own
account for the purpose of fitting himself for his entrance into law school
It is needless to say that the goal for ambition such as he portrayed is
always sure to gain its just reward, entering New Jersey Law School
in 1912, he graduated from this institution three years later as the vice-
president of his class The following two years he gained much valuable
and practical knowledge in the law offices of Isaac Sprangenthal of
Newark, and with the leading specialist, Murray Apfelbaum, also of
Newark, and in June, 1917, he passed the New Jersey State bar examinations But three months later, in September, 1917, he was called into
the service of his country and was sent to Camp Dix, later transferred
to Camp Gordon, Georgia, becoming a member of Company H, 325th
Infantry In a short time he was made sergeant major, and in March,
1918, was sent overseas, saw active service, being in many of the important encounters, was a victim of shell shock, and returned to the United
States, September, 1918 receiving his honorable discharge November,
1918, since which time he has been actively engaged in the practice of
his profession in the Ranton building

Mr Karkus is a member of the Hebrew synagogue He is unmarried and makes his home with his parents His hobby is baseball and
when in school was very clever "at the bat" He is public-spirited and
progressive, ever ready to cooperate in any movement that is for the
common welfare, or that tends to promote the material advancement
of the community, and his success, which he so thoroughly deserves, is
assured

RALPH VAN MATER GORSLINE, of New Brunswick New
Jersey, is filling a position of grave responsibility With long experience
in the mercantile world, he has reached his present high position by his
own efforts

Mr Gorsline was born in Flushing, New York, June 9, 1879, a son of
Peter Gorsline, who was an expert accountant, following this line of

endeavor through all his business career   Peter Gorsline was born in Elmhurst, Long Island, and died in Flushing, at the age of sixty-five years   He married Elizabeth Van Mater, who was born in Tennent, New Jersey, and died in Laurel Hill, New York, at the age of thirty-eight years   They had two children Eva, who died at the age of twenty-eight November 19, 1909, and Ralph Van Mater, whose career is of interest to the people of New Brunswick

Beginning his education in the public schools of Spotswood New Jersey, and continuing at the schools of Asbury Park, New Jersey, Mr. Gorsline was graduated from the Asbury Park High School in the class of 1897   Immediately thereafter the young man entered upon his business career in the employ of J J Parker a grocer then doing business in Asbury Park   This was in the capacity of counter man, and he remained in this connection until the Spanish-American War, when he enlisted in the service   He came to New Brunswick, April 9, 1902, and accepted a position with the Nelson T Parker Company, then one of the leading insurance firms of this city   Later he went on the road as special agent for the London-Lancashire Indemnity Company, thereafter holding its agency, under the firm name of the Cramer-Gorsline Company Incorporated   Mr Gorsline was president of this company, which office he held until April 9, 1917   On that date he entered upon the duties of his present position, cashier and accountant for the Reckitts Company, U S A , Limited manufacturers of laundry bluing

During the Spanish-American War, Mr Gorsline served in Company A, 3rd Regiment United States Army   For two years and a half, and until mustered out, he was captain of the local militia, Company E, 3rd Battalion, New Jersey State Militia   Mr Gorsline is prominent in various circles in New Brunswick   He is an influential member of the Board of Trade, is a member of the Young Men's Christian Association, and is a member of the Improved Order of Red Men, and of Good Intent Council Junior Order of United American Mechanics

On June 29, 1910, Mr Gorsline married Helen Brower, who was born in New Brunswick, October 1 1884   She is a daughter of Joseph Farmer and Lydia (Graham) Brower, of this city, Mr Brower being a well known contractor   Mr and Mrs Gorsline have one daughter, Jean Graham, born November 24 1912   The family are members of St John's Episcopal Church of which Mr Gorsline has been vestryman for the past ten years

---

WILLIAM WEDEEN, D. D. S.—At about the time Dr. Wedeen arrived at legal age, he received from the University of Pennsylvania, at the close of a three years' course in the Dental School of that institution, the degree of D D S With this equipment for manhood's responsibilities, the young man began his professional career in his native city, Perth Amboy, New Jersey, and is building up a good practice   He is a son of Louis Oscar Wedeen, born in Russia, where his wife, Ida Bernice (Bodine) Wedeen, and two children, were also born   After coming to the United States, they first lived in Elizabeth, New Jersey, but in a short time moved to Perth Amboy, which has since been the family home, the father now retired from active business   Four children have been born to Mr and Mrs Wedeen since coming to the United States, the two eldest born in Russia   Esther, wife of Louis E Kemler, Samuel, died in Hartford, Connecticut, aged twenty-one years, William, of further mention; Arthur, died aged seven years, Matilda, resides with her parents, and Belle, also residing with her parents

William Wedeen was born in Perth Amboy, New Jersey, June 26, 1895, and there completed grade and high school courses with graduation from grammar school in 1908, high school in 1912   He then spent a year in Pennsylvania State College, entering the dental department of the University of Pennsylvania in 1909, and finishing with the class of 1916, D D S   He at once began practice in Perth Amboy, a year, however, being spent in the United States army during the war with Germany.   Dr Wedeen entered the army in March 1918, and was stationed at Camp Wadsworth, South Carolina, until January 15, 1919, when he was honorably discharged and mustered out   He was enlisted as a member of the Medical Enlisted Reserve Corps   He is a member of Prudence Lodge No 204, Free and Accepted Masons, Perth Amboy, Amboy Chapter, No 41, Royal Arch Masons, Forest No 68, Tall Cedars of Lebanon, the Benevolent and Protective Order of Elks, the Young Men's Christian Association, the Young Men's Hebrew Association, and the Orthodox Jewish Church

---

WILLIAM PETER CLEMENSEN, prominent among the younger business men of Perth Amboy, where he is the owner of the large and flourishing flour, grain and hay business at the corner of Market and South Second streets and the Central Railroad of New Jersey, is of Danish descent and parentage, and a son of Soren and Christine (Christensen) Clemensen, both natives of Denmark, who came to the United States in early youth   The elder Mr. Clemensen received his education in his native land, and served an apprenticeship there in the baking trade Upon reaching his majority he left Denmark, came to this country and located in Perth Amboy, New Jersey, and there secured employment in a local bakery   He later founded a similar establishment, Clemensen & Nelson, on Smith street and remained at the head of that concern for four years   The success of the enterprise was considerable, but in 1913 Mr Clemensen sold his interest and established himself in the flour, grain and hay business of which his son is now the head   His death occurred in 1916, when he was but forty-seven years of age, in Perth Amboy   He and his wife, who survives him, were the parents of two children, as follows· William Peter, with whom we are here concerned; and a daughter Mamie, who became the wife of Herbert Jensen, of Perth Amboy

William Peter Clemensen was born in Perth Amboy, New Jersey, July 20, 1895   He attended the public schools of his native place until he was fifteen years old   At that age his parents removed to the town of Metuchen, New Jersey, and the lad attended the high school there for three years longer The family then returned to Perth Amboy, where his father engaged in the present line of business and took his son into partnership In 1916, on the death of the elder man, Mr. Clemensen became the sole owner of the prosperous concern and has continued to conduct it with a notable degree of success up to the present time Besides its main offices in Perth Amboy, there is also a branch of the house in Tottenville, Staten Island, New York, where a thriving business is also done Mr Clemensen is exceedingly fond of out-door life of all kinds and especially of hunting, spending much of his leisure time in the latter pursuit He is also an accomplished musician and has studied that art for two and a half years at the National Conservatory of Music in New York City He is prominent in social and fraternal life in Perth Amboy, and is a member of the Independent Order of Odd Fellows, the Danish Brotherhood, and the Benevolent and Protective Order of Elks During the great war in Europe, Mr Clemensen entered the service of his country and spent sixteen months at Forts Dix and Stewart, at the former as a member of Company D, 311th Infantry Regiment, and at the latter with the 11th Regiment United States Cavalry, to which he had been transferred

William Peter Clemensen was united in marriage, November 4, 1917, in Matawan, with Helen Isadore Kelly, a native of Matawan, New Jersey, and a daughter of Edward and Elizabeth Kelly, old and much esteemed residents of that place, where the former is engaged in business as a stone mason Mr and Mrs Clemensen are the parents of one child, William Melville born June 20, 1919

WILLIAM HENRY RUCKLE—After coming to the United States a young man, William Henry Ruckle established a bakery in the city of New York at Third avenue and Eighty-sixth street, continuing until 1895, when he located in New Brunswick, New Jersey He resumed the baking business in his new home, establishing his plant and store at Nos 101-103 Neilson street, there continuing in successful operation until his death March 19 1918 aged sixty-four. He had trained his son, also William Henry Ruckle to follow the same trade, and when the elder Ruckle passed away the young man succeeded him and the business established by the father a quarter of a century ago, is successfully conducted by the son who has greatly widened its scope and increased the output

William Henry Ruckle, Sr, married Catherine Ingner, born in Alsace-Lorraine, France, died in New Brunswick, New Jersey, December 10, 1917 They were the parents of five children· Elsie, married Simon Boyce, and resides in Weatherly, Pennsylvania, William Henry (2), of further mention, Anna Mary, a resident of New Brunswick, Everett G, a radio operator of New Brunswick, Catherine B, residing at home

William Henry Ruckle, Jr, was born in New York City New York, November 21, 1887, and there spent the first eight years of his life In 1895 his parents moved to New Brunswick and the lad attended school until eighteen years of age, then became a baker's apprentice, learning the business under the instruction of his father   He continued his father's assistant until the latter's death in 1918, then became head of the business which he yet continues   Mr Ruckle is a young man of good business ability, and during the less than two years since coming into full management has greatly increased the business   He is well liked and popular, a member of several fraternities and clubs, his favorite recreations yachting and hunting   His fraternal orders are the Elks, Red Men, Foresters and Eagles, his club the New Brunswick Yacht   He is a communicant of St John's Roman Catholic Church

---

LEWIS HOLLANDER, of Perth Amboy, New Jersey, is actively engaged in a line of business which has largely to do with the public health and well-being—the milk business

Andrew Hollander, father of Lewis Hollander, was born in Woodbridge, New Jersey, but for a large part of his life was a resident of Atlantic City   There he followed the carpenter's trade for many years, and for twenty-five years was a member of the police force   He died in Atlantic City, New Jersey, June 11, 1916, at the age of sixty years   He married Mary M Dow, who died in Brooklyn, New York, at the age of fifty-seven years   She was a woman of fine characteristics, and devoted to her family   Her mother was an Indian squaw   Andrew and Mary M (Dow) Hollander were the parents of two children   Lillian, now deceased, and Lewis, the Perth Amboy milk dealer   The grandfather, Andrew Hollander, was born in Germany

Lewis Hollander was born in Philadelphia, Pennsylvania, December 2, 1876   The family remained in that city until he was twelve years of age, when they removed to Atlantic City, New Jersey   Soon after that the boy went to work with his father in the carpenter business, continuing thus for two years   The boy then came to Perth Amboy and went to work on the Lehigh Valley Railroad   This was in 1890   He continued railroad work for three years, then entered the employ of the C Pardee Works, where he remained for five years   His next connection was with the American Smelting and Refining Company, with whom he remained for fourteen years at their plant in Perth Amboy

Knowing the city thoroughly, after his long residence here, Mr Hollander decided upon a business venture of his own   He started in the milk business, which he still carries on at No 343 Barclay street, Perth Amboy   From the beginning he was successful, and with the growth of the city and his own constant attention to business, he has placed himself at the lead in his line   He has now followed this business for twelve years, and handles a very large trade   Mr Hollander is a progressive citizen, interested in everything that affects the welfare of the community   He is affiliated with the Republican party, but has never sought nor accepted public office   When his exacting business interests give him opportunity he spends his leisure motoring   He is a member of the Woodmen of the World and the Foresters of America

Mr Hollander married, September 27, 1893, Martha G Yates, daughter of James W and Alfretta (Gardener) Yates   Mrs Hollander was born in Perth Amboy, October 25, 1874. Her father was an engineer for many years and died at the age of sixty-three years. Her mother died at the age of forty-eight years. Mr and Mrs Hollander have two children Edna M, born November 17 1896, now the wife of Michael C Burns, of Perth Amboy, and Andrew C, born August 14, 1901, who is now a clerk in the employ of the American Smelting and Refining Company. The family are members of the Methodist church, and active in all its work.

CHARLES HENRY BRUNS—Nearly everyone in the State of New Jersey is familiar with the widely known catering establishment of "Bruns of New Brunswick." The business was started many years ago by Frederick Bruns, as an ice cream and confectionery store and conducted by him personally, assisted by his sons. After his death the family continued to run the business, it being made an incorporated company under the name of "Bruns of New Brunswick," Inc, high grade caterers and confectioners.

Frederick Bruns was born in Hanover, Germany. When the lad was twelve years old he came to this country alone, landing in New York City, and started a single handed fight for a living. He eventually achieved success, conducting a catering concern at No 71 Church street for a number of years and latterly being assisted by his son Charles. Frederick Bruns married Mary Meyer, a native of Germany; they came to New Brunswick in 1888 where she died June 21, 1907, and one year later January 19, 1908 her husband died. They had four boys all living at the present time (1921) three of them now being connected with the catering business. They are Charles Henry in New Brunswick, Frederick W, in a branch store in Plainfield, Harry Edward a resident of Albany, New York Otto, in charge of another branch store at No 220 Raritan avenue, Highland Park.

Charles Henry Bruns was born February 7, 1884, in Somerville, New Jersey, but when he was four years old his parents moved to New Brunswick. Here the boy attended school, graduating from the grammar and high schools, and followed this by a course at the Wilson Business College of New Brunswick. After finishing there, Charles Henry Bruns went into his father's store, assisting him until his death, when the son carried on the business, moving in 1910 to the present establishment at No 361 George street. There may be found the most complete concern of its kind in the State, their catering work extending over a large territory and their daily deliveries being of a considerable number. Mr Bruns has a hobby—it is music, of which he is devotedly fond especially symphony concerts, chamber music, etc. He is also much interested in the Young Men's Christian Association, of which he is a member and is active in the Rotary Club. He is a member of the First Reformed Church of New Brunswick.

On January 17 1910, in New Brunswick, Charles Henry Bruns married Mabel C Harvey, born in this city March 11 1886, the daughter of Charles W and Mary C (Cole) Harvey, they reside in New Brunswick where Mr Harvey was formerly engaged as a pattern maker, but is now leading a retired life   Mr and Mrs Bruns have one child, Dorothy Virginia, born May 12 1912   Their home is at No 14 Remson avenue, New Brunswick, New Jersey

---

JOSEPH JOHN FEASTER, numbered among the successful merchants of New Brunswick, New Jersey, is the proprietor of a grocery and provision store at No 165 Throop avenue   Not only is Mr Feaster prominent in business circles, but he also takes an active part in the political life of the community, and is known throughout the city for his public spirit and interest in the welfare of the place

John Feaster father of Joseph John Feaster, was born in Germany, but was brought by his parents to this country when a baby, the family locating at once in New Brunswick   Upon reaching manhood he served an apprenticeship to the carpenter's trade, and followed this particular line throughout his entire lifetime   He died January 29, 1920   He married Caroline Feaster, whose surname was the same as his although they claimed no relationship, and to them were born six children   Mary, who married William F McGrath, of New Brunswick, New Jersey; Edward, deceased, Frank, John, Joseph John, of further mention; Nicholas, a resident of New York City

Joseph John Feaster, son of John and Caroline (Feaster) Feaster, was born June 24, 1880, in New Brunswick, New Jersey, in the old homestead   He obtained his education in the public schools of his native place and St John's Academy, and after finishing his studies at the age of nineteen established himself in his present business in which he has met with great success

The same qualities that Mr Feaster has exhibited in the conduct of his own business he has also shown in that of the city administration, which he has served so efficiently, having served as alderman from 1907 until 1915, as recorder from 1915 until 1917 and elected commissioner, March 1917, serving to 1919, when he was reelected for another term of four years   He has indeed always been very active in politics, and enjoys a wide and well-deserved popularity, and the entire community, without regard to party differences, has expressed itself eminently satisfied with his work   Mr. Feaster is affiliated with many important organizations here   among them being the Benevolent and Protective Order of Elks the Knights of Columbus the Improved Order of Red Men, and the Fraternal Order of Eagles   In his religious belief he is a Roman Catholic and attends St John's Church of New Brunswick

Joseph John Feaster was united in marriage, November 15, 1906, at New Brunswick, with Anna E Crennar, of East Brunswick township, a daughter of Joseph and Mary Crennar, both deceased   To Mr and Mrs Feaster two children have been born as follows: Anna M, born August 16, 1907, Frank J born May 16, 1910   The family reside at No 127 Throop avenue, New Brunswick, New Jersey   Mr Feaster is ardently devoted to hunting and fishing, and during the seasons for such sport, he devotes whatever time he can spare from his ever increasing business affairs to this particular line of outdoor recreation

PATRICK JOSEPH LYONS, rising by the force of his own character from the position of laborer, now owns an independent manufacturing business in Perth Amboy, building many kinds of water craft

Thomas Lyons, father of Patrick J Lyons, was born in Ireland, and came to this country alone when a very young man He came first to Jersey City, New Jersey, where he obtained employment as a sticker in a slaughter house He removed to England when the boy, Patrick J, was three years old. Some years later his wife died there, and he brought his children back to America He came to Perth Amboy, New Jersey, in 1889, and there was employed on the coal docks. He was killed there by a train, in 1901, at the age of fifty-four years He married, in Jersey City, Elizabeth Bath, who was born in Jersey City, and died in England They were the parents of three children Thomas, of Perth Amboy, who is a mason's tender, unmarried, Patrick Joseph, of whom further mention follows, and Mary, who died in Perth Amboy, at the age of thirty-four years; she was the wife of Peter Martin and the mother of nine children, all of whom now live in Perth Amboy

Patrick Joseph Lyons was born in Jersey City, New Jersey, October 15, 1875 Going with his parents to England he remained there for five years Then at eight years of age he returned to America, motherless For a time he was in Woodbridge, New Jersey, and there attended the public schools, completing the course at the age of fourteen years He then came to Perth Amboy, and began life driving a dump cart This work he followed for two years then worked in a brick factory By industry and thrift he accumulated enough money to start in business, and for eleven years he was proprietor of a hotel located on the corner of Smith and Maple streets He was always in touch with the shipping interests in the city of Perth Amboy, and when he was able to follow his tastes more closely in business he disposed of his hotel and began the manufacture of boats He has done very attractive work along this line, and is making a success of the venture. Mr Lyons is unmarried He is connected with several fraternal organizations He is a member of the Improved Order of Red Men, the Foresters of America, and the Fraternal Order of Eagles He is foreman of the Perth Amboy Engine Company In the Spanish-American War, Mr Lyons served in Company D, 3rd New Jersey Infantry of New Brunswick, New Jersey He was first sent to Sea Girt, then to Sandy Hook, then to Pompton Plains, and last to Athens, Georgia where this company was discharged from the service

---

GEORGE ROBERT BUNTEN, JR—For the past ten years the growth and development of the city of Perth Amboy, New Jersey have been so rapid that the mere providing of the materials of construction has become an industry in itself In this line of business activity George Robert Bunten Jr, stands among the leaders

Mr Bunten is a son of George Robert Bunten, Sr, formerly of Alpine, New Jersey, and for many years in the ship chandlery business, but now retired The elder Mr Bunten served in the Civil War

Geo R Linster Jr

W. K. Bunten

George Robert Bunten, Jr, was born in Alpine, New Jersey, May 9, 1876. He received his education in the public schools of Richmond Valley, Staten Island, New York. There he laid the practical foundation for a business career. As he grew into manhood he became interested in his father's business, learning all the details. This business he followed for twelve years, then seeing the opportunities for success in the handling of all kinds of construction materials, he entered this field, along the line of mason's materials and supplies. This line of business activity he has followed for the last ten years, and has made himself felt in the construction world. He is a member of the Benevolent and Protective Order of Elks, Lodge No 784, of Perth Amboy, also a member of the Elks Club, of that city

Mr Bunten married, October 16, 1900, in Perth Amboy, Margaret Connell, daughter of Patrick and Margaret Connell

---

WILLIAM RUSSELL BUNTEN —In the business world of Perth Amboy, New Jersey, one of the noteworthy men in the construction line is William Russell Bunten. He was born in Alpine, New Jersey, December 3, 1878, a son of George Robert and Mary Bunten

William Russell Bunten received his education in the excellent public schools of Richmond Valley, Staten Island, New York. When a young man he was attracted to a business career, and conducted a coal business for ten years. For the past twelve years, however, he has been actively interested in the handling of mason's materials, and his present business at No 283 Water street, Perth Amboy, has grown and developed from its early beginnings until it is one of the important factors in the construction work of this section. Mr Bunten is first a business man, but he holds affiliation with the foremost social and fraternal organizations in which he takes an active interest. He is a member of the Independent Order of Odd Fellows, the Knights of Pythias, in which order he is past chancellor, the Improved Order of Red Men, past president of the Order of Owls, and the Benevolent and Protective Order of Elks. He is an honorary member of the Washington Hose Chemical Company, of Perth Amboy, and of the Haymakers' Association. He is a member of the Elks and Odd Fellows clubs

Mr Bunten married, June 12, 1898, in Tottenville, New York, Annie Morehouse, daughter of David and Eliza Morehouse. They are the parents of eight children: William Russell, Jr, born November 2, 1899, Anna, born March 30, 1902, Helen, born April 1, 1906, Grace, born July 11, 1907, Henry born March 18, 1910, Bessie, born June 27, 1913, Mary, born March 21, 1916, and Robert, born June 2 1918. The family are Members of St Peter's Episcopal Church, Perth Amboy

---

BENJAMIN T. McNALLY —From the Atlantic ocean to the Pacific coast and from the most northern part of the United States to South America, Benjamin T McNally has visited nearly every city of importance on this continent and in addition has traveled all over Europe and Australia   A vaudeville performer, he enjoyed, by reason of his profession, unusual opportunities of seeing the world

Benjamin T McNally was born in Cleveland, Ohio, his father being Benjamin McNally, also born in Cleveland   He had always been a railroad engineer until the last few years, when he retired from so strenuous a life and is now living in New Brunswick   On August 11, 1920, the elder Mr McNally celebrated his seventy-seventh birthday anniversary   His wife was Annie (Hynes) McNally, born in Lynn, Massachusetts   She died January 19, 1912, in San Francisco, California, at the age of sixty-two years   Mr and Mrs McNally were the parents of nine children five of whom are now living, namely : John a resident of San Francisco, Benjamin T , Hattie wife of John Rogers, Louis living in San Francisco, Stephen, a vaudeville actor

Though claiming Cleveland, Ohio as his birthplace, Benjamin T McNally spent his childhood and youth in California and there he acquired an education in the public schools of San Francisco   After leaving school Mr McNally joined Sells Brothers Circus, traveling with them for one season, doing a high wire and flying trapeze act in their shows   Coming East he entered into vaudeville work and began his journeying all over the world   In 1912, Mr McNally came to New Brunswick, New Jersey, and entered into business life here   In 1917 he took over the Easton Avenue Garage and now has a flourishing plant at Nos 39-41 Easton avenue   He is a member of the actors' club, the White Rats

During the time that Mr McNally was performing in vaudeville in Buda Pesth Hungary, he met Theresia Hess, a native of Paris, France   She was also engaged in vaudeville shows   On April 23 1905 in New York City, Benjamin T McNally married Theresia Hess   They have no children

---

NICHOLAS AUGUSTA MORRISSY is a thorough musician and as an arranger of high class musical programs has no superiors   He is the founder of Morrissy's Band which has a wide reputation, for no numbers except high class selections are ever played by the organization save by request   This evidences the wide range of music with which Mr Morrissy is familiar, and the superior musicians comprising his organization

Nicholas Morrissy, father of Nicholas Augusta Morrissy, was born in Waterford, Ireland, and came to this country when a young man, locating in Brooklyn, New York, where he worked as a blacksmith for many years   He died in Perth Amboy, New Jersey, about 1895   He married Katherine Power and to them were born ten children, seven of whom are living, among them being Katherine, wife of Patrick Tierney, a resident of Perth Amboy, Mary Dugan, a resident of Brooklyn, New York, Nicholas Augusta, mentioned below

Nicholas Augusta Morrissy was born in Brooklyn, New York, May 24, 1872, and was brought by his parents to Perth Amboy, New Jersey, when he was six years of age   Here he attended the public schools until he was sixteen years old, when upon the death of both his parents, which occurred at this time, he was obliged to leave school He then served an apprenticeship to the machinist's trade, since which time he has followed this particular trade with the exception of the ten years that he devoted exclusively to music At the present time he is a machinist in the Schantz & Eckert Company He is a fine cornetist, and has devoted much of his time to perfecting himself in the playing of this instrument His hobby, which can be readily seen, is music. He affiliates with the Benevolent and Protective Order of Elks, and in religion is a Roman Catholic, being a prominent member of St Mary's Roman Catholic Church

Mr Morrissy married, in 1904, Anna Toft, daughter of John H and Mathilda (Brown) Toft Mr and Mrs Morrissy are the parents of two children Anna Katherine, and Harry Austin

---

CHARLES AUGUSTUS SCHENCK, a man who has since 1890 been a resident of New Brunswick, New Jersey, and later held for many years a prominent place among the active business men of this community, is secretary of the Brunswick Refrigerating Company, which is located on Jersey avenue

Henry Vander Veer Schenck, father of Charles Augustus Schenck, was born in New Brunswick, New Jersey, in 1833, and died here September 10, 1918, having spent his entire life in this State, largely in Newark, and for years connected with the Singer Sewing Machine Company He married Mary A Marshall of New York City, who is still living and resides at the present time, 1921, in Newark, New Jersey Mr and Mrs Schenck were the parents of three children Charles Augustus, with whom we are here concerned, being the only surviving member

Charles Augustus Schenck was born March 16, 1861, at New Brunswick, but at the age of six years removed with his parents to Newark, where he attended the public schools, graduating from the Newark High School in 1878 That same year he secured a position with the Singer Manufacturing Company and remained with them until 1885, when he resigned and went to Boston, Massachusetts, where for the next two years he furnished various office buildings throughout that city with towel supplies In 1890 he returned to New Brunswick, and became private secretary to the president of the National Water Tube Boiler Company, later being promoted to the treasurership of the organization In 1906, when this company was merged with the Brunswick Refrigerating Company, Mr Schenck continued with the latter, and in 1912 was elected to the position of secretary of the organization in which he has since continued He has been for the past twenty years secretary of the second Merchants' Building and Loan Company of New Brunswick

Mr Schenck is a member of the Royal Arcanum, life member of the Young Men's Christian Association, and also holds membership in the City Bowling Club, of which he is secretary His hobby is bowling and in recognition of his clever playing of the game he has won many tro-

phies He attends the First Reformed Church of New Brunswick, and
has served on its official board   An able business man, public-spirited,
loyal, patriotic and progressive, he is a man whom no obstacle can daunt
nor no misfortune discourage.

On December 23 1899 Charles Augustus Schenck was united in
marriage with Nellie L Cook, a native of Newark, New Jersey

FRANK BURRELL OVERTON.—A love of engineering in all its
branches prompted Mr Overton, while in the employ of a corporation
as stationary engineer, to begin the study of welding and he became
so interested in the subject that he fitted up a shop in the rear of his
home in Keyport, New Jersey, finally making electrical and acetylene
welding of metals his sole business   He is master of his art, and in his
shop at No 261 King street, Perth Amboy, he follows his business successfully   He is the son of William Willard and Julia Ann (Hutz) Overton, his father a mariner all his life

Frank Burrell Overton was born in Port Monmouth, Monmouth
county, New Jersey, on Sandy Hook bay, February 27, 1884   He
attended the village public school, and when school years were over was
variously employed until finally becoming a stationary engineer with
the Jersey Central Traction Company of Keyport, New Jersey   He was
in that employ in 1911, when he took up the study of welding metals
and finally built a shop in the rear of his home and made welding his
specialty   He began in a small way, but met with such encouraging
success that in 1918 he moved to Perth Amboy, where he opened a shop
at No 261 King street   He specializes in both electric and acetylene
welding, and is well established in business   Mr Overton is a member
of Corliss Lodge No 13 National Association of Stationary Engineers,
Raritan Lodge, No 61, Free and Accepted Masons; Perth Amboy Lodge,
No 784, Benevolent and Protective Order of Elks, Lawrence Lodge,
No 62, Independent Order of Odd Fellows, and Middlesex Lodge,
Junior Order of United American Mechanics   He is also a member of
Simpson Methodist Episcopal Church, and in politics is a Republican

Mr Overton married, in New York City, February 27, 1911, Henrietta
Mears Tooker daughter of Frank Elias and Mary Elizabeth (Farrell)
Tooker   Mr and Mrs Overton are the parents of two daughters Har-
rietta Elizabeth, born October 3, 1914 Kathryn Willard, born August
20, 1918

IRA RUTLEDGE CROUSE—A good example of the successful
business man and man-of-affairs, who has risen through his own efforts
to a position of prominence in the community, is Ira Rutledge Crouse,
a citizen of whom Perth Amboy, New Jersey, may well be proud   Mr
Crouse's descent from one of the fine old families which came to this
country many years ago is warranty of his sterling and vigorous traits
of character   The stock from which he sprang is typical of the best
traditions of American life

William Henry Crouse, father of the subject of this review, was

born on the old homestead in Hunterdon county, in 1841, and died in
1912, at the age of seventy-one Like many of the young men of his
time he served during the Civil War, he was a volunteer attached to
the Pennsylvania regiment, and was wounded at the battle of Bull Run
He married Catherine Loudenbery, born in Warren county, New Jersey,
May 6, 1842, and who died in Perth Amboy in February, 1918 Eight
children were born of this union Annie, now the wife of Harvey Trau-
ger, Harry, a gold miner of Idiarod, Alaska, John, a farmer in Hunterdon county; Edith, deceased, Walter, a farmer in Warren county, Ira
Rutledge, mentioned below Katherine, died in infancy, Frank, died in
infancy.

Ira Rutledge Crouse son of William Henry and Catherine (Loudenbery) Crouse, was born on the old homestead in Hunterdon county,
January 6, 1873 He attended the district school here until he was nine
years old, when he was brought by his parents to Mount Joy, New
Jersey, pursuing his studies there for two years and finishing at Millers-
ville when he had reached the age of sixteen In 1893 he came to Perth
Amboy and began an apprenticeship to the carpenter's trade, and at
the end of four years, after having finished his training, he established
himself in the contracting and building business together with a lumber
yard which he owns He has built many of the schools of Perth Amboy
and also the Polish church here, which is considered the finest structure
of its kind in the State The success which has attended his efforts
is due to no happy succession of advantageous circumstances, but to his
own sturdy will, steady application, and tireless energy

Mr Crouse's thorough business qualifications and his well-known
executive ability have always been in demand on director's boards, and in
consequence, he is president of the Union Garage Company, and was
formerly vice-president of the Stouck-Reaser Lumber Company of Harrisburg, Pennsylvania He is also a director of the Perth Amboy Trust
Company and of the Citizens Building and Loan Association In politics
he is a Republican and takes a lively interest in that phase of public
administration which makes for the highest good of the community
For two years he was a member of the Common Council, and later
became the president, which office he held for four years, he has also
served a five-year term on the Water Board

Mr Crouse affiliates with the Benevolent and Protective Order of
Elks, the Woodmen of the World, and with the Free and Accepted
Masons Realizing that a busy man must of necessity have recreation,
he holds membership in the Raritan Yacht Club, and the East Jersey
Club, his hobby is hunting

In 1894 Mr Crouse married Laura L Leonard, a daughter of the
late John and Jennie (Sinclair) Leonard, of Hunterdon county, New
Jersey To Mr and Mrs Crouse have been born three children. Lawrence, born November 18, 1895, now associated with his father in business, he is married and has one child, Grace, Ira, born March 28, 1901,
a student in the Perth Amboy High School, Katherine, born in November, 1911

Mid—20

Ira Rutledge Crouse is a man of quiet force, the force that accomplishes large results with little friction, the force that counts in the upbuilding, maintenance and prosperity of cities Throughout his career he has been animated by the spirit of progress, ever pressing forward to make the good better and the better best and his career may be summed up in one word—success—the result of his own unaided efforts furnishing a true picture of the upright business man

EMIL EWALD BRASS, numbered among the younger generation of business men in New Brunswick, is the proprietor of the Brass Auto Supply Company, which is located at Nos 53-55 Albany street, New Brunswick, New Jersey He was born April 16, 1898, in Brooklyn, New York, the son of Ewald and Margaret (Hoff) Brass Ewald Brass was born in Germany and came to this country at the age of twenty years, locating in Brooklyn, New York, where he became an importer in crockery He now resides with his wife in Metuchen, New Jersey, but spends part of his time at his son's business in New Brunswick To Mr and Mrs Brass were born two children Ewald, deceased, Emil Ewald, of further mention

The elementary education of Emil Ewald Brass was obtained in the public schools of Brooklyn after which he entered the Dwight School of New York City, from which he was graduated in 1916 The following year he came to New Brunswick and established himself in the auto supply business, first at No 33 Albany street, where he remained until December, 1919, when he removed to his present location and organized the concern known as the Brass Auto Supply Company Bringing into his business up-to-date methods, his success, already assured, has been founded upon untiring industry and conspicuous ability in his line together with a farseeing business judgment and an unchanging uprightness

During the World War, Mr Brass was a member of the Officers' Training Corps in New York City from September, 1918, until he received his honorable discharge, December 24, 1918 He is ardently devoted to all out-door sports, but takes a particularly keen interest in hunting and baseball He affiliates with Mt Zion Lodge, No 135 Free and Accepted Masons, the Benevolent and Protective Order of Elks, and the Improved Order of Red Men He also holds membership in the Young Men's Christian Association, in the New Brunswick Boat Club, and is secretary of the New Brunswick Motor Trade Association In religion he is a Presbyterian and attends the Second Church of that denomination at New Brunswick Mr Brass is unmarried

MATTHEW FRANCIS URBANSKI, M D.—The history of a State as well as that of a Nation consists chiefly of the chronicles of the lives and deeds of those who have conferred honor and dignity upon it, whether in the broad sphere of professional work or of public labors, or in the narrower, but not less worthy, one of individual activity If the general good has been promoted the man who has brought about this state of affairs is most decidedly worthy of mention Dr Matthew F Urbanski, while he has not yet been identified with the medical profession a great number of years, has already accomplished results which rebound greatly to his credit

Francis Xavier Urbanski, father of Dr Matthew F Urbanski, was born in Poland, in 1865, and came to this country when he was but twenty-one years of age He has made his home in Perth Amboy ever since coming to the United States, and for a number of years carried on a successful painting and decorating business here, but is now retired from active pursuits and reviews a life well spent in the interests of the community which has been his home for so many years He married Agnes Duschock, a native of Poland, and they are the parents of three children Matthew Francis, Adrian X, a student in the medical department of the University of Pennsylvania, Xavier, deceased

Matthew Francis Urbanski, son of Francis Xavier and Agnes (Duschock) Urbanski, was born in Perth Amboy, New Jersey, August 8, 1892 He attended the public schools of his native city, and after graduating from the local high school he commenced the study of medicine in the Bellevue Hospital Medical College, from which he was graduated with the degree of Doctor of Medicine in 1914 During the following three years he served an interneship of a year and a half in the Newark City Hospital and Essex County Isolation Hospital, and then for the remainder of the time was assistant medical director for the Stonywold Sanitarium In 1917 he established himself in the active practice of his chosen profession in Perth Amboy, where he is at present located and where he devotes himself almost exclusively to one particular disease tuberculosis He is president of the Board of Health, and vice-president of the Perth Amboy Medical Society Professionally he also holds membership in the National Tuberculosis Association, the American Medical Association, and the Middlesex County Medical Society

Dr Urbanski is a member of St Stephen's Roman Catholic Church, and affiliates with the Benevolent and Protective Order of Elks, Perth Amboy Lodge, No 784 He is a member of the Phi Alpha Sigma, medical fraternity, and supreme physician of the Greek Catholic Benevolent Society

The few years that Dr Urbanski has spent in Perth Amboy have been years of arduous devotion to the advancement of the medical profession and tireless endeavor for the relief of suffering, and have placed him in the front rank of the city's physicians It is sometimes said of a man the early part of whose career is indicative of more than usual promise "he will be heard from later" Dr Urbanski has already been heard from and Perth Amboy thinks that he will be heard from again and again and for many more years to come

---

GEORGE ANTON, JR, local manager of Armour & Company, was born June 28, 1880, the son of George and Rose (Smith) Anton George Anton, Sr, is a native of Germany, but came to this country at the age of fourteen years locating in Somerville, New Jersey, where he has since continued to reside To Mr and Mrs Anton have been born four children George, mentioned below, William, deceased, Charles L a resident of Cambridge, New York, J Edward, who resides in Somerville, New Jersey

The education of George Anton, Jr, was secured in the public schools of his native place, and during his spare hours he assisted his father in the latter's market in Somerville At the age of twenty-two years he went to Jersey City and there secured employment in the same line of business, remaining for two years or until he resigned to identify himself with the Childs' Restaurant Company of New York City. In August, 1919, Mr Anton came to New Brunswick from Yonkers to accept the managership of the local branch of Armour & Company in which he has since continued most successfully, his ability as a business man having been fully tested and proven for under his management the business of the concern has been greatly increased

During the Spanish-American War George Anton, Jr, enlisted in the 3rd Regiment of New Jersey Company H He is well known in social and fraternal life in New York and New Jersey, and is a member of T. D Landon Post, Spanish War Veterans, at Somerville, New Jersey, and the Masonic order, belonging to Poughkeepsie Lodge, No 266, Ancient Free and Accepted Masons, of Poughkeepsie, Royal Arch Chapter, Royal Arch Masons, Mount Vernon, Bethlehem Commandery, Knights Templar, of Mount Vernon, New York, and Mecca Temple, Nobles of the Mystic Shrine, of New York City He is also affiliated with the Tall Cedars of Lebanon New Brunswick In his religious views Mr Anton is a Presbyterian and attends the First Presbyterian Church in New Brunswick

On November 8 1906, George Anton Jr, was united in marriage with Florence Wright daughter of the late John W and Henrietta (Barton) Wright, the latter a resident of Poughkeepsie Mr and Mrs Anton are the parents of two children George W, born August 2 1907, Beatrice, born November 13, 1910 George Anton, Jr, is a young man, but his career has been one of good work and satisfactory results There can be no reasonable doubt that the years which lie before him will be filled with greater effort and more signal achievement

---

PATRICK NAGLE KENNEDY, one of the substantial citizens of Perth Amboy, New Jersey, and known throughout the community for his public spirit and interest in the welfare of the place, traces his parental ancestry from the Dalcassian race, being descended in a direct line from the second son of King Brean Born, the name Kennidi being its anglicized form, and the cradle of the race being in that part of the present county of Tipperary, Ireland, which is washed by the Shannon river

His maternal ancestors were French Two brothers, Gilbert and Jocelyn de Angula, went to Ireland as knights in the army of Strongbow, and they, like other Norman knights, married into the families of the native nobles and chieftains In time the name "de Angula" became

transformed into Nagle and Nangle, and both forms of the name as well as the original are extant in Ireland and other countries today Sir Richard Nagle, the founder of the southern Nagles, was a brilliant lawyer and statesman, being speaker of the House of Commons and attorney-general for Ireland in the government of James II Edmund Burke, the great statesman, orator and political philosopher, was a member of this branch of the family, his mother, Ellen Nagle, being a niece of Sir Richard's mother, and also the mother of the great Irish apostle of temperance. A son of the poet, Spencer, was married to one of the Nagle family, and still another member of this illustrious family was Sir Edmund Nagle, an English admiral, who later became governor of Newfoundland

Patrick Nagle Kennedy was born July 18, 1852, in Kilmalloch county, Limerick, Ireland, the son of John and Ellen (Nagle) Kennedy His education was received in the national and private schools which were located in and near his native town At the age of fifteen he took part in a revolutionary insurrection in Ireland, and after hiding for nine months he was obliged to seek refuge under the Stars and Stripes, and although this uprising failed, its moral effect had great influence in stimulating the future ambition of the people Upon landing in the United States in the latter part of this same year, 1867, he became employed in railroad construction work, and continued in this particular line of business until about ten years ago when he became engaged in highway construction, which is still occupying his attention at the present time In politics Mr Kennedy is a Jeffersonian Democrat, and has always taken a keen interest in local public affairs, but the only office which he has been persuaded to accept was that of member of the Board of Health, which he held for a period of four years In religion Mr Kennedy is a Catholic, a member of St Mary's Church, and his clubs are the Geraldine and the Washington He is a member of an Irish political revolutionary society in which he has held the offices of secretary, vice-president and president, the object of the society being to make Ireland an independent republic

Mr Kennedy married (first) in New York City, 1871, Alice O'Callaghan, and they were the parents of three children John J, Edward C, James N Mr. Kennedy married (second) Margaret A White, a native of Syracuse, New York, and the daughter of Thomas and Catharine (Buckley) White They have no issue

---

ALBERT LEON.—This name needs no introduction to a work of this sort, for as owner and proprietor of the largest store in Perth Amboy he is recognized as one of the leading citizens of the community, and takes an active interest in everything pertaining to municipal progress

Albert Leon was born in Germany, November 6, 1870, the son of Marcus and Minnie Leon, both natives of Germany Marcus Leon came to this country many years ago with his family, residing in Newark, New Jersey, in which place his death occurred in 1887 Mrs Leon is still living and resides in Newark

Albert Leon attended the schools of his native place until he was fifteen years of age, when he became eager to seek his fortune in this country and consequently sailed for America in 1885 Upon landing in New York City he secured employment in a chair factory, where he remained for a period of two years He then worked his way up from porter to domestic and foreign buyer for a large Philadelphia concern, in the meantime attending a night school. In 1905 he came to Perth Amboy and established himself in the furniture business, locating in a small store at No 134 Smith street, remaining there for eight years, at the end of which time he removed to his present location at the corner of State and Smith streets, where today he has the largest store in Perth Amboy

In addition to the above business, Mr Leon is officially connected with various other large enterprises, being president of the Standard Foundry Company, Bound Brook, New Jersey, vice-president of the Fords National Bank, Perth Amboy treasurer of the Green Furniture Company, Elizabeth, New Jersey, director of the People's National Bank of Elizabeth, New Jersey, director in the New York Furniture Realty Company, New York City, president of the Perth Amboy Building and Loan Association, director of the Perth Amboy Chamber of Commerce director in the Amalgamated Building and Loan Association of Newark, New Jersey, and president of the National Association of Retail Furniture Dealers In fraternal circles he also takes a prominent part being a thirty-second degree Mason, grand high priest of Royal Arch Masons of the State of New Jersey, and a member of Salaam Temple, Ancient Arabic Order of the Mystic Shrine, a member of the Benevolent and Protective Order of Elks and the Independent Order of Odd Fellows His clubs are the Progress and the Newark Athletic He was one of the presidential electors from New Jersey on the Republican ticket

On September 25, 1895, Mr Leon was united in marriage with Regina Meyer a native of Newark, New Jersey, and they are the parents of two children Sylvia Estelle wife of Dr. Harry S. Jacoby, of Newark, Marcus L now a student at Columbia College

Mr. Leon has brought to the shaping of his career a very happy and unusual combination of characteristics which have won for him his success as a business man His philanthropy is great and springs from the sincere kindness of his heart, which embraces all men in its regard He has many friends and among them, as in the community-at-large, he exerts a powerful influence which is always wielded on the side of justice It would be difficult to overestimate the value of such a man to a community or the presence in it of a man like Albert Leon There is scarcely a department in its affairs, an aspect of its life, in which his influence is not most potently felt, and felt invariably on the side of the public good He is a practical man of affairs, a man of the world, yet never in seeking his own business advantage does he lose sight of that of the community of which he is a member Such a man is certainly worthy of emulation.

LAWRENCE E RICE, a prominent figure in the business life of New Brunswick, New Jersey, since 1916, is a man of a naturally retiring disposition, publicity of any sort being very distasteful to him, but he has, nevertheless, had the welfare and advancement of the community always uppermost in his mind, and since coming here has espoused and given his earnest support to all movements calculated to advance business development

Lawrence E Rice was born in Cincinnati, Ohio   On January 1, 1916, he came to New Brunswick, New Jersey, where he established himself in the business of household furnishings at his present location, Nos 201-205 Neilson street.   Coming here with a vast experience which he had already gained in this particular line both in Grand Rapids, Michigan, and in Cincinnati, Ohio, his enterprise rapidly and consistently developed until it is now one of the largest of its kind in this vicinity Although Mr Rice has been located here but a comparatively short time, by his unswerving honesty and fair dealing he has won for himself not only the respect but also the admiration of his competitors

---

JOSEPH BURGER.—There is very properly full praise in this country for the man who has started at the bottom of the ladder and by means of his own effort is steadily making his way towards the top Among this number is Joseph Burger, owner and manager of a garage at No 6 Liberty street, New Brunswick, New Jersey

Joseph Burger was born August 22, 1887, in Germany, the son of Gustave and Mary (Rhode) Burger   Gustave Burger was a native of Germany, and died there at the age of sixty-seven, having followed the trade of carpenter throughout his entire lifetime   Mr and Mrs. Burger were the parents of ten children   Julius, Ida, Anna, Rose, Adolph, Elizabeth, Minnie, Mary, Joseph of further mention and Frank, all of whom reside in this country with the exception of Mary, who has recently returned to her native Germany

Joseph Burger attended the public schools of his native place until he was fifteen years of age, when he apprenticed himself to the machinist's trade, in which he continued until 1907, when he joined the navy Three years later he set sail for this country and upon landing in New York City remained there, engaging in the machinist's trade until 1912, at which time he came to New Brunswick, securing employment with the Simplex Company, with whom he remained until 1919, when he resigned to establish himself in his present business, erecting his garage in 1919   The close attention he has given to the development of his enterprise together with his mechanical knowledge and reliability, have given him the opportunity which would bring him in contact with the worth while things of life, and in consequence he is found among the loyal supporters of all progressive movements for the community's welfare   From unfavorable circumstances he has won success and standing, and is one of the most respected business men of New Brunswick, a product of democratic institutions   Mr Burger is affiliated with the Knights of Pythias and the Improved Order of Red Men

On October 24, 1912, Joseph Burger was united in marriage with Stephana Rohrich, a native of Austria, and the daughter of Matthew and Elizabeth Rohrich, the latter natives of Austria, but now residents of New Brunswick. Mr. and Mrs. Burger are the parents of two children: Matthew Joseph, born October 19, 1913, and Mary, died at the age of three years.

ARTHUR LEVY.—"Young's Jewelry Store," New Brunswick, is a corporation founded in October, 1920, by Arthur Levy, and Jack Steinfeld, both young men of Newark, New Jersey, but both experienced jewelers. Jack Steinfeld was born in Newark, September 11, 1896, son of Benjamin and Lottie (Hamburger) Steinfeld, he the eldest of their six children, Jack, Esther, Rosella, Irving, Sydney and Mamie, all unmarried and living in Newark. Arthur Levy was born in Newark, New Jersey, November 4, 1896, son of Max and Fannie (Berger) Levy, his parents residing in Newark. Mr. and Mrs. Levy are the parents of six children, all living in Newark. Jack, a jeweler; Elizabeth, wife of Murray Swartz; Ike K., Arthur, of further mention; Anna, and Louise.

Arthur Levy attended Newark public schools until fourteen years of age, and then became a clerk in a jewelry store, so continuing until arriving at legal age in 1917. He then formed a partnership with his brother, I. K. Levy, and opened a jewelry store in Newark, conducting it under the firm name, I. K. Levy, Incorporated. In October, 1920, Arthur Levy opened Young's Jewelry Store in New Brunswick, and there is becoming well established, the store and stock being beautiful and well displayed in a good location, No. 135 Albany street. Both partners are young men of experience in their business and are rapidly winning friends and patronage. They are both members of the Orthodox Jewish faith and both unmarried. They carry the best wishes of a wide circle of friends for the success of their business venture.

THEODORE HERMAN MERCKENS.—Everyone in and about New Brunswick has been for many years familiar with Schussler's confectionery and bakery, located at No. 378 George street. On September 4, 1920, Mr. F. M. Schussler sold out his entire establishment to Merckens, Incorporated, and these new owners are now conducting the old, well established business under a different management. The store has been remodelled and is now one of the most attractive of its kind in the country. The president of the company is August Merckens, who for most of the years of his business life was associated with Stollwerck Brothers, manufacturers of high grade cocoa and chocolate. He is also interested in the Norma Chocolate Company of Brooklyn, New York. The experience gained by long connection with this line fits Mr. Merckens for the work in which he has become engaged. The vice-president of the company is William Merckens, a son of the foregoing; another son, Theodore H. Merckens, is also a member of the company, and is in actual charge of the business conducted at the George street

store Mr and Mrs Merckens reside on their estate at Rivervale, Bergen county, New Jersey

Theodore H Merckens was born August 4, 1894, in New York City In his boyhood and youth he attended the public schools of Brooklyn and East Orange, and for several years after leaving school was engaged in the service of the United States Army In 1914 he joined the National Guard, and in 1916, during the trouble on the Mexican border, he was sent with the 23rd New York Infantry to the scene of disturbance, remaining on duty there for seven months In our war with Germany, Theodore H Merckens was stationed at Camp Grant in Illinois with the Black Hawk Division for six months, and was sent with the 344th Infantry to France, sailing on September 8, 1918 He was in the service there for ten months and was mustered out July 15, 1919 at Camp Grant He is a member of Charles Henry Post of the American Legion

---

MAX GIBIAN —In 1905 the business which was incorporated in 1909 as the Perth Amboy Garage Company, was started by Max Gibian, who has been its guiding head from its inception until the present (1920) His was the first garage in Perth Amboy to open its doors to the public, and the present business of the company, at No 283 Madison avenue, is the result of his long experience as a caterer to the needs of the automobile public Max Gibian is a son of Solomon Gibian, who was born in Bohemia, and with his mother came to the United States and located in Newark, New Jersey He became head of a meat and grocery business in Newark which he conducted many years He died in Newark, January 2, 1910, aged sixty-three years He married Carrie Schwartz, also born in Bohemia, who died in Newark, February 8, 1912, aged sixty-seven years They were the parents of nine children five of whom are living Rose, married Abraham Alter, of Newark, Minnie, a resident of Pittsburgh, Dora, married Gustav Wallach, of Newark, Joseph, a confectioner, and Max, of further mention

Max Gibian was born in Newark, New Jersey, April 28, 1881 and was there educated, completing high school study with graduation, class of 1898 He then spent three years in a Newark grocery store, going thence to Potts & Kaufmann of Perth Amboy, that city having ever since been his home and place of business He entered he automobile business in 1905, establishing the first public garage in Perth Amboy ; and so satisfactory were the results of his venture that in 1909 he incorported as the Perth Amboy Garage Company, with Max Gibian president, and H Brower, secretary The garage, located at No 283 Madison avenue, possesses excellent facilities for the storage and care of automobiles, while in addition to a full line of tires and accessories, automobiles are bought, sold and exchanged The company is a well-managed, prosperous one, reflecting credit upon its management Mr Gibian is president of New Brunswick Motor Car Company, subsidiary of Perth Amboy Garage Company, also vice-president of the Maple Realty Company, and of the Gibian Realty Company, his real estate interests being large and important

A Democrat in politics, Mr Gibian has served his city as assessor of taxes, and when the office of State license agent for motor vehicles was created, he was the first appointee, and is still serving He is a member of the Masonic order, affiliated with lodge, chapter commandery, shrine and consistory, also a member of the Tall Cedars of Lebanon, the Woodmen of the World Young Men's Christian Association, and Young Men's Hebrew Association In religion he is of Beth Mordecai congregation

Mr Gibian married, in 1906, in New Brunswick, New Jersey, Anna Wolff who was born in that city, a daughter of William and Fannie Wolff, her father a retired cattle dealer of Perth Amboy, her mother deceased

---

WALTER BARGER —The grandparents of Walter Barger, of New Brunswick, and New York, were residents of Vermilion, Illinois his grandmother born in Switzerland, Europe They were the parents of Martin J Barger, born in Vermilion county, Illinois, died July 17 1917, at Danville Illinois, being at the time governor of the Soldiers' Home, and prominent in local politics He was himself a veteran of the Civil War, serving with Company B, 125th Regiment, Illinois Volunteer Infantry. He suffered three wounds at Shiloh and Chickamauga, but not so serious as to shorten his life He married Mary A Steward who died soon after their only child, Walter, was born

Walter Barger was born in Danville, Illinois February 25 1870 there was educated and spent thirty years of his life, ten years of which he was employed in the County Court House He established a produce jobbing business in Danville, and later was in the same business on South Water street, Chicago Later he established in business in New York City, as a bond and investment broker, with offices at Columbus Circle In 1920 he came to New Brunswick to develop the hot house project, which has been set in motion and for which a company has been incorporated, Mr Barger being secretary Mr Barger is a member of the Benevolent and Protective Order of Elks, the Knights of Pythias, and of the Methodist Episcopal church

Mr Barger married, in Washington, D C, June 21 1905 Florence Lee Osborne, born in Bluemont, Virginia, daughter of Walter Clark and Martha Carter (Taghliaferro) Osborne, her father, deceased, her mother yet living in Bluemont, Virginia Mr and Mrs Barger are the parents of a daughter Jane Reynolds born June 12, 1917 The family home is "Ross Hall," River road, New Brunswick, a delightful old Colonial residence of the pre-Revolutionary period, which is noted as the scene of much of the action in the historical romance, "Janice Meredith "

HARRY TONER BICKFORD —About the year 1830, Samuel Morrill Bickford came from Portland, Maine, to Lock Haven Pennsylvania, via canal boat, and there established in the lumber business He was the grandfather of Harry Toner Bickford, and father of William Morrill

Bickford, who was born in Lock Haven, Pennsylvania, where he spent his short life of twenty-eight years, engaged as a lumber merchant. He married Alma S Toner, of Lock Haven, Pennsylvania, who survives him and resides in Altoona, Pennsylvania Mr and Mrs Bickford had three children Mabel, wife of Walter Laubach, of Altoona, Pennsylvania, Harry Toner, of further mention, William Morrill, of Lock Haven, now engaged in the lumber business

Harry T Bickford was born in Lock Haven, Pennsylvania, November 25, 1884, and there attended public schools until seventeen years of age He then was employed by Kistler, Lesh & Company, tanners, of Mount Jewett, Pennsylvania, remaining with that company four years, then going with the Beechnut Packing Company, of Canajoharie, New York, a company with which he remained three years For the next five and one-half years Mr Bickford was engaged in business for himself in New York City, gaining considerable reputation as a production engineer In 1914, he located in New Brunswick, New Jersey, going with the Nixon Nitration Works and remaining eighteen months He then spent three years with the Home Realty Company, establishing his present business, real estate and insurance, in May, 1920 His greatest present interest is in the new hot houses to be erected on River road, on the site of the old golf links, the plans calling for the largest hot house plant in the United States The company, which has been formed and incorporated, propose to utilize the great plant they will erect, in the growing of early small vegetables for the New York market The president of the company is Jeremiah H Nixon, secretary, Walter Barger, treasurer, Harry D MacMillian Mr Bickford is an enthusiast over baseball, football, basketball, in fact all healthful sports appeal to him He is a member of the Masonic order the Benevolent and Protective Order of Elks, and ot the Lutheran church

Mr Bickford married, in New Brunswick, December 18, 1915 Caroline Heinz, born December 15, 1890, daughter of Valentine and Louisa Heinz, her father, deceased, long with the United States Rubber Company, her mother living in New Brunswick Mr Bickford is a young man of energy and ability, progressive, and has a host of friends

---

ALBERT HARVEY TERHUNE—With the extensive mercantile interests centered in Perth Amboy, New Jersey the men in whose hands they lie form a significant factor in the prosperity of the city Albert Harvey Terhune, prosperous and progressive himself, and the son of a merchant also invariably in step with the times, is such a man as well represents the general body of business men of Perth Amboy Mr Terhune is a son of Albert Terhune, who was born in New York City, and died there, at the age of seventy-two years

Albert Harvey Terhune was born in New York City June 18, 1862 He was educated in the public schools of that city At the age of thirteen years he went to work in his father's store on the corner of Eighth avenue and Fifty-second street He remained with his father until he came to the age of maturity, then for some years was his father's partner

Later on he established a store of his own at the corner of Eighth avenue and One Hundred and Twenty-sixth street, also another on the corner of Amsterdam avenue and One Hundred and Forty-eighth street In 1915 Mr Terhune came to Perth Amboy, New Jersey, and on April 10, of that year, established the store in this city which has proved so marked a success Both Mr Terhune and his father have always been in the same line of business

Mr Terhune is a man of varied activities outside his business He is a member of the Masonic order and a member of the Veteran Association of the Seventy-first Regiment, National Guard of New York He finds his favorite relaxation in boating and fishing and owned a forty-two-foot yawl which he sailed on Long Island Sound when a resident of New York City He is a member of the Simpson Methodist Episcopal Church, of Perth Amboy, and for several years has served on the official board of the church He is very active in all the work of the church organization

---

FRANK ALOYSIUS CONNOLLY —Many years have passed since the founder of this family of Connolly came to the United States. He was Andrew Connolly, the grandfather of Frank Aloysius Connolly, and he emigrated from Ireland when quite young, coming directly to New Brunswick, New Jersey, where he made his home

His son, Michael Henry Connolly, was born in New Brunswick and has lived here all his life, he was formerly engaged in business, but now has retired from active work at the age of seventy-two years He is a member of the Grand Army of the Republic, having enlisted in the Civil War when only fourteen years old The wife of Michael Henry Connolly was before her marriage Mary Veronica McDonald, a native of New Brunswick, where she died, aged forty-four years She was the mother of eight children, four of whom are now living 1 Katherine Calista, wife of William A McConlogue 2 Clara Veronica who married James H Meagher 3 Mae V, unmarried and living at home, she is engaged in the millinery business on George street 4 Frank Aloysius

Frank Aloysius Connolly was born in New Brunswick, New Jersey, April 21, 1883 He attended the high school, then the parochial school from which he graduated in 1900, and then entered upon a business career by becoming a clerk in the dry goods store of Henry Landsberg, where he remained for a few years, then accepted a position in the dry goods establishment of the P J Young Company on George street, where he is still engaged Having been an active worker in the Democratic party Mr Connolly was appointed in 1918 to fill the unexpired term of Mayor Farrington, of New Brunswick, as city commissioner, and in May 1919 was elected to the same position, his term of office to continue for four years he being the present incumbent In addition to his business affairs and political and public work, Mr Connolly is quite active in club life, he is a member of the Knights of Columbus and of the Benevolent and Protective Order of Elks, also of the Young Men's Christian Association His membership in these organizations gives

him plenty of opportunity to indulge in his favorite amusement a good
game of billiards, and sometimes, in the season, he enjoys seeing a
baseball game.

In New Brunswick, April 27, 1907, Frank Aloysius Connolly married Anna Wilhelmina Farrington, a native of New Brunswick, the
daughter of Patrick and Mary Farrington, the former being deceased,
the latter living in New Brunswick Mr and Mrs Connolly have two
children 1 Francis Aloysius, Jr, born October 29, 1908 2 Edward
Farrington born May 11, 1916 The family home is at No 55 Remsen
avenue They are all members of the Roman Catholic Church of the
Sacred Heart.

WILLIAM DAVID HOY —There are very few figures among the
younger business men of Middlesex county, New Jersey, who have
risen more rapidly to a position of influence in the community than that
of William David Hoy, of Fords, who for several years has been in
the front rank of those who have developed the material interests of the
town and whose work for the general welfare thereof has been of extreme
value He is a native of Fords, where his birth occurred July 14, 1883,
and a son of William and Elizabeth (Smith) Hoy, old and highly esteemed residents of the town, to which place they had come just prior
to their son's birth, from Ireland and where their deaths occurred,
October 12, 1919, and April 16, 1917, respectively.

William David Hoy, only son of William and Elizabeth (Smith)
Hoy, passed his childhood at Fords, and attended the local public schools
for a number of years He then went to the Perth Amboy High School
for two years, but left there to enter Woods Business College at Newark
to prepare himself for his active career He had even at that time had
some practical experience, as he had been employed as a boy by the
Valentine Fire Brick Company and the National Fireproofing Company,
serving two years with each company Upon completing the course at
Woods Business College Mr. Hoy secured a clerical position with James
H Maddy, of New York City, and later with the Erie Railroad Company in the central offices of that corporation At the latter place he
remained for twelve years, and was rapidly promoted until he became
secretary to the vice-president He was very ambitious, however, to
become independent in business, and at the end of that period severed
his connection with the Erie, much to the regret of his employers, and,
returning to Fords, established himself in his present enterprise Since
that time he has been closely identified with the growth of the community, concerning himself with building development and the working
up of an insurance business He has met with marked success in his
line and is today regarded as one of the most energetic and capable men
of the town He is also actively interested in public affairs, and has
held a number of offices in the gift of the community, serving at present
(1921) his third term as a member of the Woodbridge Township Committee and as a member of the Board of Fire Commissioners of Fords
He is one of the leading men of the Republican party in this section

of the State, and is a member of the Republican County Committee, and represented the district at the last Republican State Convention For three years he was president of the Fords Fire Company, and is prominent in the fraternal circles of the place, being affiliated with Americus Lodge, No 83, Free and Accepted Masons, Amboy Chapter, No 41 Royal Arch Masons, Temple Commandery, No 61, Knights Templar, Salaam Temple, Nobles of the Mystic Shrine, of Newark, Jersey City Consistory, Supreme Princes of the Royal Secret; and Tall Cedars of Lebanon, Forest No 68, of Perth Amboy He is also a member of the Benevolent and Protective Order of Elks the Junior Order of United American Mechanics of Perth Amboy, the Raritan Yacht Club and the Perth Amboy and Woodbridge Republican clubs In his religious belief Mr Hoy is an Episcopalian and attends St Luke's Church of that denomination at Metuchen, of which he is a vestryman.

William David Hoy married, April 22, 1919, at Metuchen, New Jersey, Margaret May Fullerton, like himself a native of Fords, and a daughter of William H and Margaret (Bebernes) Fullerton Mr Fullerton was for a number of years one of the most prominent men of Perth Amboy, president of the New Jersey Produce Company, and served as street commissioner His death occurred October 11 1918 at the age of fifty-two years and he is survived by his wife who now makes her home at Woodbridge

JAMES MARTIN HOUGHTON —The profession of chiropractic is still of so recent a beginning that it is yet in its early stage, though each year brings fresh adherents to the doors of those who practice it One of the chiropractors of New Brunswick is James Martin Houghton, whose office at No 343 George street is the ' Mecca" for many troubled human beings Not only does he relieve suffering, but in many cases gives treatment free of charge to those who are too poor to pay for it To do this he conducts a clinic at his office between the hours of ten and twelve A M for their benefit So great is his interest in it that it has become his pet pastime

The Houghton family came from Ireland originally, settling almost at once in New Brunswick On the maternal side, the Gildeas were also of Irish parentage Dr Houghton's maternal grandfather, Patrick Gildea, was a graduate of Edinburgh University in Scotland

Dr Houghton's father, James Martin Houghton, was born in New Brunswick, but removed some time later to Jersey City where he conducts a large undertaking establishment He is greatly interested in politics, being a well known worker in the Democratic party He is also a very prominent Elk of Jersey City Dr Houghton's mother, Martha (Gildea) Houghton was born in Jersey City, March 8 1876 In this family there are five children 1 Frank A, a practicing dentist in Jersey City 2 Claire M, the wife of William J Flaherty, both Mr and Mrs Flaherty being successful chiropractors of Jersey City 3 James Martin, of further mention 4 Robert A a student at St Joseph's College, Baltimore Maryland, of the class of 1921 5 Rose M, unmarried, living at home, a student in the Jersey City High School in the class of 1922

James Martin Houghton was born in Jersey City, New Jersey, May 22, 1898, and for nearly all his life it has been his home. He attended the grammar school there, graduating from it at the age of twelve years, following this by a four years' course in the high school. He was only sixteen years old when he graduated and he very soon entered the Newark (New Jersey) School of Chiropractic, the course of study there being three years. After graduating, Dr Houghton began practicing in Jersey City, continuing to do so for over a year, going to New Brunswick later, where he opened an office at his present location. Dr Houghton is a member of the New Jersey State Chiropractic Association and since June, 1920, has been vice-president of that body. Dr Houghton is unmarried

THOMAS F DOLAN, postmaster of Sayreville, New Jersey, is connected with the business life of the community, having been for many years a successful contractor and builder here. Being a good citizen as well as an able business man and executant, Mr Dolan is ever ready to cooperate in the charitable and philanthropic enterprises of Sayreville, his native town

Mr Dolan was born in Sayreville, Middlesex county, New Jersey, December 11, 1887 the son of James and Bridget (Burke) Dolan. His father, James Dolan, has been foreman in the brick yard here for many years. The boy, Thomas F, was educated in the schools of his native place, after which he established himself in the contracting and building business. He received his appointment of postmaster in 1914, and was reappointed in 1918. It is hardly necessary to mention that he is an able man of affairs, for his present office, demanding the services of one whose ability is of a high order and whose well-balanced forces are manifest in sound judgment and a ready understanding of any problem that may be presented for solution, speaks for itself in a manner not to be misunderstood. Force and resolution, combined with a genial disposition, attract all who are brought in contact with him. He is one of the men who number friends in all grades of society. The thorough business qualifications of Thomas F Dolan have always been in great demand on boards of directors, and his public spirit has led him to accept of many such trusts. In politics he is a staunch Democrat. He affiliates with the Benevolent and Protective Order of Elks, the Knights of Columbus, the Foresters of America, the Improved Order of Red Men, the local union, No 1392, Carpenters and Joiners of America and the Musicians' Protective Union of New Brunswick. In religion he is a Roman Catholic

On September 27, 1909, Mr Dolan was united in marriage with Rose Gorman a native of Sayreville, born February 19 1888. Mrs Dolan is the daughter of Patrick and Margaret (Hughes) Gorman, both natives of Ireland. Mr and Mrs Dolan are the parents of five children Marguerite, born October 31, 1910. Bermardina, born July 10, 1913, Mary, born October 10, 1915, Rosemary, born March 1, 1918, deceased, Thomas born March 4, 1920

KLEMMER KALTEISSEN, numbered among the younger generation of lawyers in New Brunswick. New Jersey, and a man who already is making a name for himself in the public life of this region, is a native of this city, born August 5, 1894 He is the son of Peter and Sophia (Weigel) Kalteissen Peter Kalteissen was born in Worms, Germany, and was brought by his mother to the United States when he was but fourteen years of age Later he became a box manufacturer engaged in this business for many years, but is now living retired in New Brunswick. To Mr and Mrs Kalteissen have been born two children Klemmer, of further mention, George A , born November 2, 1888, with the New Brunswick Paper Box Company, which was founded by his father, is married and has two children, William K and George A , Jr

The elementary portion of Klemmer Kalteissen's education was obtained in the public schools of his native place, after which he entered Rutgers College, subsequently matriculating in the New Jersey Law School, from which he was graduated in 1917 with the degree of Bachelor of Laws Immediately after graduation he enlisted in the United States Army in Newark, New Jersey, and was sent to the officers' training camp at Camp Devens, where he was commissioned first lieutenant and was ordered to Camp Gordon, Georgia, later being sent to Camp Sherman, Chillicothe, Ohio From here he was ordered to Washington, D C , where he supervised the discharge of the enlisted men of the chemical warfare service, and was mustered out January 22, 1919 He then returned immediately to his native place and formed a partnership with William D Danberry, with offices at No 40 Paterson street He fraternizes with the Delta Theta Phi law fraternity, and with the Young Men's Christian Association His hobby is basket ball.

Mr Kalteissen is superintendent of the Livingston Avenue Reformed Sunday school, which position he has filled since he was nineteen years of age He delights in this work and is doing something worth while for the betterment of the community He is a member of the Reformed church Mr Kalteissen served as deputy surrogate of Middlesex county before forming the law partnership with Mr Danberry Politically he is a Democrat He is a member of Middlesex County and State Bar associations He is also member of Goodwill Council No 32, Junior Order of United American Mechanics, and of Union Lodge, No 19, Free and Accepted Masons

On April 26, 1918, in New Brunswick, New Jersey, Mr Kalteissen was united in marriage with Flora Jacobsen, a native of Elizabeth, New Jersey, and the daughter of the late Carl and Wilhelmina (Larsen) Jacobsen Mr and Mrs Kalteissen have no children

---

FERD GARRETSON—If those who claim that fortune has favored certain individuals above others will but investigate the cause of success and failure it will be found that the former is largely due to the improvement of opportunity, the latter to the neglect of it Fortunate environments encompass nearly every man at some stage of his career, but the strong man and the successful man is he who realizes that the

Ferd Garretson

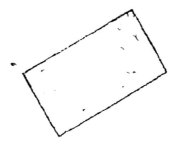

proper moment has come, that the present and not the future holds his opportunity The man who makes use of the Now and not the To Be is the one who passes on the highway of life others who started out ahead of him, and reaches the goal of prosperity in advance of them. It is this quality in Ferd Garretson, ex-mayor, and city treasurer of Perth Amboy, New Jersey

Samuel Garretson father of Ferd Garretson, was born June, 1841 Retired from active business affairs, Mr Garretson reviews a life well spent for the interests of the community in which he lives, and for the service of his country as well He holds the office of past commander of the New Jersey Volunteers, Grand Army of the Republic, having served in the Civil War with Company I, 28th Regiment For a number of years he conducted a successful real estate business, and at one time he was recorder for the city of Perth Amboy, where he resides at the present time, and where he is held in the highest esteem

Ferd Garretson, son of Samuel and Jennie A Garretson, was born at Perth Amboy, New Jersey, October 7, 1867 He attended the public schools of his native city and after graduating from the local high school, entered the Centenary Collegiate Institute, from which he was graduated For the following twenty-five years he was employed by the Lehigh Valley Railroad as telegraph operator, train despatcher and train conductor In 1905, upon the death of his father-in-law, J Ford, Mr. Garretson assumed the undertaking business formerly conducted by Mr Ford He still carries on that business together with an automobile livery and garage which he has added

Mr Garretson is a Republican in politics and has always been most conspicuously associated with the organization From 1908 until 1911 he served as coroner for Middlesex county, and was alderman-at-large and acting mayor for the year 1912 That he fulfilled this tenure most creditably, is proven by the fact that the city elected him mayor for the next four years In 1917 he was made city treasurer and custodian of the school moneys, which office he holds at the present time

Mr Garretson is prominent in fraternal organizations of his native city, being a member of Lawrence Lodge, No 61, Independent Order of Odd Fellows, a member and past master of Raritan Lodge, No. 62, Free and Accepted Masons, and past exalted ruler of the Benevolent and Protective Order of Elks, Perth Amboy Lodge, No 784 His club is the Perth Amboy Caledonian

Mr Garretson married, March 19, 1890, Elizabeth M Ford, daughter of Joshua and Amanda Ford, and they are the parents of four children Thomas A, born October 10, 1892, Donald C, born February 24, 1894, William V, born April 9, 1895, Jeannette A born December 15, 1900

Alert, alive, and progressive, Mr Garretson justly merits the success he has achieved Happily gifted in disposition, manner and taste, enterprising and original in business methods, personally liked most by those who know him best, and as frank in declaring his principles as he is sincere in maintaining them, his career has been rounded with great success and marked by the appreciation of men whose opinion is well worth having

Mid—21

WILLIAM A. CROWELL —The flour, feed and grain elevator in Metuchen, New Jersey, owned and operated by William A Crowell, is the headquarters of a prosperous business which Mr Crowell has conducted in Metuchen since 1908 This elevator is modernly planned and equipped for the particular business therein conducted, and is most capably managed by Mr Crowell and his son, Reginald B

William A Crowell is a son of William E and Phoebe M. (Dunn) Crowell, his father, born in Perth Amboy New Jersey, at one time a merchant, and later a farmer Phoebe M (Dunn) Crowell was born at Linden Heights Farm, on the Raritan river, now part of Highland Park, New Jersey

William A Crowell was born at Linden Heights Farm, August 15, 1859, and there educated in the public schools He was variously occupied until 1893, when he entered the grain business, which he has since continued with marked success. His residence on Spring street, Metuchen, was built in 1899 He is a member of the Baptist church of Metuchen, of which he was the first Sunday school superintendent, in 1902 In politics he is a Republican. Mr Crowell is a man widely known and thoroughly respected for his sterling character and upright life He is one of the founders and a charter member of the local council of the Royal Arcanum He has been active in many of the civic, charitable and other affairs of the town

Mr Crowell married, in Brooklyn, New York, October 2, 1884, Jennie W Buckley, born in Jersey City. New Jersey, February 4, 1862, daughter of Frederick and Fanny M (Wilcox) Buckley, her father born in Charleston, South Carolina, her mother born in Saugerties, New York Mr and Mrs Crowell are the parents of three children: 1 Helen born January 8, 1886 died April 27, 1891 2 Reginald B , born December 13, 1890, he enlisted in the United States Army in May, 1917, was transferred to the aviation service, and was on duty at Fort Worth, Texas, he went overseas in September, 1918, and was at the front when the armistice was signed He married, in February, 1921, Louise Crowell of Perth Amboy 3 Mildred, born March 10, 1892, she married in September, 1916, W H W Comp, a graduate of Rutgers College, who is now engaged as a sanitary engineer They are the parents of one child, Anita

---

BENJAMIN FRANKLIN SLOBODIEN, M D , numbered among the young physicians of Perth Amboy, New Jersey, was born in South Amboy, New Jersey. September 16, 1891, a son of Morris and Sophia (Triffon) Slobodien, both natives of Russia, who came from that country to the United States thirty-four and thirty-two years ago respectively The elder Mr Slobodien, upon reaching this country, settled at once in Perth Amboy where he engaged in the blacksmith and horseshoeing business and met with considerable success He met and married his countrywoman, Miss Triffon, and they were the parents of four children, as follows: Sarah, who became the wife of Charles Bardin of Perth Amboy, Michael, who is now employed in a clerical position in an establishment in Perth Amboy, Benjamin Franklin, with whom we are here especially concerned, and Bessie, who is now employed as a teacher in the public schools of the city

The early life of Dr. Slobodien was passed at Perth Amboy and it was there that he gained his elementary education, graduating eventually from the Perth Amboy High School with the class of 1909, where he had been prepared for college The young man had already determined definitely upon a medical career, and accordingly matriculated in the University and Bellevue Hospital Medical College in New York City From this institution he graduated with the class of 1913, taking his medical degree, and for the year following served as interne in the Elizabeth General Hospital, Elizabeth, New Jersey He then returned to Perth Amboy, and in 1914 began the practice of his profession in that city Here he has continued ever since and has already won for himself a reputation as a diagnostician Dr Slobodien was quick to respond to his country's need for surgical and medical service during the late war, and enlisted in the army, April 18, 1918 He was given the rank of first lieutenant in the Medical Corps and was assigned to duty, first at Embarkation Hospital, No 2, at Secaucus, New Jersey, and later at Debarkation Hospital No 3, in New York City He received his honorable discharge from the service in August 1919, and at once returned to his practice in Perth Amboy Dr Slobodien s an Independent in politics, and takes a keen and intelligent interest in all the great questions and issues of the day He is active in social and fraternal life in Perth Amboy, especially as a member of the Masonic order and is affiliated with Prudence Lodge, No 204, Ancient Free and Accepted Masons, Amboy Chapter, No 41, Royal Arch Masons, Ancient and Accepted Scottish Rite, Caldwell Consistory, Ancient Arabic Order Nobles of the Mystic Shrine, and Lodge No 784 Benevolent and Protective Order of Elks He is a member of Phi Delta Epsilon fraternity, and the Young Men's Hebrew Association His medical societies are the Perth Amboy Medical Society, the Middlesex County Medical Society, the New Jersey State Medical Society, and the Clinical Society of the Elizabeth General Hospital He is a member of the Jewish Synagogue of Shaary Tfilloh in Perth Amboy Dr Slobodien is unmarried

NATHAN ROBINS—At the age of thirteen years, in 1860 Nathan Robins, the present sealer of weights and measures for Middlesex county, New Jersey first came to Metuchen, which has now been his home for sixty years A quarter of a century ago he built his present residence, and on Thanksgiving Day, 1896, observed the feast by partaking of the first meal in the new home He is a son of Nathan and Hannah Maria (Ayres) Robins, who at the time of their son's birth were living in Oswego, New York, the father a ship chandler and later collector of customs at that port Later the family moved to Brooklyn, New York thence to Springfield, New Jersey and then to Metuchen in the same State

Nathan (2) Robins was born in Oswego, New York, December 26,

1847 He attended the public schools in Metuchen, and a private school in Flushing, Long Island, there completing his school years He has been a resident of Metuchen since 1860, and is one of the best known men of his community He has held many public and private positions of trust, and has been engaged in different lines of business activity Since 1912 he has held his present position, sealer of weights and measures for Middlesex county, and was at one time postmaster of Metuchen He is a Democrat in politics, and in religious belief an Episcopalian He is president of Eagle Hook and Ladder Company, and affiliates with Mt Zion Lodge. No 35, Free and Accepted Masons, of which he is a past master

Mr Robins married, in New York City, May 25, 1875 Mary Oakley, born January 17, 1856, daughter of Walter and Mary (Downs) Oakley Mr and Mrs Robins are the parents of six children Marie Louise, born June 6, 1876, married Frank R Savidge, and has a son, Frank R (2), Abbey Denman, born July 21 1878, Nathan, born February 16, 1881, married Cora M. Purdy, Elsa Rogers, born May 26, 1887, Caroline Nichols. born January 27. 1890 married Henry B Cook, and has a daughter, Mary Oakley Cook, Dorothy Oakley Foster, born July 30, 1894

WILLIAM D DANBERRY.—One of the younger generation of attorneys in New Brunswick, and a man who is already making a name for himself in the affairs of the community, is a native of this town, where he was born October 29, 1897, the son of William F and Julia Danberry. William F Danberry was born in New Brunswick. the son of William F Danberry, and member of a family whose progenitors came to this country in the Colonial days To Mr and Mrs Danberry have been born two children William D, of further mention. and Edmund L, deceased

William D Danberry received the elementary portion of his education in the schools of his native city, graduating from St Peter's High School, after which he attended Rutgers College He had in the meantime determined to adopt the law as a profession. and accordingly matriculated at the New Jersey Law School After completing the usual course, he graduated with the class of 1919 and won the degree of Bachelor of Laws Throughout his school and college years he had proved himself an able, intelligent student and came to the opening of his career unusually well equipped to take up the duties of his profession Immediately after graduating he returned to New Brunswick, passed his bar examination and entered the law office of Russell E Watson, where he remained until April 1 1920, when he formed a law partnership with Klemmer Kalteissen. with offices at No 40 Paterson street. While at Rutgers College Mr Danberry was a member of the Students' Training Corps He affiliates with Delta Theta Phi fraternity In religion he is a Roman Catholic and attends St Peter's Church of that denomination in New Brunswick He is unmarried

John N. Hester

JOHN N. WESTER belongs to that class of men who started at the bottom of the ladder and has made his way to the top through his own efforts Starting in this country poor in finances, but quick in shrewdness and foresight, he adapted himself readily to circumstances and took advantage of every opportunity which would bring him in contact with the worth-while things of life

Neils Wester, father of John N Wester, was born in Denmark, April 22, 1837, and died there in 1902 For many years he was a fisherman and later became a farmer, at which occupation he was engaged when his death occurred. In the war with Germany in 1864, he served in the Danish army and for his services received a medal of honor which was awarded him at that time He married Johanna Jepsen, and they were the parents of five children Bodil, wife of Neils Madsen of Los Angeles, California, Christian N, a prominent hotel man of Los Angeles, Marie N, wife of Christian Anderson, a resident of Denmark, Thomas N, a builder and contractor, and a member of the firm of Johnson & Wester, of Hartford, Connecticut; John N, mentioned below

John N Wester was born on the island of Fur in the northern part of Jutland, Denmark, and there obtained his education, which consisted of public and high school instruction At the age of twenty he set sail for America, and upon landing in New York City, went immediately to Hartford, Connecticut, where he served an apprenticeship to the brick-layer's and plasterer's trade, subsequently coming to Perth Amboy, where he worked at his trade for two years, or until 1904, when he established himself in this business He has built some of the largest residences of Perth Amboy, several churches, the grammar school, manual training school and the central heating plant

He affiliates with the Benevolent and Protective Order of Elks, Lodge No 784 He is also a member of the Building Trades Association, which grew to be one of the foremost of its kind in the State of New Jersey, and held the office of president of the organization from 1915 to 1920 In religion he is a Presbyterian In 1920 Mr Wester became affiliated with the Boy Scouts of Perth Amboy, as financial director and member of its executive committee, taking the place of the late John Penbroke, former mayor of Perth Amboy Up to 1920 he took no active part in local politics, but in that year was prevailed to run for alderman-at-large, which he did more as a civic duty than a desire to hold office He ran against former acting Mayor William Voorhees, and was elected, taking office January 1, 1920, as president of the Board of Aldermen

On November 16, 1900, Mr Wester was united in marriage (first) with Magdalena Neilsen who passed away in 1902 To them were born one child, Ethel, March 6, 1902 Mr Wester married (second) August 1, 1909, Mathilda Neilsen, a native of Perth Amboy They are the parents of two children Clifford Christian, born August 1, 1912, James Neilsen, born May 8, 1914 The family resides at No 221 Brighton avenue, Perth Amboy.

WILLIAM A. ALLGAIR, of South River, New Jersey, holds execu tive positions of large responsibility. He was born in New Brunswick New Jersey, April 17, 1887, and is a son of George and Mary Allgair The elder Mr. Allgair is in the hotel business, and has been borough collector for South River for a period of fifteen years

Educated in the local schools, and being graduated from the South River High School in the class of 1903 Mr Allgair took a course at the Rutgers Preparatory School, and was graduated in 1905 Since that time he has been connected with the business life of South River, begin-ning in the office of the South River Brick Company, where he remained until the year 1908. He then entered the office of the clerk of Middlesex county, where he was employed until 1915 With this experience behind him, and his natural adaptability for an executive position, Mr Allgair was offered a more responsible office, entering upon his new duties in 1915 This was the treasurer-secretaryship of the South River Trust Company, of which company he is also a director

Mr Allgair is widely connected fraternally, being a member of Palestine Lodge, No 111, Free and Accepted Masons, the Knights of Pythias, the Benevolent and Protective Order of Elks, and the Junior Order of United American Mechanics

On June 24, 1914, in Holy Trinity Protestant Episcopal Church Mr Allgair married Ethel Durham, daughter of Charles and Mary Durham, of South River? Mr and Mrs Allgair have one daughter, born March 6, 1916 The family are members of Holy Trinity Church

---

FRANCIS HENRY GORDON.—The firm of Howell & Gordon, of South Amboy, was composed of Benjamin F Howell, later Congress-man, and James Henry Gordon, who entered the business a boy of fifteen and later became a partner Howell & Gordon dealt in groceries and drygoods and had practically a department store, in connection with this they conducted a coal yard In 1912 the business became a Gordon property, under the name of James Henry Gordon, but upon the death of James H, his son, Francis Henry Gordon, came into control, and for eight years has successfully carried it on

James Henry Gordon was born in South Amboy, August 12, 1855, died December 26. 1912, his years, fifty-seven, having all been spent in South Amboy He entered the employ of Benjamin F Howell, a merchant of South Amboy, and so won his employer's confidence that in time he was admitted to a partnership, under the firm name. Howell & Gordon When Mr Howell was elected surrogate of Middlesex county, he moved his residence to New Brunswick, the burden of management of Howell & Gordon falling upon the junior partner He became sole owner of the business in 1912, and reorganized it under his own name He died the same year, leaving behind him an honored name and the record of a life worthily spent He served South Amboy as township collector and as councilman after South Amboy became an incorporated borough The business of James H Gordon passed to his eldest son, Francis H. Gordon, then a young man of twenty-five, but familiar with the business. Mr Gordon was a member of St Mary's Roman Catholic Church, and a fourth degree member of the Knights of Columbus He married Catherine Bowe, who died in March, 1908 They were the parents of seven children, as follows. Francis Henry, of further mention, James E , Julia, who married Thomas Pettit, Teresa, Zita, Angela, and Catherine

Francis Henry Gordon was born in South Amboy, New Jersey, May 6, 1888, and obtained his early education in St Mary's Parochial School, attending that school until thirteen years of age, when he entered the preparatory department of Fordham University, finishing in 1908 He then entered the medical department of the University of Pennsylvania, but his health failed and he returned to South Amboy He was taken into the Howell & Gordon business, and under the direction of his excellent father, became familiar with the different departments and their management Four years later, James H Gordon succeeded Howell & Gordon, and the young man was given further responsible duties In the closing days of the year 1912, he was suddenly called upon to assume full control, his father passing away with little warning

Mr Gordon is a young man of ability and energy, his standing in his community being very high He is a member of the Knights of Columbus, the Benevolent and Protective Order of Elks, St Mary's Roman Catholic Church, and is an ex-chief of the Volunteer Fire Department of his city In politics he is a Democrat, and served his city as councilman-at-large in 1917-18, and in 1918 was elected mayor, an office he held until January, 1921

Mr Gordon married, April 25, 1916, at Caldwell New Jersey, Caroline Hazel Smith, born in Philadelphia, Pennsylvania daughter of William B and Margaret (Dolan) Smith, her father a real estate dealer of Caldwell Mr. and Mrs Gordon are the parents of three children, their eldest dying in infancy, the second, Margaret, was born July 21, 1918, and their son, James Henry (2), was born December 2, 1920

Mr Gordon is a popular executive and holds to the best traditions of government He is a hard worker, but knows how to play, and spends many a day in the woods with his gun or rifle. His years, thirty-two, have been full of honorable effort, and his success has been fairly won

---

CLARK ANDERSON BUTTERWORTH, the New Brunswick distributor of the Chandler car, was born in New Brunswick, New Jersey, September 14, 1890, son of Thomas and Mary (Anderson) Butterworth, his father a grocer of New Brunswick until his death in 1892

Clark A Butterworth was educated in the public schools finishing high school in the year 1907 The same year he entered the employ of the New Brunswick Fire Insurance Company as junior clerk, and in 1913 became office manager for the New Jersey Fire Insurance Company of Newark New Jersey He remained in that position until 1916, then for about three years was connected with the county clerk's office of Middlesex county On April 1, 1919, he entered the automobile business, in which he yet continues, handling the Chandler automobile and the Mack truck

Mr Butterworth was one of the gallant lads who sailed away to maintain American honor on foreign fields during those dark days of 1917-18, and was wounded in battle He enlisted April 6, 1917, in Company F, 7th Regiment, New Jersey National Guard, a company and regiment which became Company F, 107th Regiment, United States Army He was sent overseas, saw service in the front line trenches, and at the crossing of La Selle river, east of St Souplet, in the advance on Canal de la Sombre, France, he was wounded, October 12, 1918, and sent to the Royal Sussex County Hospital in Brighton, England After recovering sufficiently from his wounds, he was returned to the United States and in due time honorably discharged Mr Butterworth is a member of New Brunswick Lodge, No. 324, Benevolent and Protective Order of Elks, Goodwill Lodge, Junior Order of United American Mechanics, and the Improved Order of Red Men

---

EUGENE SCHENCK GRIGGS, D D. S, a man who is closely identified with every field of activity in New Brunswick, whether it is in the line of business or social life, has a large patronage, with offices in the National Bank building, suite 311, at No 390 George street

The parents of Eugene Schenck Griggs were Benjamin Schenck and Sarah A (Suydam) Griggs Benjamin S Griggs was born in Dayton, New Jersey, in 1854, and was a man of many business interests, being a farmer, a miller and a large produce dealer, with headquarters at Deans, New Jersey, and at Franklin Park He died in New Brunswick, in November, 1908, at the age of fifty-four Mrs Sarah A (Suydam) Griggs still survives him, having her home at Franklin Park She and her husband were the parents of six children . 1 Bessie R, the widow of John A Bodine, she resides at Franklin Park 2 Sarah Jeanette, wife of Isaac V. Williamson, their home being at Livingston Park, New Brunswick 3 Eugene Schenck, of further mention 4 John E, living in New Brunswick, an adjuster with the Michelin Tire Company 5 Benjamin, died in infancy 6 Agnes Suydam unmarried, living in New Brunswick

Dr Griggs was born in Franklin Park, Somerset county, New Jersey, September 2, 1883, spending his early life there and receiving his preliminary education at the public schools of that town, following which he attended the New Brunswick Business College, graduating in 1900 He then took a four years' course at the Brown Preparatory School of Philadelphia, graduating in 1904 At this time he determined to make dentistry his life work and, after a three years' course, graduated from the Pennsylvania College of Dental Surgery in 1907 Deciding that there was a large field for his work in New Brunswick, Dr Griggs began practicing there, locating at once in his present offices

During the late World War, Dr Griggs was a member of the local board of examiners, giving a year and a half to this work being appointed April 16, 1918, by the adjutant-general of New Jersey. He is very fond of natural history and spends much time in the study of this subject He is also interested in the breeding and raising of thoroughbred dogs

Among his many other interests may be mentioned his enjoyment of out-of-door sports, being especially fond of fishing and hunting, and he is a member of several organizations having sporting life as their object Some of them are The Interwoven Rifle Club of New Brunswick, the New Brunswick Sportsmen's Association, and the Stillwater Hunt Club, of Canton, New York Dr Griggs is also a member of various associations connected with his profession, among them being The Middlesex County Dental Society, of which he is an ex-president the State Dental Society, the National Dental Association, and he is also a member of the medical staff of the Middlesex General Hospital He is also connected with the Dutch Reformed Church of Franklin Park

Mr Griggs married, June 3, 1916, Gertrude V Kee She was born in New York City, the daughter of Frank T. and Sarah (Rowan) Kee Mr Kee is a retired contractor and builder, making his home on Hamilton road, New Brunswick Dr. and Mrs Griggs have no children

The first known ancestor of the Griggs family came from Holland many years ago and located near what is now Flatbush, Long Island One branch of the family, who were millwrights, settled in the Somerset county district and became the founders of Griggstown, New Jersey The Suydam family is also of Holland Dutch ancestry and were among those who settled Flatbush The grandfathers on both paternal and maternal sides of Dr Griggs were fighting patriots in the Revolutionary War

---

JOE AKEN SEXTON —As manager of the South Amboy Lumber and Supply Company, and owner of a garage and automobile accessories' business, Joe A Sexton does not find time hanging heavily on his hands, neither is he a slave to his business, but by an energetic, systematic arrangement finds time to meet every business engagement and to give the duties of friendship and citizenship their proper place in life Although born in New York City, his parents moved to South Amboy when he was but two years of age, and with the exception of a few years spent in St Louis, Missouri, he has known no other home He was one of the old Camden & Amboy men of that period which antedated the Pennsylvania Railroad in New Jersey, that company only being able to enter the State by buying a controling interest in Camden & Amboy stock and then leasing the road

Joe A Sexton is a son of William Sexton, the latter born in Monmouth county, New Jersey, in 1818, died in South Amboy in 1895, a contractor and builder for many years, but at the time of his death engaged in the furniture business William Sexton married Elizabeth Aken, born in New York City, died in South Amboy, aged seventy-seven They were the parents of three children Joe Aken Sexton of this review the only one to reach mature years, the others dying young He is a descendant of the Freehold, New Jersey, branch of the Sexton family founded by John and William Sexton, who came to what is now Freehold in 1646.

Joe Aken Sexton was born in New York City, May 9, 1852, but in

1854 his parents moved to South Amboy, New Jersey, which has since been his home, excepting the comparatively short time his parents resided in St Louis, Missouri There the lad began his education, finishing his studies in the public schools of South Amboy He left school when fourteen years of age and secured a place with the Camden & Amboy Railroad Company Later he learned the carpenter's trade with his father, and, in course of time, from a capable journeyman carpenter he advanced to a building contractor, and when but eighteen years of age had executed four contracts for buildings He advanced rapidly in favor as a contractor and builder, and among the many contracts which he fulfilled was one for the erection of the South Amboy City Hall, and another for the building of an addition to Christ Episcopal Church in South Amboy With the years he took on new responsibilities in 1891 he became associated with Miller & Donnell, and the firm was known as Sexton, Miller & Donnell, dealers in building materials of all kinds Mr Miller retired about two years later and the firm name was changed to Sexton & Donnell While this firm was doing business, they established a branch in Perth Amboy under the personal supervision of Mr Sexton, this business is now the Donnell Lumber Company, and the leading lumber yard of Perth Amboy About two years after the establishment of the Perth Amboy plant they dissolved partnership, Mr Sexton taking the South Amboy yards, and Mr Donnell the Perth Amboy yards About 1905 Mr Sexton sold out his business to A J Miller, Mr Sexton deciding to retire. In 1907 he was the prime mover in the establishing of the South Amboy Lumber and Supply Company, in which he has since continued as manager, making a wonderful success of the enterprise, and in 1910 the garage and automobile supply business The South Amboy Lumber and Supply Company is a corporation, with D C Chase, president Henry Wolff vice-president: R C Stephenson, secretary-treasurer, and Joe A Sexton, manager It is a solid, substantial, prosperous concern, well-managed, and has been an important factor in the development of South Amboy The J A Sexton Garage is located at Broadway and Main street, South Amboy and there motorists can have their troubles ironed out and be sent on their way rejoicing.

In his younger years Mr Sexton was an enthusiastic yachtsman, both owning and sailing yachts, and never declining to race them The bay and river yet have charms for him, fishing a sport he frequently indulges in He is a member of the Independent Order of Odd Fellows, of which he is past grand master a member of the Knights of Pythias, Knights of the Golden Eagle, Independent Order of Red Men, a charter member of the South Amboy Yacht Club and for two years its commodore, a communicant of the Protestant Episcopal church, and for four years served his city as a member of the Board of Health He was president for two years of the Star Building and Loan Association

Mr Sexton married, at South Amboy, December 22, 1872, Lucretia Herring born in New York City, February 2, 1855, died in South Amboy June 30 1920 after a happy married life covering a period of forty-eight years She was brought to South Amboy by her parents,

James and Kate Ellen (Schenck) Herring, when a girl of twelve years, and there lived until her passing away, at the age of sixty-five. The children of Joe A. and Lucretia (Herring) Sexton, four in number, are all living, Mary Elizabeth, wife of Walter Compton, of South Amboy, Josephine, widow of Willis Fisher, James Andrew, of South Amboy, and William, a resident of Keyport, New Jersey.

WILLIAM ORR WHITNEY was born in North Adams, Massachusetts, July 1, 1889. He is the son of Charles Edward and Mary (Orr) Whitney. Charles Edward Whitney is an overseer in the Windsor Print Works in North Adams, and has always been active in the political life of that community, having formerly been a member and also president of the City Council. Mr. and Mrs. Whitney are the parents of three children: Arthur C., Anna E., William Orr, of further mention.

The preliminary portion of William Orr Whitney's education was obtained in the public schools of his native place, and after graduating from the Drury High School, North Adams, in 1907, he matriculated in the Massachusetts Institute of Technology in Boston, Massachusetts, where he remained for two years coming to New Brunswick, New Jersey, in the fall of that same year and entering the employ of the Brunswick Refrigerating Company. Here he started in to gain a thorough knowledge of the different branches of the business, and being an apt student he quickly rose to positions of responsibility, his early training standing him in good stead in his business career. In 1917 he was promoted to his present position of manager of the marine department, and continues in the management of this department, exercising the same tireless industry which has characterized his career from its beginning. Mr. Whitney is affiliated with Union Lodge, No 19, Ancient Free and Accepted Masons, Scott Chapter, No 4, Royal Arch Masons, and Temple Commandery, No 18, Knights Templar. He is also a member of the local Young Men's Christian Association, the American Society of Mechanical Engineers, the American Society of Refrigerating Engineers, the American Society of Naval Draftsmen, and the American Society of Naval Engineers.

On October 21, 1914, William Orr Whitney was united in marriage with Ruth Jenkinson Lessig, daughter of Hilary and Tamar Lessig, of Pottstown, Pennsylvania. Mr. and Mrs. Whitney are the parents of one child, Ruth Easton, born January 30, 1918.

WILLIAM H BROOKS.—The family of which William H Brooks is a descendant is of good old Jersey stock, every generation in turn showing the same substantial characteristics which are the foundation of every community worth while.

This present representative of the name, William H. Brooks, is the son of Henry and Emma B (Courter) Brooks, the former for many years employed in the ticket department of the old Camden & Amboy Railroad. Their son, William H., was born in Camden, New Jersey, December 25, 1869. After exhausting the educational opportunities of his home town, he entered Rider College of Trenton, New Jersey, of which he is now an alumnus After his graduation, Mr Brooks was for a time connected with Downs & Finch, shirt manufacturers, leaving it to accept a position in the George W Helme Company Remaining there for sixteen years he relinquished that to become, in 1905, the assistant cashier of the First National Bank of Jamesburg, New Jersey, on Buckelew avenue, where he is engaged at the present time In the political affairs of Jamesburg, Mr Brooks has not confined himself to either of the leading parties, being what is regarded as a "liberal" in his views He is popular among his townspeople, which is attested by the fact that he has been retained as the town clerk for the past twenty years, holding that office at the present time Among the many fraternal orders existing in Jamesburg, Mr Brooks is connected with but three: The Independent Order of Odd Fellows, Appollo Lodge, No 156, Free and Accepted Masons, Cranbury, New Jersey, and Junior Order of United American Mechanics He is also interested in the Presbyterian church, where he and his wife attend service

In Burgettstown, Pennsylvania, William H Brooks and Lulu Pauline Marquis were united in marriage, September 21, 1904 Mrs Brooks is the daughter of James T and Mary C. (Bucher) Marquis The maternal grandfather of Mr Brooks, William H Courter, built in 1853 a very beautiful house which has always been in the possession of some member of the family It is at the present time occupied by this grandson, William H Brooks, and his wife They have given it the name of "Brooks Crest" and are exceedingly proud of their ancestral acres, the homestead being well worthy of their natural appreciation of it It is situated on Railroad avenue, Jamesburg, Monroe township

---

SPENCER PERRY—The Perrys are an old Middlesex county family long located in the South River district of the county Spencer Perry, of Milltown, engineer at the plant of the Russell Playing Card Company, is a son of John and Patience (Bloodgood) Perry, of South River, his father a carpenter by trade

Spencer Perry was born in South River, New Jersey, September 11, 1871, and there was educated in the public schools He was variously employed until finally deciding to fit himself for an engineer's position, and steadily pursued his ambition until in possession of an engineer's license or certificate For twenty-one years he has been engineer with the Russell Playing Card Company of Milltown organizer and director of the Milltown Coal and Lumber Company, a $50,000 corporation, one of the original organizers of the First National Bank of Milltown, of which he is a director, served twenty-one years on the Board of Education of the town of Milltown, one term of three years as councilman of Milltown, and an unexpired term of two years as mayor Mr. Perry is a Democrat in politics, a member of the Order of United American Mechanics (both senior and junior), of the National Association of Stationary Engineers, and the Travel Club of America

Mr Perry married, in New Brunswick, New Jersey, August 14, 1893,

Spencer Perry

Minnie Knox, born November 25, 1869, in Trenton, New Jersey, daughter of Peter B. and Henrietta (Moore) Knox, her father born in Scotland but brought to the United States at the age of eight years Mr and Mrs. Perry are the parents of eight children 1 Spencer B , born February 27, 1894, was sergeant in Company G, 311th Infantry, 78th Division, serving from October 17, 1916, until he was killed, November 1, 1917, in the Argonne Forest 2 Jesse L , born July 20, 1895, served one year with the 203rd Regiment Ambulance Company, 78th Division, mustered out in June, 1918 3 Mahta, born January 20, 1897 4 Richard J , born February 5, 1900. 5 Arminta K , born February 9, 1902 6 Leslie E , born March 19, 1904 7. Patience E , born November 20, 1905 8 Arthur K , born July 30, 1907 The family home is at No 18 Riva street, Milltown, New Jersey

---

THOMAS SWALES.—In 1912 the city of New Brunswick, New Jersey, held what was called a "Boost Week," one of the principal features being extensive advertising of the merits and advantages of the city One of these advertisements, catching the eye of Thomas Swales in Toronto, Canada, he determined to make that city his home and is now a loyal citizen of the United States

Thomas Swales was born in Stockport, England, November 18, 1884, the son of James and Elizabeth (Crowder) Swales James Swales was a native of England, a printer's engineer by trade· he died in England Elizabeth (Crowder) Swales was also born in England and died there They had a large family of children, eight of whom are now living Mary Ellen, residing in England, Polly, also in England, Ernest, living in Canada, Daniel, also in England; James, in Toronto, Canada, Cissie and Lillie, both of these living in England, Thomas, now residing in America The eldest son, Charles, was killed during the World War, two of his sons meeting death in the same struggle, one of these, Arthur Swales, was the champion welter-weight of the British Army during his service in it

During his infancy, the parents of Thomas Swales moved from Stockport to Manchester, England, where he attended school in his boyhood, leaving it at the age of fourteen to learn the carpenter's trade When nineteen years old the young man came to America, and upon reaching Canada located in Toronto, where he worked as a carpenter during his residence there After coming to New Brunswick in 1912 he for a time continued in that line of work, then went into the building business in his own name His offices are at No 507 National Bank building, at No. 390 George street Mr Swales' ambition is to build houses in the way Henry Ford builds automobiles Having taken an active interest in the politics of his adopted home, Mr Swales was nominated for the office of township committeeman in 1920 He is also affiliated with several of the fraternal orders of the city, is a member of Mt Zion Lodge, No 135, Free and Accepted Masons, New Brunswick Forest, Tall Cedars of Lebanon, and of the volunteer fire department

At Tarrytown, New York, March 10, 1905, Thomas Swales married

Ruth Perry, a native of North Carolina She was the daughter of Isaac and Mary Ann (Missimore) Perry, farmers of Yadkin county, North Carolina. The former is now deceased, but the latter is still living in her Southern home Mr and Mrs Swales have five children, all living Helen, Cora, Thomas, Jr , James, Ruth Their home is in the Lindeneau section of New Brunswick They are members of the Protestant Episcopal church

HOWARD DAYTON LITTELL—After an experience as a salesman of coal, which gave him the information he needed to successfully conduct a business of his own, Howard D Littell established a coal business in South Amboy which he very successfully managed for twelve years, beginning a young man of twenty-three A little arithmetic proves him yet to be a young man, although a veteran in business and one of the progessive, substantial business men of his city He is a son of Frederick Meeker Littell, born in Newark, but now with the General Motors Company, and long a resident of South Amboy Frederick M Littell married Mary Dayton, born in South Amboy, of Revolutionary family, one of her ancestors a signer of the Declaration of Independence The Littells originally came to New Jersey from France several generations ago

Howard Dayton Littell, only child of Frederick M and Mary (Dayton) Littell, was born in South Amboy, October 31, 1885, and there attended public schools until thirteen years of age He completed his studies in State educational institutions, and was quite a noted schoolboy athlete, captain of his school football team He left school in 1904 and entered the employ of the Mohawk Coal Company of New York City, continuing with them as traveling salesman in New York State and Pennsylvania territory In 1908 he established the coal business which he has since conducted in South Amboy, dealing in both anthracite and bituminous coal under the firm name, Howard D Littell He is also a director of the Owners' and Investors' Building and Loan Association, and a member of the South Amboy Chamber of Commerce. Mr. Littell is a member of the Masonic order and affiliates with St Stephen's Lodge, No 63, Free and Accepted Masons, and Amboy Chapter, No 41, Royal Arch Masons His club is the South Amboy Yacht He attends the Protestant Episcopal church

Mr Littell married, in Keyport, New Jersey, November 2, 1914, Florence M Armstrong, born there, daughter of Frederick and Mary (Sillik) Armstrong, her father deceased, her mother yet (1920) a resident of Keyport Mr and Mrs Littell are the parents of two children Howard Dayton (2), born June 24, 1917, Helen Armstrong, born June 26, 1920 The family home is in South Amboy, the city in which Mr Littell was born and which has always been his home

EDWARD JOSEPH HOUGHTON.—Three generations of Houghtons in this branch have resided in New Brunswick, New Jersey, Dennis Houghton, who came from Ireland where he grew to manhood upon his father's farm, his son, James Houghton, born in New Brunswick, where he yet resides, aged seventy-seven, Edward J Houghton, now a merchant of the city, senior member of the haberdashery firm, Houghton & Strauss. The first of the family to come to the United States was the great-grandfather of Edward J Houghton, but the records do not show that he lived in New Brunswick, neither is his name known to the writer

Dennis Houghton was a brakeman in the employ of the Central Railroad of New Jersey until about 1860, when he went to New Orleans, where he died leaving sons, James and Michael, and a daughter Catherine

James Houghton, son of Dennis and Margaret Houghton, was born in New Brunswick, in 1843, and there has spent his years, seventy-seven He attended the public schools until thirteen years of age, then spent four years as a grocery clerk, followed by four years as a tinsmith In 1872 he opened a grocery store on Neilson street, which he conducted for many years, finally retired to a well earned competence He was an ardent Democrat and served his ward as alderman in 1884-1888 and faithfully represented his district He was long a member of the volunteer fire department, and as foreman was very efficient in fighting fires or any turbulent spirit who might run counter to the desires of the company He married, in 1871, Mary A Whealon, who died in February, 1902 Twelve children were born to James and Mary A Houghton, three of whom are living Margaret E, wife of William T McLaughlin, Edward Joseph, of further mention, and Sarah A. (Sadie), a resident of New Brunswick

Edward Joseph Houghton was born in New Brunswick, New Jersey, January 21, 1876, and there has passed his years, forty-five He attended both parochial and public schools, finishing his education with a commercial course in the New Jersey Business College in Newark, graduating with the class of 1893 He then entered his father's employ and for ten years was associated with him in the grocery business He was then with A Wilson & Sons, engaged in the mercantile business for twelve years, and in 1916 established the haberdashery business of Houghton & Strauss, No 342 George street, which he yet successfully conducts Mr Houghton was elected city recorder in 1908 and was twice reelected to that office In March, 1915, he was elected commissioner for a four-year term, and in May, 1919, was reelected for a similar term He has served his city well and has won public confidence to a surprising degree He is a member of the Fraternal Order of Eagles, the Benevolent and Protective Order of Elks, the Knights of Columbus, and Sacred Heart Roman Catholic Church

Mr Houghton married (first) in New Brunswick, April 28, 1898, Katherine Donahue, who died in August, 1900, leaving a daughter Katherine, who married Francis R Hays, of New Brunswick He married (second) August 17, 1908, Mary A Donahue, and they have a daughter Margaret, born December 4, 1909

ANTONIO FREDERICK MUNOZ —The Munoz family is of Spanish origin, this branch finally settling in Berlin, Germany, where Antonio Frederick Munoz, Sr, was born, but of Spanish parents Later in life he came to the United States, and located in Brooklyn, New York, where he died August 28, 1887, aged forty years. He was a man of education and ability, serving at one time as vice-consul to Venezuela, South America. He married Edwina Wiggins, born in Parkville, Long Island, died in Brooklyn, December 21, 1886, her death preceding that of her husband by less than a year. They were the parents of two children: Antonio F., of further mention, and Grace Edwina, wife of Dr. Frederick Koehler, of Philadelphia. She died in Philadelphia, aged twenty-four. She was a descendant of Whitehead Howard, a colonel in the Revolutionary army, a landowner of Long Island, and one of the pioneer stage coach drivers between New York and Philadelphia.

Antonio Frederick (2) Munoz, son of Antonio Frederick (1) and Edwina (Wiggins) Munoz, was born in Brooklyn, New York, November 28, 1877. When nine years of age he lost both parents, their deaths occurring in Brooklyn. He pursued his studies in St. Joseph's College in Canada, and in 1888 came to Perth Amboy, making his home temporarily with an uncle, Dr. H. W. Phillips. After finishing his school years, he learned the plumber's trade with Kelly & McAlinden, of Perth Amboy, and remained with that firm for seven years, becoming a skilled workman in his line. His next position was in the laboratory of the Roessler & Hasslacher Chemical Company, of Perth Amboy, but a year later he abandoned his trade to engage in stock dealing, principally horses. He so continued until January 1, 1917, when he was appointed by Common Council to his present position, street commissioner of Perth Amboy.

Mr. Munoz is a Republican in politics, and has been active in the politics of his city. For three years he was president of the Third Ward Republican Club, and is county committeeman from the First District of the Third Ward of Perth Amboy, an office he has held since 1912. In addition to his public business, he is president and treasurer of the Munoz Warehouse Company, Nos. 236-238 Sheridan street, a business established in 1898, and incorporated in 1917. His hours of recreation are usually spent in his power boat on the water of Amboy and New York bays, fishing also being one of his favorite sports. He is a member of the Benevolent and Protective Order of Elks, Foresters of America; Algonquin Lodge, No. 44, Knights of Pythias, Dramatic Order Knights Khorrasan, Exempt Firemen's Association of Perth Amboy, Sons of Veterans, Lincoln Engine Company, No. 1, and the Episcopal church.

Mr. Munoz married, in Perth Amboy, April 28, 1898, Anna D. Burchell, born in Bordentown, New Jersey, October 30, 1876, daughter of William and Emily (Thorn) Burchell. Mrs. Burchell died August 6, 1906, in Perth Amboy, Mr. Burchell surviving her, and residing in Perth Amboy with his daughter Anna D. Mr. and Mrs. Munoz had a son, Antonio Frederick (3), born December 5, 1906, deceased.

JAMES LOUIS FAGAN, M. D.—With a broadly comprehensive hospital experience, and a record of usefulness overseas, Dr. James Louis Fagan, M. D., has established himself in the practice of medicine in New Brunswick, New Jersey.

About the middle of the nineteenth century Dr Fagan's grandfather, John Fagan, came from Ireland to America, and settled in Ash Brook, Union county, New Jersey

James Fagan, his son, was born in that vicinity, July 27, 1857 He is now living in Huntington, West Virginia, and holds the position of mechanical and electrical engineer for the American Railways Company He married Helen Barry, who died July 12, 1920, they were the parents of eleven children, all of whom are now living

Dr James Louis Fagan, M D, son of James and Helen (Barry) Fagan, was born in Brooklyn, New York, September 14, 1891 His parents removed to Wilkes-Barre, Pennsylvania, and his education was begun in the primary schools of that city, continuing there up to the fourth grade Another change took the family to Huntington, West Virginia, where the boy's common school course was completed In this city also his higher education was begun, at Marshall College, Huntington, from which he was graduated 1910 He then entered the University of Louisville, in the medical department, from which institution he was graduated in 1914 Then began Dr Fagan's hospital practice, comprising a rarely extensive and varied experience In 1914 and 1915, he was interne at St Joseph's Infirmary, Louisville, Kentucky, and in 1916 and 1917 in the New York Post-Graduate Hospital In the latter part of 1917 he became resident physician and surgeon in St Luke's Hospital, New York City, shortly thereafter he went to St Mary's Hospital for Children, in the same capacity, then in February, 1918, he entered the medical department of the United States army In the course of his official duties he was detailed to the Rockefeller Institute for Medical Research, then to the Walter Reed Hospital, Washington, D C, where he remained until August 1, 1918 He sailed for France, August 31, 1918, with Base Hospital No 62. This hospital was located at Marssur-Allier, France He was thereafter given temporary duty with Camp Hospital, No 28, at Nevers, France, then later transferred to Base Hospital, No 91, at Commercy, France He sailed for the United States, July 22, 1919, and was discharged from the service in August, 1919

On December 22, 1919, Dr Fagan opened an office in New Brunswick for the general practice of medicine, at No 243 George street Although this is a comparatively recent date, Dr Fagan is rapidly placing his name among those of the successful physicians of Middlesex county Outside his profession Dr Fagan has few interests He is a member of Middlesex County Medical Association, New Jersey State Medical Association, fellow of the American Medical Association, a member of Rutgers Medical Club, and of the Phi Chi, a medical fraternity. His favorite relaxation is hunting and fishing

Dr. Fagan married, in Washington, District of Columbia, May 1, 1918, Lillian Wickenhaver, who was born in Brooklyn, New York, a daughter of John and Nettie (Wright) Wickenhaver; her father is now deceased, and her mother resides in Harrisburg, Pennsylvania The family has always been connected with the Roman Catholic church

JOHN PAXTON KIRKPATRICK, one of the successful attorneys of New Brunswick, New Jersey, and a man who has already made a name for himself and by his personal worth commands a high place in this community, was born in Jamesburg, New Jersey, January 11, 1881, the son of David and Mary (Paxton) Kirkpatrick. David Kirkpatrick was the son of John Kirkpatrick who emigrated to this country from Ballyshannon, Ireland, in 1822, and settled in St. John's Newfoundland, the former owning a large farm in Jamesburg, where he resided. To Mr. and Mrs. David Kirkpatrick have been born two children. David, deceased, and John Paxton, of further mention.

John Paxton Kirkpatrick completed the elementary portion of his education in the schools of Spotswood, New Jersey, and at the model school of Trenton, New Jersey, after which he prepared himself for college at Princeton Preparatory School, subsequently matriculating at Princeton College, from which he was graduated with the degree of Bachelor of Science in 1904. Having determined in the meantime to adopt the law as a profession, he accordingly studied in the office of Aaron E. Johnston, and was admitted to the bar in February, 1908. Throughout his school and college years he had proved himself an intelligent and painstaking student, and at the close came to the opening of his career unusually well-equipped both with natural gifts and a training that was the result of long and conscientious effort. Immediately after passing his bar examinations, he first established himself in the practice of his chosen profession in Newark, later in Elizabeth, and in 1912 came to New Brunswick, New Jersey, and opened an office at No. 46 Paterson street which has remained his headquarters ever since. He has built up an excellent practice and has handled many important cases up to the present, proving himself to be a most capable and conscientious attorney.

Besides his legal activity, Mr. Kirkpatrick has interested himself in the conduct of public affairs in the community and has come to be regarded as a leader of the local organization of the Democratic party. He was a member of the General Assembly for three years, 1912-13-14. He affiliates with Cranbury Lodge, No. 196, Free and Accepted Masons, and is an Episcopalian in religion. He holds membership in the Union Club of New Brunswick, and also in the New Brunswick Country Club.

On November 27, 1907, Mr. Kirkpatrick was united in marriage with Ethel B. Davison, of Jamesburg, New Jersey, the daughter of Isaac S. and Louise (Marsh) Davison. Mr. and Mrs. Kirkpatrick are the parents of five children: John P., born November 8, 1908, died August 29, 1909, Roger B., born June 8, 1910, Robert S., born May 3, 1914, died December 15, 1915, David E., born November 12, 1916, Malcolm S., born February 1, 1919.

EDWIN VOORHEES KENT—Among the older families in this section of the country very few can trace a straighter line to a Colonial ancestor than Edwin Voorhees Kent, of New Brunswick, New Jersey. He is the eighth in descent from the original emigrant, Stephen Kent,

who landed in Massachusetts in 1638, from England   Some records
give this as 1635, but he was known to have sailed from Southhampton,
England, in the ship 'Confidence,'' in 1638, and to have brought with
him his wife, Margery, and four servants   Settling in Newbury, Massachusetts, he was sworn a freeman May 22, 1639   For several years
Stephen Kent was a man of considerable prominence in his vicinity, and
remained there until he and his family removed to Woodbridge, New
Jersey, in 1665, so founding the family of Kent in Middlesex county

Edwin Voorhees Kent, born in New Brunswick, August 1, 1865, is
the son of John Voorhees and Ann Elizabeth (Van Derhoef) Kent   John
Voorhees Kent, born September 12, 1840, son of Clayton and Catherine
Ann (Voorhees) Kent   Clayton Kent, born August 5, 1794, son of
Phineas and Sarah (Brown) Kent   Phineas Kent, born September 11,
1756, son of William and Charity (Freeman) Kent   William Kent, born
in 1713, son of David Kent and unknown wife   David Kent, born June
30, 1686, son of Stephen and first wife, Jane Scott Kent   Stephen Kent,
born March 6, 1648, son of Stephen and first wife, Margery   Stephen
(1) Kent, born in England, in 1607

John V Kent, father of Edwin Voorhees Kent, was a native of New
Brunswick and lived there all his life, his death occurring July 30 1910,
at the age of seventy years   For many years he had been in the employ
of the Raritan & Delaware Canal Company as assistant superintendent
He married Ann Elizabeth Van Derhoef, born in New Brunswick in
1841, who still survives him, her home being in New Brunswick   They
had seven children, four of whom are now living. Edwin Voorhees, of
whom further, Mabel, wife of Milton C Mook, residing at No 48
Rector street, Metuchen, Clayton, a coal merchant living in Uniontown,
Pennsylvania, Elmer W, who resides in Passaic, New Jersey, and is
assistant division superintendent of public service with an office in
Passaic

Edwin Voorhees Kent was educated in the public schools of New
Brunswick and at the age of fifteen years left school to take a position
as clerk in a drug store, remaining so employed for six months, when
he left to become a salesman in the L. B. Tarbox jewelry store on
Church street, where he remained for two years   Following this, the
young man entered the real estate office of J Bayard Kirkpatrick, continuing this for two more years and then accepting an opening in the
National Bank of New Jersey as messenger   From this small beginning,
Mr Kent has progressed from time to time as opportunity offered, as
debit clerk, bookkeeper, receiving teller, paying teller and finally, in 1915,
as assistant cashier, a position he now holds

Mr Kent enjoys the society of his fellow-men as is evidenced by
his membership in various clubs and societies   He is quite active in
Young Men's Christian Association work, and is much interested in
the local lodges of the Free Masons, and the Independent Order of
Odd Fellows   Since May, 1920 Mr Kent has been president of the
New Brunswick Boat Club, an organization with which he has been

connected for several years. He has a particular fondness for all kinds of outdoor sports, chief among them being fishing, automobiling and hiking Though occupied with sports and pleasures, Mr Kent is a regular attendant at the Baptist church of New Brunswick He resides at No 275 George street

---

DR MORTIMER HAROLD LINDEN.—Among the younger physicians of New Brunswick, New Jersey, who are going forward to ever increasing success, is Dr. Mortimer Harold Linden

Dr Linden was born in New York City, March 11, 1887, a son of Jacob and Frances Linden, of that city Jacob Linden was for many years a prominent clothier of Brooklyn, New York, but now is retired from active business Of the five children of Jacob and Frances Linden Dr. Linden is the eldest The others are as follows: Irving B, a successful attorney located at No 299 Broadway, New York City; Bernard A, a chemist, connected with the United States Department of Agriculture at Washington, District of Columbia Arthur C, a physician located at No 5 East Eighty-fourth street, New York City and Jeannette F, of Brooklyn, New York

Gaining his early education at Public School No 147, of New York City Mortimer Harold Linden continued at the De Witt Clinton High School, then attended the College of the City of New York for one year. He then entered Long Island College Hospital, remaining until June, 1910 From September to December, 1910, he was assistant house surgeon at the New York Lying-In Hospital, then was house physician at Randall's Island, New York City, continuing there until April, 1911 He then went to England and practiced in London until November, 1915 and following this experience returned to this country and established himself in private practice in Brooklyn New York Here he remained until the interruption of the World War He began practice in New Brunswick, New Jersey, December 4, 1919, and is rapidly becoming one of the leading physicians of the city Dr Linden is a member of the Free and Accepted Masons, the Improved Order of Red Men, the Order of B'rith Abraham and of the Association of Military Surgeons of America. He is a member of the Craftsmen's Club, and of the Middlesex County Medical Society.

When United States intervention became a fact, Dr Linden was one of the first to offer his services to the Government for duty overseas He was commissioned first lieutenant in June, 1917, and called to active service, August 11, 1917 and detailed to Fort Benjamin Harrison, Indiana, then to Camp Grant, Rockford, Illinois Promoted to captain, he was appointed commanding officer of Ambulance Company No 341, and arrived overseas in France, August 13 1918. Remaining with the Ambulance Company until after the armistice, he was ordered to duty at Camp Hospital No 1 at Gondrecourt (Meuse), France Returning home he arrived in the United States, July 24, 1919, and received an honorable discharge at Camp Dix, on that date

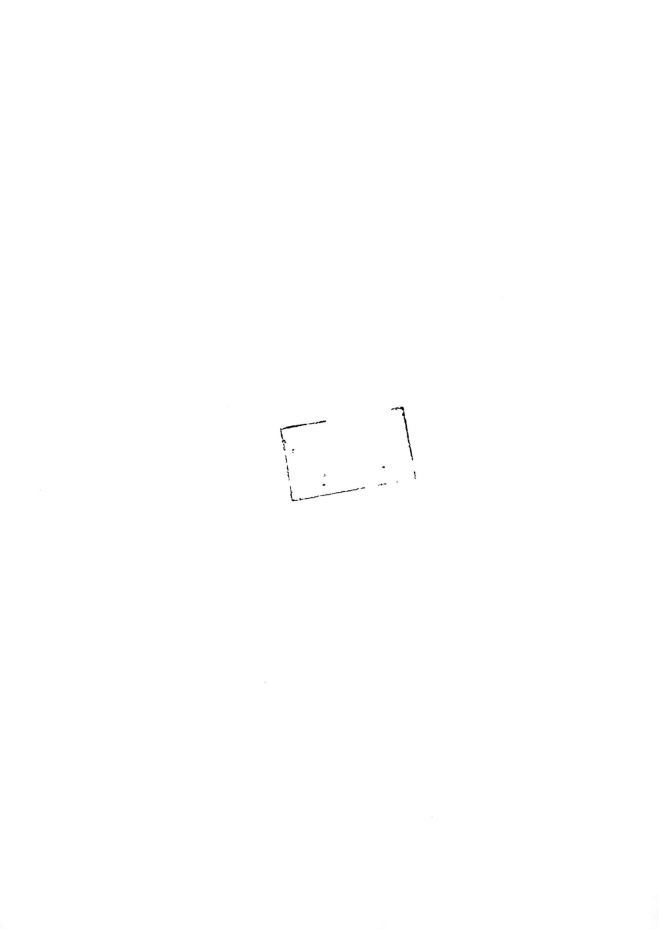

Charles M. Peterson

CHARLEY MARTIN PETERSON, head of the firm of C M Peterson & Company, dealers in coal and wood, in Perth Amboy, New Jersey, and prominent in the business and commercial affairs of the city, was born in Perth Amboy, October 15, 1879, a son of Martin and Christine (Madison) Peterson, old and highly respected residents there The elder Mr Peterson was a native of Nakshov, Denmark, and spent the first sixteen years of his life in that country He then came to the United States and settled at once in Perth Amboy, where he engaged in business as a cobbler, a trade that he followed for some thirty-eight years He later became interested in the coal business and continued therein until his death, April 6, 1914 at the age of sixty-two years He is survived by his wife, who continues to make her home in Perth Amboy Five children were born to them, as follows Frank, who died in infancy, John, who died in infancy, Charley Martin, whose career forms the subject of this sketch, Matilda, who became the wife of John W. Olson, of Perth Amboy; and Cornelia, who became the wife of Albert Hanson of Perth Amboy.

The childhood of Mr Peterson was passed in his native city, and it was there that he received his education, attending for this purpose Public School No 1 and continuing until he had taken one year in the local high school He then gave up his studies and took a clerical position in a shoe establishment and remained there for three or four years, gaining in the meantime a wide knowledge of business methods Mr Peterson was then the victim of a breakdown in his health and was recommended by his physician to seek some employment that would keep him constantly out-of-doors, so he purchased the ice business from J Neilson, which he conducted with a high degree of success for about three years In 1902, in association with his father, who had given up the shoe business, he bought the coal business of Neer & Eggert, and has continued the same ever since His father's death occurred in 1914 and since that time Mr Peterson has been in complete control of the enterprise which, under his very capable management, has grown to be the largest of its kind in the city Outside of his private coal business Mr Peterson has taken an active part in the commercial enterprises of the community and is now interested in and a director of the Trojan Coal Mining Company, the Boardman Coal Mining Company, the City National Bank, the Citizens' Building and Loan and the Perth Amboy Building and Loan associations He is also prominent in social and fraternal circles in Perth Amboy and is a member of the Ancient Free and Accepted Masons, Royal Arch Masons, Royal and Select Masters, Knights Templar, and Salaam Temple, Ancient Arabic Order Nobles of the Mystic Shrine Besides these Masonic bodies he is a member of the Danish Brotherhood, the Danish Relief Society, the Raritan Yacht Club, and the Young Men's Christian Association, being also a director of the last named organization and chairman of the Boys' Department Mr Peterson is an Episcopalian and attends St Peter's Church in Perth Amboy

Mr Peterson was united in marriage, July 21, 1904, in Perth Amboy, with Marie Magreta Therkelson, a daughter of Yen Peter and Marie Therkelson Two children have been born to them, as follows Carl Frederick and Elva Marie, born, respectively, July 15, 1907, and August 20, 1918

HORACE E BARWIS comes from an old English family who settled in Trenton, New Jersey, and vicinity before the Revolutionary War He was born in Trenton, New Jersey, April 30, 1887, the son of Alfred C and Susan R (Hoagland) Barwis Alfred C Barwis was born in Langhorne, Pennsylvania, in 1848, and is now residing in Trenton, retired For many years he was collector of the port of Burlington Susan R (Hoagland) Barwis was born in New Brunswick, July 13, 1858, and died September 6 1920, the daughter of Tunis V D Hoagland who was keeper of the New Jersey State Prison in 1862, and who served as mayor of New Brunswick at one time To Mr and Mrs Barwis were born four children Mary, wife of William Davison, of Taylorsville, Pennsylvania, Dorothy, wife of George A Pitman, of Trenton, New Jersey, Robert Elmer stenographer for the Pennsylvania railroad, Horace E, of further mention

The elementary portion of the education of Horace E Barwis was obtained in the public schools of New Brunswick After graduating from the local high school in 1905, he entered Rutgers College, where he remained for two years, and then worked for the Home Rubber Company at Trenton for three years He had in the meantime determined to adopt the law as his profession, and, accordingly, studied in the law office of George L Burton, passing his bar examinations and establishing himself in his chosen profession in 1915 He opened an office in the National Bank building in New Brunswick, and this has remained his headquarters ever since He is building up an excellent practice and already has handled many important cases, proving himself to be a most capable and conscientious attorney In politics he is a Republican, and was appointed in December, 1920, borough attorney of Highland Park

On October 9, 1918, Mr Barwis was united in marriage with Ada I Rolfe, a native of New Brunswick and the daughter of Joseph G and Mary Rolfe, deceased There is no issue

---

ROBERT SEGRAVE is a son of John Segrave, a sailor, and his wife, Margaret (Austin) Segrave, who were born in Ireland there passed their lives, and both died there They had four children, two of whom are yet living Patrick of Brooklyn, New York and Robert of whom further

Robert Segrave, born in Ireland in 1854 came to the United States in 1881, having previously been a sailor, shipping first at the age of fifteen years Upon landing in New York City he decided to go directly to South Amboy where he is yet (1921) living, at the age of sixty-six, coming here a young man of twenty-seven After coming to South Amboy he operated a coal barge for several years, then for eighteen years was engaged in the liquor business on Stevens avenue, and is now interested in the operation of a line of freight boats. He is a director of the South Amboy Trust Company, was for two years chief of the South Amboy Fire Department and still a member; for thirty years has been a member of the Ancient Order of Hibernians, and is a communicant of St Mary's Roman Catholic Church. He is also a member of the South Amboy Chamber of Commerce.

Mr Segrave married, in Ireland (returning from the United States for his bride), Mary Grimley, born in Ireland, died in South Amboy, in 1917. They were the parents of the following children Margaret M, married P Joseph McGowan, of South Amboy. Christopher, of Greenville, captain of a tug boat, Catherine T, who resides with her father at South Amboy, John, cashier of the Perth Amboy freight station of the Central Railroad of New Jersey, Mary C, also at home with her father, Francis, a student at Holy Cross College, and two children who died in infancy

---

THOMAS H HAGERTY, an able, successful lawyer, known and honored throughout the county, and especially in New Brunswick, New Jersey where he has been practicing since 1900, has since his commencement of law practice been continually in the public eye, and has won leadership in business and public life. He is a self-made man in the best sense of the word, a man of will and determination who knows not the meaning of the word failure

Thomas H Hagerty was born in New Brunswick, New Jersey, January 13, 1874, the son of Patrick and Mary A (Hughes) Hagerty, the former a native of Ireland and now living in New Brunswick, retired, at the age of ninety, and the latter a native of New York City. Thomas H Hagerty obtained his elementary education in the parochial and public schools of his native city. After attending local high school, he became a clerk in a grocery store, where he remained for two years, and then, having decided upon the profession of law for his life work, he entered the law school of the New York University, from which he was graduated in 1899, and admitted to the New Jersey bar the following year. He studied law with Hon Peter F Daily, now (1921), judge of the Court of Common Pleas. He then went to Perth Amboy, where he practiced his profession for two years, at the end of which time he removed to New Brunswick, where he has continued active ever since

In politics Mr Hagerty is a Democrat, and is chairman of the Middlesex County and Democratic executive committees. He was county collector from 1910 to 1915, and from May, 1915, up to the present time (1920), he has been city attorney. He also holds the office of attorney for the borough of Sayreville, New Jersey. He is a member of the County and State bar associations. Mr Hagerty fraternizes with the Knights of Columbus, and is a member of the Union Club of New Brunswick. In religion he is a Roman Catholic, a member of St Peter's Roman Catholic Church

Thomas H Hagerty was united in marriage, November 15, 1911, with Rose N. Langan, a native of Perth Amboy, New Jersey. They have no children

ELIAS STRATTON MASON —John Mason, grandfather of Elias S Mason, of South Amboy, New Jersey, was born on the ocean, his parents having left their native England for the United States   John Mason grew to manhood, married and settled in Cranbury township, Middlesex county, New Jersey, where his son Robert P Mason, was born, January 6, 1841   Robert P Mason was a veteran of the Civil War serving in the Twenty-second Regiment, New Jersey Volunteer Infantry   He was a ship carpenter by trade, and also for forty-five years, served as a justice of the peace in Cranbury township and South Amboy Twenty-five years prior to his death, which occurred June 4, 1917, he moved to South Amboy, and there passed away   He married Mary Stratton, born in Pemberton, New Jersey, April 11 1842, died February 18, 1921, at South Amboy, in her seventy-ninth year   The six children of Robert P and Mary (Stratton) Mason, all living, are as follows   1 Rev John R, a minister of the Methodist Episcopal church, now stationed in Moorestown, New Jersey   2 Addison H also a minister of the Methodist Episcopal church, stationed at Hamburg New York   3 Elias Stratton, of further mention.   4 Anna K married John Perkins of South Amboy   5 Eleanor S, of South Amboy   6 Charles T, a Pennsylvania railroad employee

Elias Stratton Mason, third son of Robert P and Mary (Stratton) Mason, was born in the village of Cranbury, Middlesex county, New Jersey, April 11, 1871. He attended the public schools until sixteen years of age, then became a clerk in a grocery store at Kingston, New Jersey He then began firing on a Pennsylvania railroad locomotive and for over ten years remained a fireman   He then retired from the road, settled in South Amboy, and with a partner established in the undertaking business under the firm name, Stillwell & Mason   That firm continued in business until 1917, when it was succeeded by E S Mason & Son, who conduct in addition to their undertaking business a complete furniture and house-furnishing store at No 212 North Broadway, South Amboy   Mr Mason has just completed one of the most costly business blocks to be found anywhere outside the large cities, the building 55x125 feet, with two stores and basement   Mr Mason resides in a handsome house at No 249 Second street, South Amboy

Mr Mason retains his membership in the Brotherhood of Locomotive Firemen and Engineers, and is affiliated with the Independent Order of Odd Fellows, Knights of Pythias, and the Order of United American Mechanics   He is an official member of the Methodist Episcopal church and active in church work

Mr. Mason married (first) at Kingston, New Jersey, October 18, 1889, Mary F Johnson, who died June 6, 1891, leaving a son, Robert Perrine, of whom further   He married (second) December 12, 1894, in South Amboy, Mattie Adelina Stillwell, and they are the parents of a daughter, Hazel Adelina, who married October 25, 1920, Harold Francis Stephenson

Robert Perrine Mason, only child of Elias Stratton Mason and his first wife, Mary F (Johnson) Mason, was born in Cranbury, New

Jersey, May 23, 1891, and is a graduate of the grammar and high schools
of South Amboy, finishing high school with the class of 1909 He at
once began a business association with his father, becoming a master
of that business, and in 1916 was admitted a partner of the firm of E S
Mason & Son, furniture dealers and undertakers, a very successful firm
Robert P Mason married, June 25, 1913, Nellie Lambertson, born in
South Amboy, New Jersey

GEORGE SYLVESTER McLAUGHLIN —Having had an unusual
amount of experience as an assistant in the offices of other dentists,
George Sylvester McLaughlin, D D S, was well fitted to attain the
success which has attended him since he opened his own office at No
137 Albany street, New Brunswick, New Jersey

The McLaughlin family originated in Ireland, but the great-grandfather of Dr McLaughlin came to this country many years ago, settling
in New Brunswick, where he now lies buried in one of the cemeteries
One of his grandsons, Charles A McLaughlin, was at one time in the
meat market business in New Brunswick, later giving it up to become
free to attend to large real estate speculations in which he was interested
He was born and brought up in the city, and there married Ellen
McElroy, he died in New Brunswick, in March, 1909, at the age of
seventy-one years He and his wife, Ellen, were the parents of seven
children 1 Agnes, wife of George Cathers 2 Frank A 3 Charles
A, Jr, now deceased 4 George Sylvester, of whom further 5 Eugene 6 Jennie, who married Harvey H. Moynihan. 7 Clarence A
All but one are living at the present time in New Brunswick

The fourth child of this family, George Sylvester McLaughlin, was
born in New Brunswick, July 21, 1880, residing there ever since He
was educated in the public schools, and immediately after graduating,
entered the Philadelphia Dental College, from which he was graduated
in 1901 His first step was to become an assistant in the office of the
famous dentist, Dr C W F Holbrook, of Newark, New Jersey, later
practicing with Dr R M Sanger, of East Orange, New Jersey After
a time spent in this office, Dr. McLaughlin went to Freehold to join
with Dr W E Truax, president of the State Board of Dental Examiners
All of these different engagements gave the young dentist great opportunities to advance in a practical way in his profession Wishing to
perfect himself in certain branches, Dr McLaughlin took a post-graduate course at Columbia University in advanced surgical work and
X-ray examinations During the World War, Dr McLaughlin served
as the dental examiner for Middlesex county, on the Medical Advisory
Board, his appointment coming from the governor of the State Dr
McLaughlin's office is located at No. 137 Albany street

Though a very busy man and with but few leisure hours in which
to enjoy the diversion of a club, Dr McLaughlin is frequently seen
at the meetings of the Knights of Columbus, which body he has
served as treasurer, and at the Union Club, of which he is one of the
board of governors He is also a member of the National and State
Dental societies, and former secretary and later president of the Middle-

sex County Dental Society   He and his family attend St Peter's Roman Catholic Church of New Brunswick

In Jersey City, New Jersey, on February 25, 1911, George Sylvester McLaughlin was married to Margaret C. Carroll, a native of Keyport, New Jersey, where she was born, October 13, 1885   She is the daughter of Martin J Carroll, now deceased and his wife, Catherine C (Donovan) Carroll, who is still living, her home being in Jersey City.   Dr and Mrs McLaughlin have two children, both living   Grace, born July 29, 1912, Margaret Carroll born May 4, 1914   Their home is at No. 225 Hale street, New Brunswick

---

EARL LAKE, a prominent figure in business life in Perth Amboy, president and manager of the Lake Coal Company, Incorporated, from the time of his coming to this community in 1911, has always had the welfare and advancement of Perth Amboy uppermost in his mind, and has given his earnest support to all movements calculated to advance business development

Earl Lake was born in Scranton, Pennsylvania, June 4, 1876, the son of David Crawford and Georgiana (Fitze) Lake   David C Lake was president of the First National Bank at Osage City, Kansas   The education of Earl Lake was obtained in the public schools of his native place, and after graduating from the local high school in 1894, he entered the Eastman's National Business College, completing the business and shorthand course in one year   In 1895 he secured a position as bookkeeper for the Searls Manufacturing Company, at Newark, New Jersey, subsequently becoming bookkeeper for the Elizabeth Hardware Company at Elizabeth, New Jersey, and later being promoted to office manager, where he remained until 1911, when he was appointed manager of the Perth Amboy branch of the business, which position he held until August 1, 1917   He then purchased the coal and wood business of Henry W Kinsey, and subsequently became president and manager of the company which is now incorporated under the name of the Lake Coal Company, and located at No 367 New Brunswick avenue   The enterprise has rapidly and consistently grown, due to Mr Lake's boundless energy

Mr Lake is a director of the People's Building and Loan Association, and secretary and treasurer of the City Realty and Investment Company, both of Perth Amboy   In politics he is a Republican but is in no sense of the word a politician, having avoided rather than sought public office   He is a member of the First Presbyterian Church of Perth Amboy, and president of its board of trustees   He also holds membership in the Raritan Yacht Club

On March 16, 1904, Mr Lake was united in marriage with Jessie Hanship, daughter of Edward R and Jennie Hanship, natives of Osage City, Kansas, who died October 22, 1918   Mr and Mrs. Lake were the parents of four children   Edward Earl, born March 13 1905, Jessie Kathryn, born January 17, 1908, Frederick David, born May 28, 1913, Anna Mae, born January 8, 1917   The family reside at No 98 High street, Perth Amboy.

EDMUND ANTHONY HAYES.—New Brunswick's lawyers of the early twentieth century constitute an element in her citizenship important both from a professional and a civic standpoint, and one of the most representative of these members of her bar is the man whose name stands at the head of this article Mr Hayes takes a loyal interest in everything relating to the welfare and prosperity of his native city, and can always be relied upon to do all in his power to further these ends

Edward R Hayes, father of Edmund Anthony Hayes, was born in Philadelphia, where his grandfather, Patrick Hayes, had settled on coming from Ireland Edward R Hayes was in business in Middlesex county, New Jersey He married Mary MacLaren, who was a native of New Brunswick, and of the eight children born to them the following are now living Edmund Anthony, mentioned below, the Rev John A ; Molita Barry, R Francis, and Kenneth At the age of fifty years, Mrs Hayes passed away at Highland Park, New Jersey, and her husband is still living at the same place

Edmund Anthony Hayes, son of Edward R and Mary (MacLaren) Hayes, was born May 9, 1889, in New Brunswick He graduated in June, 1905, from St Peter's High School. In June, 1912, he received his degree from the New Jersey Law School Having served a clerkship in the office of Irving Hoagland he was admitted, in 1912, at the November term of the Supreme Court, to the New Jersey bar In 1915, at the November term, he was admitted as a counsellor Ever since his admission to the bar, Mr Hayes has been continuously engaged in the active practice of his profession, having his office in the First National Bank building The professional position which he has carved out for himself proves him possessed of the essential qualities of a successful lawyer, and holds out a bright prospect for the future Devoted as he is to his profession, Mr Hayes is never neglectful of the duties of citizenship nor does he ignore the requirements of social intercourse His favorite recreations are fishing, gunning and boating, and he affiliates with the Knights of Columbus, the Royal Arcanum, and the Ancient Order of Hibernians His only club is the Catholic, of New Brunswick He is a member of St Paul's Roman Catholic Church, Highland Park, New Jersey

Mr Hayes married, April 23, 1916, at Woodbridge, New Jersey, Jane L Dunigan, a native of that place, daughter of Thomas F and Jane (Finn) Dunigan, the former a contractor of Woodbridge Mr and Mrs Hayes are the parents of one child, Edmund Anthony, Jr., born March 30, 1917

A man of keen perception, sound judgment and clarity of vision, and withal, sagacious, fair-minded and forceful, Mr Hayes is the type of man needed to insure the future of the New Jersey bar

---

JOHN SUTLIFF.—The days when New Jersey was called the State of Camden and Amboy, on account of the supposed domination of the Camden & Amboy Railroad in State affairs, are recalled by a reference to the fact that John Sutliff, when a boy of five years, was brought by his parents to South Amboy, at one time the eastern terminus of the road, and that at an early age he was employed on the freight docks, communication with New York being by steamboat All this of course antedated the coming of the Pennsylvania Railroad, which acquired the Camden & Amboy

John (2) Sutliff was born in Hightstown, New Jersey, October 19, 1858, son of John (1) and Mary Sutliff, his father born in Ireland John (1) Sutliff came to the United States when a young man and located in Trenton, New Jersey, where he married Later he resided in Hightstown, but in 1863 moved to South Amboy, New Jersey John and Mary Sutliff were the parents of nine children, six of whom are living Mrs Anna F Outten, of Brooklyn, New York, Mrs Elizabeth Morris, of Perth Amboy, New Jersey, John (2), of further mention, Jacob, of New York City, Joseph, of Jersey City; Mrs Mary E Houlihan, of New York City

When John (2) Sutliff was five years of age, his parents moved to South Amboy and there he attended public schools until twelve years of age. He then did a boy's work at the pottery nearby, and two years later entered the employ of the Camden & Amboy Railroad at their freight docks. In 1874 he was sent out with the construction train in charge of the water supply, this being followed by another period of employment in the brick yards at South Amboy Later he was connected with the New York & Long Branch Railroad, then was again employed on the coal docks, finally, on April 1, 1888, opening a grocery store at No 104 North Pine avenue Thirty-two years have since elapsed and he is still in business and at the same location His life has been one of activity, and he has richly earned the success which he has attained

A Democrat in politics, Mr Sutliff has served his city three terms of three years each as a member of the school board, and a portion of that period as president of the board He was city collector three years, 1911-1914, and for thirteen years was treasurer of the Star Building and Loan Association He is now a director of the same association, and serves the First National Bank of South Amboy in similar capacity He is a member of the Ancient Order of Hibernians, the Knights of Columbus, and the Benevolent and Protective Order of Elks, and his religious connection is with St Mary's Roman Catholic Church

Mr. Sutliff married, at Jamesburg, New Jersey, March 2, 1881, Mary A Callahan, born there February 22, 1858, daughter of John and Catherine (Mullane) Callahan Mr and Mrs Sutliff are the parents of eight children 1 Mary T., married Thomas P Farrell 2 Anna A, married James J Dwyer 3 John F, now his father's store assistant 4 Edward A, now of Cleveland, Ohio, with the National Biscuit Company, he is a veteran of the World War, served in France with the 77th Division of the American Expeditionary Forces. 5 Catherine S, married Romera R Everett, and resides in South Amboy 6 Joseph M, a priest of the Roman Catholic church, now serving the church at Gloucester City, New Jersey 7 Charles J, now his father's store assistant, he was in training at Camp Green, North Carolina, during the war period, but was not sent overseas 8 Elizabeth B, residing at home There are seven grandsons and one granddaughter in the family

CHARLES VAN LIEW BOOREAM.—The Booraem, Booream, Boerum, and Van Boerum families all spring from William Jacobse, who came from the village of Boerum in Friesland, Holland, to New Amsterdam, in 1657, and settled in Flatbush, Long Island To the Dutch *Van* (meaning from) the name of the village was added and the surname became Van Boerum, (William Jacobse from Boerum). The founder, William Jacobse, married Gertje Hendrickse, and two of their sons, Hendrick and Jacob, came to New Amsterdam with their parents

The Middlesex county family descends through the eldest son, Hendrick Willemse Van Boerum, a landowner of Flatbush, and his wife, Maria (Ariaens) Van Boerum, their son, Hendrick Van Boerum, who moved to Bound Brook, New Jersey, changed his name to Booraem, his son, Nicholas Booraem, born near Bound Brook, New Jersey, in 1714, settled near New Brunswick, Middlesex county, New Jersey, and is the founder of that branch of the family. His son Nicholas (2) Booraem, was a soldier of the Revolution, and his grandson, Nicholas (3) Booraem, was a colonel in the War of 1812, a member of the New Jersey Legislature, associate judge of the Court of Common Pleas, and for forty-two years treasurer of Middlesex county Charles Van Liew Booream is a son of John Van Liew and Caroline (Vincent) Booream, his father born in Milltown, Middlesex county, New Jersey, his mother in New York State John Van Liew Booream was for many years manager of a lumber company in Milltown, after which he became postmaster of the village, an office which he was later compelled to resign on account of ill health He is now living in Milltown, retired

Charles Van Liew Booream was born in Milltown, New Jersey, June 12, 1891, and there was educated in the public schools He began business life as an employee of the Michelin Tire Company, where he remained about two years, then joined the Milltown Coal and Lumber Company, of which his father was manager, and when he later resigned to accept the postmastership he was succeeded as manager by his capable son. Mr Van Liew Booream is a Democrat in politics, a member of the Methodist Episcopal church, the Improved Order of Red Men, United Order of American Mechanics (both Junior and Senior) and of the Michelin Club of Milltown. He is one of Milltown's popular young business men, and is deeply interested in all that concerns the welfare of the village in which his life has been spent

Mr Booream married, in New Brunswick, New Jersey, November 22, 1916, Barbara Lins, born there, December 29, 1892, daughter of Adam Philip and Catherine (Steinmacher) Lins, both born in Germany, her father coming to the United States at the age of twelve years, her mother at the age of sixteen Mr and Mrs Booream are the parents of a son, Charles Van Liew Booream, Jr

---

DR LOUIS P. KARSHMER, one of the many young progressive dentists of New Brunswick whose patrons in that city are numerous, especially among the younger set of the Hebrew population, is a native of Russia

Dr Karshmer's father, Morris Karshmer, is a retired merchant, living in New Brunswick He was born in Russia, but came to this country many years ago, locating for some time in New York City, but later, moving to New Brunswick, he opened a general merchandise store on French street, remaining there for six years His wife, Mindel Rubenstein, also was a native of Russia They had seven children 1 Harry, now a grocer in New Brunswick 2 A child who died in infancy. 3 Sarah, who died at the age of nineteen 4 Benjamin, a manufacturer living in New York City 5 Louis P, of further mention 6 Fannie, unmarried, a school teacher, living at home 7 Nathan, living at home and now a student in the medical department of George Washington University, he also is a graduate of the high school

Born in Russia, but coming to America when a very small child with his parents, Dr Karshmer has grown up to manhood in the atmosphere and with the many advantages of the United States His early boyhood was spent in New York City, where he attended the public schools, but when he was nine years old his family removed to New Brunswick and he was sent to the public schools of that city He became a pupil in the grammar school, from which he graduated in 1910, then entered the high school, taking a four years' course and graduating in 1914 For a year after this he was a student at Rutgers College, New Brunswick, taking a preparatory course for entrance in the New York College of Dentistry After a three years' course at that college he graduated, in 1918 and at once began the practice of his profession, with offices at No 360 George street, New Brunswick

Dr Karshmer has one great hobby and that is athletics in every form While a pupil in the New Brunswick High School he played on the baseball team and is equally agile in basketball or on a football team Swimming is another one of his accomplishments, and he makes it a point to keep up his practice in all these lines He is a member of the Young Men's Christian Association and of the Young Men's Hebrew Association, greatly enjoying the opportunities for athletic exercises in both organizations He and all the members of his family are members of the Synagogue

In New Brunswick, on February 22, 1919, Dr Louis P Karshmer and Rose Sheinaus were united in marriage They have one child, Robert Eugene, born February 11, 1920 Mrs Karshmer was born in New York City, and is the daughter of Abraham and Fannie (Orell) Sheinaus Mr Sheinaus is an electrical engineer in Brooklyn, in the employ of the Edison Company Dr Karshmer and his wife reside in the Highland Park section of New Brunswick, at Abbott and Eighth avenues

---

FRANK RUDOLPH NEWMAN was born in Liverpool, England, June 5, 1856 He attended the public schools there until he was seventeen years of age, when he set sail for America and upon landing in New York City went immediately to Newark, New Jersey, where he became a reporter, later an editor In 1885 he came to Perth Amboy,

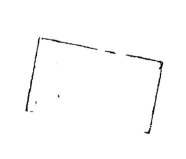

Thomas H. Riddle

New Jersey, where he has been engaged in the printing business ever since and is the pioneer here in his particular line of occupation He is a member of the International Typographical Union, No 657, and affiliates with PoAmbo Tribe, No 65, Improved Order of Red Men In politics Mr Newman was a staunch Republican until about 1902, when he opposed party machinery and affiliated himself with the 'New Idea" movement A few years later, as a member of the executive committee of both the McKinley Club and later on, the Roosevelt Progressive Club, he was actively engaged in the support of his party's candidates He never aspired to office himself, but was always in the front ranks in the securing of the best timber for offices of any importance. He takes particular pride in the possession of an autograph letter from the late President Roosevelt, sent to him in appreciation of work done in his behalf His hobby is fishing, and he also takes a keen delight in gardening, and is a great reader

Mr Newman married, September 27, 1884, Anna Louise Van Pelt, daughter of the late Joseph and Jane (Ling) Van Pelt, formerly of Rahway, New Jersey Mr and Mrs Newman are the parents of nine children Frank E J , Jennie A B , wife of J H Arrowsmith, of Albany, New York, Raymond LeRoy, Joseph J , William McKinley, Georgeanna ; Frances Ling , and a pair of twins, Harry S A and Emeline H E

Since 1919 Mr and Mrs Newman have resided in Tottenville, Staten Island, New York

The position which Mr Newman occupies in the business development of Perth Amboy represents the reward of unremitting labor and a fixed determination to achieve a responsible place, while in his advancement he has known no deviation from the strictest probity and the most upright methods

---

THOMAS HENRY RIDDLE, an Englishman by birth, and a resident of his native home for the early years of his life, has been a resident of New Brunswick for the past thirty years. His parents were born in England and spent all their lives there, his mother, Elizabeth (Cowling) Riddle, dying at Plymouth, England, in 1883, his father, Jacob Riddle, still living in Plymouth at the age of ninety-six years He was a contractor, in business there for many years, but has lived, for a long time back, in retirement Jacob and Elizabeth (Cowling) Riddle had fourteen children, but of this large family only six are now living, five of them residing in England They are Elizabeth , Thomas Henry, the only one in America , George, John, Carrie and William

Thomas Henry Riddle was born in Plymouth, England, May 12, 1860 He attended the common schools in that city until thirteen years of age, leaving them to become an apprentice in the brick laying, stone cutting and stone mason trade When the young man reached the age of twenty, he came to the United States, landing in New York City in 1880 Remaining there for the next few years, Mr. Riddle worked at his trade in various states, Pennsylvania, Kentucky and New York, but in 1891, locating permanently in New Brunswick, he entered into the contracting business, frequently his work has taken him temporarily into various sections of the country, Indiana, Illinois, Michigan, West Virginia, and Ohio, he having done quantities of railroad bridge and railroad construction work in all these States He also built the locks for the government at Ford, Kentucky, across the Kentucky river, and the power house at Sault Sainte Marie, Michigan, for the Michigan & Lake Superior Power Company

About 1912 Mr Riddle opened offices in the New Brunswick Savings Institution building, at No 102 Church street, and in the years that he has located there he has done contract work in the county of Middlesex, city of New Brunswick, and also in Essex and Monmouth counties He built the Albany street bridge, now in use, and is the contractor for the improvements going on at the present time (1920) in George street, New Brunswick Mr Riddle has erected many railroad bridges and other large works, among them being the Walnut Lane bridge, in Philadelphia, the largest span concrete bridge in the world at that time, 1906-08

While his ever-increasing business occupies most of Mr Riddle's time and attention, he always greatly enjoys a gunning trip in the way of recreation, or a good game of baseball In all matters pertaining to the work of the Free Masons, he has been particularly active, having taken all steps up to the thirty-second degree He is a member of Hamilton Lodge No 274 of Philadelphia, Pennsylvania, Scott Chapter, No 4 Royal Arch Masons, Scott Council, No 1, Royal and Select Masters, Temple Commandery No 18 Knights Templar, State of New Jersey, Lulu Temple, Ancient Arabic Order Nobles of the Mystic Shrine of Philadelphia, Philadelphia Consistory, Scottish Rite, Philadelphia, Pennsylvania, and is now (1921) grand commander of the Knights Templar of New Jersey He is also a member of the Independent Order of Odd Fellows, and of the Knights of Pythias, also the Benevolent and Protective Order of Elks, and the Royal Arcanum Mr Riddle has been active in the work of the Young Men's Christian Association, and is a prominent member of the Board of Trade He is a director of the Masonic Temple Association, also the Elks Building Corporation His clubs are the Craftsmen's and New Brunswick Mr Riddle and his family attend the First Reformed Church of New Brunswick

In Rochester, New York, on December 15 1884, Thomas Henry Riddle was married to Matilda Christ a native of Pennsylvania Three children were born of this marriage, but the last two died in infancy, the only surviving one being a daughter, Caroline Elizabeth, born December 29 1886, now the wife of Alexander W Quackenboss living on Adelaide avenue, Highland Park Mr and Mrs Riddle reside at No. 269 Seaman street, New Brunswick

---

JABEZ HOLLAND HELM —The fact that Mr Helm has been but a few years numbered among the practising lawyers of New Brunswick does not exclude him from a place on the list of the city's known and respected members of the bar In fraternal circles Mr. Helm is a figure of prominence, and as a citizen can always be relied upon to do his utmost in the promotion of any plan having for its object the betterment of community conditions

Jabez Holland Helm was born March 7, 1882, in New Brunswick, and is a son of John A and Alice (Cronk) Helm John A. Helm was a well-known carpenter and stair-builder The education of Jabez Holland Helm was received at the New Brunswick High School, and after completing his course of study he became a law student in the office of Alfred S March and Freeman Woodbridge In 1916, at the June term of the Supreme Court, he was admitted to the New Jersey bar as attorney, being admitted as counsellor at the June term of 1919 On March 19, 1917, Mr. Helm opened an office of his own in New Brunswick, in the National Bank building, and has since, by his own unaided efforts, won marked recognition both from the legal fraternity and the general public In politics Mr Helm is a Republican and has actively identified himself with the work of the organization He affiliates with New Brunswick Lodge, No 6, Independent Order of Odd Fellows, Middlesex Encampment, No. 43, Independent Order of Odd Fellows, Palestine Lodge, No 111, Free and Accepted Masons, Scott Chapter, No 4, Royal Arch Masons, Scott Council, No 1, Royal and Select Masters, New Brunswick Forest No 12, Tall Cedars of Lebanon In both the Independent Order of Odd Fellows lodges he is a past officer His clubs are the Craftsmen's and the New Brunswick Boat He is a member of Livingston Avenue Baptist Church

Mr Helm married, December 10, 1910, in New Brunswick, Florence May Smith, daughter of Benjamin I and Mary (Dunn) Smith, and they are the parents of three children. Augusta, born March 2 1912, Benjamin Holland, born September 2, 1914, and Jane, born September 10, 1916 The family home is at No 14 Stratford place

Mr Helm's career has opened auspiciously, and inasmuch as he is at the same time acquiring a lucrative practice and a well-founded reputation for ability and integrity, a bright future seems opening before him

---

CHARLES M SCHAEFER, manager of the New Brunswick branch of the Beith & Reilly Company, was born in New York City, September 18, 1880, the son of the late Henry C and Elizabeth (Overland) Schaefer. Henry C Schaefer was born in New York City, and died here, in 1890, at the age of fifty-seven years For many years he was engaged in the real estate business in his native place

The education of Charles M Schaefer was obtained in the public schools of his native place, after which he became identified with the concern with which he is still connected, first being employed with the main business, which was established in New York City in 1906, and later, in February, 1919, when this branch was established in New Brunswick, becoming its manager There never was a supply house to take care of the wants of the many factories in this community and when this one was established it proved to be of great benefit to the several manufacturing concerns of this vicinity   Henry F Teall is the assistant manager of this branch, he was born in England but came to this country when a young man and lived in Jersey City until 1919, when he accepted his present position

Mr Schaefer takes no active part in the affairs of the community, devoting his entire time to his ever-increasing business cares   He affiliates with Lodge No 278 Free and Accepted Masons but his home is his club

---

ANTHONY J GEBHARDT, a lifelong resident of Middlesex county, New Jersey, now located in the thriving borough of Highland Park, represents the progressive spirit of his community, and is one of the substantial, successful business men of his town

Anthony J Gebhardt was born in Milltown, Middlesex county, New Jersey, in 1864, and there resided until 1884 when he located in the city of New Brunswick and engaged in the grocery business   In 1889 he moved to Highland Park, Raritan township, where he opened a grocery store   He has continued in business there until the present (1921) and has in addition dealt extensively in Highland Park real estate   He is a director and treasurer of the Highland Park Building and Loan Association   He is a careful, energetic, capable business man, public-spirited in his citizenship and keeps abreast of the times.   In 1891 he was elected township committeeman of Raritan township and served three years—one term   In 1903 he was the candidate of his party for collector of taxes for Raritan township, the township at that time being strongly Republican, and he carried the township by thirty-four votes   He secured the division of the township into three lighting districts, was one of the men instrumental in securing signatures to the petition which brought the present water supply to Highland Park from New Brunswick, and was one of the organizers and a charter member of the fire department   In 1905 Highland Park was created a borough, and for six years Mr Gebhardt served as borough collector of taxes   From 1909 to 1917 he was a director of the Board of Freeholders from Middlesex county   He has been one of the men responsible for the development of the thriving borough of Highland Park, and through his influence he had the sidewalks widened on the Albany street bridge, had Raritan avenue paved by the county, and was responsible for many other improvements   He was also a member of the board that drew the plans for the present draw-bridge between New Brunswick and Highland Park   He has also made an enduring name for himself as a successful business man and public-spirited citizen

Mr Gebhardt married, May 9, 1887, Susie A Fleming, and they are the parents of four children   Mrs James L Rogers, Raymond A, at home, Mrs Joseph Ballon, and Mrs Richard Whitaker

---

JOHN HENRY INTEMANN, D D S, numbered among the younger generation of professional men of New Brunswick, New Jersey, has been for the past five years engaged in dentistry at No 336 George street.

John C Intemann, father of John Henry Intemann, was born in Germany, August 6, 1851, and died in New Brunswick, New Jersey, January 30, 1918, at the age of sixty-seven years When sixteen years of age, he set sail for the United States and upon landing in New York City remained there until 1886, when he removed to New Brunswick and established himself in the confectionery business, in which he continued until his death He married Bertha Elizabeth Hauck, a native of the province of Posen, Germany Mrs Intemann is now residing in New Brunswick Mr and Mrs Intemann were the parents of six children Edward A, a confectioner at New Brunswick, Arthur H a confectioner, Marie, deceased, John Henry, of further mention, William F, an electrical engineer of New Brunswick, Bertha, deceased

John Henry Intemann was born in New Brunswick, New Jersey, November 8, 1894, and it was here that the preparatory portion of his education was received After graduating from the local high school, in 1912, he immediately entered New York College of Dentistry, where he remained for two years, subsequently matriculating at Philadelphia Dental College, from which he was graduated in 1915 with the degree of Doctor of Dental Surgery Dr Intemann then returned to New Brunswick, where he has since been actively engaged in the practice of his chosen profession, having developed a large and high class practice, so that he is now regarded among the leaders here in his particular field of labor

He is affiliated with Palestine Lodge, No 111, Free and Accepted Masons, and is a member of the various professional organizations, including the National Dental Association, the New Jersey Dental Society, and the Middlesex County Dental Society, of which he is president, having been appointed in 1919 In religion he is a Baptist and attends the Livingston Avenue Baptist Church at New Brunswick During the World War, Dr. Intemann served on the Middlesex County Board, No 2, as dental examiner

Dr Intemann married, April 29, 1918, Margaret Ella Bartels, daughter of the late Frank and Gertrude Bartels Mrs Bartels married (second) J L McAuliffe, a resident of East Orange, New Jersey Dr and Mrs Intemann have no children Dr Intemann greatly enjoys hunting and fishing and spends much of his spare time thus employed

ARTHUR A. DETER —The mercantile and industrial activities of the town of Woodbridge, New Jersey, call for many kinds of skill in the men who are carrying the burdens of the hour Arthur A Deter is an authority along chemical lines Mr Deter was born in Woodbridge, September 30, 1878, and is a son of Anthony and Helen (Gillis) Deter, both long residents of Woodbridge

As a boy Mr Deter gained a practical and thorough foundation for future success in the excellent public schools of the town, later entered upon special courses of study along his chosen line of effort He took up chemistry and ore and copper sampling The need of this knowledge applies to many of the industries located in this part of New Jersey, and Mr Deter's work is not limited to local demands   He has won his way to a high position, and is widely sought for work demanding special knowledge of this nature   His success has been gained by steady application and patient endeavor

Mr Deter, for the past ten years, has borne a share in the public life of Woodbridge   His standing among the people of the town is clearly evinced by the fact that, while himself affiliated with the Republican party, he was elected to the Town Council from a Democratic ward   He was elected for a term of two years, in 1911, and the call of the people has held him continuously in the same position up to the present time.   Mr Deter is a member of Perth Amboy Lodge, No 784, Benevolent and Protective Order of Elks, and of the Royal Arcanum, of Woodbridge.   He is also a member of the Perth Amboy and Woodbridge Gun clubs

On January 26, 1906, Mr Deter married Anna Emhorn, and they have five children   George Horace Evelyne Irma and Arthur Robert

---

GEORGE ENGLAND BROWN was born in Worthington, Massachusetts, October 7, 1841, and died in Highland Park Illinois, April 19, 1895   He was a son of Timothy Harrington and Ermina (Drury) Brown   He was educated in the public schools of Worthington and in the academy in Sherburne Falls, Massachusetts and at a business college in the State of Wisconsin   Early in his career he taught school for two years, then entered the office employ of the New York Central Railroad Company and later transferred his services to the Pennsylvania Railroad and to other railroads of the East   He next spent two years in the lumber business in New Brunswick, New Jersey, going thence to Leadville Colorado, where he was engaged in silver mining   After returning East he located in South River, New Jersey, where he engaged in the real estate business until his passing.   Mr Brown was a Democrat in politics and served in several offices, including a term in the State Legislature   He was also called for service in several town offices, including the school board   He was a member of the Masonic order and the Knights of Pythias his religious affiliation being with the Protestant Episcopal church

Mr Brown married, in South River New Jersey, November 9 1865, Mary Elizabeth Martin, daughter of Daniel B and Sarah T Martin, her father a chief engineer and engineer-in-chief in the United States Navy, and was stationed for four years in Washington, D C   Three children were born to Mr and Mrs George E Brown: Daniel B Martin, Sarah T Martin, and Ermina Drury who married William H Kline   Mrs Brown survives her husband and continues her residence in South River

---

HENRY FRANK ZERFING, D. D S, numbered among the professional men of New Brunswick, New Jersey, admittedly occupies a leading position, gained through natural ability combined with close application and perseverance factors that have contributed the most in this country toward making our successful men   Dr Zerfing, who has been so intimately associated with the welfare of this community since taking up his residence here in 1897, and who is as well known in social circles as he is among the dental fraternity, is a native of Ashland, Pennsylvania, where he was born, May 10, 1871, the son of Aaron and Catherine (Smith) Zerfing

Aaron Zerfing, father of Henry F Zerfing, was born in Schuylkill county, Pennsylvania, October 20, 1836, and died at Scranton, Pennsylvania, in 1908, at the age of seventy-two years   He was a carpenter by trade   During the Civil War he enlisted in the Union army   His wife, Catherine Smith, was born in Schuylkill county, in 1842, and died there in 1876, at the age of thirty-four years   To Mr and Mrs Zerfing were born five children. Wilson, a dentist at Philadelphia, and director of the dental clinic in the dental department of the University of Pennsylvania, Ida, wife of Dr R J Ritz, of Scranton, Pennsylvania, Henry Frank, of further mention, Charles E, a physician at Los Angeles, California, Laura, deceased

Henry Frank Zerfing son of Aaron and Catherine (Smith) Zerfing, is a direct descendant of the Zerfing family who came to this country from Germany in the middle of the eighteenth century, the records showing that the Zerfings paid taxes at Valley Forge in 1789   The preliminary education of Dr Zerfing was obtained in the public schools of his native place   After graduating from the Ashland High School in 1888, he secured a position in the Engineers' Corps with the Reading Railroad, where he remained for two years   In the meantime, however, he had decided to adopt the profession of dentistry as his career, so with this end in view, matriculated in the dental department of the University of Pennsylvania and was graduated with the degree of Doctor of Dental Surgery in 1897   Having decided to establish himself in the practice of his profession at New Brunswick, New Jersey, he came here immediately and opened an office and in 1911 moved to the National Bank building, which has been his headquarters ever since   His practice is a large and widely extended one, and he has the affection as well as the confidence of his patients

Dr Zerfing affiliates with Union Lodge, No 19, Free and Accepted Masons, Scott Chapter, No 4, Royal Arch Masons, and being of a social nature, holds membership in the Union and Country clubs of New Brunswick   In religion he is a Baptist, and attends the First Church of that denomination

On September 2, 1897, Dr Zerfing was united in marriage with Sallie A Wylie, daughter of Robert J and Elizabeth (Dally) Wylie, both deceased, but formerly residents of Woodbridge   Dr and Mrs Zerfing are the parents of one child, Ruth, born March 7, 1901   The family home is at No 240 Lincoln avenue, Highland Park, New Jersey   Dr Zerfing's hobby is golf and much of his spare time he devotes to this particular recreation

---

JOSEPH MARK.—The office of mayor which Joseph Mark held for thirteen years was tendered him each recurring term by his townsmen with the feeling that the proper thing to do is to continue a faithful official in office He was a native son, born in South River, Middlesex county New Jersey, December 6 1865, died October 9, 1920, son of Bernard and Theresa Mark, his father a shoemaker

Joseph Mark was educated in private schools He spent his life in South River and was one of the best known business men of the borough. In 1900 he was elected mayor of South River and served thirteen years, for 13 he was successively reëlected at the expiration of each term He was postmaster of the borough for six years, and highly esteemed for his manly, upright life He was a member of the Junior Order of American Mechanics, Patriotic Order Sons of America, Knights of Pythias, Improved Order of Red Men, Benevolent and Protective Order of Elks; Nonpareil Club and the Methodist Episcopal church

Joseph Mark married, in South River, September 7, 1904, Clara Kessler, daughter of George and Marie Kessler Mr and Mrs Mark were the parents of four children Joseph George, born May 23, 1905, Bernard Francis, born October 27, 1906, Emma Theresa born February 3, 1908, Marie, born March 12, 1909

MICHAEL CARL SPINELLI—The Spinelli family of New Brunswick was founded in that city by Michael Spinelli, born in Italy, who at the age of twenty-one, in 1871, came to the United States, finding a home in Brooklyn, New York For twenty years he conducted a fruit business in Brooklyn, and in 1893 moved to New Brunswick, New Jersey, where he established a junk business, which he conducted for ten years He died August 14, 1910 Mr Spinelli married Marie Rose Zita, born in Italy, who came to the United States at the age of fourteen They were the parents of fourteen children, four of whom are here named Peter D, a member of Spinelli Brothers Garage and automobile accessories, married and has a son, Michael, Rose C, married Frank Piazzo, and has three children, Antoinetta, Salvator, and Michael, Michael Carl, of further mention, Dominick, a high school student

Michael Carl Spinelli was born in New Brunswick, December 5, 1895, and there has spent his years He attended public school until sixteen years of age, then for a time was in the employ of Johnson & Johnson His next position was with a moving picture house, remaining there two years, going thence to Easton, Pennsylvania, where he spent three years In 1916, he opened a garage at No 4 Prospect street, New Brunswick, known as Spinelli Brothers Garage, his partner being his brother, Peter D Spinelli They maintain an automobile livery service in connection with the garage, and at the corner of French and Bayard streets have an accessory store, where a complete stock for automobiles is carried. The business is a success, and Spinelli Brothers are rated as men of energy, thoroughly reliable and capable Michael C Spinelli is a member of the Improved Order of Red Men, and St. Peter's Roman Catholic Church

Mr Spinelli married, in Easton, Pennsylvania, in 1915, Mary E Mc-Laughlin, born in Pattenburg, New Jersey, daughter of John and Mary Emma McLaughlin, her mother yet living, a resident of Trenton, New Jersey Mr and Mrs Spinelli are the parents of two children Mary and Peter

RALPH ENGLISH SEAMAN, son of Frederick and Anna (English) Seaman, was born in Perth Amboy, New Jersey, December 28, 1882 He received his preliminary education in the local public schools, and after graduating from the high school in 1900 he studied for three and one-half years in Lafayette College, Easton, Pennsylvania It having been decided that he follow in his father's footsteps for his business career, he prepared himself at Columbia University College of Pharmacy, from which institution he was graduated in 1907, and immediately returned to Perth Amboy and associated himself with his father's business, which was located at that time at No 56 Smith street, in 1910 moving to the present location, No 60 Smith street Whether Mr Seaman is considered as a business man or a citizen he must be considered a success, for his business is prosperous and his standing as a citizen is high

Mr Seaman affiliates with the Benevolent and Protective Order of Elks and the Free and Accepted Masons He is also a member of the Raritan Yacht Club, and his hobby is gunning, in which recreation he engages during some of the leisure time which he can spare from his ever increasing business activities. Any reference to his appearance and manner would be out of place here, inasmuch as his years of successful business and good citizenship have made them thoroughly familiar to a large number of the residents of Perth Amboy

Mr Seaman married, in Perth Amboy, Clara Hardiman, a daughter of James and Mary Hardiman, both of Perth Amboy There are no children

---

MARINO VINCENT PALISI, JR, numbered among the younger men of the Perth Amboy business world who give promise of marked and well-deserved success, was born in Perth Amboy, New Jersey, August 12, 1894, a son of Marino Palisi, who was born in Isola Salina, Italy, and has long been a resident of Perth Amboy He is now fifty-eight years of age, but still has a fruit store at No 132 Smith street, which he established thirty years ago He came to this country at the age of twenty-one years He married, in New York City, Frances Tesoriero, who was born in his own native city in Italy They had nine children, of whom five are now living Marina, Marino Vincent, Dominick, Anthony and John

Marino Vincent Palisi, Jr, received his education in the public schools of Perth Amboy He began his life career by working in his father's fruit and grocery store at No 132 Smith street, Perth Amboy He was a natural salesman even when a young lad and was well liked by his father's customers But he was ambitious to handle larger interests, believing himself capable of going out and finding trade and building up a business on a larger scale So he became associated with P C Richardson & Company, of New York City, in the capacity of traveling salesman He remained with them for two years, then determined that whatever success he achieved in life would be for himself instead of turning it over to another So on April 15, 1920, with the beginning of perhaps the greatest motoring season in the history of mechanical vehicles, he established the National Auto Supply Company, at No 446 Amboy avenue His friends are certain that his success is assured. Unquestionably he is taking rapid strides forward, and will soon be among the leaders in his line

Mr Palisi is a man of public spirit, and prominent in the social world, being particularly active in the work of those societies which promote the welfare of Americans of Italian birth or parentage. He is a member of the Sons of Italy, and also of the Knights of Columbus He is a fine musician, playing the E-flat tuber, and for two years has been vice-president of the Musicians' Union, of Perth Amboy He is manager of the Columbus Italian Union Band, of Perth Amboy This organization gave gratis a great deal of their time in all public drives and demonstrations during the World War. He was a member of the New Jersey State Militia Reserve, and took an active part in the band of the regiment He was first sergeant, and later second lieutenant, and also took an active part in assisting after the explosion at Morgan, New Jersey

Mr Palisi married, in Perth Amboy, March 5, 1916, Amelia Rossi, daughter of Alfred and Gervasia (Occhialini) Rossi Mrs Palisi was born in Rome, Italy, her father is a modeller, living in Perth Amboy, whose work is in New York City The family attend the Italian Church of the Holy Rosary

---

GEORGE W WOOD —As cashier of Fords National Bank, of Fords, Middlesex county, New Jersey, Mr Wood is well known and popular He is deeply interested in the welfare of his adopted town and always aids or leads in every movement to make Fords a desirable place in which to locate He is the son of George R and Ida L (Hamilton) Wood, who are descendants of old Staten Island and Brooklyn families

George W Wood was born on Staten Island, New York, August 2, 1891, and after graduating from the public schools, he spent three years in high school, and next took a business course in Trainor's Private School (now Trainor's Business College), at Perth Amboy, and in 1908 entered the employ of the Perth Amboy Trust Company as clerk For nine years he remained with that institution, rising to the postion of teller, after which time he spent two years as teller with the Elizabeth Trust Company, then in September, 1919, he accepted his present position as cashier of the Fords National Bank, being the first cashier of that institution He is also secretary of the Fairfield Building and Loan Association, a member of the Masonic order, the Junior Order of United American Mechanics, the Young Men's Christian Association the Raritan Yacht Club, Junior Club, Travel Club of America, and the First Presbyterian Church of Perth Amboy

Mr Wood married, February 27, 1915, Bessie C Sofield, of Perth Amboy, daughter of John Ellis and Laura A Sofield, of an old Middlesex county family The Wood home is in Fords

RALPH JAMES FAULKINGHAM —Among the many physicians who live in New Brunswick none has a practice of wider scope than Dr Ralph James Faulkingham From his early manhood he has devoted all his energies to his beloved profession, the years spent in preparation being the necessary "foreword" of the later career

Dr. Faulkingham claims New England as his birthplace, having been born on November 26, 1884, at West Jonesport, Maine, his father, James H Faulkingham, being a fisherman of that seaport town Dr Faulkingham's mother was, before her marriage, Flora E Woodward Their son, Ralph James, was given every advantage in the way of education from the primary school to his graduation in 1904 from the Jonesport High School He remained at home for only a short time, for he desired to obtain college training and so entered Colby College, at Waterville, Maine, from which institution he graduated in 1910 Following this he matriculated at Bowdoin Medical College, where after a four years' course he became, in 1914, the proud possessor of the degree of Doctor of Medicine and with it the treasured "sheepskin."

During his college days, Dr Faulkingham took an active part in the fraternal life surrounding him, being a member of the Zeta Psi fraternity and of Alpha Kappa Kappa, of which he had the honor to be president He is also connected with a benevolent society, the Improved Order of Red Men The doctor is now giving special attention to surgery He is a member of the Middlesex County and New Jersey State Medical societies, the American Medical Association, and of the medical section of the Rutgers Club He is also a member of the medical staff of St Peter's Hospital Dr Faulkingham and his family attend the Baptist church of New Brunswick

On May 31, 1910, Ralph James Faulkingham was married to Lucy May Brown, the ceremony taking place at Waterville, Maine She was the daughter of Fred H and Clara (Dinsmore) Brown To them two children have been born Ralph Brown, born September 12, 1912, and Flora Blanche, born July 15, 1917 Their home is at No 61 Livingston avenue

THE GREENSPAN BROTHERS.—There is no name better known or more highly respected in mercantile and commercial circles in Perth Amboy, New Jersey, than that of Greenspan, represented there as it is by four brothers, joint owners of the large and prosperous mercantile establishment at No 314 Elm street, known as Greenspan Brothers Company Isadore, Jacob, Hyman and Philip Greenspan are all natives of Russia, where the first named was born, May 30, 1892, and sons of Samuel and Diana Greenspan, of that country The father, Samuel Greenspan, came to the United States with his wife and four children at the age of fifty years, having been preceded to this country by his son Hyman, who had settled in New York City and there engaged in the paper and box business The elder Mr Greenspan established himself in the milk business in Brooklyn, New York, where he met with marked success, but in 1900 removed to Perth Amboy, New Jersey, and con-

tinued in the same line until 1916, when he retired There he still
makes his home, surviving his wife, who died April 15, 1918, at the age
of sixty-eight years

Isadore Greenspan was but six years of age when he accompanied
his parents to the United States, and it was in Brooklyn that he began
his education in the public schools Two years later he came to Perth
Amboy and there continued his schooling until he was of an age to
take part in business He then founded and for two years conducted
a retail grocery store at No 200 Madison avenue, Perth Amboy, displaying an unusual degree of business ability, and meeting with a well-
deserved success In the meantime his brother Hyman, who had been
in the paper and box line for some years in New York City, had retired
therefrom and with another brother, Jacob had founded the wholesale
grocery business in Perth Amboy in 1900, and at the end of his two
years' success in the retail branch of the trade, Isadore Greenspan joined
them in the enterprise, as well as the fourth brother, Philip Since that
time the concern has grown greatly in size and importance and is now
justly regarded as one of the most important of its kind in the region,
it being engaged in wholesale groceries, importing, coffee roasting, and
as a commission mercantile house The four brothers are also active in
the general life of the community, Isadore being a member of the Masonic
order, Hyman of the Benevolent and Protective Order of Elks, while
Jacob and Philip belong to both organizations All four brothers attend
Temple B'rith Mordicai, and are members of the Young Men's Hebrew
Association

Isadore Greenspan was united in marriage, October 12, 1917 in Perth
Amboy, with Anna Davidson, a native of that place, and they are the
parents of one daughter, Diana Jacob Greenspan married Beatrice
Eiten, and they are the parents of two children, Jeannette and Mortimer
Hyman Greenspan married Jennie Borak, and they also are the parents
of two children, Abraham and Rebecca Philip Greenspan married
Frances Davidson, and they are the parents of three children, as follows
Lillian Walter and Francis

THEODORE UNKEL, late owner of the Sayreville Hotel, which
he conducted for many years, always took a keen and active interest in
the affairs of the community, and when his death occurred, November 28,
1919, Sayreville lost one of her foremost citizens Theodore Unkel was
a native of Germany, born May 22, 1870 He was the son of Rudolph
and Elizabeth (Clemens) Unkel, both of them natives of Germany Mr
Unkel was for many years a butcher in Sayreville Theodore Unkel
received his education in the local public schools, after which he became
associated with his father in business Upon coming to this country he
located in Sayreville, New Jersey, in 1884, and subsequently purchased
the hotel with which he was identified for so many years Upon his
death Mrs Unkel took over the entire charge of the house and has since
continued in its management In politics Mr Unkel was a Democrat,
and was long an important figure in public affairs, although caring noth-

ing for public office, but taking a deep interest in all that pertained to the public good. He affiliated with the Sons of Liberty, and in religion was a Roman Catholic, greatly devoted to the interests of his church.

On July 13, 1893, in New York City, Theodore Unkel was united in marriage with Anna Nagle, a native of Germany, the daughter of Sebastian and Antoinette (Hoffman) Nagle. To Mr and Mrs Unkel have been born twelve children: Max, born October 27, 1894; Theodore, born November 8, 1895; Elizabeth, born April 26, 1897; Jeanette, born December 21, 1898; Sebastian, born October 2, 1900; Gertrude, born September 4, 1904; John, born October 26, 1906; Lillian, born October 30, 1908; Augusta, born January 27, 1910; Madeline, born December 13, 1912; Randolph, born July 18, 1914, and George, born September 26, 1915.

WILLIAM MORRISON SMITH, now a prosperous plumber of Metuchen, New Jersey, son of James Benjamin and Elizabeth Smith, was born in Summit, Spottsylvania county, Virginia, fifty-three miles by rail north of Richmond, October 25, 1891. He was there educated in the public schools. Upon coming to a suitable age he learned the plumber's trade and has since followed that occupation. Mr Smith located in Metuchen, New Jersey, in 1914, and during the war period was employed in the government arsenal in Raritan. He is an Independent in politics, and a member of the Presbyterian church.

Mr Smith married, in Metuchen, June 23 1917, Ida May Compton, born in Metuchen, April 25, 1896, daughter of Charles and Phoebe K (Boylan) Compton, of an old Middlesex county family. Mr and Mrs Smith are the parents of twins, Doris and Oliver Compton, born December 23, 1918.

JAMES P GERITY.—Mr Gerity's father, Andrew Gerity, of Woodbridge, New Jersey, was born in Tipperary, Ireland. He came to the United States in 1857, and located in Woodbridge. He was married, September 18, 1864, by the Rev Edward A Braidy, at the Church of St Teresa corner of Rutgers and Henry streets, New York City, to Mary Jane Bolan. Mr Gerity passed his life in honest industry, respected by all.

James P Gerity, son of Andrew and Mary Jane (Bolan) Gerity, was born in Woodbridge, New Jersey, March 21, 1880. He attended St James' Parochial and Woodbridge public schools, but at the age of fifteen entered the employ of the Port Reading Railroad Company as an office boy under L J Barrett, then shipping agent for the company. He remained in the employ of the Port Reading Railroad Company for twenty-three years, 1895-1918, rising through the various grades of promotion to the position of general timekeeper and auditor. In 1918 he resigned as auditor to enter government service as deputy collector of internal revenue under Charles Duffy, chief of the New Jersey district. Mr Gerity was in charge of Federal taxes for Hunterdon and Somerset counties until September, 1919, when he resigned and entered business under the firm name of J P Gerity & Company, Woodbridge, opening an office in the First National Bank building, where he transacts a real estate and general insurance business

Mr Gerity is a Democrat in politics, and for three years, 1914-1917, was a member of the Town Committee, and from 1917 until the present time has been a member of the Middlesex County Democratic Committee A leader in local affairs, he has always taken a keen and active interest in the furtherance of any good movement which would be beneficial to Woodbridge He was the first to advocate permanent street pavements in Woodbridge, and largely through his efforts Main street was taken over by the County Board of Freeholders and improved with a permanent pavement He has been a director of the Woodbridge Building and Loan Association since its inception, secretary of the Woodbridge Knights of Columbus Building Association, member of the Woodbridge Knights of Columbus, serving the local council as second grand knight from 1907-1911, and in 1912-13 was district deputy He is a member of St James' Roman Catholic Church, Woodbridge, the Columbian Club, and the Woodbridge Exempt Firemen's Association

Mr Gerity has been greatly interested in athletic sports, and entire credit is due him for the field meets held under the Amateur Athletic Union in Woodbridge in 1910-11-12, when many of the leading amateurs of the county competed

Mr Gerity married, at Union Hill, New Jersey, April 19, 1907, Anna F Messenger, daughter of William T and Frances (Volkert) Messenger, her father born in New York City, her mother a native of Germany Mr and Mrs Gerity are the parents of two sons James Francis Xavier, born September 27, 1909; and George, born July 7, 1911

Mr Gerity is well and favorably known in the community with which he has been associated all his life, and is building up a good business in the lines he has chosen, real estate and general insurance

---

ALEXANDER FITZ RANDOLPH —The members of the Fitz Randolph family of New Jersey, descend from the family in England, which traces its ancestry through different branches to noble and even royal blood In this country they trace to the royal blood of New England a "Mayflower" passenger, and on both sides descent is both ancient and honorable.

Alexander Fitz Randolph of Middlesex county, is a son of Elkanah Fitz Randolph, who spent his life in New Jersey, a farmer, Seventh Day Baptist, and a Republican He was born October 9, 1797, and died in Plainfield, New Jersey, February 26, 1877 He married in Plainfield, Phoebe Drake, who was born March 21, 1802, died June 19, 1876 They were the parents of eight children, all of whom grew to adult years save one

Alexander Fitz Randolph, youngest of the children of Elkanah and Phoebe (Drake) Fitz Randolph, was born in Plainfield, New Jersey, July 4, 1844 He was educated in the public schools of Plainfield, and at Alfred University, Alfred, New York, an institution under the patronage of the Seventh Day Baptist Church After his college years were over, he returned to Plainfield, and has spent his life principally as a farmer, but for a few years was a merchant and for a time was employed in a factory His home for the past forty years has been on a farm in Piscataway township, Middlesex county, where he is living practically retired In politics he is a Republican, and for two terms served his township as school trustee He is a member of Mount Zion Lodge, No 135, Free and Accepted Masons, of Metuchen, New Market Grange, Patrons of Husbandry, and a member of the Seventh Day Baptist church

Alexander Fitz Randolph married, January 20, 1877, at Alfred, New York, Jessie Witter, born in New York State, September 3, 1856, daughter of Charles Henry and Abby K Witter, her father a farmer of New York State who gave his life for the Union cause, and died in Andersonville Prison, Georgia, April 20, 1864 Mr. and Mrs Alexander Fitz Randolph are the parents of four children 1 Phoebe Elfrieda, born October 15, 1877, she finished her education in the Plainfield High School 2 John Bryant, born December 3, 1884 3 Margaret Louise, born February 18, 1888, a graduate of Plainfield High School 4 Orson Witter, born September 26, 1892, was educated in Middlesex county public schools

---

WILLIAM A SILENCE —For more than a quarter of a century Oak Tree, Middlesex county, New Jersey, has been the scene of the business activity of William A Silence, who is meeting with creditable and well deserved success as the reward of his indefatigable labor, tireless energy and capable management He is a man whose word is as good as his bond, and whose transactions are conducted in a thoroughly business-like manner, thus insuring the continuance of the patronage accorded him in the beginning of his business career

The birth of William A Silence occurred in what was then the city of Brooklyn, New York, now the borough of Brooklyn, Greater New York November 9, 1869, a son of William A Silence, a native of the State of Maryland, a hatter by occupation, and his wife, Emma F (Depew) Silence, a native of Brooklyn, New York The schools of Brooklyn in the vicinity of his home were the means of his education, and he profitted by attending them He was a resident of his native city until the year 1894, when he removed to the State of New Jersey, locating in Oak Tree, Raritan township where he has since made his home His entire time and attention is devoted to the manufacture of cider and vinegar, which are of excellent quality, and these useful commodities are made in a plant which is suited to the purpose, modern in every particular, clean and neat in appearance, thus insuring the uniform quality of the articles manufactured Mr Silence holds membership in the South Plainfield Patriotic Order Sons of America He is a Republican in politics, and belongs to the Harding and Coolidge Club

The welfare and improvement of his community receives from him a hearty cooperation in all projects which have for their aim that object

Mr Silence married, February 22, 1893, in Oak Tree, Jane Laing, born in South Plainfield, New Jersey, August 17, 1866, daughter of Abel Laing, a native of South Plainfield, a tiller of the soil, and his wife, Cornelia C (Drake) Laing, a native of Oak Tree Two children were born to Mr and Mrs Silence, as follows Marion, born July 28, 1894, and William A (3), born March 13, 1910

HARVEY LeROY HULLFISH—When a young boy Harvey LeRoy Hullfish came with his parents to New Brunswick, New Jersey, and there has spent the years which have since elapsed. He has devoted himself chiefly to the automobile business as a salesman, and is one of the well known men of the trade He is also well known in the political field

Harvey LeRoy Hullfish was born in Jamesburg, Middlesex county, New Jersey, July 29, 1885, son of Giles H and Bertha M Hullfish, his father a merchant He was educated in New Brunswick public schools and in the Wilson Business College, New Brunswick He at once entered business life in New Brunswick, first as a grocery man, then for ten years in the automobile business, dealing both in new and second-hand cars He is still in that line as sales manager for Elwood E Waller & Son, handling Willys-Knight and Overland cars He was formerly manager for the New Brunswick Motor Car Company, was the first president of the New Brunswick Motor Trade Association, which he aided in organizing, and for three years he assisted in the management of the auto shows

In politics Mr Hullfish is a Republican, and for ten years was a member of the Middlesex County Committee, resigning to accept appointment on the Board of Elections of the Fourth Ward He was appointed clerk of the Martin Act Commission, was stenographer to the State Assembly one session, and is now a deputy sheriff and court officer holding these positions in connection with his automobile business He is a past officer of Goodwill Council, No 32, Junior Order of United American Mechanics, having served twelve and one-half years in office, and is a member of Orient Court. He is a member of the Goodwill Club, and of the Livingston Avenue Baptist Church

Mr Hullfish married, June 24, 1908, at New Brunswick, Mary C Whitfield, daughter of Jacob H and Julia Whitfield Mr and Mrs. Hullfish are the parents of a daughter, Elsie May Hullfish, born April 30, 1911

EUGENE WORDEN HOPE—For many years Eugene Worden Hope has been prominent among the prosperous business men of Perth Amboy, New Jersey, where he conducts a successful milk business and enjoys a large patronage in the surrounding community He is a member of a family that had its origin in the Island of Jersey, in the British channel off the coast of France, and which came from there and settled in Virginia in early days, where many of the Hopes continue to reside at the present time.

Mr Hope is a son of Luther Martin Hope, who was born at Modestown, Virginia, June 9, 1839, and came as a young man to Brooklyn, New York, and thence, later, to Perth Amboy, New Jersey For many years he carried on a mercantile business at the last named place, but during the latter years of his life retired and made his home on the old Billy Watson farm, now 'Hopelawn," in Perth Amboy, his death occurring there January 25, 1907 Luther Martin Hope married Katie Lee Coyle, of New York City, born February 2, 1840, and died December 15, 1907, they became the parents of nine children, as follows· Arthur H , Eugene Worden, with whom we are here especially concerned, Luther J , J Howard, Everett, who died in infancy, Annie A. who became the wife of George Liddle, of Fords, New Jersey, Mary L. who became the wife of John Harvey, of Tottenville, Staten Island, Elizabeth V , who became the wife of George Larrison of Perth Amboy Katie L , who became the wife of Edward Koch, of Perth Amboy

Eugene Worden Hope was born, June 11, 1862, at Brooklyn New York, and was but three years of age when his parents removed to Perth Amboy, where his childhood and early youth were passed As a lad he attended the Fairfield School at Fords Corners, New Jersey, but the circumstances of the family were such at that time that it became necessary for him to engage in some kind of remunerative occupation at an early age and, accordingly, when only eleven years old, he began to work for the Lehigh Valley Railroad, driving a horse and cart, receiving in compensation sixty cents a day. When seventeen years of age Mr Hope, who was of an enterprising and venturesome disposition left his father's home and went West, locating in North Dakota, where he remained for seven years, engaged in farming and raising wheat This period was the only one spent by him away from Perth Amboy, to which place he returned at the age of twenty-four, and where he has subsequently made his home Upon locating a second time at Perth Amboy, Mr Hope, who in the meantime had amassed a considerable capital, entered into the milk business and has continued successfully in this line ever since Under his skillful and far-seeing management a large and flourishing business has been built up, the conduct of which has always been along the highest standards of commercial integrity and fair play Mr Hope is a Republican in politics and takes a keen interest in all the vital issues of the day He is a member of the local lodge of the Royal Arcanum, the Eagle Athletic Club, and the Raritan Yacht Club In religious belief Mr. Hope is a Baptist, and he and the members of his family attend the church of that denomination at Perth Amboy

Eugene Worden Hope was united in marriage, September 20, 1904, at Perth Amboy, with Flora Martha Russell, a widow, and daughter of Charles and Sarah Russell, both now deceased Mrs Hope was the mother of one daughter by her former marriage, Helen, now the wife of Clarence Davis, of Staten Island Mr and Mrs Hope are also the parents of one daughter, Ruth Elizabeth, born December 27, 1917

STEPHEN FRANCIS SOMOGYI—Son of a scholarly father, Stephen F Somogyi inherited the professional instinct, and in his chosen line of activity, the law, he has built up a lucrative practice and firmly established himself in the public regard His residence and place of business is Perth Amboy, and he is one of the most successful among the younger lawyers of the county, his proficiency in the Hungarian and Slavic languages has gained for him a large clientele among the foreign born of Perth Amboy Stephen F Somogyi was born in Hungary in the city of Kassau, August 20, 1879, son of Michael and Josephine A (Oshslo) Somogyi Michael Somogyi was a professor in the Royal University of Kassau, and resided with his family in that city until his death occurred in 1882

Stephen F Somogyi received his elementary education in the schools and colleges of his native city. Assisted greatly by his scholarly father, he was well advanced in his studies when he came to America with his mother in 1890 They located first in Oliphant, Pennsylvania, where he continued his studies in the local schools until 1899, when he removed to Perth Amboy, New Jersey. Electing to follow the legal profession, he began to read law in the office of Joseph E Stricker, in the meanwhile attending the New York Law School, where he took a special course On June 3 1903, he was admitted to the Middlesex County Bar as an attorney, and immediately entered into the practice of his profession in Perth Amboy, opening an office in the Adelaide building on Smith street From there he removed his office to No 137 Smith street He was later admitted to practice as a counsellor, and now practices in the State and Federal courts of the district

For a number of years he was greatly interested in State and local politics He was county interpreter from 1907 until 1920, when he resigned from office His knowledge of European languages especially fitted him for that office in a community where a large percentage of the population is of foreign birth In 1915 he ran for the State Assembly on the Republican ticket, but as it was an out and out Democratic year, he was defeated He retains a lively interest in party affairs, and is an active worker for party success During the World War, 1917-1918, he served as a member of the Advisory Board in the Draft, and was himself enrolled in the New Jersey reserves and commissioned first lieutenant, serving until the close of hostilities During the Liberty Loan 'drives" he canvassed among the foreign born and was quite successful He is a member of the Benevolent and Protective Order of Elks, Royal Arcanum, and Raritan Yacht Club, of which he is one of the board of governors and chairman of the entertainment committee He is a lover of music and devotes much of his leisure time to that art being an unusually fine performer on the 'cello He was one of the organizers of the Dominant Society an orchestral association, and while it was in existence was its leader He is a member of the String Quintette, which has considerable local reputation, and is devoted to the study of classical music

Mr Somogyi was united in marriage, December 27, 1910, with Allie May Dayton, daughter of William and Anna Dayton, of Perth Amboy.

FREDERICK DAVID SPRUANCE, of New Brunswick, has had a somewhat varied life, both as to occupation and place of residence At the time of this writing he is engaged in the automobile business in New Brunswick

John Baylis Spruance, father of Frederick D Spruance, was born in Philadelphia and still lives there, engaged in the sugar brokerage business, with an office at Eleventh and Market streets He married Jessie McIntosh, who was born in Philadelphia Mr and Mrs Spruance have three children 1 Mabel, the wife of Charles R Fairland, of Jenkintown, Pennsylvania 2 Frederick David, of whom further 3 Florence Duncan, wife of Rev R B W Hutt, of Philadelphia

Frederick David Spruance was born in Philadelphia, January 27, 1884, remaining there and attending the primary school until he had reached the age of seven, when his family moved to Sheffield, Alabama Here he attended the public schools and later entered the Alabama Polytechnic Institute, taking the electrical engineering course, and graduating from that seat of learning in 1906 Following this he spent two and a half years in electrical construction work on the Panama Canal Mr Spruance next went West, where he was engaged in the transport service for more than a year, returning then to Sheffield, Alabama, taking up electrical construction work again for two and a half years In 1913 he went for the second time to Panama, remaining for eighteen months, when he came back to the United States and accepted a position with the DuPont Powder Company He remained with them for nearly four years, helping in the production of powder for the war work, going from this to New Brunswick and establishing a business of his own, the F D Spruance Automobile Company, at No 92 Schureman street His temperament is that of the hustler and his training has made him quick to grasp an opportunity He handles the Chevrolet, the Stearns-Knight, and the Premier cars, and also does general repair work

Mr Spruance is interested in several clubs in New Brunswick, being a member of the local lodge of Elks, the Middlesex County Automobile Club, and the Board of Trade Mr Spruance has a hobby, that of hunting, and during the season he may frequently be seen going off on an expedition with his dog and gun During a period spent in Philadelphia, he took considerable interest in military matters, being a member of the Second Regiment, Pennsylvania National Guard, holding the commission of captain

The marriage of Frederick David Spruance to Annie M Spear took place April 2, 1913 in Charleston, South Carolina, where Miss Spear was born She is the daughter of Horace P and Annie Mortimer (Cleckley) Spear, of Richmond, Virginia, where Mr Spear is engaged in the real estate business

Mr and Mrs Spruance went to Panama immediately after their marriage, and there they started their first housekeeping They now have a delightful home at No 117 South Fourth avenue, New Brunswick

There are no children of this marriage   Both are members of the Presbyterian church

The Spruance family is of French origin, the first of the name to emigrate to the United States was John Spruance, who landed at Lewes, Delaware, from France, in 1730

AUGUSTUS STELLE.—On the east side of the Raritan river, opposite New Brunswick and three miles east, lies the village of Stelton, named for the Stelle families who owned large farms in the district, and there lived most of their lives   They were among the highly regarded citizens of their times, and among their number were prominent men and women of agricultural, business, professional, public and social affairs of life

Augustus Stelle was a prominent agriculturist and large land owner. The farm mansion which he built is now (1921) the home of his daughters, who have never known any other residence than the old farm The farm came into possession of Augustus Stelle in 1840, and the house was built by him the same year, consequently the associations of a lifetime gather around the old homestead, and the place is very dear to the Misses Stelle   They are granddaughters of Isaac and Frances (Dunn) Stelle, the former born near New Brunswick, January 26, 1789, died June 6 1872, in Stelton, the latter born August 20, 1790, near New Brunswick, died March 3, 1876, in Stelton   Isaac Stelle was a farmer in this region all his life, and was well known   He and his wife were the parents of eight children   Samuel, Louis, Augustus, of whom further   Eliza, Phoebe, James, Prudence, and Alexander

Augustus Stelle, son of Isaac and Frances (Dunn) Stelle, was born October 23, 1815, in Piscataway township, Middlesex county, New Jersey, died at the homestead, January 14, 1899   He was educated in the district schools, and during his active years he was engaged in farming and in farm management   becoming possessed of many acres on the east side of the Raritan river   He was an influential Democrat, and a man of substance highly esteemed as a man of integrity and honor   He was a member of the Baptist church, which he liberally supported and regularly attended

Mr Stelle married, February 12 1840 in Plainfield, New Jersey, Maria Stelle, born in South Plainfield October 25, 1817, died January 15, 1899, surviving her husband but one day, they both being laid at rest in Piscataway Town Cemetery at the same time   Augustus and Maria (Stelle) Stelle were the parents of four children.   1 John, born June 4, 1842, in Stelton died September 29, 1914, at Hollywood, California, and is buried in the family plot in Piscataway Town Cemetery. He was a farmer until his retirement and removal to California   He married Mary Conaway, of Martin's Dock, New Jersey   She died January 16, 1920, at Washington New Jersey, without issue   2 Angelina A, born January 20, 1845, in Stelton   3 Julia R, born February 20, 1848, in Stelton   4 Spencer C born August 10, 1854, in Stelton   He has been variously occupied in life being at one time in the silk business

He is now living at Dalton, New Jersey. He married Ellen C. Conaway, a sister of his brother's wife, and two children have been born to them: Harry N., who died at the age of nine years, and Russel A., who died at the age of sixteen.

NELSON M. GILES.—After following different lines of mercantile pursuits, in which he achieved a certain degree of success, Nelson M. Giles, an enterprising and public-spirited citizen of Bound Brook, New Jersey, is now devoting his time and attention to the tilling of the soil, an occupation which calls for untiring energy, perseverance and careful management, characteristics which are fully developed in the person of the subject of this review.

Nelson M. Giles was born in Harris Lane, Bound Brook, Middlesex county, New Jersey, September 20, 1862, in the same house in which he now resides, his parents, Benjamin S. and Adeline A. (Harris) Giles, also residing in the same house, Benjamin S. Giles having been born in Middlesex county, one mile distant from the place now occupied by his son. Benjamin S. Giles was a blacksmith by trade, following this line of work profitably during the active years of his life.

Nelson M. Giles attended the common school adjacent to his home, and upon arriving at suitable age became a manufacturer of roofing material, following this occupation for twelve years, at the expiration of which time he changed his line of work and engaged in farming, and in addition to the arduous duties which falls to the lot of an agriculturist has added those of public office, serving at the present time (1920) in the capacity of collector for Middlesex borough. He is president of the borough of Middlesex Building and Loan Association, a member of the Republican County Committee, a member and trustee of the Presbyterian church, filling the latter office for two decades and a member of the order of Free and Accepted Masons, and the Knights of Pythias. He takes a keen interest in all that pertains to the growth and improvement of his native place, and well merits the confidence reposed in him.

Mr. Giles married, May 7, 1884, in Bound Brook, New Jersey, Jennie Blaine, born in Somerville, New Jersey February 1, 1864, daughter of Charles W. and Phebe (Vanarsdale) Blaine. Children: 1. Harry R., born January 16, 1886. 2. Benjamin H., born July 4, 1892. In 1917 he was drafted for service in the World War, went to camp for training, and was sent overseas, sailing from New York City, January 12, 1918. He was killed in battle, in France, October 5, 1918, thus adding another to the list who made the supreme sacrifice for their country. He had attained the rank of corporal, and was at the front for a period of five months. 3. Anna A., born September 22, 1895. 4. Albert M., born January 14, 1898. 5. Charles W., born December 11, 1900.

DENNIS FRANCIS DONOVAN came to America with his parents as a child of six years. Growing up in Perth Amboy, he is now one of the business men of the city, and well known throughout this section

Dennis Donovan, father of Dennis F Donovan, was born in County Cork, Ireland In his early manhood, he was employed on a railroad in England Upon coming to America, he located directly in Perth Amboy, and there worked on the Lehigh Valley coal docks until his death which occurred at the comparatively early age of fifty-one years Dennis Donovan married Johanna Sullivan, who was also born in County Cork, Ireland She came to this country with her husband, and died here, in 1913 at the age of sixty-five years They had eight children, of whom five are now living Anna, the wife of George Mickle, of New York City, Michael J, of Perth Amboy; Mary E, the wife of John Kelner, of Trenton, New Jersey, Dennis Francis, of whom further, and Katherine the widow of John Sleight, residing in Trenton

Dennis Francis Donovan was born in County Cork, Ireland, August 25, 1877 His education was begun at the public schools of Perth Amboy, New Jersey, when his parents came to America and took up their residence there, and was completed in St Mary's Parochial schools of that city At the age of fifteen he went out into the world to earn his own living, beginning life in the work of tile making After three years in this line, he worked on the railroad for three years, then, having saved enough to make a start for himself, he opened a hotel at No 314 Front street, Perth Amboy. The venture has been successful, and promises well for the future

Mr Donovan is a Democrat by political choice He is member of the Benevolent and Protective Order of Elks; of the Foresters of America and of the Improved Order of Red Men

Mr Donovan married, in Perth Amboy, on October 14, 1903, Helen Gertrude Smith, daughter of Peter and Margaret Smith She was born in Lambertville, New Jersey Her father died in Long Island City, at the age of sixty-five years, and her mother now lives at Whitestone, Long Island Mr and Mrs Donovan have two children Margaret Frances, born March 14, 1905, and Helen Olive, born June 11, 1909 The family attend St Mary's Roman Catholic Church

---

CHARLES GROVER WRAGE —Among the representative citizens of Dunellen, who have aided materially in its development, upbuilding and substantial progress, may be mentioned Charles G Wrage, a native of Flemington, Hunterdon county, New Jersey, born September 14, 1884, son of Henry and Catherine (Witt) Wrage, natives of Germany, from whence they emigrated to the United States in the year 1872 Henry Wrage was a contractor and builder by occupation, skillful and proficient in workmanship, just and equitable in all his transactions

Charles Grover Wrage attended the common schools in the vicinity of his home acquiring a practical education which fitted him for the duties of an active career Upon attaining a suitable age, he decided to follow in his father's footsteps, in this line of work, he gave his attention to familiarizing himself with the details, and in due course of time, in 1908, began operations as a builder and contractor, so continuing during the intervening years, and at the present time (1921) many buildings stand as monuments to his skill and ability along that line He is progressive in his methods and ideas, fully alive to the present-day needs of the public, and by giving the closest attention to the work he has chosen, noting every improvement and acting upon it, he is looked upon as a thoroughly reliable man, and is in receipt of an excellent patronage

Mr Wrage is a Presbyterian in religion, a Republican in politics, and a member of the Republican Club and the Benevolent and Protective Order of Elks He is highly respected and esteemed in the community, and exerts an influence for good upon those with whom he is brought in contact He was a member of the Dunellen Borough Council for three years, 1917-1920

Mr Wrage married, in New York City, February 12, 1908, Emma Miller born in New York City, December 30, 1884, daughter of Richard and Louisa (Raggar) Miller, natives of Germany, both now deceased Three children have been born to Mr and Mrs Wrage Beatrice, born September 8, 1910, Hazel, born August 25, 1912, Evelyn, born December 17, 1919 The house in which the family now resides, No 504 Walnut street, Dunellen, was erected by Mr Wrage in 1912

WILLARD N. APGAR—Serving Dunellen as postmaster, Mr Apgar applies to this public office the same energy and careful attention that he has given to all things connected with his busy life, and thus it can be said that he ranks among the foremost citizens of Dunellen

Willard N Apgar was born in Plainfield, New Jersey, March 22, 1876, the son of John P and Sarah (Smith) Apgar Mr Apgar has spent practically his entire life in Dunellen, New Jersey After receiving a good common school education, he became associated with his father in business and since that time has met with much success as a contractor and builder, which is the result of his untiring devotion to business

A Democrat in politics, Mr Apgar has ever taken a keen and active interest in the affairs of the local organization, and in 1916 was appointed postmaster of Dunellen, to which service he has added intense public spirit and patriotic fervor, all based upon full appreciation of his responsibility as an American citizen to whom has been delivered a profound trust Under his term of office as postmaster he advocated and had established a city delivery service in Dunellen He affiliates with the Foresters of America Junior Order of United American Mechanics, and the Patriotic Order Sons of America, is a director of the Home Building and Loan Association, and in his religious belief is a Presbyterian

On November 28, 1900, Willard N Apgar was united in marriage with Jennie M Apgar, daughter of James M and Martha (Haltman) Apgar, the former a native of High Bridge, New Jersey, the latter of Allentown, Pennsylvania Mr and Mrs Apgar are the parents of seven children W Clayton, born September 16, 1902, Sylvester M, born February 14, 1905, Clifford, born January 25 1907, Beatrice, born July 19, 1908, J Austin, born October 14 1910, Eleanor, born July 14, 1912, and Yvonne E., born December 27, 1918

JOSEPH M MAIER—The career of Joseph M Maier, proprietor of a fine grocery store in Dunellen, which he established in 1917, illustrates that success can be achieved by hard work and honorable business dealings, for today he is the owner of one of the most up-to-date business establishments of his town

Joseph M Maier was born in Dunellen, New Jersey, June 7, 1873, son of Joseph and Catherine (Eder) Maier, the former named having been engaged in a successful hotel business for a number of years

After completing the course of study afforded by the common schools of his birthplace, Joseph M Maier was the proprietor for a time of the hotel formerly conducted by his father   Later he decided that a change of occupation would be beneficial and better suited to his tastes and inclinations and accordingly, on August 21, 1917, he embarked in an entirely different line, opening up a grocery store in his native town, at No 384 North avenue, where he carries a complete stock of everything in the grocery line   His trade has increased during the past three years, which is largely the result of his energy, progressiveness, and courteous treatment of all who grant him their patronage   Mr Maier is connected with the First National Bank of Dunellen, is a Democrat in politics and a Catholic in religion

Mr Maier married (first) at Cranford, New Jersey, February 14, 1898, Anna Doyle daughter of John and Mary (Brennan) Doyle   Mrs Maier died in Dunellen, February 4, 1905   Three children were born of this marriage as follows Catherine, born January 28 1900, Joseph, born March 5 1902 John born November 6 1903   Mr Maier married (second) July 12, 1910, Anna Pfister, daughter of Philip and Mary (Bonig) Pfister   Five children have been born of this marriage, as follows William, born May 25 1912 Edward, born November 30, 1913, Robert born September 5 1915, Anna, born September 30, 1917, Margaret born February 25, 1920

JAMES EDWARD NOE, whose fifty-four consecutive years in one line of business in the same city and that his birthplace, is a fine record He is a venerable oyster dealer of Perth Amboy, New Jersey

The Noe family is one of the pioneer families of this region   Mr Noe's father, David Ogden Noe, was born and died in the old Noe homestead the same house where his son now lives, No 61 Water street He was in the oyster business, with his son as partner, and the latter continued the business after the death of his father   He married Hester Margaret Harned, and they had nine children, four of whom are now living James Edward, whose name appears at the head of this review Mrs Henrietta L Kipp, Mrs Sarah E Smith, and William Kelly, all of these are residents of Perth Amboy

James Edward Noe was born in Perth Amboy New Jersey, August 6 1845   Here he received his early education going to Pennington Seminary for advanced study, and later to Eastman's Business College, Poughkeepsie New York   Immediately after his graduation from that institution, the young man went to New York City and engaged in the

James E Noe

lumber business, being associated with Stone & Wiswall. He remained with them one year, the only period in his business career not identified with the daily life of Perth Amboy. He next joined his father in the oyster business, buying one-half of this business, and on the death of his father he continued to own the same. He was twenty-one years of age when he bought out this business, and now (1921) at the age of seventy-five years he still keeps oversight of the business, although he has been practically retired from active work since 1915.

Mr. Noe has always been deeply interested in all branches of public endeavor. He is a staunch supporter of Republican principles, and has for many years voted with this party. He was at one time elected to the Board of Education, and was made president of the board. He has also served as alderman from the First Ward. He has for many years been treasurer of the Alpine Cemetery Association, and only declined to serve longer in 1919 when advancing years made him feel that a younger man should relieve him of this charge. Since his youth, Mr. Noe has been identified with the work of the Simpson Methodist Episcopal Church. For twenty-five consecutive years he was superintendent of the Sunday school, for a long period had charge of the music for the church services, being chorister of the choir, and is still president of the board of trustees of the church.

Mr. Noe married in Perth Amboy, December 19, 1866, Annie E. Valentine, daughter of Benjamin and Elizabeth (Buck) Valentine. Mrs. Noe was born in Keasbey, Woodbridge township, New Jersey. Her father was for many years a farmer in Woodbridge. Both her parents died in Perth Amboy. Mr. and Mrs. Noe have three children, all living: Edward Valentine, of Newark, New Jersey, Margaret E., wife of William L. Anderson, of Dorchester, Massachusetts, and Katherine D., wife of William H. Hesser, of Perth Amboy.

Mr. Noe is a man whom it is a pleasure to meet. After a long life of constant and active usefulness, he is not content to sit idly and let the world go by, but takes the keenest interest in every phase of the life of which he has been a part, and in this very interest wields a strong and beneficent influence in the community.

GEORGE W. AINSCOW, of Stelton, Middlesex county, New Jersey, was born March 30, 1868, at Bay View, Maryland, son of Evan and Rachel (Brown) Ainscow, his parents both born in Wilmington, Delaware. Evan Ainscow was a contractor, a farmer, and a man of energy, and was successful in his varied business enterprises.

William Ainscow, grandfather of George W. Ainscow, was born in Bolton, England, he married in his native land, and later came to America with his wife Mary, settling in Wilmington, Delaware, where they lived and died.

George W. Ainscow was educated in the public schools, and in early life was associated with his father as his assistant. He next engaged in business as a public caterer, and for fifteen years was the proprietor of a well patronized restaurant in the city of Wilmington, Delaware. In

1898 he went to Jersey City, New Jersey, where he engaged in the grain and hay business for a time. He moved to Stelton, Middlesex county, two miles east of New Brunswick, in 1911, and there bought a farm, upon which he resides In 1920 he built a new residence on his farm, and is now building a large structure for general purposes, and for the convenience of auto tourists over the Lincoln Highway In addition to this he erected a large garage in 1916, which he conducts in connection with his other interests His gas and oil station is one of the largest on the highway between New York and Philadelphia He supplies the big auto truck transportation companies with fuel, and in the course of a year hundreds of thousands of gallons of oil and gas are handled through his station He has been successful in all his undertakings, and highly regarded in a business and social way. He and his family attend the Methodist Episcopal church of Metuchen, and take a deep interest in the life of the community

Mr Ainscow married, in Elkton, Maryland, April 30, 1890, Virgie R Lodge, born July 27, 1867, in Philadelphia. Pennsylvania. daughter of Richard and Jane (Hall) Lodge Richard Lodge was born in England, and with his parents sailed for the United States in 1847 Mr and Mrs Ainscow are the parents of four children · Marion E , born May 19, 1891, married Arthur Van Keuren, and they have two children. Virginia and Tobias, now residing in Albany, New York, Edith V , born March 24, 1893, residing at home with her parents, A Roy, born January 8, 1895, married Laura Boyd, and they reside near Metuchen, George W , Jr , born November 29, 1902, residing at home

---

HENRY S GARRETSON —From a Middlesex county farm in Piscataway township, Mr Garretson came to Dunellen, in his native county, and there entered mercantile life For nearly a quarter of a century he has conducted a lumber and coal business in Dunellen, and is one of the substantial men of his community He is a son of James and Gertrude E (Staats) Garretson, his father a farmer

Henry S Garretson was born in New Brunswick, New Jersey, October 1, 1856, and was there educated in the public schools. He grew to manhood at the home farm, and until he was about forty-five years of age engaged in farming and tilling his own acres, and he prospered About 1898 he formed a partnership with Alvah Gray in a lumber and coal business in Dunellen, which he has successfully conducted during the twenty-three years which have since intervened He is a man of strong business ability, and as a citizen his upright life is an example He is president of the Home Building and Loan Association of Dunellen, and president of the Hillsborough Mutual Fire Assurance Association, and was a member of the Board of Freeholders for nine years

In his political views, Mr Garretson is a Republican, in his church affiliation he is a member of the First Baptist of New Market, in which he has been active He is a member of the Masonic order, the Junior Order of United American Mechanics, Patriotic Order Sons of America, the Benevolent and Protective Order of Elks, and the Republican Club

Mr Garretson married, in New Market, New Jersey, November 1, 1882, Lily E Benward, born August 17, 1863, daughter of Peter and Phoebe L (Dayton) Benward, her father a farmer Mr and Mrs Garretson are the parents of three children Ethel, born June 30, 1884, J Russell, born February 7, 1890, and Lillian, born August 4, 1892 The Garretson home is in Dunellen, New Jersey, where the family is well known

FREDERICK B PEINS —For eighteen years Frederick B Peins has been engaged in the manufacture of tile flooring with the B H Lage Company, first under the partnership form, and later, in 1914, under its corporate form the B H Lage Company, Inc, of New York City, and Menlo Park, New Jersey This is one of the well known tile manufacturing companies, its offices being in New York City, the plant at Menlo Park He is a son of Henry and Margaret (Anderson) Peins, both born in Germany, where they lived and died They were the parents of eight children Ferdinand, Catherine, Sophia, Andrew, Marie, Henrietta Frederick B, of further mention, and Heinrich Four of these children came to the United States Andrew, Catherine, Frederick B., and Marie

Frederick B Peins was born in Tating, Germany, January 24, 1866, and there spent the first twenty-five years of his life He was educated in his native land, the gymnasium there furnishing training and instruction on a par with the best technical high schools in this country In 1891 he came to the United States and shortly afterward began his connection with clay manufacturing His line has been largely the manufacture of tile flooring and in that particular line of business he has specialized In 1902 he became superintendent and later manager of the B H Lage Company, of Menlo Park, New Jersey, the well known tile manufacturing company He has been connected with that company ever since, although in more recent years its ownership has changed and it is now the B H Lage Company, Inc, of New York City Mr Peins is one of the principal stockholders of the present company, and fills the same place in the management of the corporation as he did in the firm He is well known in the clay products business, and the company is well established and highly regarded in the trade

In political faith Mr. Peins is a Republican, and keenly alive to his responsibilities as a citizen, but as a citizen only, not as a seeker for office He is a member of the Benevolent and Protective Order of Elks, of Rahway, and the Independent Order of Foresters, of Metuchen, he and his family are members of the Lutheran church of Rahway

Mr Peins married, in Rahway in 1891, Anna Eseman, born in Germany, November 3, 1866, daughter of Frederick and Marie Eseman, natives of Germany, where they always resided Mrs Peins has a sister, Martha, who remained with her parents Mr and Mrs Peins are the parents of five children Anna, born February 22, 1893, Frederick, born April 8, 1895, Elsie, born June 17, 1897, died September 4, 1898, Rudolph, born September 7, 1899, Margaret born January 24, 1904, died January

29, 1904 Mr Peins and his family are among the well known and highly respected residents of Menlo Park The family home is one of the fine old mansions there, and the first house in which Thomas Edison installed electric lights

---

GUSTAV BLAUM.—A native son of Woodbridge, Gustav Blaum has all his life been connected with the town, and from boyhood has been associated with its mercantile life. He began as a grocer's clerk, and has always been partial to that business, finally, in 1905, becoming proprietor of the Hilsdorf store in Woodbridge, and one of the leading merchants of his town He is a son of Sebastian and Catherine (Lorch) Blaum

Gustav Blaum was born in Woodbridge, Middlesex county, New Jersey, April 10, 1867, and there obtained a public school education Quite early in life he clerked in different Woodbridge stores, but attended school quite regularly until about 1880 when he took a permanent position with Robert Humphrey, a long-time hardware merchant, with whom he remained until 1882 when he transferred his services to Hilsdorf & Harned, grocers, at now No 82 Main street, Woodbridge He remained with Hilsdorf & Harned until 1888, when he became a clerk with Burkett & Paterson, grocers, of Woodbridge, and three and one-half years later entered into a partnership with C W Harned and conducted a grocery business on Main street, Woodbridge, for three years

This experience seems to have satisfied Mr Blaum's ambition for a mercantile career and for five years, 1895-1900, he was agent for the Prudential Life Insurance Company, with offices in Perth Amboy In 1900 he reëntered the grocery business, accepting a position with Hilsdorf Brothers who were then running a chain of grocery stores, one of them, the old Hilsdorf & Harned store in Woodbridge, in which Mr. Blaum had formerly been a clerk He was appointed manager of that store by Hilsdorf Brothers, and successfully operated it for five years, when he purchased the business from the Hilsdorfs, and since 1905 has operated it under his own name He has been very successful has built up a good business, and is highly esteemed by his community He has other interests of importance, the most important being in the Woodbridge Building and Loan Association of which he was one of the founders in 1910 and during the entire eleven years of its life he has been the efficient treasurer

Mr Blaum has served his town as fire commissioner, and member of the Lighting Commission, is a member of the Woodbridge Fire Department the Junior Order of United American Mechanics, the Independent Order of Odd Fellows, and the Royal Arcanum Politically he is an Independent and keenly alive to his responsibilities as a citizen He is always ready to "lend a hand" in any forward movement, and displays a fine public spirit in his attitude on all questions of civic importance

Mr Blaum married, in Woodbridge, in 1900 Emma Ayres, daughter of John and Maria Ayres

CHARLES COMPTON — The farm in Raritan township, Middlesex county, New Jersey, which Charles Compton owns and cultivates has been in the family name for over a century, and the house he occupies was built by Ephraim Compton his grandfather, nearly one hundred years ago

Joel Compton son of Ephraim and Elizabeth (Carpenter) Compton occupied the old farm, and in 1860 built an addition to the old house built by his father and now occupied by his son, Charles. The Comptons came from England to Monmouth county, New Jersey, in 1667, and William Compton, the original settler became one of the original proprietors of Middlesex township, and from him sprang a large and influential family. The farm in Raritan township upon which Ephraim Compton lived and built his house adjoins the village of Metuchen, and once contained about five hundred acres, part of which is now owned and tilled by his grandson, Charles Compton

Charles Compton, son of Joel and Louisa (Campbell) Compton, was born in Dark Lane, Middlesex county, New Jersey, May 28, 1865 and was educated in the district schools. He early became his father's farm assistant and later inherited the old homestead upon which he now resides. He has been a farmer all his life and is rated one of the prosperous, substantial men of his township. In religious faith, Mr. Compton is a Presbyterian, and in politics exercises the greatest independence, voting for the man of principle which best appeals to his judgment

Mr. Compton married, April 25, 1881, Phoebe (Boylan) Mettick, born October 27, 1855, daughter of John V and Susan Terry (Newman) Boylan, and widow of Isaac Mettick. Mr. and Mrs. Compton are the parents of six children. Louisa born August 15, 1883, Mattietha, born December 11, 1885, Olive, born May 11, 1888 Mary N, born September 3, 1889 William C, born April 16 1892 and Ida May, born April 5, 1896

MARTIN GALBRAITH, JR, was born in Plainfield, New Jersey, March 25, 1879 the son of Martin Galbraith, Sr, who was born in Ireland, but came to the United States about 1859. Martin Galbraith Sr, married Julia Kilbride, and they were living in Plainfield, New Jersey, at the time of the birth of their son Martin, Jr

Martin Galbraith, Jr, was educated in the public schools of that city. He early became a hotel proprietor, and is now owner of the only hotel in Iselin, a village of Woodbridge township, Middlesex county, on the Pennsylvania Railroad. The hotel of which Mr Galbraith is proprietor was built in 1864. In politics he is an independent, in religious faith a Catholic. His fraternity is the Benevolent and Protective Order of Elks, of Rahway

Mr Galbraith married, April 1 1901, at Plainfield, New Jersey, Mary Geary born November 5, 1881, daughter of Richard and Ellen (Hughes) Geary born in Iselin. To Mr and Mrs Galbraith five children were born Dorothy born February 21, 1903 Roger, born June 9, 1905, died March 14, 1910, Eleanor, born November 16, 1909, Charles, born November 5 1911 Howard, born February 24, 1915

CALVIN CLETUS CUNNIUS, JR—Coming to New Brunswick a lad just out of high school, Mr Cunnius saw the opportunity and two years later established the business which he has since conducted—an automobile service station, his absence in the army the only interruption since 1915

Calvin C Cunnius, Jr, was born in Freeland, Pennsylvania, March 19, 1897, the son of Calvin and Mary (Nagle) Cunnius, his father is engaged in the automobile business The family later moved to Long Branch, New Jersey, where Calvin C was educated, finishing with graduation from Chattle High School He became familiar with the automobile business and was the first to operate auto-motive electrical service in New Brunswick Later, for two years, he was with the Willard Company at their New Brunswick station In 1915 although but eighteen years of age, he opened a service station in New Brunswick for his own account, and has successfully conducted it until the present (1921)

During the World War, Mr Cunnius enlisted in the United States army, September 5, 1918, and spent five months at Camp Humphries, Virginia as a private of Company K, Engineers Regiment He was honorably discharged, January 4, 1919 He is a member of the Lions Club and of Suydam Street Reformed Church

On May 5, 1918, in Suydam Street Reformed Church, Mr Cunnius married Mary Regina Deshler, daughter of John and Mary Deshler

Mr Cunnius is a young man of energy and ability, and has obtained a good start in the business world. His service station, at No 257 George street is well patronized, the service being appreciated by motorists

---

ARTHUR J HAMLEY, now cashier of the First National Bank of Dunellen New Jersey, was born in Mount Olive, New, Jersey, December 18, 1881, son of Joseph and Elizabeth (Lindberry) Hamley, his father a machinist Arthur J Hamley was educated in public schools and business college and when ready to enter business life he chose banking. He came to the First National Bank of Dunellen, January 1, 1907, and since has been its efficient cashier He is thoroughly informed in matters financial, and has the entire confidence of the public. Mr Hamley is a Republican in politics, and a member of the Presbyterian church Mr Hamley married, in 1903, in Stephensburg, New Jersey, Esther M Fleming, daughter of Albert and M Louise (Mitchell) Fleming her father a farmer Mr and Mrs Hamley are the parents of two children J Ronald, born January 15, 1905, S Elizabeth, born July 22 1909

JOHN H BECKER—As a cosmopolitan nation, America is distinctive From the four quarters of the globe men have come to her shores, many of whom have been men of unbounded integrity, of determined purpose of mental vigor and endurance, men who are both builders and conservators When one man passes another on the highway of prosperity and high standing in a community, it is because he has the power

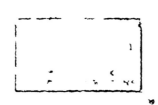

to make the most of every advantage which surround the human race. It is this power which has made John H Becker, of Milltown, New Jersey, one of the leading men of this community

John H Becker was born in Austria-Hungary, December 24, 1886, and came to this country at the age of sixteen He conducts a garage at Milltown, New Jersey, where he also does a large repair business He has won his way to success through sheer pluck and that indomitable energy which in its last analysis is the fundamental characteristic of the successful business man His career is one of those whose study affords fruitful conclusions for men who possess the combination of pluck and perseverance, and who take advantage of the opportunities open to young men in this country In politics Mr Becker is a Republican He fraternizes with the Independent Order of Odd Fellows, and the Improved Order of Red Men

On August 4, 1907, Mr Becker was united in marriage with Anna Mihalofsky, and they are the parents of five children Anna, born April 4, 1908, Elizabeth, born December 11, 1910, John, born January 6, 1912, Margaret, born June 12, 1918, Catherine, born February 25, 1920 The family home is at No 86 Riva avenue, Milltown, New Jersey

---

PATRICK F McCUTCHEON, numbered among the representative citizens of Sayreville, New Jersey, is a native of this community, where he has always had the welfare and advancement of it uppermost in his mind and given earnest support to all movements calculated to advance its development

Patrick F McCutcheon was born January 6, 1865, in Sayreville, New Jersey, the son of John and Anna (Campbell) McCutcheon He was educated in the schools of his native place, and after completing his studies entered upon his business career. For the past thirty years he has been owner and manager of a general merchandise store and has been highly successful in this venture Unswerving honesty and fairness has won for him the respect of his fellow-citizens In politics Mr McCutcheon is a Democrat, and gives to the affairs of the organization the interest demanded of every good citizen He is also prominent in fraternal circles, being affiliated with the Knights of Columbus, the Improved Order of Red Men, the Foresters of America, and the Woodmen of the World In religion he is a Roman Catholic, and has always served the church well by personal righteousness, and his means is ever contributed to his church and its benevolences

Patrick F McCutcheon was united in marriage with Catherine (Kelley) Clark, February 26, 1900 Mrs McCutcheon was born September 1, 1865, in New York City, the daughter of Martin and Margaret (Gurnan) Kelley Mr and Mrs McCutcheon have no children

---

WILLIAM P WALDRON —At Three Bridges, a village of Hunterdon county, New Jersey, on the south branch of the Raritan river, four miles east of Flemington Peter Waldron, and his son, William P, were born, that locality having long been the family seat Peter Waldron, a farmer of Three Bridges, married Louise West, born in Montgomery, Somerset county, New Jersey, and they were the parents of William P Waldron, now (1921) superintendent of the Middlesex County Poor Farm

William P Waldron was born at Three Bridges, New Jersey, November 15, 1871, and there was educated in the public schools He remained at home his father's farm helper, until coming of age, then farmed for his own account until elected to superintend the County Poor Farm at Stelton He has held that position for seven years, beginning in 1914 He is a Republican in politics, a member of Stelton Baptist Church, and of the Junior Order of American Mechanics.

Mr Waldron married, at Bound Brook, New Jersey, March 31, 1897, Carrie Moore, born at Bound Brook, July 31, 1873, daughter of John M and Mary (Wisner) Moore, her father a miller Mr and Mrs Waldron have three children: Rilla, born September 2, 1901, Beulah, born January 19, 1907, Howard, born February 20, 1910

JAMES PARKER LIDDLE —A native son of Middlesex county, Mr Liddle strayed far from his native heath, and for thirty years braved the storms that swept Dakota's prairies But storms are followed by sunshine, and the Dakota storms and sunshine produced the wonderful crops which Mr Liddle garnered year after year, until his wants were satisfied, then he met the craving he had long fought against and returned to the hills, valleys and fields of Middlesex county On a little farm not far from Metuchen (a garden in comparison with his broad Dakota acres) he located, near enough to have city advantages, far enough away to avoid the crowded feeling, and there the veteran of seventy-three years, in the house which he rebuilt and modernized, is reaping the reward of his years of toil in a life of contented ease He is a son of Joshua and Ann (Buck) Liddle, his father before him a Middlesex farmer

James Parker Liddle was born in Woodbridge township, Middlesex county, New Jersey, December 15, 1847, and there spent the years of his youth and early manhood He attended public schools, then learned the blacksmith's trade, working at his trade and farming until 1878, when he went to North Dakota, and there remained for thirty years In the early days in North Dakota few people attempted to remain on their prairie lands during the winer, Mr Liddle being one of the first to attempt it in his section He built one of the first frame houses in that country, most of the houses being made of sod, which is a house partly below and partly above the surface, the walls and roof being built of thick, tough prairie sod, making a warm and comfortable home. After thirty years in the West he returned to Middlesex county and bought a little farm of nineteen acres near Metuchen, and has there created a delightful home for his declining years In politics he is a Republican, and takes a great interest in affairs of his community

Mr Liddle married, at Fords Corners, New Jersey, December 15, 1873, Ellen Gaffney, born in Boston, Massachusetts, July 5, 1849, daughter of John and Ellen (Lavigne) Gaffney, both born in Ireland

W Guy Weaver

JOHN JOSEPH QUINN—One of the responsible executive positions in the business world of Perth Amboy, New Jersey, is filled by John Joseph Quinn Born in this city, he is a son of Terence Quinn, a native of Ireland, who spent the greater part of his life in this country

Terence Quinn was born in Tyrone, Ireland, and came here with his parents when he was a boy The family located in Philadelphia, and remained there for a considerable period of time In his early manhood young Terence enlisted in a Pennsylvania regiment, and served through the Civil War Soon after his discharge, he came to Perth Amboy, and established a cigar and candy store at No 88 Smith street He conducted this store for many years, and the building in which it was located came to be known as the "Old Quinn Homestead" It is still in excellent condition, and used for both residence and business purposes Mr. Quinn's widow still resides there. Mr. Quinn died on September 29, 1893, at the age of sixty-one He married Jane McDonnell, who was born in County Sligo, Ireland, and came to this country with her father at the age of nine years, settling in Quebec, Canada Terence and Jane (McDonnell) Quinn were the parents of the following children Mary, Arthur, Elizabeth, Terence, deceased, Anna, James, Michael, deceased, and John Joseph

John Joseph Quinn began his education in the public schools of Perth Amboy After completing the usual course, he entered the Coleman Business College, of Newark, New Jersey, and was graduated in 1903 He then entered the employ of Westinghouse, Church, Kerr & Company, engineers of New York City, as one of their statistical force, remaining with them for a year and a half, during which time he spent his evenings in advanced study at the Lenftner Preparatory School At the end of that time he went to New York University, completing his studies, and for the next five years was employed by Douglas Robinson, of Charles S Brown Company, dealers in real estate Returning to Perth Amboy, he became associated with Alpern & Company, as vice-president of their organization, remaining in this connection for three years He is now manager of the real estate department of the Perth Amboy Trust Company, and is also clerk of the District Court of Perth Amboy

Mr Quinn is a member of the Knights of Columbus, the Benevolent and Protective Order of Elks, and the Raritan Yacht Club His hobby is music, and he has a fine bass voice He is a member of the Roman Catholic church. Mr Quinn married, October 20, 1920, Florence E Donegan a teacher in the grammar school of Perth Amboy

---

W. GUY WEAVER, now general superintendent of the New Jersey plants of the National Fireproofing Company, with local offices in Perth Amboy, was born in Newark, New Jersey, December 29, 1878, son of W Guy and Elizabeth J (Brannigan) Weaver, his father a railroad man and a well known resident of Perth Amboy, New Jersey

The son, W Guy Weaver, was educated in Perth Amboy public schools, and after school years were over, began his business career, his first position being as office boy with the G B Wilson Company, in Jersey City He remained with that house four years, then, about 1896 became a clerk with the Perth Amboy Gas Light Company, continuing here until 1898 In the same year he took a position with the American Smelting and Refining Company, as a weigher in the lead department, holding this until 1902 In July, 1902, he entered the employ of the National Fireproofing Company at Perth Amboy, a connection which has grown closer and stronger as the years have passed by and which he yet continues (1921)

Mr. Weaver's first place with the above company was as a clerk in the shipping department, and promotion followed, he having been successively assistant superintendent, superintendent, and, as above stated, is now general superintendent of all the company's plants in New Jersey, one being located in Perth Amboy, two in Woodbridge township, one at Lorillard, and one at Port Murray He is a thorough master of every detail of the business over which he has direction, and is regarded as one of the best informed and most capable men in the business He is a director of the City National Bank of Perth Amboy, and of the Woodbridge National Bank, of Woodbridge, New Jersey

In politics, Mr Weaver is a Democrat, and has served the city of Perth Amboy as president of the Board of Aldermen, and as secretary of the Board of Water Commissioners He is a past exalted ruler of Perth Amboy Lodge, Benevolent and Protective Order of Elks, a member of the Knights of Columbus, Royal Arcanum; and Woodmen of the World, and his religious connection is with St James' Roman Catholic Church of Woodbridge His clubs are the East Jersey, the Raritan River Yacht and the Sewaren Land and Water.

Mr Weaver married, at Perth Amboy, October 30, 1902, Madeline R Hartung, daughter of Bernard and Theresa (Angst) Hartung, of Perth Amboy Mr and Mrs Weaver are the parents of two daughters. Ruth M, and Bernice C. Since coming to Woodbridge, after a long residence in Perth Amboy, the family home has been at No. 192 Green street

---

JOSEPH A. FURKAY.—Almost the entire section around Jamesburg is given over to farming, that portion of New Jersey having a wide reputation for agricultural development One of the numerous farms is operated by Joseph A Furkay who has been a resident for some years past, though not a native of this State

Joseph A Furkay was born in New York City, March 11, 1874, the son of John Furkay, a cigar maker of that city, and his wife, Anna (Lowda) Furkay The education of the young boy was acquired in the common schools, and when that was finished he began his farming career

In politics Mr Furkay is a liberal, and in religion he is a Presbyterian his business interests are with the First National Bank of Jamesburg, and the only organization of which he is a member is the Farmers' Corporation of Monmouth county

In Rhode Hall, February 26, 1902, Joseph A Furkay was united in marriage with Mae E Scott, born April 5, 1882, in Hightstown New Jersey She is the daughter of Addison H and Lydia A (Perine) Scott, born natives of Hightstown   The grandfather of Mae E (Scott) Furkay was James Scott and her grandmother Mary Harding, both having been born in Mercer county, New Jersey, all her family for several generations owning that county as their native place   Mr and Mrs Furkay have two children Addison S, born September 4, 1903, and Joseph A, born September 14, 1915

LEO C OSBORN, an agriculturist and market gardener in the vicinity of New Brunswick, New Jersey, is a man who has won for himself a place among the prominent and highly respected citizens of that locality, who through his industry, his upright and honorable principles, and his genial nature, well merits the confidence and esteem in which he is held by his fellow-men

Leo C Osborn was born in New Market, Middlesex county, New Jersey, May 23, 1887, a son of Peter C. and Ida E (Fulton) Osborn, the father devoting the years of his active career to the breaking and training of horses a lucrative occupation in those days when horses were used almost exclusively as a means of conveyance from place to place, in addition to being used for all kinds of work   By attendance at the common schools in the neighborhood of his home, Leo C Osborn obtained a good education, and upon the completion of his studies he turned his attention to agricultural pursuits, the farm which he now owns and resides on having been in the possession of members of the family from the Revolutionary period, he being a member of the fifth generation, and a portion of the house he resides in was built prior to the Revolutionary War, this making it one of the ancient landmarks of that locality   The work and care he has bestowed on his property is amply shown in the harvests that it yields, which is housed in commodious and modern buildings, everything kept in the best of order   In religious preference he is a First Day Baptist, and he is connected with the Junior Order of United American Mechanics, and the local Grange, Patrons of Husbandry

Mr Osborn married, October 14, 1914, at High Bridge, Hunterdon county, New Jersey, Mae Cory Titus, born April 30, 1896, at Plainfield, New Jersey, daughter of Isaac and Caroline Titus, the former named born in Ohio, and the latter named in Bound Brook, New Jersey   Mr and Mrs Osborn are the parents of one child, Gorden, born September 27, 1917

HENRY KUHLTHAU, one of the leading business men of the borough of Milltown is the successful proprietor of a coal, hay and grain store   He also carries on an extensive trade in all kinds of farm products

While Mr Kuhlthau is a descendant of German ancestry, he is of American birth, having been born in Milltown, New Jersey, April 23,

1864 After attending the public school of that town, he assisted his
father both in his general store and on the farm, growing up to manhood in the village where he was born   His father, Conrad Kuhlthau,
was born in Germany, came to this country when a young man, joined
the mad rush to the Pacific coast, and became one of the gold diggers
of California   He afterward came East and settled in Milltown, engaging in farming and conducting the village store, handling general merchandise   He bought and sold the farm his son now lives on   The
mother of Henry Kuhlthau was Myleana (Junker) Kuhlthau, also a
native of Germany

Mr Kuhlthau takes an active part in all the affairs of the constantly
growing borough, and is well regarded by his fellow-citizens   He has
been chosen president of the Milltown Building and Loan Association
He also is a member of the Junior Order of United American Mechanics
and of the Improved Order of Red Men   In politics Mr Kuhlthau is a
Republican, but not a politician, though for the last nine years he has
been one of the councilmen of the borough   He is also a member of
the Milltown Republican Club   Mr Kuhlthau and his family attend
St Paul's Church

On August 4, 1886, in the city of New Brunswick, Henry Kuhlthau
married Mamie Hughes, daughter of Thomas Hughes, a native of England   Mr Hughes came to this country many years ago and settled
in New Brunswick, New Jersey, where his daughter Mamie was born
May 28, 1869   Mr and Mrs Henry Kuhlthau have one child, May E,
born in 1887

REUNE FITZ RANDOLPH, deceased, who for many years was
a representative of the farming interests of Raritan township, Middlesex
county, New Jersey, was a lineal descendant in the ninth generation
of a family that made its home in the State of New Jersey at an early
date, the founder having been Edward Fitz Randolph, a native of
England, from whence he emigrated to New England in the year 1630
and located in the State of Massachusetts, married, May 10, 1637,
Elizabeth Blossom, and later moved to Manasquan, New Jersey   The
descent to Reune Fitz Randolph was through his son, Thomas Fitz
Randolph, his son, David B Fitz Randolph, born January 1, 1690, his
son, William Fitz Randolph, born January 10, 1716 died December 10,
1795, his son, Nehemiah Fitz Randolph, born January 3, 1745, died
January 3, 1806, married Sarah Walker, born 1750, died March 27, 1807,
their son, Peter Fitz Randolph, born December 12, 1767, died April 24,
1815, married Phoebe Blackford, born February 12, 1763, their son,
Asa Fitz Randolph, born in Plainfield, New Jersey, May 21, 1802, a
farmer by occupation, married Hannah T Drake, born August 18, 1801,
in New Jersey, they the parents of Reune Fitz Randolph, of this review

Reune Fitz Randolph was born in Plainfield, Union county, New
Jersey, February 18, 1837   He attended the schools of his native place,
completing his studies in the Plainfield High School, thus acquiring
an education that prepared him for the activities of life   He gave his
attention to farming pursuits in early boyhood, and so continued until

his retirement from labor in his declining years, thereafter enjoying to the full the rest and quiet that should follow years of strenuous effort He was a Seventh Day Baptist in religion, and a Republican in politics, and was looked upon in the vicinity of his home as a good neighbor and friend His death occurred at his home, January 25, 1914

Reune Fitz Randolph married, in Flemington, New Jersey, January 1, 1862, Anna Camp, born in Flemington, August 25, 1842, daughter of Elias Camp, who was born in Cape May, New Jersey, May 23, 1816, married, September 30, 1838, Elizabeth Ann Dills, born February 1, 1814 Three children were born of this union, as follows Ida, born August 5, 1864, Nellie, born July 5, 1866, departed this life December 27, 1901, and Etta, born January 27, 1874. They reside in the old homestead, and are honored and esteemed for their excellent characteristics

PLATT J ROWLEY, deceased, who for many years was classed among the prosperous and representative tillers of the soil of Raritan township, in the vicinity of Plainfield, New Jersey, who are noted for their excellent products, was born in Lexington, Greene county, New York, March 18 1822, a son of Nathan and Esther (Goslie) Rowley, who resided for many years on a farm there

The district schools of Lexington afforded Platt J Rowley the opportunity of obtaining an elementary education, and his active life thereafter was devoted to farming in Greene county, New York, and later in Middlesex county, New Jersey He spent a number of years on his father's farm in New York State, and later became the owner of the farm in New Jersey, whereon he spent the remainder of his days, and which since his death is occupied by his daughters He was a man of means and experience, energetic, thrifty, and painstaking, all these qualities combining to make him a successful farmer He also gave proof of his patriotism and allegiance to his country by enlisting in its service during the period of the Civil War, becoming a lieutenant in the Ulster New York Guard, which was ready for service at any moment, but was not called out for action He was a member of the First Baptist Church of Plainfield, an adherent of Republican principles, and highly esteemed by all with whom he associated, either in business, religious or social circles

Mr Rowley married, in Somerville, New Jersey, December 31, 1865, Augusta C Cubberley, born March 23 1829 daughter of Isaac Cubberley, of Bergen New Jersey, and his wife, Susanna (Van Nostrand) Cubberley, of Paterson, New Jersey The Cubberleys are an old English family, various members being found among the early settlers of Staten Island, and in the maternal line Mrs Rowley is descended from the Mercereau family, an equally well known family Two children were born to Mr and Mrs Rowley Lizzie, born February 12, 1868, resides at the homestead in Plainfield, Adelaide, born August 31, 1870, also resides on the old homestead, she became the wife of George M Banks, and they are the parents of five children, as follows Luther, Everett, Adelaide, Eunice, and George Mr Rowley died in his residence on the farm in Raritan township, August 17, 1899, and his wife died October 25, 1913

PHINNEY E. AND RUTHETTA (CURTIS-DRAKE) GRAF-FAM —In the town of Gray, eighteen miles from Portland, Cumberland county, Maine, Phinney E Graffam was born, October 5, 1852, son of Clement and Elizabeth (Ross) Graffam, his father was a farmer After finishing public school, he learned the carpenter's trade, which he followed many years He is a member of the Methodist Episcopal church, a Republican in politics, and in his younger years a member of the militia

Mr Graffam married, in Newark New Jersey, December 3, 1916, Ruthetta (Curtis) Drake, daughter of David and Katherine (Long) Curtis, and widow of David F Drake dealer in stocks, who was born in Plainfield, Union county, February 11, 1845, son of William W. Drake, Esq , a descendant of Sir Frances Drake, and Eunice (French) Drake, who was a sister of P. M French William W Drake, Esq , filled a number of important public offices during his life He was health commissioner, overseer of the poor, and county surveyor, holding these positions until the time of his death

Ruthetta (Curtis-Drake) Graffam was born in Plainfield, Union county, April 27, 1850, and has been a resident of this section all her life She traces her ancestors (all of whom were born and lived in Union county) back to the early pioneer days of the seventeenth century, her great-grandfather, Daniel Curtis having fought and died in the fight for independence

In her early life, Mrs Graffam devoted a great deal of her time to fancy poultry raising, for which she took many prizes Of recent years she has dealt extensively in real estate, and owns a large amount of property in Plainfield At the present time she and Mr Graffam reside on their farm in Piscataway township The farm is under splendid cultivation. She is a Methodist, a member of the First Methodist Church of Plainfield Notwithstanding her very active life in business, Mrs Graffam has always found time to minister to the wants of the poor and needy, and is well known for her philanthropic work

By Mrs Graffam's first marriage there are five children now living: 1 William W Drake, milk dealer, married, in Trenton, New Jersey, Lily Fermann, and has two children Eugene and Bessie 2 Minnie Drake, who lives in Plainfield, New Jersey, married John Barber Carpenter, and has two children Ethel and William. 3 Edward Drake, public service employee for twenty-one years, married, in New Brunswick, New Jersey, Mabel Curtis, and has five children Dorothy, Evelyn, Walter, Katherine and Mabel 4 Charles Drake, stock farmer, in New Brunswick, New Jersey, married Mabel Long, and has two children Nellie and Grace 5 Sarah Elizabeth, of Brooklyn, New York, married Edward Sanders, retired merchant, and has three children Gladys, Victor and Ruth.

FRANK J LAWSON.—Although Mr Lawson has been a resident of Woodbridge for a longer period than he can remember, his business is and always has been in New York City, he having been connected

Frank J. Lawson

with the music publishing business since his school days, and is now head of the F J Lawson Company, Inc, general publishers of music He is not only a practical printer, but a practical publisher and an excellent business man

Frank J Lawson is a son of Peter Lawson, a one-time music publisher of New York, who moved to Woodbridge, New Jersey, in 1867, and there died, February 21, 1899 He was born in New York, in 1817, and continued actively engaged in the music publishing business until 1898, when he retired in favor of his son, who had been his valued assistant He was a member of the famous Seventh Regiment, New York Militia, and was with that regiment in some of its noted experiences He married Rachel Lyons, of English parentage She died in Woodbridge, New Jersey, December 12, 1917 Mr and Mrs Lawson were the parents of five children James, Henry, Frank J, of further mention, Jeannette, and Elsie

Frank J Lawson was born in New York City, December 16, 1866, but in 1867 Woodbridge, New Jersey, became the family home, and there he completed public school studies He then pursued a course of study at Paine's Business College, New York City, after which he became associated with his father in business Under his father's direction he learned the printer's trade, and the methods of setting musical scores, printing, and every detail of the business He became his father's trusted assistant, and when, in 1898, Peter Lawson retired from the business, Frank J Lawson assumed sole management In 1907 the business was incorporated as the F J Lawson Company, with offices at No 350 West Thirty-eighth street, New York The business is one of the largest music publishing concerns in the country, and at the company's plant every phase of music printing is conducted Outside of his own firm, Mr Lawson is interested in other activities, among them being vice-president of the Woodbridge National Bank

Mr Lawson is a Republican in politics, and takes a keen interest in local affairs He is a trustee of the First Congregational Church of Woodbridge, is past chancellor commander of Woodbridge Lodge, Knights of Pythias, and member of the official board of Woodbridge Chapter of the Red Cross He has taken a keen interest in the affairs of the community, and is one of the esteemed citizens of the town

---

RUSSELL E RUNYON —Dunellen, New Jersey, has long been the home of this branch of the Runyon family, this review dealing with three heads of generations who have made Dunellen the seat of their business activities Eugene Runyon, his son, Walter G Runyon, and his grandson, Russell E Runyon Eugene Runyon was active in town enterprises, and one of the leading men of his day He was one of the principal organizers of the Dunellen Building and Loan Association, and conducted a large real estate and insurance business He was also a merchant of Dunellen, and a man genuinely respected He married Jersey Ann Randolph, and they were the parents of five children Walter G, of further mention, Oscar, for many years a leading merchant of Dunellen, borough councilman, and a member of the Board of Education; William, Arthur, and Randolph, all of whom died young

Walter G Runyon, eldest son of Eugene and Jersey Ann (Randolph) Runyon, was born in Plainfield, New Jersey, and for thirty years was engaged in the undertaking business in Dunellen. He also conducted a successful livery business, dealt extensively in real estate, and became influential in town affairs. He was highly esteemed and widely known as a man of integrity, public-spirited and progressive, whose labors for the good of Dunellen added much to town progress and welfare. He was a member of several organizations, social and fraternal and a devoted member of the New Market Baptist Church. He married Cora A Apgar of Cokesbury, New Jersey, and they were the parents of an only child Russell E Runyon of further mention

Russell E Runyon, son of Walter G and Cora A (Apgar) Runyon, was born in Dunellen, New Jersey, October 1, 1891, and there was educated in the public schools of Dunellen. He finished his studies in Plainfield High School and after leaving that institution, became associated with his father in business, continuing until the passing of the elder partner, when the son succeeded him as owner and manager. He has other business interests in his town, one being his connection with the First National Bank, another, the Dunellen Building and Loan Association, of which his grandfather was a founder. He is a member of several organizations of Dunellen, social and fraternal, and takes a deep interest in town affairs

Mr Runyon married (first) at Dunellen, November 18, 1914, Edna M Shirley, of Dunellen, who died December 14, 1917, the mother of two children Walter G (2), born October 3, 1915; and Edythe A, born November 23, 1916. He married (second) Mabel Brown, of Boonton, New Jersey

---

ALVAH GRAY—Among the leading residents of Dunellen who have passed from a life of usefulness and service was Alvah Gray. He was one of the town's most influential citizens, highly esteemed by all who knew him, and his death, which occurred February 9, 1918, was a sad loss to the community. He was a native of the State of New Jersey, born near Long Valley, Hunterdon county, November 18, 1849, a son of Rance H and Elizabeth (Swakhamer) Gray, natives of Long Valley, where Mr Gray was engaged in agricultural pursuits

Alvah Gray was a student in the common schools adjacent to his childhood home and being inured to farm labor, assisted his father in the work of the homestead. He gave his attention to that line of occupation until the year 1884, then took up an entirely different line of work, engaging in the lumber, coal, flour and feed business in Dunellen, Middlesex county. His business increased in volume and importance with each passing year until it ranked among the most successful in this section of the township. He was honorable and straightforward in his methods of conducting his business, energetic and enterprising, and the success which he achieved was the direct result of his own well-directed efforts. His connection as president of the First National Bank of

Dunellen for many years testified to his trustworthiness and ability He was a member of the Presbyterian church of Dunellen, and his political allegiance was given to the Republican party. For many years he was a member of the Town Board, and a committeeman of the township

Mr Gray married, in Glen Garden, near Spruce Run, New Jersey, December 18, 1869, Mary Elizabeth Bonnell, born in Clinton, New Jersey, October 20, 1849, daughter of Joseph and Sarah (Beavers) Bonnell, natives of Clinton Mr and Mrs Gray were the parents of one daughter, Sarah Louise, born in Califon, Hunterdon county, New Jersey, September 4, 1874, she married, April 20, 1898, William E Terry, born September 29, 1872, now serving in the capacity of manager of the American Felt Company in New York City, and resides in Dunellen Mr and Mrs Terry are the parents of three children Natalie, born December 30, 1901, Edwin T, born July 12, 1904, and Richard G, born July 11, 1907

TRUMAN W. BILYEU, one of the successful business men of New Market, New Jersey, is a man of excellent business and executive ability, is public-spirited and enterprising, and has always adhered to a high standard of living, both in public and private life, and enjoys the esteem and respect of all who know him

Truman W Bilyeu is a native of Brooklyn, New York, born October 31, 1847, a son of William and Sarah (Upson) Bilyeu, the former named born in Somerset county, New Jersey, a chair maker by trade, from which he derived a comfortable livelihood, and the latter named a native of New York City The common schools in the vicinity of his home afforded Truman W Bilyeu the opportunity of acquiring a practical education, and upon arriving at the age when he could depend upon his own efforts for making a living, he chose the trade of blacksmith, at which he became highly proficient He also learned the trade of wagonmaker, and to these occupations he has since devoted his entire time and energy. In 1870, at the age of twenty-three years, he established a blacksmith shop on Somerset street, in Plainfield, New Jersey, which he conducted very successfully up to the year 1910, when he moved to New Market and there erected a repair and blacksmith shop, at the same time erecting a modern house for the occupancy of his family At present he is connected with his son-in-law, Walter J Titus, in the blacksmith and wagonmaking shop at New Market Mr Bilyeu is a Baptist in religion, and is staunch in his advocacy of the principles of the Republican party

Mr Bilyeu married, June 24, 1871, in Plainfield, New Jersey, Adeline Harris, born in New Market, Middlesex county, New Jersey, December 8, 1845, daughter of John and Susan (Pope) Harris Two children have been born to Mr and Mrs Bilyeu, namely Emma Louise, born March 30, 1872, who became the wife of Walter J. Titus, of Somerset county, New Jersey, and Florence, born March 5 1882, who became the wife of George Apgar, of Plainfield, and they are the parents of two children George, Jr, and Harold Apgar

JAMES SCANLON.—At the age of thirty, James Scanlon came to the United States from Ireland and became an employee of the Pennsylvania Railroad, remaining many years with that company until an accident so crippled him that his days of usefulness to the road were ended The company most generously compensated him by placing him upon the pension list, and he now resides at Menlo Park, Middlesex county, New Jersey, a property owner, contented and free from all care He is a son of John and Katherine (Dugan) Scanlon both of whom lived and died in County Sligo, Ireland, his father a farmer The family were members of the Roman Catholic church and in that faith James Scanlon firmly abides

James Scanlon was born in County Sligo, Ireland, August 15 1853 He attended parish schools, and until 1883 resided in Ireland, employed as a farm hand and in other pursuits In that year he came to the United States and soon afterward received employment with the Pennsylvania Railroad He was badly injured in a railroad wreck on the Pennsylvania, and has since been upon the company's retired list He was a member of that old-time organization, the Knights of Labor, now but a memory but at one time very strong In politics he is a Democrat

Mr Scanlon married in Ireland, February 3, 1879, Katherine Carroll born November 27, 1850 in Ireland daughter of Mark and Bridget (Dwyer) Carroll. Mr and Mrs Scanlon are the parents of four children . 1 Mary, born November 7, 1882, she married Joseph Jan Konsky, and has eight children Katherine, Mary, John, James, Joseph, Agnes, Michael, and Edward 2 John, born July 24, 1884, deceased 3 Katherine, born February 1, 1888, she married Stephen Walker and has three children Gertrude, Katherine, and James 4 John F, born May 21, 1896

IOW R EDGAR—The Edgars were formerly a Woodbridge family, and there Freeman Edgar, the father of Iow R Edgar, was born While he was yet young, his parents moved to New York City, where his life was largely spent For a number of years he was engaged in the grocery business there, but later in life was in the same business in Metuchen, New Jersey, where he died

Iow R Edgar, son of Freeman and Sarah (Martin) Edgar, was born in New York City, March 20, 1847, and there spent the first eleven years of his youth He attended the New York City public schools until 1858, when the family moved to Metuchen, New Jersey, and there the lad attended a private school until 1862, when school days ended In that year he became a clerk in his father's general store in Metuchen, continuing in the business until 1873 He then became engaged in general merchandising on his own account for several years, later entering the clay business, a line of activity he has been in for thirty years, having clay interests in Middlesex county, New Jersey, in Florida, and in Georgia

Mr Edgar is a director of the Metuchen National Bank, a man highly regarded in business circles, and in a social way has many friends

Jour R. Edgar

throughout the community In politics Mr Edgar is a Republican, keenly alive to his duties as a citizen, and is interested in all things for public betterment He and his family are members of the Metuchen Reformed Church, where he married in 1874, Cecilia Ross Thomas, daughter of David G and Ann (Ross) Thomas, the Ross family one of the old Revolutionary families of Metuchen Mr and Mrs Edgar are the parents of two sons Harold T and David R The family home is at No 32 Graham avenue, Metuchen

CALEB DOUGLAS FRASER —The Fraser family, originating in the Scottish Highlands, was established on this side the Atlantic two hundred years ago, the original immigrant ancestor settling in Nova Scotia There the family remained for many generations William Fraser, who was born in Nova Scotia, in 1838 later came to the United States, bringing his wife and children, and located in Perth Amboy, New Jersey He was in the employ of the Pennsylvania Railroad for many years William Fraser died in Perth Amboy, in 1904 His wife, Susan Douglas, also born in Nova Scotia, survives him and is now seventy-one years of age She is a descendant of the famous Douglas clan of the Scottish Highlands The children of this fine couple, all born in Nova Scotia with the exception of the youngest, with the sturdy pioneer spirit of their ancestors, are Jessie, the wife of Frank Douglas, of Providence, Rhode Island, Caleb D, of further mention; Anne, widow of Maxwell F Lawton, of Brooklyn, New York, Edwin Grant, a sketch of whom follows, Mary, who died not long after the family left Nova Scotia, Harriet, a resident of Perth Amboy, Emma, wife of John E Sofield, of Perth Amboy, and William H a real estate man in Perth Amboy

Caleb Douglas Fraser was born in Hants county, Nova Scotia, on July 17, 1870, on the old farm where the family had lived for many years There he attended school until he was sixteen years of age, helping his father in the butcher business in his spare time. In May, 1887, the family came to Perth Amboy, New Jersey, the young man accompanying them Later he was employed in a grocery store in Brooklyn, New York Returning to Perth Amboy after a year spent thus, he was apprenticed to Thomas Langan, a carpenter He worked at this trade for a few years here in this city, then entered the employ of the American Smelting and Refining Company, and remained in that connection for ten years During that time, however, he kept in close touch with the construction work constantly going on in the rapid development of the city The outgrowth of this interest was the formation in 1907 of Fraser Brothers, real estate dealers The Fraser Realty Company was also formed of which Caleb Douglas Fraser is treasurer He is also a director and secretary of the People's Building and Loan Association

Closely identified as he is with the growth and development of the city, Mr Fraser is interested in every phase of its progress, and while always preferring to forward the welfare in an unofficial way, he was at one time induced to become a candidate for alderman of the First Ward He is a member of the First Presbyterian Church, and an elder and trustee He at one time taught in the Sunday school

Mr Fraser married, October 12, 1899, in Pluckemin, New Jersey, Margaret Huff, daughter of David and Henriette (Van Arsdale) Huff. Mrs Fraser was born in Pluckemin, and her mother now resides there, but her father died in Perth Amboy Mr and Mrs Fraser have three children, all living Mary Douglas, born August 14, 1902, Douglas, born June 12, 1904, and Margaret Melick, born February 29, 1908

EDWIN GRANT FRASER, fourth child of William and Susan (Douglas) Fraser (q v), was born in Shurbenacadie, Hants county, Nova Scotia, February 4, 1875 and there spent the first thirteen years of his life In 1888 he came to Perth Amboy New Jersey, and there completed his school years At the age of fifteen he began his business career in a Perth Amboy real estate office, and so well was he adapted to that business that he has always continued therein He began business under his own name at the age of thirty-one, in 1906 opening his first office at No 81 Smith street Later he moved to No 95 Smith street, thence to a building of his own at No 194 Smith street, and in April, 1918, to his present offices, No 210 Smith street in the Perth Amboy Savings Institution building He has been very successful in business and holds the confidence and high regard of his fellowmen He is a director of the First National Bank of Perth Amboy, vice-president of the People's Building and Loan Association, secretary-treasurer of the East Jersey Lumber and Timber Company, secretary-treasurer of the East Jersey Bridge Company, and president of the Fraser Realty Company

Mr Fraser is a Democrat in politics, and was a member of the first Board of City Assessors and president of the Perth Amboy Board of Water Commissioners He is a member of the Masonic order, the Benevolent and Protective Order of Elks, Royal Arcanum, East Jersey Club Colonial Country Club New York Athletic Club, and the First Presbyterian Church Mr Fraser is not married

STANLEY FRANK KACZMAREK —Although Jersey City was his birthplace Stanley F Kaczmarek was brought by his parents to Perth Amboy, New Jersey, when a child of five years Thus, when his law course was completed, he came directly to Perth Amboy and is there beginning the building of a career He is the son of Frank and Mary Kaczmarek, both born in Poland, Europe, his father coming to the United States at the age of twenty-eight, settling in Jersey City, New Jersey both yet living, Mrs Kaczmarek a capable and well known midwife of Perth Amboy, the oldest in the city Mr. and Mrs Kaczmarek are the parents of two children Mary, wife of Stephen Pribula, engaged in the retail meat and provision business on State street Perth Amboy, and Stanley F, of further mention

Stanley F Kaczmarek was born in Jersey City, New Jersey, October 19, 1895, his parents moving to Perth Amboy in 1900 He completed grammar school courses of study in 1910, high school in 1914, then entered the New Jersey Law School, at Newark, whence he was graduated, class of 1919 He began practice in Perth Amboy, in May, 1920, and is succeeding very well in his upbuilding of a practice, his offices being in the Board of Trade building During the interval between high and law schools, Mr Kaczmarek served in the United States army, attached to the base hospital medical corps He enlisted, May 17 1917, and after three weeks at Fort Slocum was sent to Camp Ethan Allen, in Vermont, where he performed three months' service His next assignment was at Camp McClellan, in Alabama, where he remained eighteen months, going thence to Camp Dix, New Jersey, where he was honorably discharged and mustered out, February 19 1918 Mr Kaczmarek is a member of the American Legion St Stephen's Roman Catholic Church, and fond of those royal out-of-door sports, hunting and fishing

---

PATRICK FRANCIS KENAH.—Thomas Kenah, father of Patrick F Kenah, was born in Cork, Ireland, and came to the United States a boy He found a home in Philadelphia, Pennsylvania, but in 1880 moved to South Amboy, New Jersey, where he died in 1910, aged seventy-two years He was a ship carpenter and a good mechanic He married Ellen Costigan, born in Tipperary, Ireland and was brought to the United States by her parents, they settling in Philadelphia, where she died, in 1871, aged twenty-six They were the parents of four children: Mary, died in Philadelphia at the age of thirty-seven years, Patrick Francis, of further mention; Catherine, died aged five years, James Joseph, in the employ of the government at Washington It was James J Kenah who admitted President Wilson and his daughter to the floor of the House when the officer in charge of their party was trying to find keys to unlock the door the janitor having gone home The newspapers of the country made a thrilling story out of this, saying that the officer would not admit them, not recognizing the President That story contained the usual grain of truth, but Mr Kenah knew the President well, and stole a march on the other officers by getting the House door unlocked

Patrick F Kenah, son of Thomas and Ellen (Costigan) Kenah, was born in Philadelphia, March 25, 1866, and there attended public schools until fourteen years of age His father then moved to South Amboy, where the lad obtained employment in the shipyards, continuing a worker in the yards at Perth Amboy and South Amboy for ten years In 1890 he established a cafe in South Amboy, and in 1895 erected the building he now occupies at No 128 North Broadway Personally, Mr Kenah is a man in good standing among the business men of his city, is popu-

lar with all classes and is a liberal public-spirited citizen   He is a director
of the South Amboy Trust Company, a director of fifteen years standing
in the Star Building and Loan Association of South Amboy, was secretary of the South Amboy Association, and in 1905 was elected chief of
the fire department, having then been a member of the department for
fourteen years   At the end of his term of service as chief, the South
Amboy paper described his record as one of 'conscientious service, intel-
ligently and faithfully performed"   Further, 'in many particulars his
wisdom and persevering efforts have secured important reforms in the
ranks and greater efficiency in the service."

Mr. Kenah is a member and ex-treasurer of the Loyal Order of
Moose, member of the Ancient Order of Hibernians, of the Chamber of
Commerce, and of St. Mary's Roman Catholic Church   He is always
ready and willing to "lend a hand" in any movement tending to advance
the interests of South Amboy, and is interested in many of the city's
enterprises not mentioned in this review

Mr. Kenah married, in Philadelphia, December 27, 1888, Mary A
Campbell, born in that city, daughter of John and Mary Campbell, her
parents both deceased

HENRY GUNTHER—Frederick (1) Gunther, father of Henry
Gunther was born in Wittenbac, Germany, and served as cashier in the
post-office of his native city   In 1850 he left his native land, coming to
the United States and settling in the vicinity of Metuchen, New Jersey,
where he purchased a farm, consisting of one hundred and fifteen acres,
and built thereon a candle factory, which he operated for a number of
years   The building was later destroyed by fire and never rebuilt   He
also erected a substantial house, which is now (1921) occupied by his son,
Henry Gunther, the present owner of the farm   The elder Mr Gunther
prospered as a farmer, and knew a freedom and independence previously
but dreamed of.   Frederick Gunther married Pauline Fischer, and they
were the parents of three sons and two daughters, as follows   1 Frederick (2), born in Germany, now deceased   he accompanied his parents
to the United States, in after life he resided in Philadelphia, Pennsylvania; married Hannah Drake, of Metuchen, New Jersey, and they were
the parents of three children   Frederick (3), Lillian, and Bertha   2
Gustavus, born in Germany, and accompanied his parents to the United
States, he enlisted in the Union army and fought throughout the Civil
War, he had followed the life of a farmer, his home near Metuchen, New
Jersey, he married Sarah Langstaff, and they are the parents of three
children: Laura, Charles, and Julia   3. Johanna, born in Germany, and
accompanied her parents to the United States   She married Frederick
Manning, of New Durham, New Jersey and they are the parents of three
children. Stelle, Harry and Pauline   4 Henry, of further mention   5
Julia, born in the old homestead near Metuchen, married Alvin F Randolph, of Piscataway, New Jersey, and they are the parents of four children   Paul F, Gertrude F, William F and Julia F

Henry Gunther was born near Metuchen, New Jersey, September 11, 1850 He obtained a good education in the district schools He bought the old farm, his birthplace and has lived there for the past thirty-five years The farm lies about one mile from Metuchen, on the road to New Brunswick, opposite the Pines Hotel Mr Gunther is a prosperous, substantial farmer, well known in his community In politics he is a Republican, and in religion a member of the Dutch Reformed Church

Mr Gunther married, April 9, 1877, Josephine Randolph, born March 20, 1853 daughter of Azael and Jane (Gibson) F Randolph, and a member of a prominent New Jersey family

HARLEY IRWIN WOOD —On the border line between Middlesex and Union counties, in the vicinity of Rahway, New Jersey, a city which is noted for its many manufactures, there have been few families which in successive generations have been more highly respected than that of Wood the man whose name heads this article being a representative in the third generation of the family to reside on the same farm whereon there are two substantial commodious houses, equipped with all the necessaries of modern life

Harley Irwin Wood, son of Samuel F and Sarah Jane (Clark) Wood, the former named a carpenter and joiner by trade, was born in New Dover, New Jersey, October 5, 1873 He was a student in the common school of his birthplace, making good use of his opportunities and becoming well-grounded in the fundamentals and then he followed in the footsteps of his father, from whom he obtained a thorough insight into the mysteries of carpentering to which he added building, conducting both lines with equal success and profit Integrity, activity and energy have been the factors in the success he has achieved, and his enterprise has been of decided advantage to the community, promoting its material welfare in no uncertain manner He holds membership in the New Dover Methodist Episcopal Church and in the Junior Order of United American Mechanics, and his political affiliations are with the Republican party

Mr Wood married, June 26, 1901, in Plainfield, New Jersey, Adda Belle Huselton, born in Kings, Hunterdon county, New Jersey, October 1, 1880 daughter of Henry and Margaret (Rupell) Huselton, the former named serving in the capacity of conductor on the New York Central Railroad Children of Mr and Mrs Wood· Dorothy M, born July 15, 1903, Isabel H, born July 18, 1904: Ruth L, born January 16, 1909, Marjorie J, born February 9, 1911, Harley S, twin of Marjorie J, and Norman H, born June 25, 1918

WILLIAM H. VAN WYCK —Agriculture has from time immemorial been the chosen occupation of many men, the greater portion of whom have achieved not only success in a material way but a strong, healthy body and an alert, active mind, capable of coping with the various problems of life, and among this number is the man whose name heads this sketch, William H Van Wyck, an enterprising and progressive agriculturist of Colonia New Jersey

William H Van Wyck is a native of Flatbush, Long Island, New York State, born July 24, 1872, youngest son of Z B and Catherine (Mitchell) Van Wyck, the former born on Long Island, and the latter at Oyster Bay, Long Island, New York State. They were the parents of five other children, namely Frank B, born May 24, 1858, Samuel H, born December 25, 1859, George M, born November 8 1861, Elizabeth M, born August 3, 1863 and Doritha M, born March 28, 1874

William H Van Wyck attended the common schools in the vicinity of his home in Flatbush, in which section he resided until the year 1890, when he was eighteen years of age, and then changed his place of residence to the State of New Jersey, locating on a farm in Colonia, Woodbridge township, Middlesex county, where he has made his home ever since a period of three decades He is devoting his entire attention to the raising of a general line of farm products, and the neat and thrifty appearance of everything pertaining to the property, including his residence and out buildings, indicates the careful supervision of a master hand Mr Van Wyck is not hampered by affiliation with any of the great political parties, but casts his vote for the men who in his opinion are best qualified for the office for which they are nominated His religious affiliation is with the Dutch Reformed church, in the work and activities of which he takes an active interest, and wherever he is known he is held in high regard for his genuine worth, his loyalty to his duties of citizenship and his trustworthiness in all relations of life He is unmarried

---

EDWARD W COOPER—Prior to the birth of their son, Edward W his parents, Frank and Anna (Haley) Cooper, left their home in Ireland and came to the United States, Frank Cooper being at that time a young man of thirty They settled in Iselin, Middlesex county, New Jersey, and there a son, Edward W Cooper, now a prosperous dairy farmer of the same town was born, July 22, 1863 Edward W attended the Iselin public schools, and early in life began farming He now owns a farm of forty-three acres near Iselin station on the Pennsylvania Railroad, in Middlesex county, and rents about two hundred adjoining acres which he cultivates, and also uses as pasture for a herd of thirty-two cows, for since 1902 he has been a successful dairy farmer He is a Democrat in politics, and a member of the Protestant Episcopal church

Mr Cooper married, in Oak Tree, New Jersey, June 14, 1893, Jane W Dickson, born in Scotland, February 5, 1870, daughter of Thomas and Jane (Wilson) Dickson her father a farmer, born in Scotland Mr. and Mrs Cooper are the parents of five children Frank, born April 6, 1894, Jeannette, born July 10, 1896, Helen, born June 12 1901, Edward, born April 27, 1907, died April 29, 1907, and Ethel, born January 1, 1911.

RICHARD J FAGAN, a lifelong resident of his native State, New Jersey, a representative of its agricultural interests, a man of integrity and honor, esteemed and respected by his fellow-townsmen, was born in Raritan, New Jersey, April 20, 1860, a son of John and Frances (McGuire) Fagan, the former named born in Ireland, November 11, 1827, the latter named born in New York City, and they were the parents of ten children, as follows Sarah, born July 2, 1855, James, born July 27, 1857; Richard J of this review, Julia, born July 18, 1861, John, born February 24, 1863, William, born April 17, 1867, Thomas, born October 21, 1868, Henry, born August 26 1870, Arthur, born May 6, 1872, and Charles, born July 21, 1874

Richard J Fagan obtained his preliminary education in the public school in the vicinity of his home, and completed his studies in the Rahway High School His father was the owner of a farm consisting of two hundred acres, upon which all his children were born, hence Richard J, being the second oldest son, was inured to farm labor, assisting his father in the work of planting cultivating and reaping, in addition to the many other tasks that fall to the lot of a farmer and thus was thoroughly competent to carry on the work on his own account when attaining the suitable age The property is well improved and gives every indication of a master's hand in its management and cultivation His residence and outbuildings are neat and attractive in appearance, and are equipped with everything needful for comfort and convenience Mr Fagan is a member of the Roman Catholic church a member of the Knights of Columbus, a Democrat in politics, and a staunch supporter of community interests He is unmarried

---

FRED JENSEN —The Danish Home for the Aged, at Metuchen was founded in 1913 and at that time a fine private residence and seventy-two acres of land were purchased from the Smith estate and has since well served its purpose The home and farm has all modern improvements, and is maintained by various Danish societies

---

FRANK WALLACE KIESSLING, son of Joseph Charles and Rachel Jane (Bell) Kiessling, was born in New Brunswick, New Jersey, December 27, 1874, and there educated in the public schools Since May, 1920, he has been a deacon of the First Presbyterian Church of New Brunswick, New Jersey

Mr Kiessling married, in Bellport, New York, June 3, 1905, Anna Evelyn Osborne, daughter of George Tomlinson and Anna Eliza (Selover) Osborne Mr and Mrs Kiessling are the parents of a daughter, Elizabeth Osborne Kiessling, born January 16, 1909

JAMES B POWER —John Power, father of James B Power, was born in Waterford, Ireland He came to the United States, about 1870, and settled in Metuchen, New Jersey, a harness-maker by trade He married, in New York State, Ellen O'Callahan, and they were the parents of five children   David, John, Edward, Nellie, and James B, whose career is herein traced

James B Power was born in Metuchen, New Jersey, October 25, 1875 and there completed a high school education   He was variously employed in his earlier years, and since 1903 has been with the Vaccum Oil Company in official capacity   He is a Roman Catholic in religion, a Democrat in politics, and a member of the Independent Order of Foresters

Mr Power married in Southampton, Long Island, November 23, 1904, Anna McTurnin, born in Water Mill, Long Island, January 20, 1883, daughter of Frank and Mary (Boyle) McTurnin, her father born in Ireland, but coming to the United States at the age of fifteen years   Mr. and Mrs. Power have no children.   Their home is in Metuchen, New Jersey

---

CHARLES SMITH EDGAR —The Edgar family, of which the late Charles Smith Edgar was a descendant, came to the United States from Scotland, about 1680, and settled in Middlesex county, New Jersey   The members of this family were mostly men of business and farmers, and in each generation produced worthy men and women who transmitted to posterity the sterling traits of character which distinguished their early Scotch ancestors   Mr Edgar's Grandfather Tappen's home at Bonhampton, New Jersey, was once the headquarters for the British army during the Revolution   Afterwards, a British cannon ball was found in the house and is yet kept by Mrs Edgar as a souvenir   Mr and Mrs Edgar's great-grandfather, Thomas Edgar, served during the Revolution

Charles Smith Edgar, a clay miner and manufacturer, was a son of Albert Edgar, born in New Jersey, who became a successful farmer of Bonhampton, New Jersey, where his wife, Susan Tappen, was born.

Charles S Edgar was born in Bonhampton, New Jersey, September 22, 1848, and died in Metuchen, New Jersey, May 15, 1917. He obtained a good education in the district schools, and grew to manhood at the home farm, later becoming a landowner   A clay bed was found on his property, and he made the mining, washing and production of clays his life s business   The production of his mines was used in the pottery industry   He developed a very profitable enterprise, and secured a fortune through his initiative and executive ability   He continued in business until his passing away   He was a man of sterling character, and was held in high esteem by his townsmen and his business associates   In politics he was a Republican, and in religion a member of the Metuchen Dutch Reformed Church

Mr Edgar married, in Metuchen, New Jersey, December 20, 1882, Frances Emily Edgar, born May 22, 1848, daughter of Freeman and Sarah Elizabeth (Martin) Edgar, both parents born in New York City, where her father was a merchant   One son was born to Mr and Mrs. Edgar, Albert Charles Edgar, born May 27, 1898, who attended Rutgers

Andrew Keyes

College, New Brunswick, and is now (1921) a student at Pratt Institute, Brooklyn, New York During the World War he was with the Twenty-eighth Regiment, New Jersey Engineers, and served in France Mrs Edgar survives her husband and continues her residence in Metuchen, her home, at No 31 Graham avenue, a handsome residence built in 1889 by Mr Edgar Mrs. Edgar is a member of the Metuchen Dutch Reformed Church, as was her husband She is a lady highly esteemed in the community in which she has so long resided, and has been active in community affairs

ANDREW KEYES —A half century ago William and Mary (Irvine) Keyes came from Ireland to the United States, where William Keyes engaged as a farmer at Englishtown, New Jersey Later they moved to Rahway, New Jersey, where their son Andrew was born, he now a successful contractor of Woodbridge, Middlesex county, New Jersey, and an esteemed citizen.

Andrew Keyes was born in Rahway, New Jersey, June 15, 1883, and there attended the public schools Later he completed a course in the New Jersey Business College, Newark New Jersey, entering the clerical employ of the Pennsylvania railroad immediately after graduation He continued a clerk in the Newark freight office of the Pennsylvania until 1906, when he became a lineman with the Public Service Corporation at Perth Amboy, and six years later, in 1912, began business in Woodbridge, New Jersey, as a contractor, and there continues a prosperous business

In politics Mr Keyes is a Republican and since 1911 has been township clerk, now serving his tenth consecutive year He is a member of the Masonic order, the Knights of Pythias, Royal Arcanum, and the Benevolent and Protective Order of Elks He and his family are members of St Paul's Protestant Episcopal Church of Rahway, New Jersey

Mr Keyes married, in Rahway, in 1905, Mary A Marson, daughter of John and Mary Ann Gordon (Bunch) Marson, her parents of English birth, they coming to the United States a half century ago Mr and Mrs Keyes are the parents of two children John Andrew, and Behatta Alice

The family home is in Woodbridge, where the family are highly esteemed Mr Keyes has proven a most efficient town clerk and has given to his office the same careful attention that he gives to his private affairs In his business relations he is honorable and upright, holding public confidence to a remarkable degree

ARTHUR EDWARD WARNER, president and manager of the Perth Amboy Printing Company, who in the last three years has become prominently identified with the business life of Middlesex county, and politics of New Jersey, particularly of Union county, is a member of a New England family and a native of East Providence, Rhode Island, where his birth occurred May 15, 1878 His father, Edward Pike

Warner, was also born in that town in 1843, and resided there during his entire life. The elder Mr. Warner was engaged in business at East Providence, and was connected with the Department of Roads for many years, being one of the prominent residents of the town. His death occurred there in 1919, at the age of seventy-five. He married Sarah Medbury, by whom he had two children. Alvah F., now a newspaper man of Schenectady, New York, and Arthur Edward, of whom further.

Arthur Edward Warner attended the local schools of East Providence as a lad, and was prepared for college at the high school, from which he graduated in 1898, at the age of twenty years. Later he matriculated at Dartmouth College, and was graduated from there with the class of 1904, having in the meantime done considerable work in connection with various Rhode Island newspapers. After completing his studies he did not, however, at once continue with his journalistic work, but accepted a position as vice-principal and instructor of mathematics and sciences at the Newport Academy, Newport Vermont. He found that the more active life of the newspaper man made a stronger appeal to him, and after one year in the above position became editor of the "Daily Eagle," of Lawrence, Massachusetts. His next post was as city editor of the "Telegram" of Bridgeport, Connecticut, and after six years in this position he became acting editor of the Hartford "Post." He was later associated with the New Haven "Register." This was Mr. Warner's last New England paper, and from New Haven he came to New Jersey to take the post of assistant editor of the "Daily Journal" of Elizabeth. From the latter place he went to Newark and became associated with the 'Star-Eagle' of that city, remaining with that publication until 1917. In that year he severed his connection with the 'Star-Eagle" and gave up direct newspaper work in order to establish the Perth Amboy Printing Company, of Perth Amboy, his present concern, with himself as president and manager. This company is the successor of the job department of the Perth Amboy "Evening News," and its career as a separate organization under the directions of Mr. Warner has been eminently successful. The shop and offices are located at No. 70 Smith street, and there a large business is done in the printing of periodicals, catalogues, job work and stationery, the firstclass quality of the work and service recommending it highly to the community. The establishment is carried on in a most efficient and businesslike manner the equipment being of the most modern type and adequate to care for every kind of highclass and fancy printing.

Since coming to Perth Amboy, Mr. Warner has interested himself actively in local and State politics, and his grasp of practical affairs has already carried him far. He is associated with the local organization of the Republican party and in 1918 was elected a member of the New Jersey State Legislature, a post in which he has served the best interests of his constituents and the community-at-large in a highly efficient manner. He was appointed by Governor Edge, in 1919, as a member of the commission to urge upon Congress a Federal appropriation for the Intra-State canal from Bordentown to Morgan, and was chairman of the House Commission on Domestic Relations and Juvenile Courts, besides serving on the Appropriations Committee of the State of New Jersey for three years

Mr Warner is also prominent in social and fraternal circles, and is a member of the Loyal Order of Moose, the Improved Order of Red Men, and the Junior Order of United American Mechanics His clubs are the Dartmouth of New York City, and the University of Bridgeport, Connecticut Mr Warner is a Baptist in religious belief, and is a member of the Central Church of that denomination of Elizabeth, New Jersey

Mr Warner was united in marriage, September 4, 1901, at Riverside, Rhode Island, with Nellie Benning Allen, a daughter of Samuel and Helen (Reynolds) Allen, now both deceased

JOSEPH JOHN KEENEN, proprietor of the successful boiler-making establishment at No 396 Division street, Perth Amboy, New Jersey, one of the rapidly growing enterprises of the city, is a native of California, his birth having occurred in the city of San Francisco, December 8 1865 He is of Irish parentage, his father, Jeremiah Matthew Keenen, having been born in Ireland, and there spent his childhood days

The elder Mr Keenen came to the United States in company with his parents when quite young, the family settling for a time at Hackensack, New Jersey Later, however, the young man went to California, and, settling in San Francisco, there developed a boiler-making business, in which he continued successfully for a great number of years He now resides in that city at the venerable age of eighty-two years Jeremiah Matthew Keenen married Hannah Kennedy, in San Francisco, and they were the parents of seven children, as follows James, who now occupies the position of chief engineer with the Pacific Mail Steamship Line Company, William, who is a member of the City Fire Department of San Francisco, Thomas, who volunteered for service in the Spanish-American War, and met his death in action during that conflict in the Philippine Islands, Joseph John with whose career we are here especially concerned, Mary, who married John Howley, and they reside in San Francisco Ellen, who married Robert James Kennedy, and they make their home in Seattle, Washington, and Catherine, who married John Douglass, and they make their home at Auckland, New Zealand

Joseph John Keenen passed his childhood in his native city of San Francisco and attended the parochial school of St Francis Xavier's Church until he had reached the age of seventeen years He then entered his father's boiler-making shop and there learned the trade that he has followed ever since After serving an apprenticeship of several years, he came to Perth Amboy, New Jersey, in 1902, to take the position of foreman in the boiler-works of P White & Sons, and continued to hold the same for a period of twelve years, during which time he not only perfected his knowledge of every detail of the work, but also gained considerable familiarity with the business side of the establishment In 1914, having amassed a sufficient capital, he terminated his association with that firm and engaged in the same line of business on his own account   Mr Keenen met with success from the outset of his venture, and now owns a large and developing business, with shop and office at No 396 Division street, Perth Amboy   The scrupulous honesty with which he has always conducted his affairs, together with the quality of his work and the materials which he uses have gained for him the well-merited esteem of the business and industrial world, and a reputation which is the basis of his success

Mr Keenen has always interested himself in the questions and issues of the day, as well as in local affairs, but although his fitness for public office is apparent, and he has had several opportunities to become a candidate, he has consistently refused all offers of the kind and confined himself to the conduct of his business affairs   He is a Democrat in politics, and is well known in local social circles, being a member of the Benevolent and Protective Order of Elks the Knights of Columbus, and the Ancient Order of Hibernians   In his religious belief Mr Keenen is a Roman Catholic and attends St Mary's Church of that denomination at Perth Amboy   He is an active member of the parish and belongs to the Holy Name Society connected with his church   Mr Keenen has always taken keen pleasure in open air sports and pastimes, especially in hunting and fishing, his favorite hunting ground being his native State of California, where he delights to stalk the big game of the region, making occasional trips to that section

Mr Keenen was united in marriage June 18, 1908, at Perth Amboy, with Mary F Smith a native of that city   She is a daughter of James Smith, a proprietor of one of the oldest blacksmith shops of the city, situated on King street   He served at his trade when Perth Amboy was but a village, for some sixty years   He died July 3, 1920

JOSEPH BRUCK—In the retail distribution of fine footwear, one of the most complex of any one line of merchandising, Joseph Bruck, of Perth Amboy New Jersey, meets an everyday need of the people

The name of Bruck is an old one in Hungary.   Maurice Samuel Bruck, Mr Bruck's father, owned a large jewelry store in the city of Unghvar, Hungary   He was a prosperous and highly respected citizen, and besides this mercantile establishment he handled extensive government contracts   He lived and died in Hungary, reaching the age of fifty-five years   He married Mary Weinburg, also a native of that country   She survived her husband for a long time, and died at the age of seventy-three, in Hungary   They had ten children. Johanna, deceased, Sigmund, deceased, Cecilia, now a resident of New York City, and the widow of Max Blau Caeser deceased, Antonia, married and lives in the city of Rosenau, Hungary, Rosalia, a widow, resides in Budapest, Hungary, Isador, a resident of Brooklyn, New York   Joseph, of further mention, Louis, deceased, and Samuel, now living in Brooklyn New York

Joseph Bruck was born in Hungary January 1, 1863   He attended school there until 1879 when his ambition leaped ahead of the opportunities he saw in that environment and he came to the younger country across the seas   He located in New York City, where he obtained work in a book bindery Realizing the importance of practical education in the struggle of life, he was a regular attendant at evening school, making the most of this opportunity to become thoroughly familiar with the language and customs of the country With mental equipment won by diligent application, he secured a position on the road in the employ of a grocery house, holding same for two years At the end of that time he was ambitious to branch out for himself, so started a store and auction room in New York City He followed this successfully for two years, then removed to Perth Amboy and started a wholesale and retail grocery store on State street This was in 1893, and he continued in that business for ten years Then, in 1903, he established the present business on Smith street For the past fifteen years he has been at his present location at No 140 Smith street, and this has come to be recognized as the largest shoe store in Middlesex county

Apart from the shoe business, Mr Bruck has extensive real estate interests, and takes great interest in the building up of unimproved districts He is a keenly enthusiastic motorist, and few people have a greater familiarity with the topography of the surrounding country He is a member of the Ancient Free and Accepted Masons, and of the Knights of Pythias

Mr Bruck married, March 7, 1893, Stella Eisner, daughter of Emanuel and Barbara (Gottlieb) Eisner, of Bohemia, she born in that country, June 19, 1864 Her father died in Bohemia after which her mother joined her in Perth Amboy, and there her mother died Mr and Mrs Bruck are the parents of three children, Mary, who died in infancy, Irene Agnes Sarah, who was born May 2, 1895, and Maurice Samuel, born July 29, 1896 The family worship at Temple Beth Mordecai

---

WILLARD PAYNE MELICK —The Melicks of Woodbridge, New Jersey, were early interested in the clay industry, and there, engaged in that industry, Joel Melick spent his life He was born in Woodbridge, September 5, 1838, and there died, August 31, 1890 He married Anne E Payne, born in Woodbridge, October 7, 1841, and they were the parents of Willard Payne Melick, secretary of Powell's, Inc , No 411-415 Canal street, New York City

Willard Payne Melick was born in Woodbridge, New Jersey, October 2, 1870, and there completed the grade and high school courses of study, finishing with high school graduation, class of 1888 He then increased his educational advantages by a full course at the Coleman Business College, Newark, New Jersey. After graduation, in 1889, he was variously employed, and in November, 1890, entered the employ of A M Powell, at No 154 Chambers street, New York City He began as a bookkeeper and cashier, and has never severed his connection with the business that first claimed him in 1890 In 1910 the business was incorporated as Powell's, Inc with the following officers Alexander M Powell president, Joseph B Powell, vice-president, Robert J Powell, vice-president; Willard P Melick, secretary, and Alexander W Powell, treasurer The business of the house is wholesale confectionery, and they are also proprietors of Powell's Chocolate Mills

Mr Melick is a Republican in politics, and a member of the First Presbyterian Church of Woodbridge

Mr Melick married, in Woodbridge, May 18, 1892, Edith Jeannette Lawson, daughter of Peter and Rachel (Lyons) Lawson Mr and Mrs Melick are the parents of a son, Edwin W, and a daughter, Jeannette

Edwin W Melick enlisted in the United States army during the World War, 1917-18, serving with the Motor Section Headquarters Troops First Army of the American Expeditionary Forces, attaining the rank of sergeant He was honorably discharged and mustered out in June, 1919 The family home is at No 204 Green street, Woodbridge, New Jersey

---

COLONEL J BLANCHARD EDGAR—The Edgars, since coming from Scotland to Middlesex county, New Jersey, about 1720, have varied farming with business operations, the heads of each generation having been either men of large affairs or substantial farmers Thomas Edgar was the first of the family in Woodbridge, and he received a large tract of land, upon which a homestead was erected, which in its day was one of the handsomest and most substantial in the county The land adjoining and surrounding the homestead was extensive and a considerable portion descended to William Edgar, the great-grandfather of Colonel J B Edgar, and to his son, Major William Edgar, one of the leading men of his day, a member of the New Jersey Legislature, a founder and first president of the Farmers' and Merchants' Bank of Rahway He married Phoebe S Baker, and they were the parents of thirteen children, one of these being John B Edgar father of Colonel J Blanchard Edgar, who built the home in which his son was born, and where the family resides

John B Edgar was born at the old Edgar homestead, in 1809, and died at his farm in April, 1882 He attended the district school, and from youth was employed about the farm later adopting agriculture as his life work, he became one of the successful, substantial farmers of Woodbridge He bought his own farm when quite young, and built a comfortable residence thereon He made a specialty of blooded cattle, sheep and swine, and was a large exhibitor at the fair held at Trenton by the New Jersey State Fair Association, of which he was a charter member He was a man well read and well informed, public-spirited and energetic, particularly interested in road improvement, a subject upon which he was far in advance of his neighbors He could never be prevailed upon to accept any other office than that of overseer of roads, and that he was always willing to take, as it enabled him to accomplish needed improvements He was a Presbyterian in his religious belief, a Whig and later a Republican in politics He loved his farm not as a farm, but as his home, and there hospitality abounded

Mr Edgar married (first) Anna Louise Ross, who died in 1863, daughter of William M Ross, a merchant of New York City, and later in life lived at Metuchen, New Jersey, where he was an elder of the Presbyterian church A sister of Mrs Edgar married Amos Robins, a

leading Middlesex county Democrat, who sat in both houses of the Legislature, and for several terms was president of the Senate Mr. and Mrs Edgar were the parents of six children Eugene R , Rufus N , J Blanchard, of further mention, Margaret, Josephine, and Catherine Mr Edgar married (second) Catherine Bevier, of Ulster county, New York, who with her infant child passed away

J. Blanchard Edgar, the last survivor of the children of John B and Anna Louise (Ross) Edgar, was born at the homestead built by his father at Woodbridge, New Jersey, May 7, 1843, and died December 28, 1920 After preparation at Rev David H Pierson's School, at Elizabeth, New Jersey, he entered Rutgers College, whence he was graduated in the class of 66 He decided to become a lawyer, and so entered the offices of Parker & Keasby, of Newark, New Jersey, as a student, but pressing calls were made for his help in the management of the home farm, and he gave up his own ambition to become his father's assistant Some years later he was appointed to a position in the United States Custom House, New York City, a position he held several years. He then spent ten years in charge of the lumber interests of the Domestic Sewing Machine Company of Newark, New Jersey, then operated on his own account in West Virginia and other timber sections The lure of the land then proved the stronger, and he became owner of the homestead upon which he was born, and there resided until his death. He operated the farm as a dairying proposition largely, maintaining a herd of seventy-five cows, and serving a choice class of customers in Rahway with the products of his dairy

Colonel Edgar was a member of the State militia for over twenty years, serving at one time as a member of the general staff of the governor's, with the rank of colonel, and for several years was a member of the Woodbridge Board of Education His college fraternity was Zeta Psi, and he was a member of the Masonic order Politically he was a Republican

Colonel Edgar married Harriett B Collins, of New Britain, Connecticut, and they were the parents of five children: Anna Louise, who is the wife of Willard C. Freeman, of Rahway, New Jersey, Blanchard Collins, who resides at Nashville, Tennessee, and is vice-president and general manager of the Tennessee Power Company, Gertrude, the wife of Cornelius T Myers, of Avenel, New Jersey, Marguerite, the wife of Henry D Tucker of Rahway, New Jersey, and Natalie, who is now (1921) at home Colonel Edgar was interred in the cemetery at Rahway, New Jersey

---

JOHN ELLIOT BRECKENRIDGE—From the time he received his degree from Yale University more than a quarter of a century ago, Mr Breckenridge has been engaged in the chemical industry, being now chief chemist of the American Agricultural Chemical Company, and an authority on many matters connected with his department He has written extensively on chemical topics, his articles appearing in current chemical journals

John Elliot Breckenridge, son of John Albert and Harriet (Kellogg) Breckenridge, was born at Palmer, Massachusetts, May 4, 1873 He completed public school education with graduation from Palmer High School, class of 1891, then entered Yale University, whence he was graduated with honors in chemistry, class of 1896 Immediately after graduation from Yale University, he began professional work with the Liebig Manufacturing Company continuing with that company as chemist until accepting his present position, chief chemist of the American Agricultural Chemical Company, at No 2 Rector street, New York City. The company is an important one, Mr Breckenridge having seventeen laboratories under his charge and direction He is a member of the American Chemical Society, Association for the Advancement of Science, Society of Chemical Industry, and was for several years chairman of the fertilizer division of the American Chemical Society

In politics Mr Breckenridge is a Republican, and was chairman of the township committee of Woodbridge township, Middlesex county, New Jersey, for two years 1918-19 He is an elder of the First Presbyterian Church of Woodbridge, member of the Independent Order of Foresters, and Yale Alumni Association

Mr Breckenridge married, October 26, 1898, Amanda G Edgar, daughter of William and Amelia (Gray) Edgar They are the parents of two children Marian Edgar, born December 26, 1900 now a junior at Wellesley College class of 1922· and Harriet Amelia, born May 31, 1906 The family home is at No 198 Green street, Woodbridge, New Jersey.

J EDWARD HARNED —Active in the community life of Woodbridge, New Jersey, a locality in which he drew his earliest breath, Mr Harned has through his business activities and personal characteristics won the respect and confidence of all who knew him, and that includes practically everyone in the town

Mr Harned is a son of the late Dr Samuel P and Fannie C (Bloodgood) Harned, his mother of old New Jersey family, a daughter of James Bloodgood, of Woodbridge Dr Harned was a medical practitioner in Woodbridge many years, continuing until his death in 1898 He was the son of William Harned, of ancient New York family, who came to Woodbridge in 1856, his son, Samuel P, then being a young man Dr Samuel P Harned there practiced his profession with success and honor for a long term of years, passing away at the age of sixty-two, after having been a resident of Woodbridge for nearly half a century

J Edward Harned was born in Woodbridge, New Jersey, October 15, 1875, and there passed all the grades of the public schools, graduating from the high school with honors in 1891 The year following his graduation he entered the grocery business in Woodbridge as clerk, continuing until 1898, when he entered the employ of the Central railroad at Sewaren In 1901 he took a position as bookkeeper with Faverweather & Ladew, of New York City, then the largest manufacturers of leather belting in the world   He continued in the employ of this firm for several years, finally becoming head accountant and assistant secretary. He later became associated with the publishing house of Frank A Munsey & Company, as an accountant   His engagement with Mr Munsey was a brief one, his health failing a few months after he made this connection to such an extent that it was necessary for him to work in the open air   As he was not in a position to finance a long period of rest, even for health purposes, he secured an out-of-door position with the Prudential Life Insurance Company   He acted as collector and agent for that company at Woodbridge for three years, 1909-1912, then resigned and opened a real estate office in Woodbridge under his own name

Since 1912, Mr Harned has operated a successful real estate business, his office now being in the Post Office building   He was one of the organizers of the Woodbridge Building and Loan Association, of which he is now a director   A Democrat in politics, he has long been connected with public civic life   From 1906 until 1912 he was town clerk, 1912-13, township treasurer, 1913-16, secretary of the Middlesex County Board of Taxation, and since April, 1918, has been postmaster of Woodbridge

Mr Harned married in "The Little Church Around the Corner" in New York City, September 20, 1906, Mabel E Stell, daughter of William and Emma (Huber) Stell   Mr and Mrs Harned are the parents of four children Warren P, Helen E, Katherine V, and Emily L   The family are attendants of the First Congregational Church of Woodbridge

---

WALTER GREEN QUACKENBUSH —Good roads form one of the big issues of the day, not only in State and county politics, but in the daily welfare of a large percentage of the population   Middlesex county, New Jersey, takes a justifiable pride in her excellent roads, and since 1918 Walter Green Quackenbush has been at the head of this important branch of the county business

The name of Quackenbush dates back several generations in New Jersey   Allen Peter Quackenbush, father of Walter Green Quackenbush, was born in Monmouth county, and died in Middlesex county, at the age of seventy-three years, he was a lifelong farmer   He married Mary Magee, who was also born in Monmouth county, and died in Middlesex county, at the age of sixty-seven   They were the parents of thirteen children of whom seven are now living   Richard, Experience, William, Luther, Ella, Allen and Walter Green, of whom further

Walter Green Quackenbush was born in Madison township, Middlesex county New Jersey on August 31, 1867, on his father's farm, the old family homestead   He attended school in the nearest district, then worked on the farm with his father until he was twenty-two years of age. He then went to Matawan New Jersey, where he learned the trade of mason   He followed this trade for a number of years, going about wherever fine construction work offered interesting employment, and thus covering a large part of the State   Then, in 1901, he came to Perth Amboy, where he remained until 1918 in the same line of work, and also doing a very considerable amount of road construction In 1918 he was elected road supervisor of Middlesex county, which office he now holds

Mr Quackenbush is a Republican by political affiliation He is a member of the Benevolent and Protective Order of Elks of the Knights of the Golden Eagle, and of the Improved Order of Red Men His main hobby is of the outdoor kind, that of hunting, and he is a member of the New Brunswick Shooting Club, and considered an excellent shot

Mr Quackenbush married, in Freehold, New Jersey, May 11, 1887, Annie Grace Preston, daughter of Henry and Ellen (Miller) Preston, who was born in Hawkeshead, England Her parents were both born in England, and both died in Matawan, New Jersey Mrs Quackenbush's grandfather, John Preston, died in Middlesex county, near Old Bridge, New Jersey, at the age of one hundred and four years, five months and ten days He always voted the Republican ticket Mr. and Mrs Quackenbush are the parents of four children, all living Arlie, born on January 9, 1888, and now the wife of Alfred Therkelsen, of Perth Amboy, Maud, born on September 20, 1890, and now the wife of Abram Mason Percy James born on January 4, 1897, who was graduated from the University of Michigan in the class of 1920 and Walter Earl, born on January 8, 1907 The family are members of the Episcopal church, and active in all the social and welfare work of the same

---

VICTOR HERBERT GILLIS—Among the well known ship-builders of New Jersey and New England is Alexander Gillis, father of our subject, who was born on Prince Edward Island, Canada, in 1851 He learned the ship carpenter's trade and was employed in Nova Scotia, Canada where his son, Victor H., was born, and later in Perth Amboy, New Jersey, and Providence Rhode Island, dying in the last-named city in 1920 He married Anne Ellis, and they were the parents of Victor Herbert Gillis, now holding executive position with the Roessler & Hasslacher Chemical Company of Perth Amboy, New Jersey.

Victor Herbert Gillis was born in South Maitland, Nova Scotia, Canada, March 12, 1882 Soon afterward his parents moved to Perth Amboy, New Jersey, where he was educated in the public school, finishing with the high school graduating class of 1899 He entered business life with the Tietjen & Lang Dry Dock Company, but after a few months, shipped before the mast for an ocean voyage and for eighteen months remained at sea He tried various occupations, remaining two years in the freight department of the Central Railroad of New Jersey as clerk, 1902-05, then from 1904-07 was with the C Pardee Company of Perth Amboy, finally in 1907 forming a connection with the Roessler & Hasslacher Chemical Company of Perth Amboy He has risen to an important position with that company and is highly regarded by the company's officials He is an independent in politics, a member of the Raritan Yacht and Chemical clubs of Perth Amboy, and the Bentley Yacht Club of Tottenville, Staten Island, New York He and his family are members of the Presbyterian church of Perth Amboy

Mr Gillis married, in Perth Amboy, New Jersey, in 1905, Laura Tunis, daughter of Charles S and Ella (Peacock) Tunis. Mr and Mrs. Gillis are the parents of three children. Helen G., Marjorie, and Catherine S.

BERNARD M GANNON—A familiar figure in the business world of Perth Amboy, New Jersey, is Bernard M Gannon, of Gannon & Sheehy, the leading haberdashers of Perth Amboy.

Mr. Gannon is a son of John and Mary (Clancy) Gannon, both of whom were born in Ireland, and emigrated to this country early in life. They made their home in Port Jervis, New York, Mr Gannon entering the employ of the Erie railroad, where he was continuously employed for fifty years.

Bernard M Gannon was born in Port Jervis, New York, where he attended school until fifteen years of age. Being active and full of spirit, the boy started out to make his way in the world, taking the line of railroad work as his choice. He entered the yards of the West Shore railroad, wiping engines for a beginning. He remained with the West Shore for four years, then went on the New York Central railroad as a fireman. While working in that capacity he had an accident which deprived him of the use of his right hand, and thereafter, during his connection with the New York Central, was a station agent. He came to Perth Amboy in 1893 and acted as joint agent for the Staten Island railroad and the United States Express Company.

In 1903 Mr Gannon became associated with his present partner, and the firm of Gannon & Sheehy was formed for the purpose of establishing a retail business in men's furnishings and haberdashery. The venture was successful from the very beginning, and the attractive store at No 92 Smith street has become the popular shopping mart for the fastidious men of Perth Amboy and its vicinity.

Mr Gannon has long been interested in the public matters of the city, having been called upon repeatedly to serve in public capacities. In 1901 he was elected alderman from the Second Ward, in 1902, elected assemblyman, in 1907 again elected alderman, in 1909 county clerk, which latter office he has held continuously ever since. He is a Democrat in his political affiliation and a member of the Perth Amboy Democratic Club. He is a member of the Benevolent and Protective Order of Elks, of the Knights of Columbus, and of the Hibernians. He also is a member of the East Jersey Club, of the Raritan Yacht Club; and of the Union Club, of New Brunswick.

Mr Gannon married, in New York City, in 1900, Catherine Maher, who has since died. Mr Gannon has three children. Catherine, John, and Mary. He resides in Metuchen.

SAMUEL S. BURLOCK.—To the intelligence, industry and thrift of her agriculturists more than to all other causes combined, does Middlesex county, New Jersey, owe her remarkable development. The farm owned by Samuel S Burlock and his wife was brought to its present condition by Louis Kolb, a native of Germany, who came to this country in 1853 and settled in Newark, New Jersey, where at the age of twenty-one he became a citizen of the United States, and where he worked at his trade, that of hat finishing In 1861 Mr Kolb married Christina Schaffer also a native of Germany, and they were the parents of five children, two sons and three daughters, all born in Newark, in the public schools of which place they received their education Mr Kolb had the misfortune to lose his arm, so was compelled to give up his trade He bought the farm which had laid idle for over twenty years, and by hard work succeeded in clearing it He built a residence thereon, and set out the grounds with all kinds of fruit trees suited to that climate In 1900 Mr and Mrs Burlock purchased this farm and made it their home, Mr Burlock remaining, however, with the Pennsylvania railroad

Samuel S Burlock is a native of Philadelphia Pennsylvania born September 4, 1843, a son of Samuel DeForest Burlock, a native of New York City, and Lydia Ann (Smith) Burlock, a native of Philadelphia, Pennsylvania The elder Mr Burlock was an enterprising business man, devoting his entire time and attention to the publishing trade, from which he derived a lucrative livelihood

Samuel S Burlock was a student in the public schools of Philadelphia He learned the trade of book binding in his father's publishing house, becoming thoroughly expert in that line, but he did not follow it for his active business career, as he entered the employ of the Pennsylvania railroad, in whose service he continued until he attained the age limit for their employees, then was retired on a pension

Mr Burlock is a veteran of the Civil War He enlisted in Philadelphia, Pennsylvania, August 7, 1862, serving sixteen months, when he was honorably discharged He is a member of the Protestant Episcopal church, and whatever conduces to the betterment of the community receives from him an earnest support.

Mr Burlock married (second) in New York City, April 10, 1889, Catherine Christina Kolb, born in Newark, New Jersey, January 13, 1862, a daughter of Louis and Christina (Schaffer) Kolb, the former owners of the Burlock farm By a former marriage Mr Burlock has a son, Horace V Burlock, who is employed by the New York Central railroad, he is the father of two sons and one daughter, the latter a teacher in the public schools of New York City Also, by a previous marriage, Mrs Catherine C. (Kolb-Wenzler) Burlock had a son, Harry Wenzler who was raised by Mr Burlock and given the name of Burlock, he was born in Newark, New Jersey, May 25, 1883 He is a prosperous farmer and the father of four children, two sons and two daughters who represent the third generation of the Kolb family born in America

---

PHILIP LEO SCHWARTZ, D D S, is more than usually well supplied with talents by which he may earn a livelihood He has been on the staff of a daily periodical, has written upon professional subjects for magazines, is at present an instructor upon medical subjects;

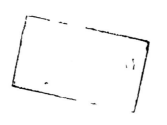

and also is a dentist with a large practice which occupies most of his time

Born in New Brunswick, Dr Schwartz is the son of Herman Schwartz, a cigar manufacturer in New Brunswick, where he has conducted an establishment for many years at No 84 Albany street, his home being at No 19 Kirkpatrick street   Mrs Schwartz was Malvina Rosenberg, the daughter of Rev Daniel Rosenberg, a prominent divine, located in New York City   Mr and Mrs Herman Schwartz have six children, all living at the present time   Their son, Philip Leo Schwartz, has enjoyed the advantages arising from a good, fundamental education, having been a pupil in the grammar schools, from which he graduated in 1909, followed by a four years' course at the high school, graduating in 1913   Immediately after leaving school, the young man held the position of assistant advertising manager of the New Brunswick "Daily Times"   After a short business experience, Dr Schwartz entered the New York College of Dental Surgery, which institution, after a complete course of instruction, conferred upon him the degree of Doctor of Dental Surgery in 1917   For six months after his graduation from college, Dr Schwartz was located in Trenton, but at the end of that time he opened an office in New Brunswick, in October, 1917, and began the practice of his profession here, his office being at No 101 Albany street, in the Montalvo building

Dr Schwartz is at the present time assistant oral surgeon at the Vanderbilt clinic in New York City, and instructor in anesthesia at Columbia University in the post-graduate course of dental surgery   Dr Schwartz also devotes part of his time to charitable work, being a member of the staff on oral surgery at St Peter's Hospital, New Brunswick   His particular work is in the line of dental surgery, using the X-ray in connection with his work   Dr Schwartz has also contributed several excellent articles treating on professional subjects to the "Dental Cosmos Magazine" one being "The Treatment of Facial Neuralgia by Alcoholic Injections" and another article upon "The Removal of Redundant Tissues of the Mouth"

The various societies having connection with professional matters are some of Dr Schwartz's many interests   He is a member of The Middlesex County Dental Society of which he is secretary, the New Jersey State Dental Society, the National Dental Association, and the Middlesex County Professional Guild being treasurer of same   In club life he is also quite active, being a member of the New Brunswick Lodge of the Benevolent and Protective Order of Elks, and the New Brunswick Country Club, this last affording him the opportunity to indulge in his favorite game of golf   Dr Schwartz is not married

---

EPHRAIM CUTTER —As a legal practitioner at Woodbridge, New Jersey, Mr. Cutter has passed his professional life, which began in 1877 with his admission to the New Jersey bar   He opened an office in Woodbridge, in January, 1878 and has since practiced there   That period however, does not cover his connection with Woodbridge, for there he first saw the light of day, and there his father was born, and his forefathers, back to Richard (2) Cutter the first of his family to leave New England and establish a home in New Jersey

The Cutter family is of English origin Elizabeth Cutter, a widow, came to New England about 1640 with her three children, William, Richard and Barbara

Richard Cutter, son of Elizabeth Cutter, died at Cambridge, Massachusetts. June 16, 1693 He married (first) about 1644, Elizabeth Williams He married (second) February 14, 1662-63, Frances (Perriman) Amsden, widow of Isaac Amsden Fourteen children were born to Richard Cutter, seven by each wife, William Cutter, of whom further, being among the children of his first wife

William Cutter, son of Richard and Elizabeth (Williams) Cutter, was born at Cambridge, Massachusetts, February 22, 1650, and died in Cambridge, April 1, 1723 He married Rebecca Rolfe, and they were the parents of Richard (2) Cutter, of whom further

Richard (2) Cutter, son of William and Rebecca (Rolfe) Cutter, was born November 13, 1682 As before mentioned, he was the first of the Cutter family to leave New England and establish a home in New Jersey He settled in Woodbridge township, Middlesex county, where in 1709 in company with John Pike, he built what is believed to be the first mill erected in that township That mill stood on then Pike, now Woodbridge creek, at what is now the Cutter and Prall dock He married, August 20, 1706, Mary Pike, and they were the parents of fourteen children Richard (2) Cutter died in December, 1756, aged seventy-five years From this ancestor sprang the Cutters of Woodbridge prominent in the clay mining and manufacturing business, in farming and merchandising.

Ephraim (2) Cutter, of Woodbridge, is a son of Ephraim and Mary (Stansbury) Cutter, his father a farmer of Woodbridge township, who died in 1854, at the age of forty-seven years He was an officer of the Presbyterian church, and was greatly respected Mary (Stansbury) Cutter belonged to an old Woodbridge family, the Alston The farm upon which Ephraim and Mary (Stansbury) Cutter first lived came into the Cutter family in 1750 They were the parents of four children: William Mary H, deceased, Sarah, who married Daniel S Voorhees, of Woodbridge, and Ephraim (2) of further mention

Ephraim (2) Cutter was born at the farm in Woodbridge, New Jersey August 11, 1854, this farm having been the home of his father and grandfather The farm has been known for many years as the Spa Spring Farm Ephraim (2) Cutter began his education in Woodbridge public schools, passing thence to a private school in Elizabeth, New Jersey of which Dr David H. Pierson was the head, continuing there during the years 1867-68 He then spent a year in Rutgers Preparatory School at New Brunswick, New Jersey, and in the fall of 1870 entered Rutgers College, taking a classical course, remaining until graduation, when he received his A B with the class of 1874

After his graduation he at once began another term of close application, registering as a law student in the office of Andrew Dutcher, in

Elizabeth, New Jersey. After a year's study under Mr Dutcher, he entered the office of William J Magie and Joseph Cross, also at Elizabeth Mr Magie was afterwards chancellor of New Jersey He continued in this office as a student for two years At the November term, 1877, of the Supreme Court, Mr Cutter was admitted to the New Jersey bar as an attorney, and the following January he opened an office in Woodbridge, and began the practice of law At the June term, 1881, he was admitted as a counsellor, and has since been admitted to practice in all the Federal courts of the district He has been continuously in the practice of law in Woodbridge from 1878 to 1921, and holds honorable position at the Middlesex county bar He served as township attorney in 1884-1889, and again in 1906-1913, inclusive He has a good practice along general legal lines, and holds the confidence and esteem of his community He has been engaged in much important litigation

A Democrat in his political faith, he has always taken an active interest and part in local public affairs He represented the First Assembly District of Middlesex county in the New Jersey State Assembly in 1888 and 1889, and from 1884 to 1889 was a member of the township committee In the years 1896 and 1897 he was president of the Woodbridge Board of Education Mr Cutter has always been one of the leading supporters of every forward movement, and in all things, progressive and public-spirited He is a member of the official board of the First Congregational Church of Woodbridge, a society he aided in organizing in 1874, and of which he has been a member for forty-seven years

Mr Cutter was one of the charter members of the Salmagundi Literary Society of Woodbridge organized in 1882, and has been a member of that society since that time. He has always taken a keen interest in State and National affairs

---

JUDSON G COTTRELL, a prominent physician of Perth Amboy, New Jersey, and one of the leaders of his profession in Middlesex county is a member of an old and highly esteemed family in this part of the State, where for four generations it has held a conspicuous place, his great-grandfather, James Cottrell, being one of the early settlers of Madison township His grandfather, Garrett Cottrell, and his wife, Hannah (Herbert) Cottrell, also lived here and were well known in the life of the community in their time.

Dr. Cottrell is a son of William H and Louisa (Ely) Cottrell, the former a prosperous farmer of these parts, and the latter a native of Hightstown, New Jersey, and now a resident of Asbury Park They were the parents of eight children, as follows Harvey, who died at the age of twenty-four years, Ely, now engaged in business as a merchant in New York City, Laura, who became the wife of C W Waltman, of Asbury Park; Emily, who became the wife of C T Warner, also of Asbury Park, Herbert, who now follows the occupation of farming in Middlesex county; Willard and Frank, twins, the former a practicing physician at Rutherford, New Jersey, and the latter a farmer in this region, Judson G., with whom we are here especially concerned.

Dr. Cottrell was born on the old family homestead in Middlesex county, New Jersey, June 14, 1883 and after attending the local district schools as a lad, entered the Glenwood Collegiate Institute, at Matawan, New Jersey, and was graduated from the same in 1902 He had in the meantime determined to follow medicine as a profession, and accordingly matriculated at the New York Homœopathic College, where his brother Willard was a sophomore After his brother's graduation at New York, he entered the Hahnemann Medical College of Philadelphia, Pennsylvania where he graduated with the class of 1906, and received the degrees of Doctor of Medicine and Doctor of Homœopathic Medicine For eighteen months Dr. Cottrell served as interne at the Metropolitan Hospital on Blackwell's Island New York, and there gained a wide practical experience in his work, which has been of inestimable service in his subsequent career. In 1908 he removed to Perth Amboy, New Jersey, and on June 25th of that year, began the general practice of his profession there, with offices at No 288 Madison avenue He has continued in this place uninterruptedly up to the present time, and has in that period built up one of the largest practices in the region, and come to be regarded with the highest respect alike by his professional colleagues and the community-at-large

During the World War Dr. Cottrell volunteered his expert services in the cause of his country and the world and served for eight months as surgeon in the United States Army Debarkation Hospital, No 3, at the headquarters of the Port of Embarkation at Hoboken, New Jersey. Dr. Cottrell is a man of wide interests and has always given much attention to the general problems and issues, social and political, of the day He is a Republican in politics but does not allow himself to be bound by partisan considerations in casting his ballot, but judges for himself of each issue and candidate with the greatest of independence He is very fond of outdoor life and spends much of his leisure in automobiling, to which he is greatly devoted Dr. Cottrell is a prominent member of the Masonic order having reached the thirty-second degree in Freemasonry, and is affiliated with Raritan Lodge Free and Accepted Masons the commandery Knights Templar, Salaam Temple, Ancient Arabic Order Nobles of the Mystic Shrine, and New Jersey Consistory Besides those Masonic bodies, he is a member of the local lodges of the Royal Arcanum and the Order of Maccabees, Tall Cedars of Lebanon the Perth Amboy Medical Society, the Middlesex County Medical Society, the New Jersey State Medical Society and the American Medical Association Other societies with which Dr. Cottrell is affiliated are the American Institute of Homœopathy, the New Jersey State Homœopathic Society, the New York County Homœpathic Society, of which he is an associate member; the Alpha Sigma Alumni Association and the Association of Military Surgeons He is a member of the Colonial Country Club of Colonia, New Jersey, and the Middlesex Golf Club at Woodbridge

HON JAMES KEARNY RICE —From the beginning of the legal activity of the young attorney of 1876 to the death of the ex-Judge and ex-United States District Attorney in 1920, there is no period in the life of the Hon James Kearny Rice that does not measure up to the highest of professional and private standards. There is written below the outline of his busy, purposeful career, and the words of appreciation of his closest associates are quoted. Were there means of recording and preserving the testimony of all who knew and loved him, from the humblest to the most influential, then and then only could there be reared the perfect memorial to one of the first citizens of Middlesex county and New Jersey.

James Kearny Rice was born in Washington, D C, November 20, 1849, son of Nathan and Eliza W (Warren) Rice, his mother a daughter of John Warren, of New York City, one of the first members of the New York Stock Exchange. James Kearny Rice was graduated from Lawrenceville High School in 1865 and for several years was engaged in business in New York City. He began the study of law in the office of Woodbridge Strong, and in 1875 was admitted to the bar of New York, becoming an attorney in New Jersey in 1876. After graduation from the Law School of the University of New York he was admitted as counsellor in New Jersey at the November term, 1880, and two years later, in 1882, his long career in public life began. In this year he was appointed by Governor Ludlow prosecutor of the pleas for Middlesex county, was reappointed at the expiration of his term by Governor Green, and in 1890 was appointed law judge of Middlesex county by Governor Abbett. He was reappointed by Governor Werts in 1895.

Mr Rice was the first law judge who ever sat and held the Circuit Court in New Jersey after the passage of the act authorizing law judges to sit in the circuit, and after that act was passed until he stepped down from the bench, nearly all of the circuit business was tried before him under the assignment of Chief Justice Beasley. Judge Rice was also the first law judge who ever sat in the Oyer and Terminer alone, without a justice of the Supreme Court, in a capital case, under the provisions of the act of 1894. This was the case of the State vs Aragio and Spina, charged with the murder of Antonio Prisco. It was first tried in the Middlesex Oyer and Terminer, December term, 1894, before Judge Rice. After two weeks' trial the jury disagreed, another trial was held at the April term, 1895, and the defendants were convicted of murder in the first degree. The case is somewhat celebrated, both because of the facts connected with it and from the fact that it was the first time in the history of the commonwealth when a capital case was presided over by anyone except a justice of the Supreme Court.

In February, 1896, Judge Rice resigned his judgeship of the Court of Common Pleas of Middlesex county to accept the post of United States Attorney for the district of New Jersey, tendered him by President Cleveland, and this place he filled with eminent satisfaction until 1900.

Judge Rice's talents were not alone those of the attorney, advocate, and jurist, for he was the possessor of exceptionally keen business judgment, and in connection with several important receiverships and trusteeships, proved his ability in most commendable accomplishment In 1904 he was appointed by the United States Circuit Court receiver for the Great Eastern and the National Clay Company, near South River, the other receiver being the New York Trust Company, Otto T Bennard, president The affairs of these companies were administered so successfully that within one year more than $90,000 was made for the creditors, reorganization being made and a new concern formed, which, in later years, was absorbed by the trust In December, 1907, Judge Rice was appointed by Judge Lanning, in the United States Circuit Court, receiver of the Arizona Smelting Company and of the Consolidated Arizona Smelting Company, a corporation capitalized at $15,500,000, with offices in New York and plant in Humboldt, Arizona He was subsequently made receiver by the New York and Arizona courts, his duties in this relation taking him to Arizona a number of times The companies were thrown into bankruptcy, Judge Rice was elected trustee, the plants were sold and a new company was organized, now continuing in operation

In July, 1917, Elmer E. Connolly, treasurer of the Michelin Tire Company, and Judge Rice, were asked to accept positions on the Federal Draft Board of New Brunswick New Jersey, in the place of the mayor and the city clerk, who were disqualified by reason of being within the draft age Both expressed their willingness to serve, and Judge Rice was elected chairman of the board, and Mr Connolly secretary They continued in service with Dr Cronk, the medical advisor, during the remainder of the war, until the signing of the armistice and their discharge by orders from Washington in the spring of 1919 Few persons, who did not experience it, realize the heavy drain upon the members of the various draft boards, the burden of responsibility they bore, and the disadvantages under which they labored During long periods the government furnished insufficient help for the work, and assistance had to be obtained elsewhere The Michelin Tire Company, Johnson & Johnson, and the Interwoven Stocking Company, at times furnished clerical help without charge, and Judge Rice, on occasions of importance, gave the services of his expert stenographer to the government. A feature of the draft board work in New Brunswick, which was probably different from that of other boards, was the keeping of the record of every person who appeared for examination, showing the results of the physical examination whether or not exemption was claimed If exemption was claimed, the findings of the board were noted, while in cases that were contested a full report of the testimony was given This was the course adopted at Judge Rice's suggestion before the questionnaire system was adopted, and after that system was introduced, every case that was investigated for validity, and every case where the board on its own motion directed that testimony be taken regarding alleged claims for exemption, was recorded by Judge Rice with the aid of his stenographer, who was especially adapted ior such work Before any case was decided the person concerning whom the hearings were ordered had his or her "day in court," and in every case that was heard Judge Rice wrote an opinion, his recommendations being submitted to the other members of the board for their decision thereon before the final judgment was given In other words, the Federal Draft Board of New Brunswick required that every man have his "day in court," just as in a trial in a court of law, before decision was rendered A stenographic report of the proceedings was kept and forwarded to Washington with the general records

In the summer of 1918 the work of the board was particularly strenuous, and Judge Rice was advised by his physician, the late Dr Donahue, that his own welfare required his resignation Judge Rice, in his zeal and devotion to patriotic ideals, disregarded this counsel although his colleagues on the board lightened his responsibilities as far as possible, and with the close of hostilities he gave up actual participation in the daily routine, but retained his place on the board In 1919 he had been appointed a member of the State Board of Conservation and Development, serving thereon with the conscientious fidelity that marked his administration of every public trust

Judge Rice married the eldest daughter of Theodore G Neilson, of New Brunswick The family home for many years was at No 82 Carroll Place, New Brunswick, New Jersey He died in New Brunswick, January 14, 1920 The following is a minute of the Middlesex Bar Association, adopted January 16, 1920

This minute is a slight expression of the love and esteem of the members of the bar of Middlesex County for their brother and friend, so long their companion and advisor their leader as President for many years

His was a strong and sturdy personality,—a man of decided opinions, reticent, brief in speech, a deep thinker, an ardent lover of the profession of the law and ever ready to preserve its dignity and traditions, a thorough student of the law, an earnest advocate, a tireless defender of the State and fearless prosecutor of offenders of its laws, an able and impartial judge Loyalty to his client, thoroughness in preparation and earnestness in presentation, were his distinguishing legal characteristics

We knew him to love him He was the first to congratulate us upon every success in public or private life, and the first to express the word of sympathy in personal loss or failure His word of counsel in many a difficult situation will be remembered and appreciated by us all

As a public official his high sense of duty and responsibility for whatever office he filled was strongly marked He sacrificed his personal practice upon the altar of official duty

What more fitting climax to his long and splendid career than to have given his time and talent in his declining years to patriotic service of his country upon the Federal Draft Board,—the great test of our democracy, where without fear or favor America's youth proved its belief in equality and sprang to its country's service

The memory of Judge Rice's personality, his faithfulness in private and public affairs, and his love of his profession will be an inspiration to those of us who remain.

W E FLORANCE, Chairman,
GEO S SILZER,
CHARLES T COWENHOVEN,
ADRIAN LYON,

PETER F DALY,
FREDERICK NEIGEL,
EDWARD W HICKS,
FREEMAN WOODBRIDGE

MONSIGNOR JOHN A O'GRADY.—From the time when as a youth of sixteen years he felt the urge to his holy calling, until as a Christian veteran of seventy years he laid aside a completed task Monsignor John A O Grady lived a life of single-hearted devotion that has its rich fruits in the thousands he has influenced toward righteousness The glorious history of the church is but the composite record of such loyal, faithful followers of its great head as he and it is from such example that the great body of its people have derived inspiration for lives of unselfish service, of brotherhood with all men His parish has many physical evidences of splendid work accomplished under his vitalizing leadership and in the minds and hearts of the multitude in Middlesex county and throughout the State whose privilege it was to work with him, there remains in unfailing strength and beauty the memory of a Godly man An editorial tribute in the "Daily Home News" of New Brunswick at the time of his death spoke thus of this beloved churchman.

Probably no New Brunswicker has rivalled in warmth of affection or in distinction the life and achievements of Monsignor John A O'Grady He was conspicuous in church and civic affairs in this city for nearly half of his life of three score and ten years, and as a faithful churchman, a mighty molder of public opinion, a scholar, and a friend, he was noteworthily esteemed by the vast majority of our citizens The record of his personal accomplishments is amazing The untiring and restless energy of his mind vied with and even exceeded that of his indefatigable body—for long after the inroads of ill-health had made necessary a curtailment of physical exertion his mind was as clear and his discourse as illuminating as at any period of his career

Monsignor O'Grady was a churchman of noble stature and a leader whose rare sagacity and diplomacy won many victories for the cause of civic righteousness and spiritual and moral uplift An orator of power and tremendous conviction, he proved a potent leader, and while his victories were mainly those secured through peaceful conquest, he never shirked a fight against evil in any form, and his splendid influence was always to be counted upon for the betterment of all mankind. As a theologian he ranked with the highest, while as an administrator and financier his works will long remain as monuments of unusual efficiency He was, in his heart's core, a lovable man, adored by all who shared his intimacies Guided by an overwhelming love for his Master, with a masterful intelligence and a profound knowledge of men and motives, he was a born leader Scintillant in his many-sided genius, he almost was gifted with what Hugo termed the cube of human faculties He was among his fellowmen a star of the first magnitude, an Orion in the firmament of mankind

A strange, great light exhausted its vital ray when Monsignor O'Grady's lamp of life flickered and went out A community testifies its sense of personal bereavement An imposing, dominating and rugged figure has passed from view

Monsignor John A O'Grady was born at Montague Sussex county. New Jersey, July 3, 1849 He was sixteen years of age when he determined to give himself to the priesthood, and he entered St Charles College at Ellicott City, Maryland Upon the completion of his course in this institution he entered Seton College for the study of theology and philosophy, and was ordained May 30, 1874, becoming private secretary to Bishop M. A Corrigan of the diocese of Newark, New Jersey Later, he was sent to St Patrick's Cathedral, Newark, and two years afterward to St Peter's Church, New Brunswick, New Jersey, as curate, Rev Father Rogers then serving as pastor After two years at St Peter's, he became rector of the church at Boonton, and in 1881 returned to St

Peter's for his long and richly blessed pastorate, Father Rogers' advanced years having made necessary the relinquishment of his heavier ecclesiastical burdens   Father O'Grady, during the long years of his New Brunswick residence, became more than a denominational figure, for his sympathies and interests extended into all fields affecting the welfare and happiness of his fellowmen, irrespective of race or belief, and his admirers were found in all classes alike   At one time he was a member of the City Park Commission, and he was a member of the Board of Trade   He was a devoted friend of Rutgers College, and for several years prior to his death was the donor of an annual oratory prize, known as the "O'Grady prize"   At the 1918 commencement exercises the degree of Doctor of Letters was conferred upon him, *in absentia*, illness keeping him at home

Father O'Grady's pastorate at St Peter's covered a period of thirty-seven years, a period of vast material expansion and spiritual growth   Among the accomplishments of his long term of service whose physical evidences remain, were the purchase of a new organ, the redecoration and furnishing of the church, the building of a commodious sacristy, the enlargement of the rectory and convent, and the acquisition of additional ground for the cemetery, whose area he more than doubled   A notable event of his ministry was the erection of the splendid equipped parochial school, known as Columbia Hall, and the construction of a large addition to that building a few years prior to his death   The purchase of the former Russell property at Somerset and Hardenbergh streets, and the founding of St Peter's General Hospital on the site, was due in large measure to Monsignor O'Grady, who gave the institution watchful care from the first and contributed heavily to its success

When Father O'Grady assumed charge of the parish of St Peter's it was staggering under a debt of almost one hundred thousand dollars, a disheartening handicap for a young priest to take up   Nevertheless, in addition to paying off this debt, he paid off the old and new debt of Columbia Hall, the hospital grounds, and several acres of hospital property which, with interest, amounted to nearly three hundred thousand dollars   All of this was paid by the close of 1911, when the parish was entirely free from debt   With barely a breathing space, this zealous man of God and his devoted followers undertook a new program of advancement, and in order to meet the demand for more hospital room a fine home for the nurses was erected and later a separate maternity hospital, containing a children's ward

Father O'Grady was an earnest supporter of the movement to provide a convenient church home for the Catholics of Highland Park, and the formal opening of St Paul's Chapel resulted from this interest   Out of St Peter's parish was formed the German parish of St John the Baptist in 1865, the Sacred Heart parish in 1883, the Hungarian parish of St Ladislaus in 1904, and the Italian parish of St Mary of Mt Virgin in 1905   Father O'Grady was raised to the dignity of dean by the late Bishop O'Farrell and was made a domestic prelate with the title of Monsignor by His Holiness, Pope Leo XIII, predecessor of the present Pope Pius X For a number of years he occupied the position of Rural Dean of the northern section of the diocese of Trenton, and as such was the valued advisor of the bishop and the warm personal friend of every rector in his district

On the occasion of the twenty-fifth anniversary of his ordination celebration, ceremonies of four days concluded with a banquet, at which he was presented with a silver box containing one thousand dollars in gold and fifteen hundred dollars in bills, all of which he at once applied toward the work of refurnishing the church His fortieth anniversary, in 1914, was likewise the occasion of a season of celebration by his parishioners

Monsignor O Grady died January 15, 1919 His funeral was held in the church of which he had been pastor for so many years, and was attended by thousands of men, women and children in every walk of life It was the largest funeral service ever held in the city of New Brunswick, and many of the mourners, who filled the church to overflowing, together with hundreds of children attending the parochial school, accompanied the cortege to St Peter's Cemetery, where all that was mortal of this saintly man was laid to rest The solemn High Requiem Mass was celebrated with Rt Rev. Monsignor B J Mulligan, celebrant, Rev Thomas Roche, of Asbury Park, deacon; and Rev Dr. William P Cantwell, of Perth Amboy, sub-deacon Rev Thomas B Hagerty, of Hampton, master of ceremonies Rev Father Neal A Mooney, of Trenton, thurifer, Rev Fathers James A Harding, of Phillipsburg, and J Arthur Hayes, of Trenton, acolytes

---

DR. SAMUEL MESSINGER.—Among those who coming to this country from other lands, have not only made a successful career for themselves but have reared and educated a family for future usefulness to themselves, their country, and the nation, Leon and Helen (Baum) Messinger, parents of Dr Samuel Messinger, of Roosevelt, New Jersey, have rendered a distinct service Leon Messinger was a manufacturer of furniture in Austria, and a well known citizen in his native town Czernowitz Capable, energetic, and ambitious, he found conditions somewhat hampering in the Old World, so decided to try his fortune in the newer land to the westward, where opportunity was greater and where there were fewer long-established customs to fetter the ambitious man who wished to rise In 1891, with his wife, Helen, and four children, Morris, Henrietta, Samuel, of whom further, and Hattie, he came to America and settled in New York City, where he engaged in the furniture business, first as a mechanic, and later, in 1894, as a manufacturer There were difficulties that called for all the courage and determination he possessed, and there were times when his business venture seemed doomed to failure, but the initiative, and the steady courage which had brought him into a new country never failed him Against heavy odds, he succeeded, building up a business which not only supplied their immediate needs, but which enabled him to give his children the best education obtainable In addition to the four children born in Austria, four more, Mildred, Isadore, Rose and David, were born in America, and both Leon Messinger and his wife were determined that their family should have all the advantages which the new country could give To this end they had toiled, economized, and achieved business success Leon Messinger died March 14, 1920, survived by his wife A hard worker, honest and sincere in his every purpose, Leon Messinger was a devoted father and a true citizen, and in the hearts and lives of his children his influence will long continue to be of service to them

Samuel Messinger, son of Leon and Helen (Baum) Messinger was born at Czernowitz, Austria, July 7, 1887, and came to America with his parents, while still a small child Taking full advantage of his father's desire that the children should obtain the best education possible, and also of the opportunities offered in the land of his adoption, he attended the grammar and high schools of New York City and then entered the College of the City of New York, first pursuing a general course of study and then studying medicine and surgery in the Eclectic Medical College of the City of New York, from which he graduated in 1912, receiving the degree of Doctor of Medicine and Surgery He then entered upon his professional career in New York City, where for a year he practiced in various hospitals and infirmaries, specializing along certain medical lines He then left New York City and for three years engaged in general practice in Jersey City, New Jersey In 1915 he located in the borough of Roosevelt, Middlesex county, New Jersey, where he has remained and here has built up a large and successful practice He is one of the leading physicians of this section of the county, and has rendered valuable service to his community, both in professional and in public life The poor and afflicted have found in him a "great physician," tender and sympathetic, always ready to meet a real need, regardless of the probabilities of renumeration

Dr Messinger has taken a keen interest in civic affairs in the borough of Roosevelt, and is held in high esteem by his many friends During the World War he was a member of the Officers' Reserve Corps, holding the rank of lieutenant He is a member of the visiting staff of the Rahway Hospital, of which he was one of the founders He is also a member of the Middlesex County Medical Society, and of the National and State Eclectic Medical societies

Dr Messinger is highly talented as a musician He studied the violin under Nathan Manor of New York City, and his mastery of this instrument is still fresh in the minds of those who have heard him play while in the concert world

Dr Messinger married, December 11, 1911, Sonja Carsch, daughter of Aaron and Frances (Wexler) Carsch of New York, and Boston, Massachusetts To Dr and Mrs Messinger three children have been born Walter, October 19, 1913, Edith Barbara, March 28, 1920, and Leonard, May 29, 1921 Dr Messinger's fine residence and well-fitted clinic is located at Nos 29 and 31 Roosevelt avenue, corner of McKinley avenue, borough of Roosevelt, Middlesex county, New Jersey

AARON GROSS—Among the prominent business men and citizens in the progressive little town of Fords, New Jersey, may be mentioned Aaron Gross He is a son of Nathan and Rebecca Gross, and was born in Hanusfolwa, Austria, October 23, 1870 In early life his father followed the occupation of a farmer in that country, and about 1887 he and his wife came to the United States with their children, among whom were William, now a prominent business man at Fords, Terrie, now the wife of Max Goldberger, of Perth Amboy, Aaron, of further mention; Sallie, now the wife of Jacob Gluck, of Cold Spring, New York, Mollie, now the wife of Julius Kohn of Perth Amboy, David, a business man of Newark, New Jersey, and Herman, deceased, who was a practicing physician at Metuchen, New Jersey

Aaron Gross passed the years of his boyhood in Austria, where he received a good education in the schools of his home town At about the age of eighteen he accompanied his parents to the United States, where he secured employment in New York City, remaining there for some time Later, he moved to Perth Amboy, New Jersey, where he secured a position in a local grocery store After about six years in this line of business he gained much experience, and with a little capital, embarked in business on his own account

It is now about twenty-five years since he came to Fords Corners, and in that time he has built up the largest mercantile business in the town He carries a large line of high-grade groceries and meats, and deals extensively in many other commodities Mr Gross has established a reputation for himself by his honorable and upright dealings. His store is modern in all its details and one of the finest in this section of the State He takes a keen and active interest in the affairs of his town, and is well known throughout the county Besides his own business, Mr Gross is interested in other affairs, including the Fairfield Building and Loan Association, of which he is a director, and he is a large stockholder in the Fords National Bank He is a member of the Republican party, the Masonic order, and the Woodmen of the World

Mr Gross married, July 7, 1895, at Brooklyn, New York, Bertha Goldberger, a native of Austria, the daughter of Samuel and Sara (Goodman) Goldberger, who came to the United States when their daughter was a child, and eventually made their home at Perth Amboy, New Jersey Mr and Mrs Gross are the parents of four children Mollie, born March 27, 1896, Irene, born March 5, 1899, Nathan, born April 1, 1902; and Joseph, born May 31, 1907

MATTHEW A HERMANN—When a man passes practically his entire life in one community and gives freely of his time, his energy, and his talents to the upbuilding of the interests of the group with which he lives, he makes for himself a large place in the life of the community and in the hearts of his fellow-citizens, a place which, when vacated, cannot well be filled by another When he passes from among his life-long associates, his friends and fellow-citizens suffer deep loss. Such

Matthew A Hermann

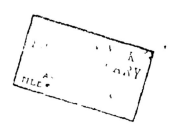

loss has been experienced by the citizens of the borough of Roosevelt, New Jersey, in the death of Matthew A Hermann

Mr Hermann was born in Carteret, now the borough of Roosevelt, New Jersey, and received the fortunate heritage which often results from the union of two nationalities From his father, Matthias Hermann, born in Baden, Germany, he received the German thoroughness, steadiness, and earnestness of purpose, from his mother, Bridget (Kelly) Hermann, born in County West Meath, Ireland, the quickness of sympathy, the wit, and the genial warmth of the sons of Erin These characteristics of two nations blended in one personality, staunchly and intensely American, produced a fine type of American manhood and a life that was exceptionally valuable to friends and community

Matthew A Hermann attended the schools of his district and then went to Miss Arrowsmith's Private School at Blazing Star Landing As a boy, he worked on the farm with his father, where, undaunted by the long hours of hard work, he developed strength and determination, and nourished his ambition for larger things His parents encouraged his aspirations, and when he decided to study telegraphy, helped in every way they could The lack of means of transportation in those days, however, made impossible the fulfillment of many a young dream, and the vigorous, ambitious, clear-seeing boy soon realized that his plan was impracticable. He kept at his studies, watched for his opportunity, and filled his days with earnest work at whatever his hand could find to do until the general contracting business offered the chance for which he had been waiting He formed a partnership with his brother, Joseph A Hermann, and for many years the firm of Hermann Brothers has carried on a large and successful business as dealers in builders' materials In recent years he also individually conducted a large construction business, and never failed to complete a contract satisfactorily and on time Many big improvements, public and private, in the Roosevelt section of the county have been the result of his work

Politically, Mr Hermann was a loyal Democrat, actively interested and influential in the councils of the party Always devoted to the best interests of his community, he served on the Middlesex county grand jury, and was a member of the local Board of Education since the incorporation of the borough in 1906 He was also an active and faithful member of St Joseph's Roman Catholic Church, a member of the Holy Name Society, and of the Knights of Columbus The Fire Department found him an efficient, faithful member of its corps of defenders of the homes of the borough, and his fellow members of the Order of Red Men loved him for his wit and for his genial friendliness Earnest, honest, unassuming a constructive worker for the improvement of social and economic conditions in his home town, and in the surrounding district, Mr Hermann will long be missed and his influence will long be felt

Mr. Hermann is survived by his mother, Bridget (Kelly) Hermann, his brother Mayor Joseph A Hermann, and his sisters, Elizabeth, Barbara, Margaret, and Catherine Matthew A Hermann died May 3 1921

HON JOSEPH ANDREW HERMANN.—Long one of the forceful, outstanding figures in the business and public life of the county of Middlesex is the Hon Joseph Andrew Hermann, mayor of the borough of Roosevelt, New Jersey

Born in the borough, in the section then known as Carteret, son of Matthias Hermann and Bridget (Kelly) Hermann, pioneers in the development of this section of the county, he first attended the local public school and later Miss Arrowsmith's Private School Reared on a farm until his early youth he left to assist in the management of his uncle's mercantile business in New York City for about five years, returning to engage with his brother in the masons' materials business, which he has conducted ever since, developing it into one of the largest of its kind in the county He has reached the position of one of the leading business men of the county, recognized throughout for his probity, energy and high abilities He was one of the first directors of the First National Bank of Roosevelt, and is the vice-president of the Carteret Building Loan Association In the direct personal making of the great growth in the business, industry and realty improvement of this section of the county, Mr Hermann stands second to none

Mr Hermann served as township committeeman of the township of Woodbridge, New Jersey, from 1901 to 1906. Following a long continued desire and some spasmodic efforts, a definite movement was organized in the last-named year by Mr Hermann to effect the incorporation as a distinct municipality of all that portion of Woodbridge township extending along Staten Island Sound from Port Reading to the Rahway river, a distance of about three miles, and running back from the Sound about one and one-half miles This territory included the settlements known as Carteret and Chrome, and embraced many large manufacturing enterprises along the water front A committee of twenty-five of the leading men of the community was formed, representative of all parties and elements that went to make up its civic, business and industrial life, for the purpose of incorporating it by legislative enactment as the borough of Roosevelt Mr Hermann was made its head and he gave all that was in his heart and mind to the work and success of the movement Active, persistent and formidable opposition from outside the proposed new municipality had to be met, but the movement did succeed and the borough was incorporated by the act of the Legislature, approved April 11 1906 And, admitted by all, the success was largely due to the brain, the leadership, the work and the organizing genius of Joseph A Hermann, so much so that he is called the father of the borough

Mr Hermann was elected the first mayor in 1906 and has continuously held the office ever since having been elected eight times in succession This is an unprecedented record in this respect, and shows the measure of the man and what the people think of him During his time as the executive of the municipality (fifteen years), the population has increased from 1 500 to 11,049 the tax values from $1,000,000 to $10,196,000, miles of roads, sewers sidewalks and curbing have been

Joseph A. Hermann

P. L. Ryan

laid, and the borough today has not over $25,000 municipal bonded indebtedness, an indebtedness based on tax values incomparably lower than any like municipality in the State of New Jersey This indicates the kind of a man and official and the quality of the service he has rendered

In 1920, Mayor Hermann was appointed by Governor Edwards a member of the Middlesex County Board of Taxation and this year, 1921, he was elected its president In this important office he has demonstrated his special fitness for the work and the soundness and impartiality of his decisions

Mr Hermann is a member of Carey Council, Knights of Columbus, was its grand knight for six years and has been a district deputy of the order, Court Carteret, Foresters of America, Division No 7, Ancient Order of Hibernians, Holy Name Society of St. Joseph's Church, its vice-president, Quinnipiac Tribe, Improved Order of Red Men, past sachem, Rahway Lodge, Benevolent and Protective Order of Elks; Friends of Irish Freedom, Middlesex Grove, Ancient United Order of Druids, St Vincent De Paul Society, its president, and the Roosevelt Fire Company, No 2 He is also director of St. Elizabeth's Hospital, Elizabeth, and the City of Rahway Hospital

During the World War Mayor Hermann was the recognized leader of the borough in the work of all the agencies and drives recognized and approved by the United States Government, and to his masterful efforts, militant Americanism, and able executive direction, was largely due the fact that no similar community surpassed the borough of Roosevelt in the intensity and success of all the movements organized to help win the war

---

PATRICK L RYAN —Among the well known clay miners and manufacturers of Middlesex county, and a man highly regarded and esteemed for his sterling character and uprightness, was the late Patrick L Ryan, of Woodbridge, New Jersey

Patrick L Ryan was a native of Ireland, born December 31, 1838, the son of good parentage He received a good education in the home schools of that country When he was about twenty years of age he came to the United States with members of his family, and shortly afterwards located at Kreischerville, Staten Island, New York, where he began his long and honored career in the clay business For a time he was employed at the old Kreischer Brick Works there and in 1860 removed to Woodbridge, New Jersey Here he followed the occupation of clay mining, being variously engaged for many years by some of the well known clay operators of the region, among them being Frederick W Meeker, of New York City, with whom he remained several years By strict application, thrift, and the savings of his labors, he was able to purchase Mr Meeker's clay mining interests in 1890, which consisted of about ten acres This venture proved so successful that as time went on he added to his original holdings until he had about six hundred acres of the finest fire-clay producing mines in the State of New Jersey.

In 1900, with his sons, Patrick J and John F, he helped organize The Mutton Hollow Fire Brick Company of Woodbridge, of which he was president until the time of his death

Mr Ryan was a broad-gauged man, and had a wide view on business and other conditions which he came in contact with As one of Woodbridge's most influential citizens, he did his best to further any cause that would be of benefit to the community in which he lived Aside from his clay mines, he was the holder of valuable real estate in and about Woodbridge

While he did not take an active part in political life, he was a staunch Democrat, and abreast with the political affairs of his day A loyal churchman, he was one of the original supporters of St James' Roman Catholic Church of Woodbridge

Mr Ryan married, about 1867, in Rahway, New Jersey, Catherine Doyle, like himself a native of Ireland, born April 10, 1845, coming to the United States in 1867 To Mr and Mrs Patrick L Ryan the following children were born, all in Woodbridge 1 Margaret, born August 3, 1870, married Eugene L Romond, of Woodbridge, who is now connected with The Mutton Hollow Fire Brick Company 2 Mary, born September 28, 1871, married James L Dalton, of Metuchen, also connected with the above company, they are the parents of five children. Catherine, deceased; Margaret, Helen, Anna, and James 3 Patrick J, of further mention 4 John F, of further mention 5 Rev Richard T, of further mention 6 Julia J, born March 6, 1879, married Richard P Grace, of Woodbridge, now a superintendent with The Mutton Hollow Fire Brick Company, they are the parents of three children Catherine Julia, and Anna 7 William A, of further mention 8 Lawrence C, of further mention 9 Catherine, born December 28, 1885, married P H Gallagher, of Allentown, Pennsylvania, now well known in business circles in New York City Patrick L Ryan died April 28, 1912, and his wife, Catherine (Doyle) Ryan, June 20, 1913, at Woodbridge, New Jersey The passing away of these two people was a sad bereavement to the community

Patrick J Ryan, first son and third child of Patrick L and Catherine (Doyle) Ryan, was born March 10, 1874 He was educated in the public schools of Woodbridge and the Coleman Business College at Newark, New Jersey At the age of thirteen years he began to learn the clay mining business under the direction of his able father, and has continued in this line of activity to the present date with much success In 1900, with his father and brother, he helped organize The Mutton Hollow Fire Brick Company, and became its treasurer He was instrumental in going before the officials of the Philadelphia & Reading railroad and convincing them of the logic of extending a branch freight line about two miles long into the clay mining district of Woodbridge This line was officially opened September 6, 1901, to the miners and manufacturers in the district, and since that time traffic has greatly increased in volume and it has proven to be one of the profitable branches of the railroad company During the World War Mr Ryan was selected one of the eight members

to serve on the War Service Committee of the National Clay Miners and Producers Association

Politically a Democrat, Mr Ryan is one of the leaders at the executive councils of the party in Middlesex county He is a member of the Knights of Columbus, Middlesex Council, No 857, of Woodbridge, and an attendant of St James' Roman Catholic Church

Mr Ryan married, in Woodbridge, December 3, 1913, Helen Golden, daughter of William and Margaret (Hackett) Golden To them two children have been born Catherine, and Patrick J, Jr

John F Ryan, second son and fourth child of Patrick L and Catherine (Doyle) Ryan, was born November 1, 1875 He was educated in the public and St James' Parochial schools of Woodbridge and the Coleman Business College of Newark, New Jersey. He first began work with the Standard Fire Proofing Company in their Perth Amboy offices, where he remained five years becoming a chief clerk and auditor In 1900, with his father and brother he helped in the organization of The Mutton Hollow Fire Brick Company, of which he became secretary and general manager, a post he has held with credit to the present time In addition to his manufacturing interests, John F Ryan is president of the newly organized Woodbridge National Bank, vice-president of the Woodbridge Building and Loan Association, and secretary and treasurer of the Woodbridge Realty Company

In politics a Democrat, Mr Ryan was appointed postmaster of Woodbridge by President Wilson, serving from 1913 to 1917, and during his administration the new post office was erected here During the World War he was active in various Liberty Loan and other war work activities He is a member of St James' Roman Catholic Church, past grand knight of the local council, Knights of Columbus, and secretary and treasurer of their Building Association

Mr Ryan married, in Woodbridge, October 21 1908, Alice E Mara, daughter of John I and Ellen (Paterson) Mara Mr and Mrs Ryan are the parents of eight children John P, Helen M, Richard T, Robert V, deceased, Patrick L deceased, Catherine F, Alice, and Mary D

Rev Richard T Ryan, third son and fifth child of Patrick L and Catherine (Doyle) Ryan, was born August 29, 1877 He received his education in the public and St James' Parochial schools of Woodbridge, Seton Hall College, South Orange, New Jersey, and St Mary's Seminary, Baltimore, Maryland He was ordained to the priesthood at Trenton, New Jersey, June 1, 1901, subsequently becoming a curate at various Roman Catholic churches He was appointed to Long Branch, New Jersey, June 6, 1901 transferred to Phillipsburg, October 5, 1901; appointed to Sandy Hook, February 21, 1905, and August 1 1910, was made pastor of the Church of the Immaculate Conception at Somerville, New Jersey He is well known in Somerville and beloved by friends in and outside of the church He is chaplain of Somerville Council, Knights of Columbus, member of the Somerville Gun Club, and the Somerset Golf Club

William A Ryan, fourth son and seventh child of Patrick L and

Catherine (Doyle) Ryan, was born March 12, 1881 He was educated at the public and St James' Parochial schools of Woodbridge, and the Coleman Business College at Newark, New Jersey. Like his father and brothers, he started in the clay mining and manufacturing business and has followed it ever since, and is now superintendent of mines of the Ryan estate at Woodbridge Aside from the clay business, he is in the general contracting business and has built up a large and growing enterprise He is general contractor on road work, excavations, and building construction, being well known in the trade Mr Ryan is a Democrat in politics, member of the local lodge, Knights of Columbus, and St James' Roman Catholic Church

Mr Ryan married, in Woodbridge, November 25, 1907, Elizabeth Jelicks, daughter of Frank and Elizabeth (Dunn) Jelicks They are the parents of four children Elizabeth, Patrick L, Catherine and Margaret

Lawrence C Ryan fifth son and eighth child of Patrick L and Catherine (Doyle) Ryan, was born April 8 1883 He received his education in the public and St James' Parochial schools of Woodbridge, and the Coleman Business College of Newark, New Jersey Since leaving school he has been identified in the clay mining and manufacturing business He is now assistant secretary of The Mutton Hollow Fire Brick Company, and takes a leading part in the management of this large and successful firm

Mr Ryan is a Democrat in politics During the World War he was actively engaged on the Registration Board in Woodbridge He is a member of the local council, Knights of Columbus the Foresters of America and St James' Roman Catholic Church

Mr Ryan married, in Woodbridge, May 2, 1909, Mary Geis, daughter of Henry and Anna (Soder) Geis Mr and Mrs Ryan are the parents of the following children Lawrence C, Patrick J, Anna M and James H

This historical record of the family of Patrick L and Catherine (Doyle) Ryan shows the strong character and family stapleness of all its members They began in a modest way and have built up large business interests and a sound social standing, which reflects much credit upon them individually and as a whole throughout the region

---

THE WOODBRIDGE LEADER—One of the foremost institutions of Woodbridge is the Woodbridge Leader," a weekly paper devoted to the encouragement of all movements, having for their object the advancement of the best interests of the town 'The Leader" came into being on March 1, 1910, succeeding 'The Register," which was at that time edited by R Uhler and Harry B Rollinson. The necessity for a paper of the type of "The Leader" was pressing at the time, because of the rapid growth of the community and the absolute need of an organ that would at all times speak for and defend the best interests of the people Such a purpose could not fail of success and from the start "The Leader" was accepted as the reliable and fearless mouthpiece of the citizenry of Woodbridge

The first editor was Mark J Boyle, newspaper man of many years'

Francis H. Monaghan

experience At present, the paper is ably edited by John A Flood; business manager, L A McLeod "The Leader" is owned and controlled by a corporation known as the Woodbridge Printery, Inc, composed of the following men. P J Ryan, J E Harned, L M Campbell, J F Ryan, C A Campbell, J S Dooley

"The Leader" is at present recognized as the official news medium of the town, having expanded from a circulation of three hundred to more than a thousand copies weekly

FRANCIS A MONAGHAN —Among the sons of men prominent in the life of South Amboy, New Jersey, who are beginning careers of usefulness and promise, is Francis A Monaghan, son of James and Catherine (Carson) Monaghan James Monaghan, the father, has for many years been prominent in the mercantile life of South Amboy, where he and his family have lived practically all their lives. Francis A Monaghan, the son, has given evidence of ability and steadiness of purpose which will carry him far in his chosen profession, and which has caused him already to be numbered among the able and prominent young lawyers of his section

Francis A. Monaghan was born July 23, 1893, at South Amboy, New Jersey He attended the grammar and high schools of that place, and then went to Villanova College, at Villanova, Pennsylvania where he received the degree of Bachelor of Arts in 1915, and Master of Arts in 1917 He then began his law studies at the New York Law School of Columbia University, serving from 1915 to 1916 as clerk in the law offices of Senator Thomas Brown, of Perth Amboy He was admitted to the New Jersey bar, April 8, 1920, and is now engaged in active service, having his offices at Roosevelt, New Jersey, but residing with his parents in his home town, South Amboy In both towns he is well known as one of the promising young men of his profession

During the World War, Mr Monaghan enlisted as a private, and received his training at Camp Syracuse, Syracuse, New York, where he became first sergeant of his company He was transferred to the Air Service, Aircraft Production, and sent to Elizabeth, New Jersey, from which service he was honorably discharged, March 17, 1919 Mr Monaghan is a member of the Luke A Lovely Post of the American Legion, South Amboy, and of St Mary's Catholic Church, also located at South Amboy, New Jersey

SAMUEL LEDERER, a native of Bohemia, Austria, was one of the first of his nationality to settle in Englishtown, Monmouth county, New Jersey Later he went to New Brunswick, New Jersey, where he became an influential citizen He was born October 1, 1824, of good parentage, received his education in the gymnasium schools in his home town, and there learned the trade of tanner of leathers, after which he traveled through various European countries, working at his trade until about 1850, when he came to America, locating in New York He resumed his trade, working on Jacob street, where he remained a few

years He built up a substantial leather business in New York, which
he disposed of about 1855, going to Englishtown, New Jersey, where
he conducted a tannery until about 1864 He next removed to New
Brunswick, New Jersey, where he likewise conducted a tannery for
a number of years, subsequently becoming a dealer in hides and skins
and a manufacturer of fertilizer. He was known all over the country
for the excellence of his work and made the first lamb skin apron used
by a lodge of Free and Accepted Masons in the United States As a
business man he was highly regarded both at Englishtown and at New
Brunswick, and socially he was esteemed by his many friends He
continued business through his long life, and was "in the harness" until
the time of his death, June 16, 1916 He built up an immense business
for those early days, and during the Civil War devoted much of his time
to the preparation of leather for the government He was a well informed
man, a great reader, and a linguist of note, speaking eight languages
Few citizens of New Brunswick were better known than Samuel Lederer,
and he was one of the "grand old gentlemen" of the town He had
various fraternal and social connections, being one of the oldest Masons
in the State of New Jersey at the time of his death He was a firm
believer in religious life and principles, and was one of the original
supporters of the Anshe Emeth Temple, of New Brunswick, being vice-
president of that temple for years

Mr Lederer married, in New York City, October 10, 1852, Marie
Abels, a native of his own country, born December 19, 1833 It is of
interest to note that this grand old couple celebrated their golden wed-
ding anniversary, October 10, 1902, at New Brunswick To the marriage were born eleven children 1 Samuel M, now a prosperous
contractor in St Louis, Missouri, married Augusta Bodenheimer, of
New York City, and became the father of four children· Jeannette,
Lucille, Marie, and James. 2 Rose, married Edmund Bayer, of New
York City, prominent in the insurance business; they have four children·
Clarence, Jessie, Alice and Grace 3 Josephine, married Simon Bar-
doch, a tobacconist of New York City, and has two children. Charlotte
and Monroe 4 Julius, now a real estate dealer in New Haven, Connecticut, married Martha Posner, of New Brunswick, and they have four
children David, Milton Harold, and Charles 5 Max M, a sketch of
whose life follows 6 Clara, married Morris Baumann, of New Haven,
Connecticut, a rubber manufacturer; they have three children Irving,
Gertrude and Robert 7 Louise, deceased, married Morris Somerfeld,
a business man of New York 8 Flora, deceased, married Ignatz Fox,
a merchant of New York City, and left three children. Theresa, Arthur,
and Flora 9 David J, associated with the American Tobacco Company,
of Yonkers, New York; married Hattie Zabinsky, of Yonkers, and has
two children Marie and Cora 10 Henry A, a traveling salesman, of
New York City, married Deborah Levy, of New York City 11 George
W, a traveling salesman, of New York City, married Nettie Grodell,
and they have one child, Samuel Mrs Lederer, the mother of all these
children, died at a venerable old age at her home in New Brunswick, June
24, 1909

Saml Lederer

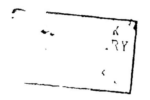

MAX M LEDERER, one of New Brunswick's prominent citizens, long identified with the leather, hide and fertilizer business, was born in Englishtown, New Jersey, August 18, 1860 When he was very young his parents moved, with their family, to New Brunswick, New Jersey, where the life of the son has been spent He received his education in the schools of New Brunswick, and as a young man entered the business of his father in which he has been engaged practically ever since For the past twenty years he has had the sole management of the business started by his honored father, and in 1906 he purchased the entire interests of the firm The business, started under the name Samuel Lederer & Son, still bears the original title and enjoys a well known reputation in the industrial life of the community under the direction of Max M Lederer

Mr Lederer is well known fraternally, being a member of the Free and Accepted Masons, of the Independent Order of Odd Fellows, and of the Knights of Pythias, and having served as a chancellor in the latter order, Friendship Lodge, No 30, of New Brunswick He is a member of the Republican party, and like his father a member of Anshe Emeth Temple, of which he was a trustee for seventeen years

Mr Lederer married, March 29, 1892, Henrietta Sontheimer, daughter of Mayer and Regina (Scheld) Sontheimer, of Elizabeth, New Jersey, well known residents of that city, the father having been treasurer of the Board of Trade there, president and treasurer of the Building and Loan Association, a county freeholder and had other important connections Mrs Lederer is one of the active women of New Brunswick, being secretary of the Middlesex Hospital Aid Association, a member of the Board of Visiting Nurses' Association, a councilor of the Girl Scouts, and prominent as a Red Cross worker To Mr and Mrs Lederer have been born three children Marie, now the wife of Sidney J Kauder, of Newark, New Jersey, they having one child, Warren G ; Edith, married Harry Strauss, of New Brunswick, and they have one child, Robert L , and Mayer S , a student, now living at home with his parents

---

GARFIELD A HUNT.—Son of a contractor and builder, Mr Hunt was early inducted into the building trades, but chose plumbing as his line He is a son of Mansfield and Maria (Quinn) Hunt, formerly of Brooklyn, New York, his father a skilled mechanical contractor and builder In 1910 Mansfield Hunt and his family moved to Queens, Long Island, where they yet reside

Garfield A Hunt was born in Brooklyn, New York, August 13, 1881, and there attended public schools until becoming a plumber's apprentice He became a skilled plumber and was employed in various places, but always followed his trade In 1910 he located in Dunellen, New Jersey, and there is well established in business for himself, and is prosperous He is a Republican in politics, a Presbyterian in religious faith, a member of the Republican Club and the Patriotic Order Sons of America

Mr Hunt married, in Brooklyn, New York, September 8, 1901, Margaret Hignett, born in that city January 17, 1881, daughter of William and Anna (Williams) Hignett. Mr and Mrs Hunt are the parents of five children Garfield, born October 8, 1903, Marguerite, born February 20, 1906, Warren, born November 22, 1908, Clinton W, born November 22, 1910, Gilbert T, born July 4, 1912

HYMAN WEDEEN —The firm of Hyman Wedeen & Son, Inc, was founded in Perth Amboy by Hyman Wedeen, who was born in Russia, January 19, 1870, but in 1889 came to this country, and since 1890 has been a resident of Perth Amboy, New Jersey He spent the first eighteen months of his American residence in New York City, where he attended school, then moved to Perth Amboy He began his business career as a pack peddler, traveling that section of New Jersey with his pack for four years He had a fixed ambition, and by carefully husbanding his resources he was able at the end of four years to abandon his route and open a small store in Perth Amboy on lower Smith street The store at No 275 Smith street was operated very successfully for eleven years, until 1904, when he opened a department store at Nos 271-273 Smith street In 1912, he added to the business a shoe store at No 279 Smith street. In 1915 he enlarged his department store by building back sixty feet, doubling the floor space, and bringing in the shoe department, and continued to conduct a prosperous modern department store He is a large owner of Perth Amboy real estate, a stockholder in the Perth Amboy Trust Company, and one of the prosperous business men of his city

Hyman Wedeen married, in New York City, February 22, 1883, Esther Bella Borak, also born in Russia They are the parents of nine children: Nathan, of further mention; Nettie, Mollie, wife of David Metzendorf, of Perth Amboy, Jennie, deceased, Sarah, Rose, Pearl, Alvin, and Isabelle, all residing with their parents in Perth Amboy except Mrs Metzendorf

Nathan Wedeen, son of Hyman Wedeen, was born in Perth Amboy, May 9, 1895 He was educated in the public schools, graduating from Perth Amboy High School, class of 1912, and spent a year at the College of the City of New York He has been associated with his father in business for several years, and is a member of the firm of Hyman Wedeen & Son, Inc He is now taking a course in finance at New York University, attending evening classes During the war with Germany, Nathan Wedeen was in the United States service in the medical supply department at Camp Merritt, on duty for thirteen months He is a member of Prudence Lodge, Amboy Chapter, Scottish Rite Consistory, and Salaam Temple, Shriners, of the Masonic order, Tall Cedars of Lebanon, the American Legion, Young Men's Christian Association, Young Men's Hebrew Association The family are members of the Shaseh Tephiloh Synagogue congregation

---

MICHAEL POLLAK —Among the best known and highly esteemed citizens of Woodbridge township, Middlesex county, New Jersey, a

Michael Pollak

ABOVE—The Old Moores Homestead on Rahway Avenue, Woodbridge, about 150 Years Old, Purchased by Michael Pollak in 1908.
BELOW—The Pollak Residence, Formerly the Moores Homestead, Remodelled and As It Appears Now, 1921.

builder of some note in his vicinity, which is called the Rahway Homestead, a man who has always stood out and has led many good movements in his community, is Michael Pollak

Mr Pollak was born in Nona, Hungary, February 22, 1873, the son of Charles and Lena (Danzinger) Pollak, old and highly respected residents of that city His father was a large landholder and a rancher there, a man of influence

Michael Pollak was given the best educational advantages, receiving his learning at the gymnasium schools of his native town, was later at the University of Vienna, and finished at the famous Heidelburg University, Germany, where he pursued courses in mechanical and chemical engineering

In 1896 Mr Pollak decided on a touring trip to America After a short time in this country he felt so much at home that he decided to remain, and so established himself in business in New York City The subsequent years were spent in that city, where he followed his profession, that of a mechanical and construction engineer, with success In 1906 Mr Pollak removed to Middlesex county, New Jersey, locating near Woodbridge, where he has since resided He purchased one of the old landmarks of the county, which he reconstructed, and today it is one of the show places, pictures of which appear in this work. He eventually acquired a large parcel of land, which he named the Rahway Homestead. Formerly, most of this was vacant land, but today there are many substantial houses built thereon, many of which were constructed by Mr Pollak Aside from his building activities, he has many other important interests, among them being president and founder of the following companies Rahway Homestead Company; the Pollak Building and Construction Company and the Nocan Soup Company of Newark, New Jersey, which is making dehydrated soups in powdered form and which is revolutionizing the food industries of the world Mr Pollak has had many important financial connections, and various other activities

Mr Pollak married Laura Dupca, in the town of Kadar, Hungary, March 16, 1894, the daughter of Anton and Elizabeth (Heffner) Dupca Her father was a director of lands and an owner of much property

Mr and Mrs Pollak are well known socially throughout the region, and are especially active in church work and charitable affairs During the World War Mr Pollak was very active in the many drives and campaigns, and showed the quota of his district on every occasion

---

RENSSELAER CLARK KENYON.—Several generations back the Kenyon family came from England and settled in Rhode Island, some of them later living in Pennsylvania on a farm known as the "Old Kenyon Homestead"

Rensselaer Clark Kenyon was born March 9, 1870, in Fell township, Lackawanna county, Pennsylvania, and there he grew up on the farm of his father, D. C Kenyon, who was born in Pennsylvania, in 1845, and is still living on the homestead farm with his wife, Louise (Johnson)

Kenyon, also born in Pennsylvania. She is now about seventy-five years old. They had a family of six boys, all living at the present time (1920) 1 Rensselaer Clark, of whom further. 2 Thomas, living in Edge Hill, Pennsylvania, treasurer of the Edge Hill Silica Rock Company 3 Edward N, residing in Portland, Maine, a soldier in the United States army, and also engaged in the real estate business 4 Howard D, living in Edge Hill, Pennsylvania, where he is engaged in the sand business, he is a veteran of the Philippine War 5 Robert W, at Edge Hill with his brother Howard D 6 William J, a resident of Highland Park, New Jersey, and superintendent of the Johnson & Johnson plant in New Brunswick, same State

The eldest son of this family, Rensselaer Clark Kenyon, attended the schools in the township where he was born, and assisted his father upon the farm until he reached the age of seventeen years, then, coming to New Brunswick, the young man entered the employ of Johnson & Johnson, the well known chemists. For twenty-six years Mr. Kenyon remained with this company in their clerical department and as auditor in the credit department, leaving it to become manager of the Edge Hill Silica Rock Company of New Brunswick He is now president of the company, as well as manager.

Mr Kenyon is very greatly interested in everything pertaining to New Brunswick For a time he was on the School Board, and has been active in the work of the Young Men's Christian Association, also is a member of the Craftsmen's Club, of New Brunswick, the Junior Order of United American Mechanics, and of the local lodge of Free and Accepted Masons

In June, 1898, in New Brunswick, New Jersey, Rensselaer Clark Kenyon married Mary Jane Henderson, the daughter of Robert and Sarah (Brown) Henderson, natives of England, where also their daughter was born Both Mr and Mrs Henderson died in this country some years ago Mr and Mrs Kenyon have three children, all living: 1. Rensselaer C, Jr, born May 10, 1901, a student at Rutgers College in the sophomore class 2 Evelyn Mildred, born February 13, 1903, a graduate of the Livingston Avenue High School in the class of 1920 3 Mary Alice, born August 27, 1917 Mr and Mrs Kenyon reside at No 29 Adelaide avenue, Highland Park, New Brunswick They and their family are members of Christ Protestant Episcopal Church

---

REV. WILLIAM A. GILFILLAN.—As pastor of the Church of Our Lady of Virtues, Sayreville, Middlesex county, New Jersey, Father Gilfillan is performing the mission in life for which he prepared and which it is his highest ambition to worthily fulfill He is a son of Joseph and Ann Gilfillan, who at the time of the birth of their son, William A, were living at Milford, Massachusetts

William A Gilfillan was born November 22, 1869, and began his education in the public schools of Worcester, Massachusetts He then entered Holy Cross College, Worcester, whence he was graduated B A, class of '94 He finished preparation for the priestly office at Grand

P'

TLD

K

Seminary, Montreal, Canada, and at the close of his theological studies he was ordained a priest of the Roman Catholic church, December 22, 1894 During the years he has been in orders, Father Gilfillan has been assigned to various phases of priestly duty, and as before noted, his present connection is as pastor of the Church of Our Lady of Virtues at Sayreville. New Jersey. He is a member of the Knights of Columbus, and is highly regarded in his community without regard to creed His parish is a large and prosperous one, all departments being in a condition of usefulness

BERNARD DUNIGAN —The name of Bernard Dunigan will long be remembered in Woodbridge, and also Middlesex county, New Jersey, as one of the pioneers of his nationality to settle in Woodbridge township, where in later years he was one of the leaders in the industrial, political, and social life of the community He was a native of Ireland, born about 1832, and as a young man came to America, soon afterward settling in Woodbridge, his home until his death, in January, 1904 During his early residence he was variously employed in the district, and by toil and thrift in the following years accumulated a little capital, which he invested in a strip of land

During the early days of clay mine prospecting he became interested in this field of activity and upon his own property found rich deposits of clay, which he mined and shipped, becoming one of the prosperous clay operators of the region He was a man of energy and sound business ability, and his splendid traits of character found expression 'n the works of good citizenship A Democrat in politics, he took a leading part in party affairs in his district, and at one time was a town committeeman and a member of the School Board He was a devoted member of the Roman Catholic church, and a fruitful, blameless life placed him high in the esteem of his fellowmen

Bernard Dunigan married, in Woodbridge. New Jersey, in 1852, Julia Ryan, also a native of Ireland Their life together was most happy and contented, and they celebrated the golden anniversary of their marriage in 1902 surrounded by their family and friends Children, all born in Woodbridge Edward P, deceased. John M, a resident of Tottenville. Staten Island, Thomas F, deceased; Ellen, married L A Conley, deceased, of Jersey City, New Jersey, Jane, married W H Nash, of Woodbridge, both deceased. Marcellia, died in infancy, Anna, died aged seventeen years. Margaret L, married B Whalen, of Carteret New Jersey, both now deceased. Catherine J, married E J. Flannigan, of Woodbridge; Bernard J, a sketch of whom follows, and Morris P, now (1921) living in Woodbridge

BERNARD JOSEPH DUNIGAN, son of Bernard and Julia (Ryan) Dunigan (q v), was born in Woodbridge, Middlesex county. New Jersey, October 26, 1875 After completing his education in Woodbridge public schools he entered business life and later became associated with his father in the clay business at Woodbridge, mining and shipping clay from their own clay beds In 1904 the senior head of the business passed away and the burden of management fell upon the young man then twenty-nine years of age Seventeen years have since passed and the business is still conducted by Bernard J Dunigan in a most efficient manner

Mr Dunigan, a Democrat in politics, has always taken an active part in public affairs, and since January 1, 1913, has been assessor of Woodbridge township an office he capably fills He possesses a wealth of friends and is held in high esteem both as a business man and a citizen Mr Dunigan is a member of the Royal Arcanum, the Knights of Columbus, the Columbian Club, and St James' Roman Catholic Church all of Woodbridge

Mr Dunigan married, June 19, 1907, at Woodbridge New Jersey, Julia A Whalen daughter of Thomas and Julia (Bray) Whalen Thomas Whalen was well known in Woodbridge, having resided here for many years after his coming as a young man from Ireland He was engaged in the fire brick industry until his death, in May, 1898 Bernard Joseph and Julia A (Whalen) Dunigan are the parents of four children Margaret Geraldine Julia Veronica, Bernard Joseph, Jr, and Thomas, all born in Woodbridge

---

WILLIAM VAN NUIS, JR, prominent among the younger generation of business men in New Brunswick, New Jersey, is secretary and treasurer of The Neilson T Parker Company, insurance brokers If describing a man as a leading citizen is equivalent to saying that he possesses intelligence of a high order and touches life at many points, then Mr Van Nuis is of this type

William Meeker Van Nuis father of William Van Nuis, Jr, was born in New Brunswick, New Jersey, in 1854, and now (1921) resides in New York City where he is at present connected with the Pennsylvania Hotel For many years he was engaged in the wholesale liquor business in New Brunswick He married Emma Strong, and they are the parents of three children: William, Jr, of further mention, Irene, a resident of New Brunswick, Leon Lyle, a traveling salesman and a resident of New Brunswick Lyle Van Nuis, grandfather of William Van Nuis Jr was a prominent citizen during the early history of New Brunswick, and conducted a carriage factory on Washington street New Brunswick, for many years He was mayor of New Brunswick during the years 1856 and 1857, 1861 and 1862, 1877 and 1878.

William Van Nuis, Jr, was born in New Brunswick, New Jersey, March 15, 1886 He attended the local schools, including the high school, until 1903, when he became identified with the Knickerbocker Trust Company, with whom he remained until 1907, when the company failed. Mr Van Nuis was immediately invited to go with the Guarantee Trust Company of New York on account of his knowledge of New York City securities In May, 1914, he entered the employ of The Neilson T. Parker Company, and two years later was promoted to fill the positions of manager and secretary of the company, and during the year 1921 became secretary and treasurer He is an able manager and executive, keenly alert to every changing phase of the business He is a man of foresight, swift and sure in his decisions, and most progressive in his policies

In politics Mr Van Nuis is a Democrat, and takes an active interest in political matters He was elected alderman from the First Ward in 1914 and served the city for one term He is a member and treasurer of the Board of Trade of New Brunswick, New Jersey He is a director of the Provident Building and Loan Association and also of the New Brunswick Building and Loan Association His hobby is golf, and he is also keenly interested in water sports, holding membership in the New Brunswick Country Club and in the New Brunswick Boat Club, serving as trustee of the latter He is also an active member of the Rotary Club of New Brunswick Mr Van Nuis is a Mason, being a member of Union Lodge, No 19, Free and Accepted Masons; Scott Chapter, No 4, Royal Arch Masons, Temple Commandery, No 18, Knights Templar, Salaam Temple, Ancient Arabic Order Nobles of the Mystic Shrine of Newark, New Jersey, Forest No 296, Tall Cedars of Lebanon, Craftsmen's Club of New Brunswick, New Jersey, member of Christ Episcopal Church, and of the Young Men's Christian Association

Mr Van Nuis married, September 19, 1918, Blanche Marie Crenning, daughter of Charles C and May (Allen) Crenning Mr and Mrs Van Nuis are the parents of one child William Lyle, born February 10, 1920

Mr Van Nuis, who is a young man, has progressed very rapidly and is considered an authority on insurance matters There can be no reasonable doubt that the years which lie before him will be filled with greater effort and more signal achievement

---

GEORGE I APGAR, JR—Among the younger generation of successful business men of Dunellen, New Jersey, is one of her native sons, George I Apgar, Jr Since 1905 Mr Apgar has been engaged in the contracting and building business, the same line of business followed by his father for many years

George I Apgar, Jr., was born June 18, 1889, at Dunellen, New Jersey, the son of John P and Sarah (Smith) Apgar He attended the public and high schools of Dunellen, and upon leaving school he became associated with his father in business He has followed the same line of business ever since, and is well known in and about Dunellen.

A Republican in politics, he is keenly interested as a voter in all the political issues of his town, State and county He affiliates with the Benevolent and Protective Order of Elks, the Junior Order United American Mechanics, the Patriotic Order Sons of America, and is a member of the Republican Club of Dunellen In his religious belief he is a Presbyterian

Mr Apgar married, November 17, 1913, at Dunellen, New Jersey, Emma Voorhees, a native of Chester, New Jersey, her birth having occurred there March 2, 1890, a daughter of Theodore and Anna (Blaine)

Voorhees Mr and Mrs Apgar are the parents of two children. Eleanor, born September 25, 1914, George. born January 9, 1918 The family reside at No 604 Lincoln avenue, Dunellen

---

REV. ERNEST RAMON BROWN, pastor of the First Presbyterian Church at Dunellen, New Jersey, has won many friends in his administration of the affairs of his charge He is a son of John Busham Johnson and Emma Caroline (Crow) Brown. his father a farmer and a water commissioner of Rahway, New Jersey

Ernest R Brown was born in Woodbridge, New Jersey, August 4, 1871 He was educated in Rahway public schools, Moody Bible Institute. Oberlin College, and the Reformed Theological Seminary, New Brunswick, New Jersey.

Rev Mr Brown served the city of Rahway as a member of the Board of Education He is a member of Anchor Lodge, No 149, Free and Accepted Masons, of Plainfield. New Jersey, and of Washington Camp, Patriotic Order Sons of America, of Dunellen, New Jersey

Rev Mr. Brown married at Rahway, New Jersey, in the First Presbyterian Church February 27, 1901, Alice Louise Avery, daughter of Charles Henry and Susan Frances (Wood) Avery, her father a retired officer of the United States navy. Rev and Mrs Brown are the parents of five children· Dorothy Frances. born November 20, 1901, Ernest Thornell, born April 5, 1903, Roger Woodruff, born April 7, 1905, Edward Payson, born July 30, 1907, and Alice Louise, born January 11, 1912

HANS M. K. HANSEN was born in Perth Amboy, New Jersey, October 8, 1886, son of Christian and Christine Hansen He was educated in the public schools, finishing with high school graduation in 1905 He was in the employ of the Central Railroad of New Jersey, in the traffic department at Perth Amboy, and also in the traffic department of the American Can Company in New York City. but his ambition was for a professional career and he entered New York University Law School whence he was graduated LL B, class of 1914 He was admitted to the bar in June, 1915, as an attorney, and opened offices at No 119 South street, Perth Amboy. He formed an association with George J Plechmer, lawyer, at No 390 George street, New Brunswick, which still continues He was later admitted a counsellor, and practiced in the State and Federal courts of the district During the World War, 1917-18, he served in the United States army as an infantryman

Mr Hansen married. December 15 1920, Mabel F Randolph, daughter of Samuel S and Lillian F Randolph.

ELIAS SHAPIRO, D D S —In 1904, even before the World War had made such havoc among the nations of Europe, Israel Shapiro found Russia a most undesirable place of residence, and with his wife, Hannah (Arkus) Shapiro, and his children, came to the United States, the land of promise to the oppressed then as now He settled in Bayonne,

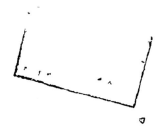

New Jersey, where he is now engaged in the automobile business Mr. and Mrs Shapiro have four children Elias, of further mention, Ida, living at home, Morris, in business with his father in Bayonne, and Rebecca, residing at home

Elias Shapiro was born in Russia, April 28, 1896, and when eight years of age was brought to the United States by his parents. The family resided in New York City for a time, and in that city he attended Public School No 64 He completed his public school courses in Bayonne, New Jersey, with graduation from high school in 1911, then was a student in the City College of New York, finally, in 1918, receiving the degree of D D S from the New York College of Dentistry. He began the practice of his profession in New York City, but in January, 1920, located in South Amboy, New Jersey, where he is building up a satisfactory practice

During the World War period he enlisted in the Medical Reserve Corps, and met every demand of citizenship He is a member of and for two terms was president of the Cosmos Club of New York City, and is a member of the Knights of Pythias

---

MILTON ALBERT EDGAR, son of Albert and Susan (Tappen) Edgar, was born in Bonhampton, Middlesex county, New Jersey, November 17, 1850 He acquired a sound education through his own efforts and application, availing himself of every opportunity for mental training and regularly walking five miles to school He overcame the disadvantages encountered in those days by youth's ambition for education, and in the public schools near New Brunswick, and Rutgers Preparatory Academy of the same place, he cultivated tastes that were naturally scholarly, devoting himself with especial interest to classical languages and science At the age of sixteen years he passed the examination for teachers and for two years taught in the schools of New Durham and Bonhampton His inclinations were toward the world of practical affairs, and with his brother, Charles Smith Edgar, he engaged in clay mining near Metuchen, meeting with excellent success This partnership covered a period of two years, and his savings at the end of this time purchased an interest in a well known mercantile establishment in Perth Amboy, with which he was connected for two years, during this same period conducting an independent clay mining business in Perth Amboy and Woodbridge In 1877 he again joined his brother and they purchased a clay mining property near Fords, New Jersey, which they operated until disposing of it by sale in 1885

Since that time Mr Edgar has been generally engaged, independently and in association with others, in clay mining, clay washing, and manufacturing, his activity in all these lines attended by a generous degree of success He is an expert on geological phases of clay formation, and his counsel has guided his associates in clay mining in Middlesex county and other places Mr Edgar is one of the most prominent figures in the ceramic trade, known locally and nationally, and is president of the American Clay Producers' Association He is president of the Edgar

Brothers Company of New Jersey and Georgia vice-president of the Edgar Plastic Kaolin Company, of Edgar, Florida, and Metuchen, New Jersey, president of the Lake Park Improvement Company, of Metuchen and Red Bank, New Jersey, and has numerous other business interests.

For many years Mr Edgar was chairman of the Middlesex County Republican Committee, and for forty years he was a delegate to every State convention of his party In 1883 he was appointed by President Arthur collector of customs for the port of Amboy, holding that office until the close of the Arthur administration He was a member of the old Perth Amboy Board of Aldermen at the time that the city was divided into wards When the trolley roads were first projected through Middlesex county, he was a member of the Board of Freeholders, and as chairman of the committee on street railroads and public roads did much to establish these lines upon a firm, equitable, and permanent basis Mr Edgar has been a keen observer and student of life's problems, has read much of the best literature of all time, and has travelled extensively throughout the United States, Canada, and the Southern republics After many years of extremely useful service he continues active in the management of his diverse business interests He is well known socially and fraternally, holding membership in various Masonic bodies and other orders and clubs

Mr Edgar married (first) in February, 1873 Frances E Thomas, daughter of William and Phoebe (Moore) Thomas, a member of an old New Jersey family long resident in Perth Amboy She died in July, 1907 She was the mother of Eva W, who married F W Johnson, of New York City ; Albert J, Frederick W, and Charles S, the last three deceased Mr Edgar married (second) in September, 1908, Nellie G Rock daughter of William G and Emma Rock, also old residents of Perth Amboy Children of this marriage · Milton A, Jr, and Jeannette E

LAURITZ WILLIAM SMITH.—The province of Schleswig-Holstein was taken from Denmark by Prussia The province is formed of Schleswig in the north, Holstein and Lauenburg in the south The province is traversed by the Kiel Canal, built by the deposed Kaiser Wilhelm, which connects the Baltic and North seas The people of North Schleswig, at a plebiscite taken under the terms of the treaty of Versailles, negotiated after the disastrous defeat of the Germans at every point of contact with the allies, voted to return to the government of Denmark, from whom Prussia and Austria wrested Schleswig-Holstein at the close of the War of 1864 When Germany and Austria fought in 1866 Germany took the province from Austria and held it until compelled to return the northern part of it to its own people, and they are now safely attached to their ancient mother Denmark, into whose possession the province had passed in the eleventh century

In the city of Christiansfeld, North Schleswig, now Denmark, Lauritz William Smith, now owner of the firm, Smith & Ostergaard, Fords, Middlesex county, New Jersey was born December 5, 1876, son of Peter and Maren (Zeuthen) Smith He was educated in the public

schools of his home town, and after completing school years, in 1892, he came to the United States and settled in Middlesex county, New Jersey, finding his first employment at the plant of the National Fire Proofing Company at Keasbey (the plant formerly operated by the Isaacs Company) For one year he continued with that company, then became an employee of the Pardee Works, manufacturers of fire brick, at Perth Amboy Four months later he left the works and began learning the carpenter's trade, becoming in time an expert workman In 1909 the firm of Smith & Ostergaard, contractors and builders, was organized at Fords, and there has since conducted a prosperous business Mr Smith as the managing head has proven both a reliable, skillful builder and a business man of high type He is a director of the Fords National Bank, and interested in all that pertains to the welfare of his village

Mr Smith is a member of the Masonic order, the Benevolent and Protective Order of Elks the Master Builders' Association, the Singing Society "Frem," of Perth Amboy, the Raritan Yacht Club, and the Lutheran church of Perth Amboy In politics, he is a Republican He is a man of high reputation as a citizen and business man, and is highly esteemed in his community

---

CALVIN CUNNIUS—Two men of the name Calvin Cunnius, father and son, are engaged in the automobile business in New Brunswick, New Jersey, and whether one or the other is patronized, good service and courteous treatment attend the transaction, and the needs of the car are fully met Calvin Cunnius, Sr, came to New Jersey from Pennsylvania, his father being a native of that State, and there the son spent his youth and earliest years of manhood, and there married

John M Cunnius, father of Calvin Cunnius, Sr, was a contractor and builder of Freeland, Luzern county, Pennsylvania, now (1921) retired He married Laura Santee, and they were residing in Freeland, Luzerne county, Pennsylvania, at the time of the birth of their son, Calvin, Sr, now of New Brunswick, New Jersey

Calvin Cunnius, Sr, son of John M and Laura (Santee) Cunnius, was born in Freeland, Pennsylvania, December 18, 1873, and was educated in the public schools After leaving school he learned the carpenter's trade, became an expert wood-worker, and there continued until after the birth of his son, Calvin, Jr, when the family moved to Long Branch, New Jersey, where he engaged in the automobile business In 1911 he located in Brooklyn, New York, continuing there in the same business until 1914, when he moved to New Brunswick, New Jersey, and opened an auto service station, namely, Depot Garage, located on Albany street After that he was located for three years on Dennis street but is now (1921) located at the corner of George and Oliver streets Mr Cunnius is a Republican in politics, and a member of Highland Park Reformed Church

Mr Cunnius married, at Freeland, Pennsylvania, August 11, 1894,

Mary D. Nagle, daughter of Jacob and Elizabeth Nagle. Mr and Mrs Cunnius are the parents of five children   Percy, Calvin, Jr , of previous mention in this work , Laura, Ruth, and Naomi, the daughters residing with their parents

---

JEAN DuBOIS, business manager of the Roessler & Hasslacher Chemical Company of Perth Amboy, New Jersey, and a well known figure in the business and industrial life of that city, is a native of Switzerland, his birth having occurred at Le Locle, in that country, November 24, 1869   He is a son of Philippe Henri and Louise (Andreae) DuBois, the former born at Le Locle and the latter at Frankfort-on-the-Main, Germany   The elder Mr DuBois now lives retired with his family at Neufchatel, Switzerland, and has attained the venerable age of eighty-four years, his wife being three years younger   To Mr and Mrs DuBois eight children have been born, as follows   1 Cecile, now the wife of Dr Henri Steinhauslin, of Le Locle, Switzerland   2 Philippe, now a resident of Rhodesia South Africa   3 Louise, deceased   4 Alice, now the wife of the Rev Herman de Montmollin, of Courcelles, Switzerland   5 Jean, of whom further   6 Albert, who resides at Neufchatel, Switzerland   7 Georges, who resides at Frankfort, Germany   8 Hugo, deceased

The childhood of Jean DuBois was passed in his native town of Le Locle, Switzerland, and there as a lad he attended the local public schools, passing through grammar and high school grades, and in the latter being prepared for college   He then entered the University of Neufchatel, in the city of the same name in Switzerland, and took a course in law   graduating with the class of 1890   After completing his studies at the latter institution, he removed to South Africa and remained in that country for eight years, being interested in mining operations on an extensive scale   While there he at one time lodged a complaint against the natives of the Blauberg region on account of their depredations, and afterwards joined the Boer army and was with their forces in the field during the South African campaign   In the year 1900 he came to the United States, and located in Florida, where for four years he was engaged in the phosphate business in association with a French company   Returning to Europe for three years, he was occupied with the building of a large chemical plant in France, but in 1911 came once more to the United States   Here he became associated with the Roessler & Hasslacher Chemical Company of Perth Amboy, his wide knowledge of industrial chemistry making him a most valuable member of the staff of the great concern   He was appointed to the responsible position of factory business manager, and continues to hold that office at the present time, making his home at No 105 High street, Perth Amboy   Mr DuBois has always been actively interested in the general business development of the community in which he has elected to reside, and since coming to Perth Amboy has been a prominent member of the local Chamber of Commerce, and for six years its vice-president   He is also a member of the Drug and Chemical Club of New York City, and the East Jersey Club. In his religious belief, Mr DuBois is a Presbyterian, and attends the church of that denomination at Perth Amboy

Mr DuBois married, in 1895, Mattie Schreiber, a native of New York City, and a daughter of Dr. Henry and Cora (Gulick) Schreiber, also natives of that place. Dr Schreiber is a physician who has retired from the active practice of his profession, and now makes his home at Hopewell, New Jersey. Mrs Schreiber died in New York City. Mr and Mrs DuBois are the parents of two children, as follows: Jean Claude, born March 30, 1898, served in the World War with the United States Naval Reserves, in which he now holds the rank of second officer; Cora Alice, born October 26, 1903

COLBY DILL, one of the most successful of the younger business men of Perth Amboy, New Jersey, where he is associated with the great organization of the Roessler & Hasslacher Chemical Company, was born December 29, 1882, at Boston, Massachusetts, and is a son of Joshua Martin and Catherine (Bassett) Dill of that city. Both the Dill and Bassett families are old ones in New England, Mr Dill's father being a native of Wellfleet, Massachusetts, where he was born January 31, 1850, and his mother of Bridgewater, in the same State. The elder Mr Dill has been an educator for many years. He now lives retired from active life with his wife at Newton, Massachusetts. They were the parents of four children, as follows: Martin Bassett, M D, now a practicing physician at Newton Center, Massachusetts; Colby, with whom we are here especially concerned; Helen Baker, who became the wife of Walter A Forbush of Brockton, Massachusetts; and Nathaniel Lothrop, who died May 8, 1903, at the age of sixteen years

Colby Dill passed his childhood and early youth in his native city of Boston, and there attended as a lad the Boston Latin School, from which he was graduated in 1900. Having completed his preparation for college at that institution, he entered Harvard University, taking the usual academic course and was graduated with the class of 1904 with the degree of A B. He had early taken a strong interest in scientific and technical subjects, and desiring a career of this kind, entered the Massachusetts Institute of Technology at Boston, from which he was graduated in 1906 with the degree of B S. Another year of postgraduate work brought him the degree of M S from the same institution, and he thereupon secured a position with the United States Geological Survey as chemist. He was employed in this capacity at Pittsburgh, Pennsylvania, for six months and then resigned his government post to accept an offer of the position of works manager with the Perth Amboy Chemical Works. This was in 1908, and the efficiency with which he discharged his responsible duties soon brought him to the attention of the owners of the Roessler & Hasslacher Chemical Company also of Perth Amboy. He did not sever his connection with the smaller concern, however, until January, 1917, when he accepted the post of assistant to the second vice-president of the Roessler & Hasslacher Chemical Company, which he holds at the present time Mr Dill has always interested himself actively in the general life of his adopted community, and is affiliated with many important orders and clubs, both here and in New York City, especially those of a professional character He is a member of the Masonic order, and the East Jersey Club, of New Jersey, the Chemists' Club, and the Harvard Club of New York City, the American Institute of Chemical Engineers, the Society of Chemical Industry, the American Chemical Society, the Association of Harvard Chemists, and the New England Society In his religious belief Mr Dill is a Congregationalist and attends the church of that denomination at Perth Amboy He has always been very fond of outdoor sports and pastimes of all kinds, and takes especial pleasure in hunting and fishing, spending most of his leisure time in this manner

Colby Dill was united in marriage, July 30, 1911, at Greenville, Michigan, with Elsie DeLamarter, a native of Kalamazoo, in that State, and a daughter of Dr Louis and Mary (Baker) DeLamarter Dr DeLamarter now makes his home at Lansing, Michigan, where he is engaged in active practice as a physician Mr and Mrs Dill are the parents of four children as follows· Donald Lothrop, born May 28, 1912, John Harding, born in 1913, Catherine Elizabeth, born in 1915, and Eleanor, born in 1917.

ROBERT A HARKINS —The father of our subject, Hugh Harkins, a veteran of the Civil War and a farmer, was a resident of Weston Mills, New Jersey. He married Jane McCune, and they were the parents of a son, Robert A Harkins, now a contractor and builder of Milltown, New Jersey

Robert A Harkins was born at Weston Mills, New Jersey, December 13 1858, and educated in the district schools Upon arriving at a suitable age he learned the carpenter's trade and later located permanently in Milltown, where he has engaged as a carpenter and builder until the present (1921) He is a skilled mechanic and has proved his ability and reliability to the abundant satisfaction of hundreds of patrons In politics he is a Republican, and for twenty-one years has been borough clerk He is a member of the Order of United American Mechanics, the Improved Order of Red Men, and of the Methodist Episcopal church He is still actively engaged in business, and is highly regarded in his community

Mr Harkins married, in New Brunswick, New Jersey, May 24, 1879, Anna Reed, born September 22, 1858, daughter of Randolph and Harriet (Black) Reed, her father born in Hightstown, New Jersey, a rubber mill worker Mr and Mrs. Harkins are the parents of five children 1 Hannah Wilhelmina, born February 27, 1882, married Charles C Lins, and has three children Percy, Robert, and Dorothy 2 Dorothy L, born November 22, 1883 3 Oscar B, born October 13, 1885 4 Harriet A, born March 31, 1889, married Clarence H Hill, and has a son, Clarence H (2) 5 Claude W, born September 7, 1899

JOHN VANDURSEN OUTCALT—A "son of the soil" indeed is John Vandursen Outcalt, for he was born and raised in the county and State in which he has always lived, on the farm where he remained until he reached manhood

On August 20, 1869, John Vandursen Outcalt was born in Milltown, New Jersey, his parents being Frederick Richard and Mary (Vandursen) Outcalt The elder Mr Outcalt was at that time a farmer, but some years later he went into the butcher's business, which he carried on for a time, eventually retiring from active occupation in the latter years of his life.

The education of John Vandursen Outcalt was acquired in the public schools at Carharts Corner He learned to be a farmer with his father, continuing this work until 1890, when he went to live in New Brunswick, New Jersey Having a brother there, James V Outcalt, who was a carpenter, Mr Outcalt entered his shop, learned the trade, and served as an apprentice for three years, after which he continued to work at it for the next fourteen years In 1907 Mr Outcalt started in business for himself as a contracting carpenter and builder and is continuing it at the present time

Having spent his early life in the country, Mr Outcalt is especially fond of animals, their care having been a part of his daily home life He is also devoted to music, claiming that his particular enjoyment is to listen to good banjo playing, minstrels, or to be with a gathering of entertaining company of musical ability

Of a social temperament, Mr Outcalt has become a member of several of the fraternal organizations of New Brunswick, among them being: Goodwill Council, No 32, Junior Order United American Mechanics, Relief Council, No 40, Order United American Mechanics, Knights of the Golden Eagle, and in connection with his business, the Master Builders' Association Mr Outcalt and his family are members of the Livingston Avenue Baptist Church

In New Brunswick, New Jersey, on June 15, 1898, John Vandursen Outcalt was married to Leila May Leonard, the ceremony being performed by the Rev C A Jenkins Mrs Outcalt is the daughter of William Milton and Katharine (Cornell) Leonard, of New Brunswick. Three children have been born to Mr and Mrs. Outcalt Willard Milton, deceased, Everett Stanley, and Rutherford Clifton The family home is at No 144 Jones avenue

---

GEORGE ANTHONY VIEHMANN, for many years one of the best known and most influential citizens of New Brunswick, New Jersey, and a leader of the bar in that State, whose death occurred at Briarcliff Lodge, New York, October 12, 1918, was a son of Anthony and Louisa (Litterest) Viehmann Anthony Viehmann was born in Germany, but came to the United States in early youth, and settled in New York City He was an expert wood carver, and produced fine furniture which he sold in the local market He married Louisa Litterest, a native of New York City Later Mr Viehmann, Sr removed to New

Brunswick, New Jersey, and it was at that place that his son, George Anthony Viehmann was born, November 29, 1868

The education of George Anthony Viehmann was begun at the local public schools, and he then became a student at Rutgers Preparatory School, from which he graduated in 1882, and was prepared for college Mr Viehmann then matriculated at Rutgers College, New Brunswick, where he took the usual classical course, graduating with the class of 1886, and gaining his Bachelor's degree In the meantime the young man had determined to adopt law as his profession in life, and accordingly entered the law school in connection with Columbia University, in New York City, from which he was graduated Immediately after, he was admitted to the practice of law in New York and New Jersey, and also to practice before the United States Court Mr Viehmann then began the active practice of his profession and maintained offices both in New York City and New Brunswick, carrying on a very large legal business in both of these places He was recognized by his colleagues as an attorney of profound learning and unusual natural acquirements, and possessed of an unusual brilliant delivery, which made him an effective trial lawyer But Mr. Viehmann never depended upon these qualities in the prosecution of a case but gave to it in each case a most careful study and examination, and possessed himself beforehand carefully of every point in its favor This is a combination difficult to overcome, and it is no wonder that such important litigation was entrusted to him in both the New York and New Jersey courts He was a man of distinctly judicial temperament, and was noted as an expert interpreter of the law The fact that Mr Viehmann was also actively engaged in a large number of successful business enterprises gave him much experience and a keen insight into litigation involving business elements

It has already been mentioned that Mr Viehmann was connected prominently with the business world, and was an officer in a number of important concerns in the region of New Brunswick and Newark, New Jersey He was a director and officer in the Perth Amboy Trust Company, of Perth Amboy, New Jersey; vice-president of the Middlesex Title Guarantee Company, of New Brunswick director of the Federal Trust Company of Newark New Jersey, and in addition was the owner of the following industrial concerns The Cronk Manufacturing Company of New Brunswick, and the Highland Park Building Company He was also the owner of the New Brunswick Opera House, and all of these enterprises met with a substantial success He was also president of the New Brunswick Fire Insurance Company, the New Jersey Fire Insurance Company, of Newark New Jersey, and several other important concerns He always maintained a keen interest in the business welfare of the community-at-large and was one of the organizers and for many years served as president of the New Jersey Chamber of Commerce, in which capacity he was very active in promoting enterprises of all kinds in this State. Mr. Viehmann was also a conspicuous figure in the social and club life of New Brunswick and the surrounding district, and was a member of the New Brunswick Country Club, the Union Club of New Brunswick, and the local lodge of the Benevolent and Protective Order of Elks, serving as first exalted ruler of the latter

It is probable, however, that Mr Viehmann was even better known in connection with public life and politics in this region than he was as an attorney or business man, and for many years he was one of the leaders of the Democratic party He was possessed of a large personal following in New Brunswick, and in 1900 was elected mayor of this city on the Democratic ticket He served in that capacity for two years and was one of the most capable and efficient executives that this city has ever had He continually interested himself in carrying out measures calculated to improve the general welfare of the community, and one of his acts was the compelling of the Pennsylvania Railroad Company to elevate its tracks through New Brunswick, as a measure of safeguard to the inhabitants It was Mr. Viehmann also who arranged for the foundation of a handsome Carnegie Library, which this city now possesses, and during his administration many of the streets were adequately paved He was regarded as a very progressive man, and his fellow-citizens universally regarded him as their friend Mr Viehmann was also nominated on a number of occasions as governor of the State by the Democratic party In his religious belief, Mr Viehmann was a member of the First Reformed Church of New Brunswick, and was very active in his support of the work of this congregation

George Anthony Viehmann was united in marriage, November 28, 1898, at Concord, New Hampshire, with Mary Abbott, a native of that place, born November 7, 1870, and a daughter of Franklin Augustus and Asenath Austin (Dow) Abbott Both of Mrs Viehmann's parents were natives of New Hampshire, her father having been born at Concord, August 1, 1836, and her mother April 4, 1831 Mr Abbott died August 4, 1910, but his wife survives him. Mr and Mrs Viehmann are the parents of the following children Ruth Abbott, who became the wife of Augustus Lemuel Gladding, of Lincoln, California, where they make their home, George Anthony, Jr, born February 6, 1903, and Mary Alice, born June 29, 1905

Mr. Viehmann was a man of unusually strong personality, and possessed a remarkable grasp of practical affairs He was, however, of a very kindly and genial temperament, and won the affection and esteem of all with whom he was associated He was a man of large proportions and commanding presence, and nature seemed to have intended him as a leader of men His instincts were intensely domestic, and he found his chief happiness among the members of his own family by his own hearthstone

---

WILLIAM C. KELLY was born at Oak Tree, New Jersey, August 17, 1837, the son of Christian L and Jeannette E. (Campbell) Kelly, both Campbell and Kelly families being among the oldest families of that section

William C Kelly was educated in the public schools of Oak Tree and

Plainfield, New Jersey, but at an early age he was thrown upon his own resources and compelled to make his own way in the world. He learned the carpenter's trade, but soon abandoned it, going to Illinois, where he spent four years on a farm. During these years he accumulated a small capital which he invested in a tract of pine timber in Wisconsin. He continued the purchase of timber tracts, with profit in lumbering, and eventually owned thousands of acres. Finally, Mr. Kelly sold most of his timber land and removed from Wisconsin to Cadillac, Michigan where he erected a large mill, and there manufactured timber on a large scale. He continued there about five years, then, in accordance with his wife's wishes, sold out and removed to Asbury Park, New Jersey, there engaging in the wholesale lumber business, under the firm name of Kelly & Palmateer, this firm continuing in business until 1895. Mr. Kelly then sold his business and returned to Oak Tree, New Jersey the place of his birth, where he purchased a large farm, upon which he resided until his death. He was a man of strong character, energetic and capable, winning success through his own ability. He was a Democrat, but never took an active part in politics. He accumulated a fortune which he wisely used in creating and providing for the future maintenance of a home for those dear to him. He was very liberal and gave much to charity, was genial and neighborly, fond of books, and most hospitable.

Mr. Kelly married, in 1864, Bessie M. Palmateer, of Albany, New York, and they were the parents of a daughter, Eva Lena Kelly, born at Oak Tree New Jersey, July 8, 1865. She married, June 27, 1888, John Henry Campbell, a sketch of whom follows.

JOHN HENRY CAMPBELL, son of Ellis A. and Louisa H. (Fink) Campbell, was born in Plainfield, New Jersey, June 25 1861, his father a contractor of Plainfield. He was educated in the public schools of Plainfield, finishing with high school, then entered business life with the Clifton-Campbell Company of Plainfield wholesale produce merchants. He established in a minor position, but soon was advanced to higher rank, finally becoming an official of the company, his term of service covering a period of thirty years. He retired from business about 1910. Besides his connection with the Clifton-Campbell Company he had other business interests, including land in Florida and extensive orange groves. The product of his orange groves in Florida he disposed of through the Clifton-Campbell Company, large shipments being made daily during the season.

About 1911 he removed from Plainfield to Oak Tree, Middlesex county, New Jersey, there occupying the farm owned by William C. Kelly, and bequeathed by him to his daughter, Mrs. Eva Lena (Kelly) Campbell. Mr. Campbell assumed the management of the estate left by Mr. Kelly, and there he has spent a very pleasant and profitable decade of his life. The estate at Oak Tree has been largely converted into building lots, and disposed of most advantageously. Mr. Campbell has closely adhered to his business interests and has taken little active part

Robert L. McKiernan

in public affairs. He is a member of the Presbyterian church, and in politics is a Democrat

Mr Campbell married, June 27, 1888, at Oak Tree, New Jersey, Eva Lena Kelly, born July 8, 1865, daughter of William C and Bessie M (Palmateer) Kelly, whose sketch precedes this Mr and Mrs Campbell are the parents of two children Bessie, born April 25, 1890, married Harvey Nash, and resides in Newark, New Jersey, William K, born June 2, 1894, married Gail Tichenor, and resides with his parents at Oak Tree, his father's business associate

---

ROBERT LEWIS McKIERNAN, M D.—Although but a comparatively short time has elapsed since his coming to New Brunswick, the name of Dr Robert Lewis McKiernan is already familiar and most favorably known to many of the residents of this community Dr. McKiernan has during these two years thoroughly identified himself both as a physician and a citizen with the progressive element here

Robert Lewis McKiernan was born February 1, 1891, in New Haven, Connecticut, the son of Daniel and Catharine (De Heslin) McKiernan He attended the Sacred Heart Parochial School of his native place until 1905, when he entered the New Haven High School, and after completing the prescribed four years' classical course was graduated with the class of 1909 Having in the meantime decided to adopt medicine as a profession, he matriculated in the medical department of Tufts College and was graduated with the degree of Doctor of Medicine in 1914. He then spent some three years in hospital work In 1916 he was appointed instructor at Cornell University in hygiene, where he remained for six months, then in February, 1917, entered the United States navy as lieutenant in the Medical Corps, serving during the war with Germany until January 5, 1920 He then came to New Brunswick, New Jersey, and established himself in the practice of his profession

Dr. McKiernan specializes in Urology, and is a member of the staff of the Middlesex Hospital, also the Hospital for Joint Diseases, of New York City He is a director of Gradwohl Laboratories of New Brunswick He is also a director of the State clinic, and general supervisor of the Public Health of New Brunswick

Dr McKiernan belongs to the Professional Guild of Middlesex county, the American Medical Association, the American Urological Association, the New Jersey State Medical Association, the Middlesex County Medical Society, the Essex County Anatomical and Pathological Society, the medical section of Rutgers College, is a member of the Sigma Alpha Epsilon, a college fraternity, and Tufts College Club, Hartford, Connecticut He is a charter member first secretary and a director of the Rotary Club of New Brunswick, and also holds membership in the Business Men's Club of the Young Men's Christian Association, the Raritan Valley Country Club, the New Brunswick Country Club, and the Diomedian Club of New York City. In religion Dr McKiernan is a Roman Catholic and attends St Peter's Church of that denomination at New Brunswick   He is a member of Charles Henry Post, No 59, American Legion, also American Officers of the World War   He is a member of the Reserve Corps of the United States navy, with the rank of lieutenant, senior grade

Dr McKiernan married, January 29, 1919, Marie Cathryn Schafer, daughter of Henry G and Rebecca Schafer, and they are the parents of one child, Marie Louise, born May 12, 1920

HELEN (GLIDDEN) TOMBS, of Sewaren, is among the prominent women in the social and club life of Woodbridge township, Middlesex county, New Jersey

Helen (Glidden) Tombs, daughter of Captain Samuel G and Martha A. H (Fisher) Glidden, both of distinguished ancestry, was born in Brooklyn, New York   The Gliddens came, in early Colonial days, from Hampshire county, England, where they had long been seated, a family of French and Norman descent, who came into England with William the Conqueror about the year 1066

Captain Samuel G Glidden, the father, was a native of Newcastle, Maine, and in the states of New Hampshire, Massachusetts, Maine, and Ohio, the family has always taken a leading part in the pioneer movements.   Early members of the family were partly responsible for the name given the State of New Hampshire, named for the County of Hampshire, England   In 1820, when the part of Massachusetts now called Maine became a separate State, the Gliddens were active in bringing about the separation, and the name Glidden is likewise well represented in the State of Ohio.   The family for centuries were large landholders, but were also engaged in maritime pursuits, Samuel G Glidden having been for years a master mariner   After retiring from the sea, he became a very successful commission merchant in New York City, and was a man of influence until his death at the age of fifty-three, in Brooklyn, New York   He was well educated, being a college graduate, a dignified and commanding personage, yet genial and a sympathetic friend   His wife, Martha A H (Fisher) Glidden, was born in Taunton, Massachusetts, daughter of Julius and Mary Wheeler (Horton) Fisher, of Franklin and Wrentham, Massachusetts, a descendant of Sir Daniel Fisher, who came to America in early days and founded the town of Dedham, Massachusetts, and of the celebrated physician of that day, Dr Nathaniel Miller, a friend of General Lafayette   The English ancestry of the Fisher family dates back for many centuries to the town of Syleham, Winston, near Cambridge, England, where they were knighted for valor by their liege lord   The Gliddens, Fishers, and all their allied families were patriots of the Revolution and of early Colonial days, and veterans of later wars   John Glidden, father of Captain Samuel G Glidden, served in the War of 1812 at old Fort Pemaquid on the coast of Maine

Mrs Helen (Glidden) Tombs, the subject of this review, was educated in Brooklyn, New York, and there resided until 1898, when a resi-

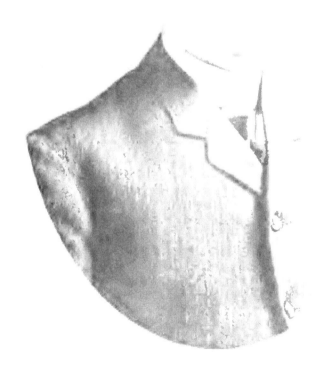

Frederic Firman Grant

dence was established in Sewaren, New Jersey. Her beautiful home, Strathspey Hall on Cliff Road, Sewaren, is the abode of hospitality and culture, her friends being many Mrs Tombs is the founder and organizer of the Sewaren History Club and of the local Civic Club, two organizations which have been of great value to the community It was through her efforts that a memorial stone dedicated to George Washington was placed in the belfry tower of the Memorial Cathedral at Valley Forge by the History Club, of Sewaren, New Jersey Like "Tabitha" of old, she is active in numerous good works An enthusiastic Red Cross worker, she also finds time to give generous support to all worthy charitable and philanthropic movements She is a member of the Fort Greene Chapter, Daughters of the American Revolution, of Brooklyn, New York, an honorary member of Camp Middlebrook Chapter, Daughters of the American Revolution, of Bound Brook, New Jersey, of the New England Women's Society, of New York, the New Jersey Historical Society, the Women's Branch of the New Jersey Historical Society, and of the Monmouth County Historical Society. She is also a member of St John's Episcopal Church, of Sewaren.

Mrs Helen (Glidden) Tombs was twice married (first) to Frederic Firman Grant, whose life history follows in this work, and (second) to William Henry Tombs, born at Rahway, New Jersey, son of William H and Margaret (Ayres) Tombs The Tombs family came from England and first located at Toms River, New Jersey, later settling at Rahway in the same State. Mr Tombs' maternal ancestors, the Ayres family, are related to the well known Coreys, of Elizabeth, and Halseys, of Newark, and to the Davis family, of Elizabeth, New Jersey Mr. Tombs is an inventor and has devoted his life to mechanical research and practice

---

FREDERIC FIRMAN GRANT was born in Hobart, New York, June 18, 1837, and died at his home in Sewaren, New Jersey, July 26, 1915 He was the son of Philander Sweeton and Caroline R (Greene) Grant, being descended on the paternal side from Matthew Grant, who came to America from Strathmore, Scotland, settled early at Windsor, Connecticut, and from whom General Ulysses Grant also descended On the material side, the line of descent includes the progenitors of General Nathaniel Greene, of Revolutionary fame

While still very young, Frederic Firman Grant came with his parents to Albany, New York, where he was educated in the public schools and in the old Albany Academy. Upon leaving the Academy, he went to work in a local bank where he remained until his real opportunity came, when George F. Baker, a close friend of his and later a great financier, invited young Grant to join him in his banking activities in New York City. Mr Baker had just organized the First National Bank, of New York, and the opportunity offered was a valuable one Thus Frederic Firman Grant entered upon the important banking career in which he remained until his death, a period of more than half a century He saw the First National Bank of New York City grow from what might be termed an acorn to a mighty oak, and much of the growth of that institution may be attributed to those who, like Mr Grant, so faithfully and ably filled its important offices

Mr Grant was a loyal and good business man, having many firm friends and affiliations in business and financial circles   The social side of his life was varied   Being a constant reader and possessed of much humor, he was the life of most gatherings of which he formed a part   He was held in high esteem by his many friends and acquaintances, and having a genial and sympathetic nature, combined with insight and good judgment, his advice and counsel were much sought   During the Civil War days he was a member of that famous old military body, the Albany Zouaves   He was a member of various societies, orders and clubs, among them being the Albany Society, and the Salamagundi Society, of Woodbridge, New Jersey, of which he was president for a time   He was a staunch Republican and a leader in the Republican Club, of Brooklyn, New York   When he established his residence in Sewaren, Middlesex county, New Jersey, he took a leading part in all movements for the welfare of the community, and here he had a host of warm friends   At Sewaren and at Woodbridge he was well known, socially and otherwise, and was a prominent member and a warden of St John's Episcopal Church, of Sewaren, New Jersey, and St James, of Brooklyn, New York

Mr Grant married Helen Glidden, of Brooklyn, now a prominent figure at Sewaren, New Jersey, whose life story is told in the preceding sketch

---

RARITAN TRUST COMPANY—The history of the Raritan Trust Company dates from June 6, 1916 when the institution was incorporated under the laws of the State of New Jersey, with a capital stock of $100,000   The company is owned and controlled by residents of Perth Amboy and vicinity, and the degree to which the public confidence is held is shown by a gratifying annual increase in the business of all its departments   The Raritan Trust Company performs all the service of the modern trust company, and in addition to its banking business has come into that intimate touch with the community that such an institution, through the very nature of its organization, can best attain.

There have been only a few minor changes in the official personnel of the company during the four years of its life, and its place of business continues at the corner of State and Fayette streets   The statement prepared at the close of business, June 30, 1921, showed deposits of well over $1,500,000, and all its items indicate a healthy growth and vigorous condition   The officers of the Raritan Trust Company are Sidney Riddlestorffer, president, A Greenbaum, vice-president, Abel Hansen, vice-president, A Clayton Clark, vice-president, W. Parker Runyon, vice-president, Harry E Comings, secretary-treasurer, and I R Solt, assistant-treasurer   The directors are A. Clayton Clark manager of the Raritan Copper Works, Leo Goldberger, city attorney, M S Gold-

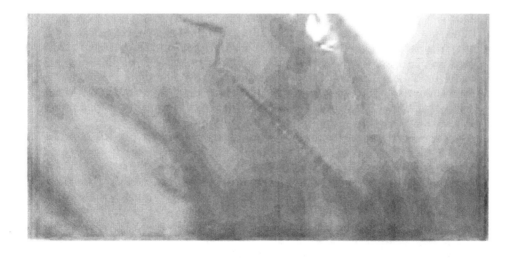

berger, merchant, A Greenbaum, president of the Metuchen Realty and Improvement Company, Abel Hansen, proprietor of Fords Porcelain Works, M M McHose, treasurer of L H McHose, Incorporated, Anton Massopust, real estate and insurance operator, S Riddlestorffer, mortgage and investment broker, I R Robins, dealer in lumber and building materials L M Rossi, works manager of the General Bakelite Company, W Parker Runyon, president of the P A Dry Dock Company, Dr C I Silk, physician, Frank Stas, treasurer of the Slovak League of America, Max Wurtzel, of Wagner & Wurtzel, wholesale merchants The company has found a wide local sphere of influence, and has taken a responsible place among the financial institutions of the county

---

FRANK HENRY VAN SYCKLE—Among the most prominent of the young business men of Perth Amboy, New Jersey, is Frank Henry Van Syckle, owner and manager of the Frank Van Syckle Garage, located at No. 162 New Brunswick avenue His meteoric rise, from a modest beginning at the bottom of the ladder to the topmost rung of success in the automobile business of the county and State, is a matter of much favorable comment by his fellow-citizens His interest in all that concerns the welfare of the community is deep and sincere, and wherever substantial aid will further public progress, it is always freely given

Mr Van Syckle was born in Perth Amboy, New Jersey, July 26, 1884, son of Peter H and Catherine Van Syckle, of New Brunswick New Jersey He was educated in the public schools of Perth Amboy, and took a further course in mechanics with private tutors At the age of fourteen years he made his first venture in the business world by selling newspapers in his home town At seventeen, he began mechanical work as a machinist in the employ of Thomas Lingel on Kings street His next employment was with the Ramsay Ship Building Yard. From there he went to the Raritan Copper Works, where he was foreman of the machine shop, and finally became master mechanic for the Barber Asphalt Paving Company, remaining with that company until he was twenty-six years old

Like many another ambitious and energetic young man, Frank H. Van Syckle was not satisfied to eke out an existence in the employ of others, he wanted to establish himself in a business of his own, where he could garner the fruit of his labor and energy, and establish for himself a position in the business world, so on October 1, 1910, with a small and borrowed capital back of him he started in the automobile business of repairing and selling of automobiles, locating in a small frame building—little more than a shanty—at the corner of Fayette and High streets He was successful from the start, the business soon outgrowing its limitations, he was obliged to seek more spacious quarters, and in 1911 removed to New Brunswick avenue, to the John Donaghue building, then known as the City Market now the New Auditorium, and there engaged in the sale of automobiles, under the firm title of the Frank Van

Syckle Garage These quarters he rented for five years, when they again proved too small for the ever-expanding business, so in 1913 he began to erect the handsome building on the corner of New Brunswick avenue and Jefferson street, where he is now located, one of the largest automobile concerns in the State This building, completed in 1914, and perfectly fitted out in every detail for the automobile business, with its spacious showroom, finely equipped garage and beautiful offices, is indeed a monument to the energy, business ability and good taste of its owner. Mr Van Syckle moved his business to these new quarters, then in 1917 he purchased the New Auditorium building, where he had formerly conducted his business The business still expanding, he erected a building in New Brunswick, and opened a new branch of the business, under the title of the American Auto Company

Among other enterprises in which Mr Van Syckle is interested is the A G Belknap Company, of Plainfield, New Jersey He is also vice-president of the Fords National Bank at Fords, New Jersey Mr. Van Syckle is now thirty-six years old, and in ten years of his business career, starting at the bottom with a borrowed capital of but three hundred dollars, he has risen to be the owner of the above mentioned concern, the largest of its kind, and still expanding

During the World War Mr Van Syckle furnished the government with fifty automobiles for its use at Camp Raritan at a mere nominal rental, keeping them in condition and supplying all parts and supplies, and was one of the largest purchasers of Liberty bonds during all the drives In religion he is a Roman Catholic, and a member of St Mary's Church, of Perth Amboy He holds membership in the East Jersey Club, Benevolent and Protective Order of Elks, Knights of Columbus, Foresters, and New York Canadian Club Mr Van Syckle is married and has one son, Frank H , Jr

It may be said of Frank Henry Van Syckle that he has been the architect of his own fortune, and is building up a name that will endure He is an able business man, public-spirited and progressive, and the place he occupies in the community is well deserved

---

THOMAS FRANCIS DUNIGAN, who for many years was a leader in the business, financial and political life of Middlesex county, was one of the esteemed and representative citizens of Woodbridge New Jersey, until his passing away, April 30, 1921

Mr Dunigan was a son of Bernard and Julia (Ryan) Dunigan, also prominent in the community life of Woodbridge He attended the public schools of Woodbridge and the parochial schools of Perth Amboy subsequently completing his education at St John's Academy, Fordham, New York Mr Dunigan at first started in business with his father, who was a prosperous clay miner and contractor with properties in Woodbridge, but remained with him but a short time His next connection was with the Ostrander Fire Brick Company Fords, New Jersey, as a foreman in their clay banks. Here he gained much experience,

T. F. Dunigan

and after being thus associated for a few years, he was tendered an offer to become associated with the Henry A Maurer & Sons Company, Maurer, New Jersey For a time he acted as foreman, but later contracted with this company in mining clay This connection was a pleasant one, and quite permanent, for he remained with the company for some twenty-eight years, until his health required him to relinquish it, much to the regret of the Maurers While associated with them he established, during the year 1898, a retail coal and wood business, which grew rapidly to large proportions, and still later added builders' supplies, which also proved a success His next venture was that of a contractor on road construction work, and in all of these activities he became a leader and known throughout the State of New Jersey

Mr Dunigan was a director and vice-president of the First National Bank of Woodbridge, a town committeeman, president of the fire commissioners, and a county freeholder He was a staunch Democrat, and a leader in the councils of the party In his religious belief he was a Roman Catholic, being a member of St James' Roman Catholic Church, Woodbridge, of which he was a trustee up to the time of his death Mr Dunigan was equally well known in fraternal circles, being a member of New Brunswick Lodge, No 324, Benevolent and Protective Order of Elks, the Knights of Columbus, of Perth Amboy, the Royal Arcanum, of Woodbridge, and the Catholic Benevolent Legion of America

Mr Dunigan married, in Woodbridge, May 28, 1884, Jane M Finn, daughter of Robert and Margaret (Meagher) Finn, who were among the first settlers of Irish ancestry in Woodbridge The following children were born to Mr. and Mrs Dunigan Florence, now the wife of James J Dunne, of Brooklyn, New York and they have three children James J., Jr, Jane M., and Regina M., George, now living at Woodbridge; Jane L, now the wife of Edmund A Hayes, and they have two children Edmund A, Jr, and Jane, Anna B, who resides with her mother.

In the passing away of Thomas F Dunigan, Woodbridge lost one of its most substantial sons and citizens, a man who was a good father, a firm friend and neighbor, and a builder in every sense of the word, which means so much to any commonwealth

JOHN H RINEHART—The Rineharts are a Hunterdon county, New Jersey, family, George Rinehart being a farmer there until his death He married Mary Ann Hackett, also of a Hunterdon county family, and among their children was a son, John H Rinehart, father of George Rinehart, the latter now conducting a prosperous ice business in Dunellen New Jersey

John H Rinehart was born in Hunterdon county, New Jersey, April 10, 1863 He was educated in the public schools, and became a cooper by trade, but for many years was in railroad employ Mr Rinehart was brought up in the Roman Catholic church, in politics always a Democrat

Mr Rinehart married in Hunterdon county, February 14, 1880, Anna Hallanhan, born in Ireland, March 17, 1864, daughter of Patrick and

Catherine (Hapney) Hallanhan Of this marriage seven children were born 1 Francis J, born May 29, 1881   2 Mary, born February 10, 1882, died August 20, 1888   3 George born April 10, 1885, he is now well established in the ice business in Dunellen, New Jersey, employing in his enterprise two large trucks, in his earlier years he learned the machinist's trade, which he followed for some time   4 Anna, born October 3, 1889   5 Sylvester, born December 13, 1893   6 John, born June 26, 1895   7 Catherine, born January 16 1898

EDWARD J HEIL—Teutonic strength steadiness and patience, have long been adding their contribution to the diverse elements which make up the life stream flowing into this country from across seas, and they have built valuable material into the life of the nation   When Henry and Caroline (Schardt) Heil came to the land of opportunity about 1860, from Fulda, Germany, they brought their worldly goods with them, and they came to stay   Since that time, in thorough-going, practical fashion they have built themselves into the life of the communities in which they have lived, first at Newark, New Jersey, and later at Linoleumville, New York   Mr and Mrs Heil were the parents of six children Edward J of further mention, Henry A, Margaret, Anna, Caroline, and Mary   Mr and Mrs. Heil are now both deceased

Edward J Heil was born in Newark, New Jersey, September 13, 1869   He attended the public schools of Linoleumville, New York, later the private school of Mrs Simonds of the same town, finishing at St. Benedict's College at Newark, New Jersey   Since that time his busy years have been passed mostly at Carteret, Middlesex county, New Jersey, where he is widely known as an active, progressive and extremely successful real estate and insurance man   The carrying on of a very large and successful business, however, does not prevent him from serving his community in many valuable ways   He has been president of the Board of Education since 1907, and of the Board of Health since 1913   He has also been president of the Exempt Firemen's Association since 1903, and of the Sinking Fund Commission since 1915   Mr Heil has been serving as president of the Roosevelt Realty and Investment Company, Inc, since the beginning of its existence in 1913, and of the Carteret Building Loan Association for ten years

Politically, Mr. Heil is a Democrat, is president of the Carteret Democratic Club, is a member of the county executive committee, and has been local judge and recorder since 1915   Fraternally, he is affiliated with Elizabeth Lodge Benevolent and Protective Order of Elks, the Foresters of America, the Improved Order of Red Men, the Knights of Columbus, and with the Woodmen of the World   Mr Heil was secretary of the Committee on Incorporation of the borough of Roosevelt in 1906   With his multitudinous business, civic, and social responsibilities, Mr Heil finds time for active church duties   He is a member of St Joseph's Roman Catholic Church, and is president of the Holy Name Society

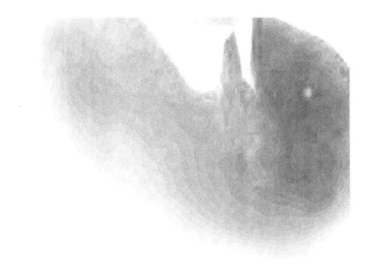

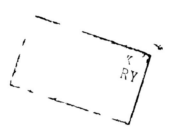

Mr Heil married Rose Frances Kreger, daughter of Joseph and Anna Frances (Brown) Kreger, of Dover, New Jersey, and they are the parents of two children: Edward J., Jr, born August 9, 1900, educated in the public schools of Roosevelt, the high school of Rahway, Seton Hall Preparatory School, and Seton Hall College, South Orange, New Jersey, and Helen F, born February 3, 1905, educated in the public schools of Roosevelt, and Mount St Mary's Academy, of Plainfield, New Jersey

---

LLOYD PERCY JOHNSON.—The name Johnson is an old and honored one in Perth Amboy, New Jersey, the first settler in this branch, James Johnson, great-grandfather of Lloyd P, being of the Newark Johnson family, founded by Thomas Johnson, who in May, 1666, came with the thirty families from Connecticut to Newark, New Jersey, where the first town meeting was held, May 21, 1666 Thomas Johnson was one of the committee of five from Newark who met John Ogden, Robert Treat, and others from Elizabeth, New Jersey, to settle boundary disputes He became one of Newark's most influential citizens, active in church and State His residence in Newark was on the northeast corner of Broad and Walnut streets, on the site of the present Grace Church Thomas Johnson was a son of Robert Johnson, who came from Yorkshire, England, and was one of the founders of the New Haven Connecticut, colony James Johnson, of the eighth American generation, was proprietor of the Old Tavern at the foot of High street, and is buried in Perth Amboy His son, Jeremiah Johnson, was born in Perth Amboy, and both he and his son, Abraham Johnson, were engaged in oyster planting in the Raritan river and in the bay Abraham Johnson married Margaret Isdell, born and married in Perth Amboy, which city is still her home at the age of sixty-five years Mr Johnson died an accidental death, September 23, 1907, aged sixty years Children, all born in Perth Amboy Elwood, chief clerk with the Lehigh Valley Railroad Company, married and has a son, Elwood, Mattie, married Ferdinand Hall, of Perth Amboy, and has a son, Ferdinand L Hall, Lloyd Percy, of further mention, Viola, deceased, who married W L McCready, and Caroline, who died unmarried

Lloyd P Johnson, youngest son of Abraham and Margaret (Isdell) Johnson, was born in Perth Amboy, New Jersey, August 15, 1880, and was there educated in the public schools After leaving high school, he was engaged in the oyster planting business with his father for eighteen months, and then entered the employ of the Perth Amboy Gas Light Company, where he remained for two years, then worked for the Public Service Corporation for a year and a half at the end of which time he entered the employ of the Central Electric Company, later returning to the Perth Amboy Gas Light Company He then continued in the employ of that company for eighteen years, rising from office boy to the position of assistant manager In 1914 he resigned his position to engage in the insurance business under the firm name, The Johnson Company In 1919 he purchased a half-interest in the business of Pierce & Son, one of the largest fire insurance agencies in the country now operated as the Pierce-Johnson Company. Mr. Johnson opened up Keasbey Heights, an addition to the city as his personal promotion and has other interests of similar nature. He is fond of sports of the forest and field, hunting being his favored recreation. He is a member of the Baptist church and a man highly esteemed for his sterling qualities. Mr. Johnson is a Republican in politics and ran for the State Assembly on the Republican ticket in 1918.

Mr. Johnson married, in Perth Amboy, Johanna Margaret Koyen, born in Perth Amboy, daughter of Emil and Marie Koyen, both residing in Woodbridge, New Jersey, her father a retired builder.

JOHN H. DAYTON —One of the well known business and professional men of Middlesex county, New Jersey, having offices in Perth Amboy and residing in Woodbridge, New Jersey, is John H. Dayton. He was born February 10, 1881, in Perth Amboy, the son of Spencer and Mary E. (Walters) Dayton, his father for many years a prominent contractor and builder in Perth Amboy.

John H. Dayton attended the grammar and high schools of his native city and then studied architecture with private tutors, passing the examinations required to practice as an architect in the State of New Jersey in 1902. Since that time he has followed that profession with pronounced success, having prepared plans for many of the well known buildings of Middlesex and surrounding counties.

Mr. Dayton is a member of the State Board of Architects. Politically he is a Republican. He is affiliated with the Free and Accepted Masons, the Benevolent and Protective Order of Elks, the East Jersey Club, and the Raritan Yacht Club.

On June 20, 1906, Mr. Dayton married Amy B. McEwen, daughter of Joseph and Sarah McEwen. They have one child, Dorothy Dayton.

THOMAS J. SCULLY for eight years representative for the Second District of New Jersey in the Congress of the United States and at present mayor of the city of South Amboy, New Jersey, is one who has steadily endeavored to make after-election performance square with pre-election promise. In so doing he has found that he who would achieve must struggle and his Congressional career has been an eventful one.

Born in South Amboy, New Jersey, September 19, 1868, he attended the public schools of that city and then went to Seton Hall College. Upon leaving college, he was taken into the towing business which his father had established in 1871. Always energetic, ambitious and capable, he directed his full energy into the upbuilding of that business with the result that the Scully Towing and Transportation Company developed into an important maritime enterprise owning more than fifty ocean going tugs and barges and carrying more than a million tons of freight annually to all parts of the world.

Devotion to his business, however, did not prevent Mr. Scully from taking an active part in the life of his community Always ready to aid in any project which seemed to him well calculated to further the interests of the city, he early gave evidence of executive and administrative ability, and when, in 1898, Dr. Ambrose Treganowan resigned his office as mayor of South Amboy, the Council appointed Mr Scully to finish the unexpired term Mr Scully had already served the city most acceptably and faithfully as a member of the Board of Education for a term of three years, and in filling out the unexpired term as the chief executive of the city, he so commended himself to the people that in 1909 they elected him to serve for a full term In discharging the duties of that office he displayed the same vigor and fearlessness that had made the Scully Towing and Transportation Company a success He improved the dock facilities and the sewer system of the city and reorganized the fire and police departments In 1908 he went as a Democratic delegate to the National Convention that named William J Bryan for President, and he was also a candidate on the Bryan ticket for presidential elector He was also a delegate to the National Convention which nominated Woodrow Wilson in 1912

It was in 1910 that Mr Scully first appeared as a candidate for Congress, securing the nomination against the Republican candidate Benjamin F Howell, who had represented the District of Washington for sixteen years, and defeating him by a plurality of nearly 4,500 So acceptably and ably did he represent his district that he was reëlected in 1912-14-16 In 1916 the result of the contest between himself and the Republican candidate, Robert Carson, was in dispute for many weeks after the election The returns as filed with the county clerks by the election boards of the district credited Mr Carson with fourteen more votes than were credited to Mr Scully Mr Scully demanded a recount, and because a tie between the parties in the National House of Representatives was threatened, the result of the recount was awaited with keenest interest throughout the country The recount disclosed a majority in favor of Mr. Scully and he retained his seat, preventing the tie between the parties in the House

Since completing his most honorable and faithful term of Congressional service, Mr Scully has not become inactive, but continues to further the economic, social, and political interests of his community, state, and nation in every way possible His long and eventful experience in the legislative halls of the nation make him an unusually valuable citizen, and in many fields of endeavor his influence is felt and will continue to work for the upbuilding of intelligent and efficient civic life He is the present mayor of South Amboy an office to which he was elected shortly after the expiration of his Congressional term, and to which he was again returned at the last city election

THOMAS L SLUGG.—One of the well known citizens of Carteret, Middlesex county, New Jersey, is Thomas L Slugg, who was born in Huntingdon Valley, Montgomery county, Pennsylvania, January 16,

1860 He was educated there in the grammar schools, and upon completing his school years he became a telegraph operator and station agent In 1888 he came to Carteret, where he followed the same occupation for three years About 1892 he engaged in the real estate and contracting business here, which he continued until his retirement from same in 1916 He is now supervising foreman for the United States Metal Refining Company at Carteret

Mr Slugg has been active in a public way, being a justice of the peace since 1890, and once postmaster and recorder of Carteret Fraternally, he is a member of the Independent Order of Odd Fellows, and a member of the Junior Order of United American Mechanics

Mr Slugg married, March 3, 1880, in Philadelphia, Pennsylvania, Margaret J Robinson, of Norristown, Pennsylvania and they are the parents of the following children Morris L, now (1921) superintendent of the American Agriculture Chemical Company at Belfast, Maine, Bessie E, now Mrs. Howard W Thorn, of Carteret, New Jersey, Fannie P, residing at home with her parents, Julia R, now Mrs L Bergheim, of Dunellen, New Jersey, Margie, a teacher in Perth Amboy public schools, Ruth M, a trained nurse in the employ of Mrs M Barron, of Woodbridge, New Jersey, who is now (1921) 104 years old, and Clarence H, now supervising foreman for the United States Metal Refining Company at Chrome, New Jersey, and a councilman for the borough of Roosevelt, New Jersey

---

PETER ANDREAS JOHANSEN —The ancestry of Peter Andreas Johansen, president and treasurer of the Perth Amboy Foundry and Machine Company, extends far back into Danish history, the American record of the line dating from his own arrival, via the Danish West Indies, in 1884 He is a grandson of Peter Johansen, of Horsens, Denmark, and son of Julius Johansen

Julius Johansen was born in Copenhagen, Denmark, in 1826, and died in 1900 He was an iron molder by trade, and served as a sergeant of infantry in the Danish army In 1848, while serving in this military capacity during the Danish-German War, he married Carolina Thessen, born in 1828, died in 1885, the marriage taking place under royal decree by order from King Frederick VII The Thessens were silversmiths throughout many generations Julius Johansen and his wife were members of the Lutheran church

Peter Andreas Johansen was born in Aarhus, Denmark, August 26, 1859, and after attending public schools, was graduated in marine engineering at the Royal Navy Yard In 1873 he entered the machinist's trade, and in 1881 was placed in charge of a sugar plant in St Croix, Danish West Indies (Virgin Islands United States), and in 1884 he came to the United States Following the trade of machinist in Yonkers and Ossining, in New York State, for a time, he later came to Perth Amboy as superintendent of McCullough & Company's Machine Shop In 1892 he entered the employ of Patrick White & Sons, and later was superintendent of same In 1905 he founded the Perth Amboy Foundry and Machine Company and is president and treasurer of same Mr Johansen is connected with the First National Bank of Perth Amboy, New Jersey, with the Perth Amboy Trust Company, and bears throughout his community the reputation of an able, substantial progressive man-of-affairs His technical talents have been turned to industrial advantage, and the concern of which he is the head ranks high among organizations of its kind in the locality

From 1897 to 1901 Mr Johansen was an alderman of Perth Amboy, and from 1902 to 1906 he was a member of the Board of Freeholders of Middlesex county He has numerous fraternal affiliations, and has held all offices in Algonquin Lodge, No 44, Knights of Pythias, while he holds the thirty-second degree in the Ancient Accepted Scottish Rite of Masonry, his lodge, Raritan No 61, Free and Accepted Masons of Perth Amboy. He is also a noble of Salaam Temple, Ancient Arabic Order Nobles of the Mystic Shrine, of Newark He is a member of Perth Amboy Forest, Tall Cedars of Lebanon, and is also a member of the Young Men's Christian Association He and his family are communicants of the Protestant Episcopal church

Mr Johansen married, in St Paul's Church, Ossining, New York, Mary Louise Rex, who died January 1, 1921, daughter of William and Louise Rex, her father a lawyer of the Virgin Islands Children of Peter Andreas and Mary Louise (Rex) Johansen 1 Wilson, born in Perth Amboy, educated in the Perth Amboy High School and Stevens Institute of Technology, Hoboken, New Jersey, was director and scenario writer of his own moving picture company, co-editor of Street and Smith's "Picture Play," and a writer of short stories under the *nom de plume* "Rex" He was a young man of literary and dramatic talent, and his death, May 12, 1916, at the age of twenty-two years, deprived his calling of a most promising man 2 Hessie Louise, born in Perth Amboy, educated in the Perth Amboy High School, a graduate of the New York College of Music

---

LUCIUS PORTER JANEWAY —The great wallpaper business conducted under the corporate title, Janeway & Carpender, is distinctively a Janeway enterprise, the Carpender interest having been extinguished in 1889 by purchase For a period of eight years, 1892-1900, it was a department of the National Wall Paper Company, but was redeemed from trust control in 1900 and incorporated as Janeway & Carpender, Colonel Jacob James Janeway, president, yet remaining its head although in years long past the age when men lay down business cares through physical infirmities To that company, in 1904, came Lucius Porter Janeway, youngest of the children of Colonel Jacob James and Eliza Ann (Harrington) Janeway, as vice-president, and in association with his honored father in the president's chair, and his brother-in-law, Rev Charles Scudder, at the secretary's desk, the Janeway control is absolute The company runs on a plan of independent action and is the largest of all wallpaper manufacturers outside the combined companies The business has grown to immense proportions and is a wonderful monument to the business acumen of the men who have been its directing heads

Lucius Porter Janeway was born in New Brunswick, New Jersey, June 18, 1881 He was a student at Rutgers College Preparatory School, Lawrenceville, until graduation in 1900, going thence to Princeton University, there receiving the customary Bachelor's degree with the class of 1904 When college years were over, he at once became associated in the management of Janeway & Carpender, serving that corporation as vice-president For sixteen years he has held that office, and is one of the strong men of the wallpaper manufacturing business He is devoted to his business, and has few outside interests

Mr Janeway married, in New York City, November 4, 1915, Lila Fairchild, daughter of LeRoy Cholwell and Julia Louise (Moore) Fairchild, and they are the parents of a daughter, Juliana Louise Janeway

---

ROBERT R VANDENBERGH.—One of the prominent business men and active citizens of Prospect Plains, New Jersey, is Robert R Vandenbergh Active in promoting all movements planned for the advancement of his community, he has worked for the economic and civic upbuilding of his native city in various ways, and has made his influence felt among a wide circle of friends and fellow-citizens

Robert R Vandenbergh, son of Robert M and Elizabeth S. (Maitland) Vandenbergh, lifelong residents of Monroe township, New Jersey, was born in Monroe township, Middlesex county, New Jersey, at the home farm, April 26, 1871. He attended the public schools of his district and then went to work on his father's farm Having by experience gained a thorough knowledge of the business, he took over the management of all his father's farm properties, and for several years managed them most successfully In 1901, however, he turned his attention to another line and engaged in the hotel business at Prospect Plains, continuing this business until 1917, when he retired He is still, and has been for many years, very active in the community life and in civic affairs as well as in political affairs He supports the Republican party, was county tax assessor from 1900 to 1920, has been a member of the Middlesex county Board of Freeholders since February 15, 1920, and takes a prominent part in the political life of this part of the State Fraternally, he is affiliated with the Benevolent and Protective Order of Elks, of New Brunswick, New Jersey, and with the Improved Order of Red Men, Ahander Tribe, of New Brunswick, New Jersey

Mr Vandenbergh married, at Cranberry, New Jersey, December 16, 1901, Mary E Doty, daughter of Louis E and Sarah (Montgomery) Doty, well known residents of Bernardsville, New Jersey, and one son has been born of this marriage, R Maitland, born September 25, 1905

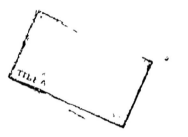

TILL A

Isaac Alpern

ISAAC ALPERN —There is no more illuminating commentary upon the economic, social, and political fabric of this country than is the lives of those who have come to us from other lands Those who question the assertion that America is a land of opportunity, and that energy, application, ability, and thrift, are the only capital necessary for the building of a business career, have only to search the life histories of those who coming to this country without capital, without friends, without acquaintance with the customs of the country, and without even the ability to use the language of the land of their adoption, have yet risen to high positions of usefulness and power

One of these wonder stories is that of Isaac Alpern, son of Jacob and Sadie Alpern Born June 6, 1883 in the humble home of his parents, near Warsaw, Russia, he grew strong vigorous, enduring inured, even as a lad, to hard work long hours, and small compensation That he shouldered his share of the burdens without complaint did not prevent his alert mind from seeing clearly the limitations of his environment, and meagre as was the education he received, it was enough to enable him to gain a knowledge of other lands where opportunity was greater and oppression and injustice less dominant Visions of a better life in the land to the westward early floated before his mind and as, from time to time, letters and reports of letters from those already in the distant land deepened his desire to try the great adventure to turn the dream into a reality determination strengthened into action, and when he was twenty-one he sailed away to the westward in search of a fortune and a career He landed in New York City, the nerve center of the "Land of Opportunity" where he remained for a time doing whatever he could find to do and getting acquainted with his new world Then he went to Brooklyn New York where working at whatever jobs he could find to do in the daytime he attended school in the evening quickly mastering the English language With a genius for hard work, and a thoroughness in mastering detail, as well as a clear grasp of essentials his increasingly ready command of the English language removed the last barrier to the first rounds of the ladder of success, and the character of the positions he held improved with each change Of a studious nature he used his spare moments in reading, and rapidly acquired a working knowledge of the customs the history and the political and civic institutions of his adopted country

By 1904 Mr Alpern felt prepared for a change of occupation, and removing to Perth Amboy New Jersey began teaching Hebrew in one of the schools connected with the Sharai Tefiloh Temple It was characteristic of the man that during his career as a teacher when he was working long hours for small pay he still strove to improve his own fitness for his work, making nightly trips to New York City, where he continued his studies in the evening schools He continued his teaching for about three years when having by strict economy saved a little money he entered the real estate and insurance business first being employed by Pratt-Brown & Company of Perth Amboy, New Jersey and later buying out the interests of that firm He continued

M_{10}

business under the Pratt-Brown name for a time and then changed the firm name to Alpern & Company As a real estate and insurance man he was very successful, and as his business grew and prospered, his services came to be sought by other interests He was made a director of the Perth Amboy Trust Company, later becoming its vice-president, and in 1919 became president of this large and growing institution He is also vice-president of the People's National Bank, of Elizabeth, New Jersey, and is connected with various other important concerns. As his banking interests became more and more exacting, demanding larger and larger portions of his time, he finally sold out his real estate and insurance business in order that he might devote his time to the offices of trust which had been conferred upon him

In addition to the exacting demands of his business connections, Mr Alpern finds time to serve his community in various ways He is president of the Young Men's Hebrew Association and also a member of the Young Men's Christian Association. Fraternally he is a member of the Benevolent and Protective Order of Elks, is affiliated with various Masonic bodies, and is a member of the Raritan Yacht Club, all of Perth Amboy He is prominent in church work interested and active in charitable enterprises, and during the World War was a leader in the various drives for the raising of funds

Mr Alpern married, March 4 1910, in New York City, Lena Pauline Coble, daughter of Louis and Rebecca Coble, of New York City, and they are the parents of two children Ruth S , born January 1, 1911, and Frances born April 28, 1917.

Mr Alpern is well known in banking circles, and is a widely known and highly esteemed citizen of Middlesex county Coming from a foreign land, with only his faith, his courage, his ability, and his willingness to work he has built for himself a life and a career which speak eloquently of the character of the man, and at the same time vindicate the right of his adopted country to its best-loved title—the "Land of Opportunity "

WALTER G DUNN —To the intelligence, industry and thrift of her agriculturists more than to all other causes combined, does the county of Middlesex, New Jersey owe her remarkable development, and of this large and useful class of her population Walter G Dunn, of New Market, is a worthy exponent

Walter G Dunn was born July 19, 1870, in New Market, Middlesex county, New Jersey, on the farm he now resides on, the house being two hundred and fifty years old, the shingles thereon being the same as when first built, they being shaved by hand and nailed on with hand-made nails that being before the day of machinery for every conceivable line of work The house is one of the landmarks of the neighborhood being kept in good repair by its present owner, who is very proud of its antiquity His parents were Louis C and Aurelia Dunn, the former named born in New Market, November 11, 1844 the latter born November 6, 1846 Louis C Dunn was a tiller of the soil, conducting his operations on the farm where his son now resides

Walter G Dunn attended the common schools of Piscataway township From childhood he assisted in the labors of the farm, and early in life became familiar with all the duties pertaining to the life of the agriculturist, and when the time arrived for earning his own livelihood he chose the line of work followed by his father His birthplace has become his permanent place of residence, and the neat and thrifty appearance of the farm, coupled with the handsome competence he receives from his labors, plainly indicate that his vocation was wisely chosen He is a member of the Seventh Day Baptist church, in which he takes an active interest, and his political allegiance is given to the Republican party He is a member of the Order of Foresters

Mr Dunn married, February 13, 1889, in Dunellen, New Jersey, Ella T Larkin, born April 3, 1870, daughter of George and Anna Shepard (Tithwarth) Larkin, the former named born in Connecticut, September 26, 1827 Three children were born to Mr. and Mrs Dunn Myrtle T, born March 26 1892, Jennie F, born March 20, 1893; and Marjorie, born March 23, 1895

SARAH E M TOMS —One of the landmarks of Middlesex county, New Jersey, is the residence of Miss Toms, located in Melrose Park, which was erected by her grandfather on the paternal side in the year 1797 and remained as erected until the year 1835, a period of thirty-eight years, when an addition was made thereto by the father of Miss Toms, and thirty-four years later he built another addition, this making it a very commodious and substantial structure, now equipped with all appliances for the comfort and convenience of its inmates The property is now very valuable, having enhanced in value in the past few years, and this was left to Miss Toms by her father at his death, she taking a particular interest in it by reason of its antiquity and associations

Sarah E M Toms was born in Rahway, New Jersey, a daughter of Joseph and Sarah Jane Toms, the former named born February 12, 1802, died July 7, 1867, and the latter named born December 12, 1819, died October 10, 1895 having survived her husband for more than a quarter of a century They were the parents of another daughter, Ellen Jane, born August 2, 1843, died August 12 1873

Miss Toms attended the common school adjacent to her home, this knowledge being supplemented by careful reading and observation She is a member of the Methodist Episcopal church of Melrose Park, taking an active interest in its activities, and her many friends in the community honor and respect her for her many excellencies of character

---

ROBERT LAWSON STOTESBURY.—In solving the complex problems of everyday existence. Robert Lawson Stotesbury takes a most practical part Under the name of the Middlesex Sanitary Laundry he takes one of the heaviest burdens from the shoulders of the housewives of this vicinity.

Mr Stotesbury's father, Robert Hall Stotesbury, was born in Waterford, Ireland   He came to America when he was twenty years of age, and was accompanied by his three sisters   Ellen, Mary and Ann, all of whom are now deceased.   Their brother survived them until 1919, when he died in Brooklyn, New York, at the age of ninety-two years Robert Hall Stotesbury married Frances L Van Cleef, who was born in New Jersey, and is now (1921) a resident of Brooklyn   They had six children, four of whom are now living   Robert Lawson, William, May, who married Peter Elling, and resides in Brooklyn, New York, and Hattie, who married J H Byington, and also resides in Brooklyn.

Robert Lawson Stotesbury was born in Brooklyn, New York, on May 11, 1882   He received his education in the public and high schools of Brooklyn, and when eighteen years of age took a position as book-keeper in Brooklyn, later filling a similar position in New York City He was ambitious to branch out for himself in an independent business, and to that end bent all his energies   By industry and economy he laid by enough capital to make a start in 1915, when he came to Perth Amboy, New Jersey, and established the Middlesex Sanitary Laundry   Just at this time an up-to-date, well equipped laundry was a crying need in Perth Amboy, the existing industries of this kind being utterly inadequate to handle the volume of business waiting to be done   Mr. Stotesbury met this real necessity in a most satisfactory manner, and his success was assured from the beginning   His first place of business was small, and located on King street, but in 1917 he removed to his present commodious quarters, where he has installed every available kind of equipment for the rapid and faultless handling of all kinds of laundry work   His location at No 5 Gordon street is most desirable for this line of business

Mr Stotesbury is a man of public spirit, and interested in every movement for the public welfare   He is a member of the Perth Amboy Board of Trade.   He is also a member of the Independent Order of Odd Fellows, of which organization he is district deputy grand master. He spends his leisure time in motoring   Mr Stotesbury was married in the fall of 1920

PATRICK JOSEPH ROCKS —The man of merit and distinction, who by his own efforts has attained a prominent position, and by his personal worth commands a high place, is certainly worthy of biographic honors, and as ʼsuch a one we present Patrick Joseph Rocks   Especial comment is unnecessary upon his high standing in the community, but the outline of his career cannot fail to be of interest

Patrick Joseph Rocks was born in Ireland, March 17, 1873, the son of Patrick J. and Mary Ann (Berry) Rocks, both natives of Ireland His father died in Baltimore, Maryland, at the age of fifty-six years. They were the parents of five children, and Patrick J (2) is the only surviving member of the entire family

Patrick J (2) Rocks attended school in Ireland for a time, but in 1881 was brought by his father to this country, their landing place being New York City   After attending the public schools of Perth

Amboy, New Jersey, where his father finally settled, at the age of thirteen he began his career in the business world by carrying water in the coal docks In 1893 he entered the local fire department and drove one of the department's teams for two years, and for the past fifteen years has been engaged in his present business

In politics he has always been a staunch Democrat, taking an active interest in the affairs of the local organization He affiliates with the Benevolent and Protective Order of Elks, Loyal Order of Moose, Improved Order of Red Men, and the Knights of the Golden Eagle He is also president of the New Jersey Third Congressional District of the Exempt Fire Department In religion he is a Roman Catholic

On July 12, 1912, Mr Rocks was united in marriage with Annie A. Hill, daughter of Charles and Louise Hill They are the parents of one child, Dorothy, born June 20, 1913

GEORGE A. SCHENCK—A conspicuous figure in the business life of New Market, New Jersey, is George A Schenck, who has carried on a successful ice business here since 1895 With but little else in the way of capital save a clear head, stout heart and a strong body, and these reinforced by hard work and a clear vision, he has attained to his present position as the reward of his efforts

George A Schenck was born December 19, 1864, at Centerville, New Jersey, the son of John H., who was a painter by trade, and his wife, Rebecca (Skilman) Schenck After obtaining his education in the schools of his native place he came to New Market, and in 1895 established himself in the ice business The venture proved successful, the business consistently increasing until it has reached its present large proportions Mr Schenck is eminently respected for the unimpeachable integrity of his dealings, and is a leader in movements which have for their end the advancement of civic conditions

In politics Mr Schenck is independent, not having identified himself with any political party, preferring to remain free from all partisan influences in the exercise of his own judgment on public issues. He has long been a prominent member of the Baptist church of New Market, and affiliates with the Junior Order United American Mechanics. He also holds membership in the Owls Club

On January 18 1895, at Somerville, New Jersey, George A Schenck was united in marriage with Lillian R Soper, a native of South Plainfield, New Jersey, her birth having occurred there, August 4, 1878 To Mr and Mrs Schenck have been born three children Clifford Earl, born November 8, 1899, Doris, born February 11, 1904, Marjorie, born November 18, 1914 During the World War, April 23, 1917, Clifford Earl Schenck enlisted in the United States navy, and was located for a time at the Mare Island navy yard, California He served on a United States-French mine sweeper, also on the "President Grant," crossing the ocean fourteen times, carrying soldiers to and from the United States

JACOB DALLENBECK—A stranger in a strange land, unused to the customs of his adopted country and with scant knowledge of its language Jacob Dallenbeck was heavily handicapped when he left his native land to make a new home in the United States, yet, with the quiet perseverance and determination for which his countrymen are noted he has made good and today is one of the recognized business men of the community where he lives

Jacob Dallenbeck was born in Switzerland, June 10 1866, the son of Ulrich and Ferana (Bernhard) Dallenbeck They lived on a farm which the father tilled, and the boy learned farming as he grew up, attending the common school until, when of suitable age, he entered the army, serving for ten years, though that is not the full length of service required of each man in Switzerland

For the past seventeen years Mr Dallenbeck has been a farmer in the Milltown section of Middlesex county, New Jersey, and during part of the time has been engaged in the sand business which he now operates and has owned for the last four years Mr Dallenbeck and his family are members of the Protestant church of that town He is not allied with either of the leading political parties, preferring to be liberal in his views and uninfluenced in his choice

While in France, Jacob Dallenbeck was married, May 30, 1897, to Alice Tometo, born April 8, 1869 She was the daughter of Thomas and Margaret (Spcher) Tometo, both natives of Switzerland Of this marriage six children were born Fred, Alice, Walter, Claria, Jacob, and Alma The family home is on Riva avenue, in Milltown

---

HOWARD CHARLES ANDERSEN is a native of Perth Amboy, New Jersey, the son of Frederick Bernhard and Elizabeth (Peterson) Andersen Frederick B Andersen, born in Norway in 1860, came to Perth Amboy a boy of sixteen and has ever since been a resident of the city a carpenter and building contractor He married, in Perth Amboy Elizabeth Peterson, who died in 1900 They were the parents of eight children, all born in Perth Amboy Anna, who married M Stricker of Woodbridge New Jersey Edward, a railroad contractor of Red Deer, Alberta, Canada , Louise, married D Wynans, of Matawan, New Jersey, Dora, married Henry Anderson of Woodbridge, New Jersey, Henry, a machinist of Newark, New Jersey , Howard Charles, of further mention , William, a confectioner of Newark, New Jersey ; and Edna, who resides at Scranton, Pennsylvania

Howard Charles Andersen was born in Perth Amboy, New Jersey, November 3, 1892, and has always made that city his home. He was educated in the public schools, finishing with grammar school at the age of fourteen When fifteen years of age he began his connection with the automobile business as a machinist and became so proficient and capable that on April 19, 1920, he was appointed manager of the Robert Treat Garage Later he entered the employ of the Castle's Ice Cream Company, Inc , of Perth Amboy

In 1914 Mr Andersen enlisted in the 12th Company, Canadian

Mounted Rifles Later he was transferred to the American Expeditionary Forces and he became sergeant in the Air Service He is a member
of the Danish Lutheran church, in politics he is a Republican

Mr Andersen married June 30, 1920, Blanche Riveley, born in Tottenville Staten Island, New York, daughter of Louis and Martha Anna
Riveley

JOSEPH WINIGER—For nearly a quarter of a century, Joseph
Winiger has conducted a livery business in Metuchen, New Jersey, a
community in which his nearly sixty years have been spent, his father,
John Winiger, having been a small farmer of Metuchen

Joseph Winiger was born in Metuchen, New Jersey, November 23,
1862, and there attended public schools Twelve years of his life prior
to 1898 were spent in the employ of the Lehigh Valley railroad and the
Public Service Corporation, he establishing a livery business in Metuchen
in 1898 That business has since been his sole activity, and although the
coming of the automobile has changed its character somewhat, he is
still its successful owner and manager He is an Independent in politics,
and a member of the Reformed church of Metuchen

Mr Winiger married, December 22, 1885, Elizabeth Brackett, born
June 2, 1865, daughter of Henry and Maria Brackett, of Brockton,
Massachusetts Mr and Mrs Winiger are the parents of six children:
Louisa, born May 7, 1887, Joseph, born September 27, 1888, married
Harriet Ackley, Nettie, born January 11, 1891, married W Edwards,
now deceased, Herbert, born December 19, 1892, died January 13, 1919,
married Jessie ———, and left a son Herbert; Julia, born December 13,
1894, Lloyd, born December 11, 1897

MATHIAS TEN EYCK.—All his life a farmer of Raritan township,
Middlesex county, New Jersey, Mr Ten Eyck has at the present time
the largest farm in the township, and is the largest landowner in the
Metuchen district He is a son of John V and Mary J (Honeyman)
Ten Eyck, his father also a farmer and landowner Mr Ten Eyck is
a member of Oak Tree Presbyterian Church, and in politics is a
Republican

Mr Ten Eyck married, in Elizabeth, New Jersey, in 1889, Ida Bennett, daughter of George W and Mary E (Smith) Bennett The Smiths
come from an old family of Galveston, Texas Mr and Mrs Ten Eyck
are the parents of two sons: Harry H , and Edward M , who married, in
Rockaway, New Jersey, Lillian B Yetter, of Rockaway

JOHN PENNY, a long time farmer of Middlesex county, New
Jersey, now deceased was born in Somerset county, New Jersey December 12, 1830, died at his farm in the town of Rahway, Middlesex county,
May 15, 1913, son of Ezra and Nettie Ann (Covert) Penny, his father
a farmer of Somerset county

John Penny was educated in the public schools, and early in life
became a practical farmer, an occupation he followed very successfully

all his life. He became the owner of a good farm in Rahway, upon which he was living at the time of his death That farm, bought in 1871, is yet the home of Mrs John Penny, his widow, and its present owner In politics Mr Penny was a Democrat, and in religious faith a member of the Rahway Methodist Episcopal Church He was an honorable, hard-working man, whose years eighty-three, were well spent

John Penny married, December 8, 1856, Catherine Davis, born February 27, 1840, daughter of William G and Sarah (Van Ness) Davis Mrs Davis survives her husband and continues her residence at the old farm, which has been her home for half a century (1871-1921) Mr and Mrs Penny were the parents of a large family 1 Ezra, born November 1, 1858, died November 8, 1913 2 Silas, born February 15, 1860, married Rose Fox, and has two children: Howard, born December 25, 1898, and Clarence, born April 11, 1911 3 Mary Ella, born August 2, 1863, died March 7, 1881 4 Anna Elizabeth, born October 21, 1871, married Carl Hanson, and has six children· Clinton, John, Carl, Kate, Hance, and Anna 5 John B, born September 27, 1875, married Hattie Dayton

---

OTTO WILLIAM LINDBERG.—One of the most prominent and influential citizens of the town of South River, New Jersey, is Otto William Lindberg, who since taking up his residence in this community, has interested himself in all that makes for the welfare and advancement of South River

Otto William Lindberg was born in Sweden, July 29, 1868, the son of John and Anna (Swanson) Lindberg John Lindberg was a sea captain for many years and owned several vessels The boy Otto was brought by his parents to this country in 1880, and upon landing in Boston remained there for several years, where he attended the local public schools, after which he served an apprenticeship to the copper-smith's trade He is now engaged in filling large plumbing contracts for the government

Mr Lindberg is the oldest member of the Board of Public Works of the borough of South River, and is vice-president and manager of a newly formed corporation, The Deerland Company, Northwest Florida. He affiliates with the Masons, having attained to the thirty-second degree, and also fraternizes with the Improved Order of Red Men and with the Benevolent and Protective Order of Elks Lodge In religion he is an Episcopalian and attends the church of that denomination in this community

On June 7, 1896, Mr. Lindberg was united in marriage with Margaret Mary Wright daughter of the late Silas and Emma (Britton) Wright, of New Brunswick New Jersey Mr. and Mrs Lindberg are the parents of one child, Margaret Emma, born March 28, 1910 Mrs Lindberg has always taken an active part in the affairs of South River, being president of the Woman's Club, and member of the Chamber of Commerce of this place She is past matron of Ruth Chapter, No 12, Order of the Eastern Star of the State of New Jersey That she is certainly

Otto W. Lundberg

fulfilling her position as helpmate to her husband is proven by the fact that she has met with great success in her management of the Washington Hotel, which her husband owns but has been unable to care for owing to his extensive contracting business *Died Oct, 1933 Saybrook, Conn.*

PAUL CHESTER KEMENY, numbered among the promising young attorneys of Perth Amboy, is a man who is making a name for himself in the public life of this community, and who has already won the regard of his brethren of the profession, who accord him full recognition

Mr Kemeny was born in Nagy Leta, Hungary, July 10, 1897, the son of Louis and Vilma Kemeny Louis Kemeny was born in Hungary, and came to Perth Amboy, New Jersey, in 1900, where he has since been engaged in the jewelry business, he is mentioned elsewhere in this work The boy, Paul Chester, was brought by his parents to this country when he was very small, and upon settling in Perth Amboy attended the public schools of that place, graduating from the Perth Amboy High School in 1914 He then entered Rutgers College, matriculating with the class of 1918, and having in the meantime determined to adopt the law as a profession he entered the New Jersey Law School and won the degree of Bachelor of Laws in 1920 Mr Kemeny served his clerkship and studied law in the office of his brother, George Kemeny, and when the latter sailed for France with the American Expeditionary Forces, Paul C completed his clerkship in the law office of Senator Thomas Brown Throughout his school and college courses he had proved himself an intelligent and painstaking student, and at the close came to the opening of his career fully equipped both with natural gifts and a training that was the result of long and conscientious effort Immediately after graduating from the New Jersey Law School he passed his bar examinations and came to New Brunswick, where he established himself in the practice of his chosen profession He opened an office at No 101 Albany street, and this has been his headquarters ever since During the World War he enlisted in the United States army, but was unassigned, and was honorably discharged, December 7, 1918 He affiliates with the Benevolent and Protective Order of Elks, Lodge No 784 Mr Kemeny is unmarried

---

HARRY LYON WOLFF—The significance to the public of every form of useful activity is a matter of profound interest, but when a man of force and initiative definitely and directly bends his energies toward the upbuilding of the community in which he lives, the people owe him a large measure of respect Harry Lyon Wolff, of Perth Amboy, New Jersey, although still a young man, has by his own efforts placed himself among the foremost men of the city.

Mr Wolff's family comes from the famous old Russian city of Riga, where he himself was born, August 15, 1882 His father, William Wolff, born in Russia, came to this country while a young man, bringing his wife and young children with him He went immediately to New

Brunswick, New Jersey, where he established a home for his little family, and after patient application and untiring industry achieved gratifying success as a wholesale butcher His wife, Fannie (Schuss) Wolff, was also born in Russia She died in Perth Amboy, New Jersey, in September 1917, at the age of sixty-five years Mr Wolff died in 1921 They were the parents of six children all of whom are now living in Middlesex county, New Jersey. Lena, wife of J H Friedman, residing in New Brunswick, Rose, wife of Samuel Mandel; Harry Lyon, of whom extended mention follows; Ada, wife of Harry Brower, Anna, wife of Max Gibson and Rae, wife of Samuel Tucker, all but the eldest being residents of Perth Amboy.

Harry Lyon Wolff was eight years old when he came with his parents to America He received his education in New Brunswick, New Jersey, mostly under the care of private teachers He was quick to learn, and at an age when most lads are entering high school he was making a start in the world of business When only fourteen years old he made his first venture in the marketing business, in New Brunswick, under the firm name of Wolff & Friedman, and two years later the ambitious firm opened a branch market on the corner of State and Center streets, Perth Amboy At the age of eighteen, the young man made a radical change in his line of business entering a field of effort that appealed not only to the practical but to the idealistic side of his nature The city was enjoying a period of great prosperity and rapid growth, and residences, business locations, and all kinds of real estate were in great demand Mr Wolff entered this field and found broad scope for his energies At twenty-one years of age he was the largest operator in real estate in the city In 1906 he went to New York City, where he engaged in the same line of business, remaining in that city for ten years He then returned to Perth Amboy and formed the Maple Realty Company, in which he is now president, dealing in real estate investments, and in many cases handling the construction operations on real estate in which they are interested Mr Wolff, in association with Max Gibian, built the Perth Amboy Garage, but his most important interest is Averse Park of which he is the builder There $500,000 has been expended and men who are considered authorities in real estate say that a population of ten thousand people may confidently be expected to gather there within the next decade

Mr Wolff is exceedingly fond of music and devotes considerable time to it, but he finds it impossible to separate entirely his recreation and his business, for his keenest delight, and the pursuit in which he finds most genuine pleasure, is the building up of communities—the creating of residences and charming landscape effects where before were only barren wastes. Mr Wolff is an attendant at Beth Mordecai Synagogue, is socially popular, and is interested individually as well as in a business way, in every public movement that tends toward progress.

THEODORE EMIL ANDERSON—The story of Theodore Emil Anderson's life is the story of a self-made man. In the busy life of Perth Amboy, New Jersey, he is a well known figure

He was born in Christiansand, Norway, February 9, 1877 His father was August Anderson, an upright, industrious man, a ship's carpenter by trade He was born in Sweden, and came to America in 1884 to provide a better home and better opportunities for his little family They located in Tottenville, New York, but remained there for only one year, going then to Perth Amboy, New Jersey There the father died when the boy Theodore E, was fourteen years of age August Anderson married Ingeborg Jorgenson, who was born in Norway, and died in Perth Amboy at the age of seventy-two years They were the parents of five children. Andrew, Theodore Emil, Magnus, Ella, now Mrs Thomas Olesen, all of the above being residents of Perth Amboy, and William, who died in infancy

Theodore Emil Anderson came to America at the age of seven years, and received nearly all his education in the public schools on this side the water He attended the Perth Amboy schools until he was sixteen years of age, when he entered the employ of the S S White Dental Works, of that city, where he remained for one year He then worked as clerk in a grocery store for four years At the age of twenty-one, he began work for the United States Express Company At twenty-five he determined to make a start in life for himself Knowing the city thoroughly, and seeing the possibilities in the express business in a growing city, he started along that line Beginning in a small way, he has increased his business and enlarged its scope until now he handles a large share of the express business of Perth Amboy and vicinity, besides conducting a well equipped garage. His location at No 49 Smith street is an advantageous one, and with the assistance of his son he covers a wide field of useful activity

Mr Anderson does not allow business to absorb all his interest He is always well informed on the topics of the day, especially matters of broad or National import He is a Republican by political choice, but has always declined office In his recreations he is apt to choose active out-of-doors sports, being especially fond of horses. At one time he was chief of the Perth Amboy Fire Department, and then he owned some of the finest horses in this section He is a member of the Raritan Yacht Club, and of the Benevolent and Protective Order of Elks.

Mr. Anderson married, in Perth Amboy, Rosette Seguine, daughter of Alexander and Celia Seguine Mr Seguine was connected with the custom house, furnishing his own power boat Both Mrs Anderson's parents lived and died in Perth Amboy, and this is her birthplace. Mr and Mrs Anderson have three children Gladys, born in 1899, Lester, born in 1901, who is associated with his father in business, and Eleanore, born in 1907 The family are members of the Baptist church, and active in all its social and benevolent organizations

---

LEO KAHN, one of the best known jewelers of New Brunswick, New Jersey was born in Riga, Latvia, Russia, May 20, 1887, a son of Hyman and Rebecca (Feldman) Kahn The elder Mr Kahn was also born in Riga, where the family is a prominent one He was a prosperous lumber merchant of that city, came to America, retired from business, and died in Cleveland, Ohio, October 6, 1912, at the age of sixty-five years. His wife now resides with her son Leo. They have seven other children now living. David, Edward, Isadore, Charlotta, Henrietta, Rose and Jennie.

Leo Kahn received his education in the schools of his native country; then at sixteen years of age came to the United States, locating in Erie, Pennsylvania. There he entered the employ of his brother, David, who is one of the old established jewelers of that city. Continuing with him for five years, the young man then went to Irvin, Pennsylvania, with a jewelry firm there. In 1914 he made the change which is proving so materially to his own advantage, coming to New Brunswick. Here he bought out the Printz Jewelry Company and started in business at the corner of Neilson and Albany streets, which has come to be a recognized center of fine jewelry effectively displayed. Mr Kahn has trebled the stock of jewelry handled, and more than trebled the volume of trade. He is already a leader in this line in New Brunswick. Still a young man, and with the best years of life yet before him, he bids fair to place the stamp of his individuality on the business world of Middlesex county. Mr Kahn is a member of the Board of Trade of New Brunswick, and is widely known fraternally. He is a member of the Benevolent and Protective Order of Elks, the Fraternal Order of Eagles, the Loyal Order of Moose, the Young Men's Christian Association, and the Young Men's Hebrew Association. He attends the services of Temple Ansch Emeth. In his leisure time, Mr Kahn indulges his taste for music, to which art he is devoted. He is also an enthusiast in out-door sports.

Mr Kahn married, in New York City, August 24, 1914, Fannie Lapidus, who was born in New York, and died in New Brunswick, New Jersey, February 9, 1920. She left a little daughter, Irma, born August 21, 1915.

LOUIS KEMENY, Perth Amboy's most prominent jeweler and a man highly respected for his substantial and public-spirited citizenship, is a native of Hungary, his birth having occurred in the city of Solmos in the county of Ungvar, March 10, 1870. He is a son of William and Marion (Berkowitz) Kemeny, of Hungary, the former being a wealthy farmer who carried on general agricultural operations on a large scale in the vicinity of Solmos in which he employed several thousand hands and two hundred teams of horses. He and his wife, who both lived and died in their native land, were the parents of three children, as follows: Gedeon, who died at the age of twenty-six years; Ethel, who became the wife of Nandor Scilagyi, a school director in Hungary, and Louis, with whose career we are here engaged.

Louis Kemeny passed his childhood and young manhood in his native region, and attended as a child the local educational institutions. It was his father's original intention that he should follow in his steps and become an agriculturist, and with this end in view he entered the Agricultural College in Ungvar, from which he graduated in 1891. He then served in the 16th Regiment of Austrian and Hungarian Cavalry for one year, during which time, being of an enterprising nature, his attention and ambition was turned toward the great republic of the West, where he believed great opportunities lay   In 1900, when twenty-nine years of age, he came to the United States and after spending one year in New York City came to Middlesex county, New Jersey, and settled in Perth Amboy and established himself in his present business   His first store was situated on State street, but in 1913 he removed to No 112 Smith street, but his business continued to grow until it became too large to be transacted there, so he removed to his present fine store at Nos 117 and 119 Smith street   This store is now the best appointed and carries the largest stock of any establishment of its kind in Middlesex county, and the business is still developing rapidly   Mr Kemeny has always taken an active and intelligent part in the conduct of local affairs, and is prominent in several fraternal orders and clubs in the city, notably the Masonic order, in which he has attained the thirty-second degree He is affiliated with the Ancient Free and Accepted Masons, Royal Arch Masons, Royal and Select Masters, Knights Templar; Ancient Arabic Order Nobles of the Mystic Shrine, and the Sovereign Princes of the Royal Secret   Besides these Masonic bodies, he is a member of the local lodge, Benevolent and Protective Order of Elks, and the Perth Amboy Progress Club   Mr Kemeny attends the Temple Beth Morchi in Perth Amboy   In his early youth he was devoted to the sport of hunting but of recent years has given this up to a certain extent and now takes a keen interest in the modern development of dramatic art   He is a Republican in politics

Louis Kemeny married (first) 1894, Vilma Berger, (second) 1899, before coming to this country, Sidonie Altman, a native of Austria   Mr Kemeny had one child by his first wife, and two by his second wife, born in Hungary, as follows   1 George, born September 22, 1895, now a practicing attorney in Perth Amboy, during the World War he entered the United States army and served with the 311th Infantry Regiment of the 78th Division, being attached to the headquarters company, he served in France during the closing episodes of the campaign, and upon the signing of the armistice entered the University of Paris, where he continued the legal studies he had already commenced in the United States, in July, 1919, he returned to this country and is now established in Perth Amboy in the practice of his chosen profession with offices in the Raritan building   2 Paul Chester, now a practicing lawyer in New Brunswick, New Jersey. 3 Mitzie, born February 3, 1900, now resides with her parents   None of Mr Kemeny's children are married and the entire family make their home at No 152 High street, Perth Amboy

In the conduct of his most successful business, Mr Kemeny is seconded by the work of several capable assistants, the chief of whom is Mr Herman Lieberman who, like his chief is a native of Europe, having been born in Austria August 22, 1885   Mr Lieberman came to the United States, September 24, 1917, and after residing in New York City for three months, came to Perth Amboy and entered directly into his association with Mr Kemeny   He married Dora Kessler, of New York City, and they are the parents of one child, Leonard S, born June 29, 1917   Mr Kemeny's second assistant is Mr W Edward Roberts, a native of Wales, born December 13, 1892   He came to the United States in 1913, and married Minnie A Pheil of Perth Amboy

---

HENRY MORAFF—The family of which Henry Moraff is a member is an old one in the city of Odessa, Russia, where they have lived for several generations   some of the men being prominent in military affairs and some of them engaged in the legal profession

Henry Moraff was born in Odessa, Russia, February 12, 1877   His parents were Meyer and Sarah (Jacob) Moraff, natives of Odessa, the former having been a successful lawyer there   He came to the United States in 1891, bringing his wife and children with him, and settled in New York City, where he continued to live until his death in 1915, at the age of seventy-eight years   His widow, Mrs Sarah (Jacob) Moraff, is still living at her home in New York   She and her husband had seven children·Israel, Isaac, Morris, Henry, Irving Francis, Dorothy, all are now living in New York City with the exception of Henry Moraff, who lives in New Brunswick

When in 1891, Henry Moraff landed in this country, he was only fourteen years old, but he found employment in a dry goods store in New York where he received a salary of three dollars a week   About twenty years later Mr Moraff went to Jackson, Michigan, where he opened a gentleman's furnishing store in 1912   During the time he lived there he held the office of trustee of the Synagogue for five years   Coming East again Mr Moraff became interested in New Brunswick, New Jersey, entering into business in that city   He opened a clothing store at No 349 George street, in September, 1919, and gave it the name of "Henry's Clothing Shop."   It has proved to be a successful venture, Mr Moraff having made many friends in his new location

When the Rotary Club was organized in New Brunswick, Henry Moraff was one of the charter members of it, he is also active in the Benevolent and Protective Order of Elks, and in the local Board of Trade, he attends the Temple, and is much interested in the Young Men's Hebrew Association, of which he is a member   During his boyhood, Henry Moraff was particularly interested in bicycle riding, and as a member of the Lincoln Wheelmen won many medals in competition affairs   When this club was organized, Mr Moraff was one of the charter members   He has always been fond of all out-door exercise, at present his chief pleasure being to take long trips in his automobile, sometimes covering five hundred miles a day.

In New York City, October 2, 1904, Henry Moraff married Belle Levy, daughter of Morris and Rose Levy, formerly residents of New York City, where their daughter Belle was born   They are both deceased   Mr and Mrs Henry Moraff have one child, Richard J, born in New York City, July 8 1905   Their home is at No 227 Power street, New Brunswick

SAMUEL BELIKOVE, who was a prominent and well known merchant of Perth Amboy, where he was engaged in the wholesale produce business until January 1, 1921, and then retired, was a native of Russia, born December 1, 1866, died May 17, 1921 He was the son of Philip and Fannie (Zolotoroff) Belikove The elder Mr Belikove was born in Russia, and for many years was engaged in cattle raising He married Fannie Zolotoroff, now living in Perth Amboy, having come from Russia fifteen years ago They were the parents of one child, Samuel, mentioned below

Samuel Belikove was educated in the schools of his native place, and at the age of twenty-three years set sail for this country Upon landing in New York City he came direct to Perth Amboy, New Jersey, where in 1894 he established himself in the grocery and fruit business at No 409 State street, later moving to No 452 State street His business rapidly and consistently developed until it became the largest of its kind in the community He affiliated with the Foresters of America, the Hebrew Progressive Association, and the Loyal Association

On June 11, 1894, Mr Belikove was united in marriage with Dora Weinblatt, who died March 20, 1918, and they were the parents of four children Philip I, now engaged in the auto business in Perth Amboy, Emily, born August 13, 1900, Ralph, born March 1, 1906, Sidney, born August 25, 1913 The family home is at No 99 Lewis street, Perth Amboy Mr Belikove found his chief recreation in motoring

---

SAMUEL GINDIN—There is very properly full praise in this country and time for the man who has started at the bottom of the ladder and by means of his own efforts made a way to prominence in the business world New Jersey has its share of such men and to this list may be added the name of Samuel Gindin Real estate is the line of business in which Mr Gindin has made his success

Samuel Gindin was born in Russia, October 17 1882, the son of Leon and Anna Gindin His father, Leon Gindin died in Russia, but his mother resides with him To Mr and Mrs Gindin were born seven children of whom there are but three living Samuel, of further mention, Celia, who married Barnard Kahn, of New Brunswick, New Jersey, Anna, who married Harry Sullivan, of New Brunswick

The education of Samuel Gindin was obtained in the public schools of his native place and here he remained until he was twenty years of age, when he came to the United States He located first in Philadelphia and here engaged in the carpenter's trade, having served his apprenticeship in his native place Four years later, in 1906, he came to New Brunswick and established himself in the real estate business at his present location, No 41 Paterson street The position which he occupies represents the reward of unremitting labor and a fixed determination to achieve a responsible place, while, in his advancement, he has used the most upright methods

Mr Gindin has no taste for political life, never sought public office, and clings closely to business He is affiliated with Mt Zion Lodge,

No 135. Free and Accepted Masons, the Improved Order of Red Men, and the Young Men's Christian Association He also holds membership in the Craftsmen's Club, of New Brunswick

On November 28, 1911, Samuel Gindin was united in marriage with Lillian Shanholtz, daughter of the late Joseph Shanholtz. Joseph Shanholtz was a native of Pittsburgh, Pennsylvania, and died in New Brunswick, in 1920, at the age of fifty-six Mrs Shanholtz resides with her daughter Mr and Mrs Gindin are the parents of three children. Irving, born September 16, 1915, Russell, born October 28, 1917, and Jerome, born in April, 1920 Mr Gindin is a popular and highly-regarded member of the community and active in the advancement of the interests of New Brunswick He finds his chief recreation in motoring

---

VICTOR PETER CHRISTOFFERSON—Among the representative citizens of Perth Amboy perhaps there is no man who stands out more prominently than Victor Peter Christofferson, who has ever been a conspicuous factor in everything pertaining to civic betterment

Waldamer Christofferson, father of Victor Peter Christofferson, was born in Copenhagen, Denmark, and there learned and worked at his profession of landscape gardening until he came with his family to this country, settling first in Bangor, Maine, and then for the last twenty years of his life he worked at his profession in Plainfield, New Jersey He married Mary Hansen, a native of Copenhagen, and they became the parents of six children, of which number four are still living. Victor Peter, of further mention; May, widow of William R. Harsell, Cornelia, a resident of Philadelphia, Nellie, wife of William Herren, of Philadelphia

Victor Peter Christofferson was born in Copenhagen, Denmark, July 4, 1872, and was brought by his parents to this country when a baby He attended the schools of Bangor, Maine, and Plainfield, New Jersey. From 1904 until 1917 he was in business in Perth Amboy as an electrical engineer having chosen that profession for his special line of work At present he is connected with the Manufacturers' Liability Insurance Company, Jersey City Politically Mr Christofferson is a Republican, giving to public affairs the interest and attention demanded of every good citizen, but taking no active part in the affairs of the organization He was the first secretary of the Board of Trade of Perth Amboy, was the first incorporator of the Home for the Aged of Middlesex County, and was one of the originators of the Community Market in Perth Amboy, being chairman of the first committee It is also interesting to note here that Perth Amboy was the first place in the United States to start a "Safe and Sane Fourth of July," and Mr Christofferson claims the honor of being the first agitator of that He is affiliated with various associations He served as secretary of the Employing Builders' Association of New Jersey for fourteen years

Mr. Christofferson married (first) in June, 1901, Katherine Fisher, who died in 1912, leaving no issue He married (second) January 3, 1914, Edith M Frey, daughter of the late Orin C. Frey, of Perth Amboy

Victor V. Christofferson.

Mr and Mrs Christofferson are the parents of one child, Victor O W , born March 19, 1915

We have not said that Mr Christofferson is a good citizen for that fact is self-evident He is without doubt one of the most prominent men of the region, widely recognized as a charitable and conscientious worker and a man of the highest ideals

AMBROSE KLAUSER, one time proprietor of the South River Hotel and for many years a well known figure in business circles here, was born in Germany, December 6, 1839, and died June 17, 1905 He was educated in his native land, and on completing his studies became a cabinet maker, which trade he followed for many years In 1863 he came to this country, and nine years later purchased the South River Hotel, continuing to manage it until his death in 1905, when his wife became his successor and the business passed entirely into her hands, since which time Mrs Klauser has done much in the development of this enterprise

But it was not only in his particular business that Mr Klauser expended his time and energy On the contrary, there was no one more interested in the welfare and advancement of the community's affairs than he and as a staunch Republican he always took the active interest in political life that is demanded of every good citizen In religion he was a Roman Catholic and attended Our Ladies of Victory Church of this denomination at South River

On April 1, 1869, at New Brunswick, New Jersey, Ambrose Klauser was united in marriage with Pauline Mark, she was also a native of Germany, her birth having occurred there October 26, 1848 Mr and Mrs Klauser were the parents of five children Amelia, born December 14, 1870, married Elward Serviss, who died January 31, 1911, Anna M , born October 5, 1872, married A W Bissett, and they are the parents of one child, Julia Elizabeth Caroline, born January 20, 1874, married Foreman Bissett, to whom she has borne three children, Susy, born May 18, 1876, died April 8, 1915, Elizabeth, born March 17, 1884, married Raymond D Booraem to whom she has borne two children Raymond and Warren

SAMUEL SEIDEN, of New Brunswick, New Jersey, is filling a very practical place in the life of the city, in the conducting of one of the cleanest and pleasantest restaurants in this part of the State

Mr Seiden was born in Austria, September 15, 1883, and is a son of Mandel and Sarah Seiden, both born in Austria Mandel Seiden is now a resident of New York City and is a prosperous manufacturer of neckwear, having a modern plant on the corner of Broadway and Ninth street His wife died in the old country when the children were young They had six children, all now living in America and all married, Louis Frank Helen Samuel, Eva and David By a later marriage Mr Seiden has three sons Abe, Carl and Harry

Samuel Seiden attended school in his native country until he was fifteen years of age, when he came to America and located in New York City There he worked in restaurants as a boss waiter, then as steward, then as manager He followed along this line in New York for eighteen years and became widely known in this business During all this time his ambition was pointing toward a future of independence when he should turn his experience and ability entirely to his own profit In 1918, he made the start, coming to New Brunswick, New Jersey, where he established a restaurant located at No 86 Albany street He made the place so attractive, and keeps it so neat and clean that success is rewarding his endeavors in generous measure In addition to the regular restaurant trade, Mr Seiden has developed a considerable business in catering This branch of his establishment is constantly growing and promises even greater success in the future Mr Seiden is active in various interests outside the business to which the greater part of his time is devoted He is a member of the New Brunswick Board of Trade, a member of the Fraternal Order of Eagles, and of the Young Men's Christian Association. He worships at the Jewish Synagogue

On February 24 1911, Mr Seiden married, in New York City Bessie Isabella Rosen who was born in Roumania Her father died in the old country, but her mother, Esther Rosen now makes her home with Mr and Mrs Seiden

---

LEO S LOWENKOPF.—In November, 1897, Samuel and Lena (Schoen) Lowenkopf left their native land. Hungary Europe, and with their infant son, their first born, came to the United States, making their home for seven years in New York City They then moved to Perth Amboy, New Jersey, where the father died, in October, 1918, aged fifty-two He was engaged as a butcher for a long time, but during the last eight years of his life kept a hotel in Keasbey, New Jersey. Children Leo S, of further mention, Jacob, engaged with his brother, Gertrude and Theresa, yet school girls

Leo S Lowenkopf was born in Hungary, August 18, 1897, and three months later was brought by his parents to the United States New York City was the family home until 1904 when the family removed to Perth Amboy New Jersey Here he completed his elementary education, finishing in grammar school in 1911, and high school in 1915 He spent one year at Rutgers College New Brunswick, New Jersey then entered the New Jersey Law School at Newark. and three years later, in June 1920, was graduated with the degree of Bachelor of Laws. He was admitted to the New Jersey bar as an attorney in December, 1920, and on January 1, 1921, began practice in Perth Amboy, New Jersey, with offices at No 224 Smith street in the Dana building

During the World War 1917-18, he served on the Legal Advisory Board for the Metuchen district, and rendered other service He is a member of the Phi Epsilon Pi, a college fraternity, and also the Lambda Alpha Phi, a legal fraternity and the Benevolent and Protective Order of Elks He is a devotee of all out-of-door athletics, his own specialties being running and high jumping In 1915 he was the East Jersey High School high jump champion, and in 1920 won the same honor in the New Jersey Young Men's Hebrew Association competition He also won the broad jump championship of the Young Men's Hebrew Association in that year

JACOB SMERLING—From far away Russia came Jacob Smerling when but fifteen, and in the land of freedom and opportunity he has improved the advantages offered, and since 1907 has been engaged in mercantile business in Perth Amboy, New Jersey He is a son of Chanon Smerling, born in and yet living in Russia, a lumber dealer, and his wife, Sarah (Smulak) Smerling, also living in Russia They were the parents of seven children, all living in the United States except one who remains in Russia with his parents Of the other six children three are in Pennsylvania, one in Michigan, one in New York, the other in Perth Amboy, and all are married

Jacob Smerling was born in Russia, and there passed fifteen years of his life prior to coming to the United States He remained in New York City for some time after coming to this country, and in the city night schools acquired the English language and an English education During those years he was employed in selling goods on the installment plan, being his own employer, for during his entire life in the United States he has worked on his own account In 1907 he closed out his New York ventures and located in Perth Amboy, establishing with his limited capital a small tobacco and confectionery store at No. 327 State street For nine years he remained at that location, and by energy and thrift made the store pay He increased his lines and built up a good patronage that continued loyal to the little shop that served them so well In 1916 he moved to his present store, No 148 Smith street, changing his line with his location, and now deals entirely in musical instruments, including phonographs and accessories He is a member of Beth Mordecai Congregation, Perth Amboy, is an independent in politics, and a member of several local societies, Brith Abraham, Zion and Loyal Association

Mr Smerling married, in New York City, July, 1900, Sarah Levine, born in Russia, where both her parents died

FRANK STAS, of Perth Amboy, New Jersey, in choosing the line of business in which to make his own strike for success in America, placed himself where he is able to be of great service to his countrymen who come to our shores In his steamship ticket agency, and also in his city office as notary public, many come to him who are glad to find this common bond

Joseph Stas, father of Frank Stas, was born in Czechoslovakia, and died in Perth Amboy, New Jersey, at the age of sixty-nine years, February 11, 1919 His mother, Anna (Kokoska) Stas, also died in Perth Amboy, January 25, 1895, at the age of forty-one years Joseph and Anna (Kokoska) Stas were the parents of eleven children, three of whom are still living Theresa, wife of Emerick Karas, residing in Budapest Frank, of Perth Amboy of whom extended mention follows, and Josephine, who lives in New York City

Frank Stas was born in Budapest, July 17, 1878 He received his education in that city and learned, in part, the trade of machinist He came to America with his mother when he was fifteen years of age, and was soon foreman of the lighterage department of the American Smelting and Refining Company. In 1900 he returned again to his trade of machinist, his natural mechanical ability qualifying him for work in that line, with the training he had received in the old country He remained with the American Smelting and Refining Company, in their machine shop, of which he was foreman for some time

Having won the confidence and respect of the people of Perth Amboy, Mr Stas was becoming known in political circles He was elected notary public and later, in connection with the duties of this office, he established an agency for the handling of steamship tickets This business has developed until with his duties as notary public, his time is fully absorbed during business hours Mr Stas is interested in broad public activities outside his business He is a faithful worker in the Republican party, which nominated him for alderman in 1914 He is now a member of the Water Board He is a director of the Raritan Trust Company and North Amboy Building and Loan Association He is a member of the Benevolent and Protective Order of Elks, the Improved Order of Red Men, and is a chief in the Haymakers' Association But his greatest interest lies in those organizations through which his fellow-countrymen uniting to find mutual help in the new country, learn the principles of Democracy He is supreme secretary of the Slovak Gymnastic Union Sokol (Falcon) is a member of the Slovak National Society, and national treasurer of the Slovak League of America He is also founder of the Slovak Roman Catholic church in Perth Amboy, and one of its first trustees As relaxation from these multiplied activities, Mr Stas indulges, occasionally, in hunting and fishing

Mr Stas married, in Perth Amboy, May 28 1901, Anna Balak, daughter of John and Elizabeth Balak. She was born in Slovakia, her father died in Perth Amboy, New Jersey, but her mother survives him, and makes her home with the daughter Mr and Mrs Stas have four children Anna, born November 17, 1902, Frances, born August 7 1903, Milan, born December 7, 1908, and Edward H, born October 5, 1910

FREDERICK CHRISTIAN CHRISTENSEN —From the sturdy blood of Northern Europe come many of the upright, hard working Americans, who help constantly to renew the life and vitality of the Nation Frederick Christian Christensen is a man still in the prime of life, who, coming from Denmark, has made a substantial success in the country of his adoption in constructive lines which make for the prosperity of the community

Mr Christensen is a son of Jens Peter Christensen, who was born and died in Denmark He lived to the age of eighty years He was a carpenter, as was his father, Christian Jensen Mr Christensen's mother was Karen Marie (Andreasen) Christensen She also was born and died in Denmark, having lived until nearly eighty years of age They were the parents of ten children, of whom seven are living Frederick Christian, of whom extended mention follows, Sophia, Peter, Julius, Christina, Christian, and Viggo. The eldest is the only one who left Denmark

Frederick Christian Christensen was born in Udby Lundley Station, Denmark, September 27, 1862 There he attended school, and later began to work with his father, learning the trade of carpenter He perfected himself in his trade in Copenhagen remaining there and continuing to work along the same line for seven years He next spent six months in Hamburg, Germany In the year 1888 he came to America, bringing his wife and eldest child, Ellen Mary He located in Perth Amboy, New Jersey and began working at his trade as journeyman carpenter He continued working thus, and by industry and economy laid up a little capital In 1902 he went into business on his own account He has been successful from the first, and is now doing business under the name of The Fred Christensen Construction Company, Incorporated, at No 218 Madison avenue Perth Amboy He handles large contracts in a workmanlike manner, and no bit of construction is too small for his careful attention Among the many important buildings erected by The Fred Christensen Construction Company may be mentioned· School No 9 Perth Amboy, and Nos 10 and 11, Woodbridge, remodelled Knights of Columbus building on High street, Perth Amboy

Mr Christensen takes a keen interest in all the activities of public life In political affiliation he is a Republican He is a member of the Ancient Free and Accepted Masons, and a member and active worker in those societies which lend a helping hand to his countrymen who come seeking a home and livelihood in this country These are the Danish Brotherhood, the Danish Relief Association, the Danish Hundred Men Society, and the Danish Singing Society Frem He also serves as secretary of the Building Trades Association of Perth Amboy, having formerly served as president of that body The family are members of the Danish Lutheran church

Mr Christensen married Ellen Margaret Dagmar Hansen who was born in Denmark Both her parents died there Their four children are as follows 1 Ellen Mary, wife of Edward J Koster, of Metuchen, New Jersey 2 John C, associated with his father in business, secretary of the company, he saw eighteen months service in France during the World War, in the Air Squadron, and at the time of his discharge was first class sergeant of the 469th Air Squadron, he is a member of the Masonic order 3 James Andrew, enlisted as a private in the service of the government during the World War, and at the time of his discharge was inspector of gas at a camp near Baltimore, Maryland, he is a member of the Masonic order 4 Caroline Sophia, twin of James Andrew, wife of John Young Hunter, of Perth Amboy

FRITZ JAHNKE—Among the well known business men of Perth Amboy, New Jersey the name of Fritz Jahnke deserves conspicuous mention for the energetic part he has taken in its commercial life where, as proprietor of the Standard Garage, he has won well merited success. Mr Jahnke is a native of Bremen, Germany, born June 19, 1888, a son of Carl and Emma Jahnke The elder Mr Jahnke was born in Berlin, Germany, and has long been engaged in the hotel business in that city, where he is well and favorably known He and his wife are the parents of three children, as follows: Agnes, who became the wife of Herman Scholtz, of Bremen, Margaret, who became the wife of Adolph Beyer, of Berlin; and Fritz, of this sketch

As a child Mr Jahnke attended the schools of his native land, and afterwards learned the trade of machinist there, gaining unusual proficiency in the craft for one of his age He was only twenty years old when he determined upon the step of leaving his home and seeking his own fortune in the New World Accordingly, he came directly to the United States and went to Buffalo, New York, where he found employment in his trade, remaining about twelve months Being a skilled machinist he had no difficulty in finding work, and his next step was to return to the East, where the next four years were spent in Jersey City, New Jersey, and New York Coming to Perth Amboy, he spent a similar period in the same line of work, and in 1917 opened a garage on Smith street and prospered greatly from the start In the month of May, 1919, he removed to his present location at No 361 New Brunswick avenue, where the Standard Garage is now numbered among the best known and most largely patronized establishments in the neighborhood The success of Mr Jahnke has been due entirely to his energetic and intelligent conduct of the business he has built up, and equally to his good reputation for honesty and good service that he has won. He wholly merits the esteem and confidence of his fellow-citizens, which have been accorded him in large measure; as he is yet a young man the notable success he has already won can be confidently counted upon as but a prophesy of a still greater achievement for the future Mr Jahnke has participated actively in the social and fraternal life of the community where he dwells, and is affiliated with the Order of Owls

Fritz Jahnke was united in marriage, September 30, 1909, in Germany, with Emma Schultz, a native of that country, a daughter of Emil and Emilia Schultz Mr and Mrs Jahnke are the parents of one child, Vernon, born March 5, 1911

MARTIN AMARESCU since childhood has been interested in the violin and has made a thorough study of the instrument Upon reaching manhood he began to manufacture this musical instrument, which has resulted in his having attained considerable fame as a violin maker

Martin Amarescu was born in Roumania, February 18, 1883, the son of John and Catherine (Whitman) Amarescu After receiving a common school education he came to this country and located in South River, New Jersey, where he has established himself as a barber, devoting all his spare time to the manufacture of violins Active in his business relations, with a ready courtesy and sympathy for all, he commands the esteem of the entire community In his religious affiliations Mr Amarescu is a Presbyterian, and he is a member of the Improved Order of Red Men *Ɛ FАⱯм. +243 Ʒo.Ʀɪⱱⱳ.*

On February 8, 1906, Mr Amarescu was united in marriage with Julia Korporetch, a native of Slavonia, her birth having occurred there, April 8, 1887 Mr and Mrs Amarescu are the parents of the following children Martin, born August 10, 1907, and Mary, born February 2, 1909 Mr Amarescu is devoted to his home and finds his greatest pleasure in the circle of his own fireside The family home is on Main street, Mr Amarescu having purchased this home in 1916

PHILIP SISKIND —Among the successful business men of Perth Amboy, New Jersey, there is none better deserving of mention than Philip Siskind, who in spite of difficulties and obstacles of all kinds has worked his way from the humblest of positions to the prominent place he now occupies in the community Mr Siskind may truly be called a self-made man in the best sense of the term, for all that he has and is has been the result of his own unswerving efforts, efforts that were continued through years when circumstances were such as to daunt most men and turn them from their objects

Philip Siskind was born September 10, 1873, in Maxtavo, near Janavo, Russia, of Jewish parents, and as a child met with the various difficulties which the ruling class in that country placed in the way of his oppressed people His education, in both Hebrew and Russian, was obtained through the offices of private teachers, and upon completing his studies he was taken by his father into the latter's wood and lumber business He remained in partnership with the elder man until his death two years later, and then for three years longer he conducted it by himself He found, however, that competition with larger concerns in the same region resulted in a steady decrease of his trade, and he eventually abandoned it and secured a position with a very large concern worth a quarter of a million, engaged in the same line He won the regard and affection of the superintendent, who personally taught him all the details of the business and imported to him all his knowledge The young man proved an apt pupil, and in the five years during which he was connected with the concern managed by dint of the greatest industry and thrift to save up a considerable sum of money In one of the slack seasons he returned to his home to visit his mother and there found that his eldest sister was engaged to a young man of fine character who had won the entire respect and approval of the young lady's family She was short of funds, however, and to make up the deficiency Mr Siskind made her a present of his hard earned savings At the same time he determined to leave his native land and journey to the United States, of the fame of which he had continually heard as a land where all men were free and equal and which, as he has himself expressed it, drew him like magic

He set sail for the land of his desires, August 1, 1893, and landed in New York harbor in due course and in good health and spirits, and was met by a cousin who displayed great friendliness and aided him in securing a position He received at first only eight dollars a month in wages, but his industry and intelligence gained him promotion, and three months later his salary had been doubled About this time he was married, and with the assistance of his wife, he engaged in business on his own account   In this venture, however, he was unsuccessful and nine months later was obliged to close up his store, having lost his entire capital With the most praiseworthy courage, Mr Siskind determined to start again on the humblest scale and came to Perth Amboy, New Jersey, where he secured a temporary position at nine dollars a week He worked at this employment for about seven months and then once more started an enterprise of his own as a dealer in clothing, which he sold on the installment plan This time his affairs prospered and he soon became well known in the town of Perth Amboy on account of his friendly and cheerful disposition and the strict honesty with which he conducted all his transactions On January 1, 1900, he opened a store on State street and here he continued his clothing business with a marked degree of success for about eighteen months By that time his trade had increased so greatly that he began negotiations for a larger store and soon began the construction of his present place of business at Nos 324 and 326 State street, a modern, well equipped building, which was successfully opened in October, 1902

It was about this time that Mr Siskind's greatest misfortune occurred in the shape of a severe sickness which nearly proved his death He first noticed its approach by the symptoms of great nervousness and severe colds which as he was at that time working day and night, grew constantly worse He consulted a number of specialists, but received no benefit, and his trouble was brought to a climax by a business trip taken in most inclement weather to Staten Island He returned from this very ill and was carried from his carriage to his house in a state of paralysis which continued uninterruptedly for seven months During this time the splendid devotion of his wife saved the situation as well as his life She was indefatigable in caring for him and at the same time attended to the store and outside business and altogether proved herself a woman of the noblest character and great resources Mr Siskind's condition grew steadily worse and at length, on the eve of Easter, 1903 he became so desperately ill that Mrs Siskind had to hurry for medical aid in the emergency She was unable to find a doctor for some time but eventually she secured Dr. Stafford and he hurried to the bedside, only to find a man of whose life he nearly despaired A medicine prescribed by him proved to be unobtainable, but Mr Siskind fell into a deep sleep which continued the remainder of the night He recalls vividly to this day that during that sleep he dreamed a curious dream in which his father appeared to him and brewed him some medicine which he drank and which brought him relief Nevertheless, when the doctor visited him the following morning he was so weak that it required electric tests to discover life and even these were for a time unavailing Finally, however, the physician concluded that life was yet present, and as the disease was broken, it required only great care and constant nursing from that time on to insure his recovery That he recovered at all appears to be due about equally to Mr Siskind's great natural strength and to the devotion of his brave wife, whose attentions never flagged Mr Siskind eventually went back to work, although for some time he was obliged to get about on crutches and later with a cane, but in course of time his cure was complete and today he is as well as ever His pleasant relations with his friends and patrons were resumed, and he is undoubtedly at present one of the most popular and successful merchants of the city, enjoying a reputation for integrity and honesty second to none and reaping in full measure the results of his virtues He is a member of Shary Telfilah Temple and order Sons of Zion, being a trustee of the former and the presiding officer of the latter He is also a member of the Fraternal Order of Eagles and of the Order of Owls

Philip Siskind was united in marriage April 3, 1897, in New York City, with Rachel Weiner, a daughter of Benjamin and Tema Weiner, of that city He and his wife are the parents of one daughter, Sarah, born February 5, 1909, in Perth Amboy New Jersey

Mr Siskind has been a frequent contributor to the local newspapers, some of his articles attracting considerable attention, especially one on woman's suffrage and one predicting in 1914 a general European war Mr Siskind has made it his policy to please his customers, and his advice to all men is characteristic of his own cheerful and optimistic nature To all men he says 'Be happy do not lose confidence, never say I am lost, approach everybody with a smile don't lose self respect, honor everybody and love your neighbor as yourself "

HARRY WOLF GREENSPAN—Brought by his parents to the United States when a boy of six years, Mr Greenspan, now a substantial resident of Perth Amboy, New Jersey, and established in the grocery business at No 265 Smith street, has but a dim personal knowledge of any other land than this He is a man of energy, has prospered through his own efforts and enterprise, and fairly won his way to success

Harry Wolf Greenspan was born in Russia the son of Philip and Rebecca (Uterman) Greenspan, who are both residents of New York City Harry W Greenspan, upon being brought to this country by his parents attended the public schools of New York City until he was fourteen years of age, when he entered the business world in the capacity of grocery clerk in Perth Amboy, New Jersey, where he remained until he was twenty years old He then went into business on his own account and established himself in the grocery business at No 265 Smith street, and has continued with success in this ever since In the affairs of the community he holds an intense interest, but has never entered politics He is a member of the Young Men's Hebrew Association and is also a member of the Jewish Synagogue

Mr Greenspan married May Spewack, September 15, 1920 In business activities and in his life as a citizen, Harry Wolf Greenspan has made himself one of the men who count in his community, and everything indicates that the years to come will bring him larger opportunities of service resulting in successes more noteworthy and more fruitful than those of the past

---

TYCHO THORVALD FILSKOV —With a number of brothers and sisters residing in Denmark and with his mother, Agatha Filskov, still living at her home in that country, Tycho Thorvald Filskov is the only member of a large family of children to come to the United States The father, Johannes Filskov, was the proprietor of a general store in his home town in Denmark, where he died many years ago. He and his wife were the parents of nine children Johanne, a school teacher in Denmark, Alfred, a minister, Elisabeth, Lorenz, Johannes, president of a bank in Denmark Christine Axel, a steamship engineer, Tycho, the editor of a newspaper, and Tycho Thorvald, of further mention

Tycho Thorvald Filskov received an excellent education in his native land, first in the public schools and later in the University of Copenhagen, from which he graduated when twenty-one years old Coming to this country almost immediately after his graduation Tycho Thorvald Filskov landed in New York City, in 1892, and for some time was located there In 1894 he went to Jersey City, where he was employed with the Lehigh Valley Railroad Company, remaining with them until 1896, then returning to New York City, he was engaged in several different engineering concerns for a number of years, eventually coming to South Amboy to accept a position with the Raritan River Railroad Company as chief engineer This was in 1914 and two years later he was appointed superintendent of the railroad still serving as its chief engineer Mr Filskov afterwards became a director of the company and is still holding this office with them

In addition to his business interests, Mr Filskov is a lover of out-of-door amusements, driving his own automobile being his favorite form of recreation He and his family are all members of the Presbyterian church

Tycho Thorvald Filskov married in Jersey City, New Jersey, in 1894, Marie Holm a native of Denmark where her father and mother were born and where they died Mr and Mrs Filskov have had two children, both now living   1 Harold, born August 13, 1896 a graduate of Stevens Institute of Technology at Hoboken in the class of 1918, receiving the degree of mechanical engineer, he is employed in the office of the Raritan River Railroad Company with his father, as assistant engineer 2 Alfred born June 11 1898 a graduate of Stevens Institute, class of 1919, he is in the office of a consulting engineer in Newark, New Jersey The family home is at No 302 Main street, South Amboy.

JACOB GOLDBERGER —In that part of Hungary now the independent State of Czecho Slovakia, Samuel Aaron Goldberger was living at the time of the birth of his son Jacob, now a successful business man of Perth Amboy, New Jersey. Samuel A Goldberger was a merchant and a land owner in his native land, and served his years of enforced military duty in the Hungarian army, his branch the infantry He married Jennie Klein, and later they came to the United States, he engaging in business in New York City as a merchant After his retirement, he moved to Perth Amboy, New Jersey

Jacob Goldberger was born December 13, 1861, in Tuchrina, Czecho Slovakia (formerly Hungary), Europe, and there passed the first seventeen years of his life He was educated in private schools and advanced so rapidly that at the age of thirteen he was himself a teacher, tutoring children At the age of sixteen he was engaged in clerical work in Miskolcz, Hungary, there continuing until August, 1878, when a flood devastated that section and swept away all his possessions. He then returned to the parental home but not long afterward came to the United States, sailing from Hull, England, on the steamship "Queen Ann," arriving at Castle Garden in New York Harbor November 13, 1878 His first year in New York was employed in serving a newspaper route, after which he learned a trade at which he was employed six years Afterward he was engaged with a wholesale produce house in Hudson street, New York, until March 12, 1888 (the period of the great blizzard in New York City) when he removed to Perth Amboy, New Jersey, that city ever since having been his home.

After locating in Perth Amboy he opened a grocery store with a foreign exchange department, at the southwest corner of High street and DeKalb avenue (the site now occupied by the Standard Underground Cable Company) his brother, Max Goldberger, being his business partner For three years they continued at the original stand, then erected a three-story brick building at the corner of State and Washington streets, where they continued the same lines until 1905 when the brothers dissolved partnership and divided the business, Jacob taking the foreign exchange and steamship ticket brokerage business and continuing at the old stand State and Washington streets He is duly authorized to conduct a banking business under the laws of the State of New Jersey and successfully conducts a banking department in connection with foreign exchange and steamship tickets He conducts a general business in the sale of steamship and railroad tickets, purchase and sale of foreign money, making remittances to all parts of the world issuing letters of credit and travelers' checks He is agent for all companies of the Mediterranean and Continental Conferences and negotiates a general business along these lines He is also a director of the Perth Amboy Trust Company, and has other business interests

In politics Mr Goldberger is a Republican In religion, he with his family worships with the Congregation Beth Mordecai, of which he was one of the founders, first vice-president and now a trustee He is affiliated with Lawrence Lodge No 62 Independent Order of Odd Fellows United Hebrew Lodge, has been treasurer of the Order of Brith Abraham, director of Young Men's Hebrew Association, and member of Young Men's Christian Association His clubs are the Progress and Republican, of Perth Amboy

Mr Goldberger married, in New York City, December 2, 1888, Jennie Fried, daughter of Leopold and Hannah Fried Mr and Mrs Goldberger are the parents of five children Morris L, born October 1, 1889, Hannah Sarah, born December 25, 1890, married Maurice P. Rosenberg, Dorothy, born August 23 1892, married Joseph Goodman, Bernard, born June 1, 1896, Regina Hilda, born August 2, 1904

SIDNEY JACOBSON, proprietor of the Hub Clothing Store, and one of the successful merchants of Perth Amboy, New Jersey, was born October 10, 1890, in Russia, and is a son of Ireen and Sarah (Novoi) Jacobson, who were likewise natives of that country The elder Mr Jacobson was engaged in the business of lumber transportation for many years, and died at his home in Russia at the age of sixty-two years He and his wife had the following children Nathan, Samuel, who now resides in Perth Amboy Leo, also of that city, Sidney, with whose career we are here concerned, Becky, who became the wife of Morris Wilkin, of Perth Amboy, Rose, who makes her home in Perth Amboy, Solomon, who also resides there After the death of her husband, Mrs. Jacobson left Russia came with her family of children to the United States and settled in Perth Amboy, where she still resides.

The first thirteen years of Sidney Jacobson's life were passed in Russia, and there he gained his early education, but he was still a boy when the family removed to this country after his father's death, and when the new home was made in Perth Amboy he continued his studies, attending night school in New York City His brother, Nathan Jacobson, started a clothing store in the neighborhood, and the lad worked for him as a clerk for eight years, and during that time gained a very complete knowledge of the business He was then offered an excellent position with the Hub Clothing Store, which he accepted For two years he acted as manager of that thriving establishment, and on February 24, 1915, purchased the business and as its proprietor continued his personal supervision thereof Since becoming its owner Mr Jacobson has more than doubled the size of the store and greatly enlarged its stock and equipment In 1919 he purchased a store adjacent to his own and thus increased his space to a degree that was more commensurate with his developing business Yet more recently he opened a branch establishment at Nos 84 and 86 Main street, Woodbridge, New Jersey, which has already developed a prosperous trade in that community Mr Jacobson has always interested himself in the general life of his adopted community, and is a member of the local branches of the Royal Arcanum and the Order of Maccabees

Sidney Jacobson was united in marriage, October 10, 1915, in Brooklyn, New York, with Anna Finkel, a native of New York City, a daughter of Hyman and Esther Finkel, the former deceased and the latter still a resident of that place Mr and Mrs Jacobson are the parents of two children, as follows Mortimer, born November 1, 1916, and Adele, born November 5, 1920 He resides at No 150 State street, Perth Amboy

AUGUST ROHDE—A prominent figure in the life of Sayreville, New Jersey, is August Rohde, who since coming to the community in 1881 has always espoused and given earnest support to all movements calculated to advance its welfare

August Rohde was born June 10, 1861, in Germany, the son of Charles and Annie (Young) Rohde When a young man he came to Sayreville, and in 1890 purchased the Peoples' Hotel, which he has continued to manage ever since Mr Rohde is also owner and manager of the Arctic ice plant in New Brunswick The success which has attended his efforts has been self-made in the truest sense of the word, the result of his own indefatigable effort and his own unfailing belief in his ability to succeed In politics he is a staunch Democrat, and takes an active part in the affairs of the organization, serving at the present time (1920), as chairman of the township committee and president of the Board of Health Mr Rohde is also a director of the South River Bank He is well known in fraternal circles, being a member of St Stephen's Lodge No 63, Free and Accepted Masons, the Independent Order of Odd Fellows; and New Brunswick Lodge Benevolent and Protective Order of Elks His religious affiliations are with the Presbyterians

On July 24, 1887 Mr Rohde was united in marriage with Margaret Houlthausen, a native of New York City, born April 28, 1868 Mr and Mrs Rohde are the parents of four children · William, born December 8, 1890, Anna, born June 14, 1894, Richard, born July 21, 1896; Nina born July 31, 1899

GEORGE SIMON—Automobile owners in the vicinity are becoming well acquainted with George Simon's garage, on New Brunswick avenue, Perth Amboy Mr Simon is a genial, alert man of business, and skilled in handling the automobile work Although only comparatively recently in this line of business, he is already winning success

Mr Simon's father was born in Austria, and came to America when a young man He is now a resident of Fords New Jersey, having retired from the milk business, in which he has spent practically all his life His wife, Annie (Ondrick) Simon, was also born in Austria-Hungary, and died in Fords, at the age of sixty-two years They were the parents of seven children, all of whom are living in Perth Amboy or Fords except Lizzie They are as follows Mary, George, Bertha, Lizzie Alice, Annie, Joseph

George Simon was born in Austria-Hungary, March 1, 1882 He came to America alone, in 1907, to join his father, who had made the change two years previously Mr Simon worked for a time as a grocery clerk, but not caring for the business obtained work on the wrecking train This work he followed for some years, and in 1918 branched out and established a business venture of his own This is proving a decided success as all who see the young man in his garage at No 567 New Brunswick avenue will acknowledge Mr Simon is well fitted for the work and is meeting the needs of a wide range of people

Mr Simon married, in Fords New Jersey, September 14, 1902, Annie

Woga, who was born in Austria-Hungary. Her father was born and died there. Her mother was also born there, she survives him still residing there. Mr and Mrs Simon are the parents of seven children, but one died in infancy. Those living are Julius, born in 1903, John, born in 1905, Alice, born in 1907; Alexander, born in 1910, Steve, born in 1913 and William born in 1916. The family are members of the Greek Catholic church.

HARRY S EISNER—There is still alive in the world the spirit that founded in the Western Hemisphere a government where men might find independence of speech and action, and this is exemplified in Harry S Eisner who left Russia for America at the age of seventeen to join his brothers and sister.

Isaac Moses Eisner, father of Harry S Eisner, was born, and is now living in Russia. He is a scholarly man and a successful school teacher. He married Sarah Trachefsky, also a Russian by birth, who died in Russia in February, 1904, at the age of fifty-six years. They were the parents of eight children all of whom are now living.

Harry S Eisner was born in Russia, March 11 1889. He received a thorough education there, completing the high school course. Coming to America when seventeen, he located directly in Perth Amboy New Jersey and took a position in one of the factories. Knowing himself capable of better things, he took the first opportunity that offered in the business world, becoming salesman and collector for the Singer Sewing Machine Company, throughout Middlesex county. He followed this business for nine years, winning valuable experience, and by industry and economy accumulating a small capital. In 1916 he established a wholesale confectionery and stationery business. He had formed a wide business acquaintance, and with his natural business ability success was merely a matter of time, and the venture promised well from the start. Then came the world appeal to American manhood, and Mr Eisner was one of the first to respond. He gave up the business into which he had put all his hopes for the future, and enlisted for the cause which demanded America's best. Fortunately he returned, and undaunted by the first loss, he began again under the name of the Lorraine Sweets Company, along the same line of business. His friends look with gratification upon the promising new start. His war record, in outline, comprises his enlistment in 1918 in the United States army. He was in the service nine months serving in the infantry at Camp Dix, then was transferred to the Emplacement Camp, Lee, Virginia. He returned on January 11 1919 and established his present business.

Mr Eisner is a member of the American Legion, Post No 45, the Benevolent and Protective Order of Elks, Perth Amboy Lodge No 784, the Young Men's Hebrew Association, the Young Men's Christian Association, and the Hebrew Progressive Association.

Mr Eisner married, October 26 1919, Elizabeth, daughter of Solomon and Sarah Papov. She was born in Boston, Massachusetts. Her parents now reside in Dorchester Massachusetts. On August 18, 1920, they be ⋯

MICHAEL ZYLKA —The life story of Michael Zylka, of Perth Amboy, New Jersey is an interesting one which had its beginning in Galicia, Europe, more than half a century ago. He came to the United States a stranger, learned the language perfectly, absorbed American ways, and after many years of work and thrift can view with satisfaction the results he has attained. He is a prosperous undertaker of Perth Amboy, doing business in his own building and is a substantial citizen. He is a son of John and Theodosia (Bajko) Zylka, both of whom were born, spent their lives and died in Galicia. They were the parents of ten children, Mary, Marko, and Tekla yet living in Galicia, Simon in New York City, and Michael in Perth Amboy.

Michael Zylka was born in Galicia, September 28, 1869 and there spent the years of his minority. In 1891 he came to the United States and made his way to McKeesport, Western Pennsylvania. From there he went to Wilmerding, Pennsylvania, where he worked in the Westinghouse shops for two years, also studying and mastering the English tongue without a teacher. In 1897 he came to Elizabeth, New Jersey, and three years later went with the Singer Sewing Machine Company, remaining six years. He then took up the undertaking business studied embalming and on April 17 1905, opened an undertaking establishment at No. 531 State street Perth Amboy, later moving to No. 526 State street, and in 1912 to his present location, No. 511 State street; he also owns the adjoining property No. 513. He has a well improved plant with modern equipment. For two terms Mr. Zylka served as a member of the Perth Amboy Board of Health, and since 1911 has been a member of the Benevolent and Protective Order of Elks. He is a member of the Greek Catholic church and of the Roman Catholic societies.

Mr. Zylka married, in Elizabeth, May 21, 1900, Rose Gadek, born in Galicia her parents both dying there before their daughter's marriage. Mr. and Mrs. Zylka are the parents of eight children William died aged eighteen years, John died aged four years Olga now a high school student; Irene, now a grammar school student, Stephania, in grammar school Daisy in intermediate grade, Antone in intermediate grade, baby, died in infancy.

JENS TOFTE HANSEN, a successful merchant of Perth Amboy, New Jersey where he is engaged in business as a clothier and haberdasher is a native of Denmark. His father Hans Hansen was born in Denmark and his mother Mette Christina (Tofte) Hansen was a native of Copenhagen. To Mr and Mrs Hansen were born six children: Christian, deceased, Eilen Petrea Carl; Jens Tofte, of further mention and Johannes.

Jens Tofte Hansen, son of Hans and Mette Christina Tofte) Hansen, was born in Denmark July 18 1863. He obtained his education in the public schools of his native place and then worked on his father's farm for a few years. In 1888 at the age of twenty-five years he set sail for America and upon landing in New York went immediately to Omaha, Nebraska, where he remained until 1890. when he came to

Perth Amboy, New Jersey, and secured employment as a clerk in a local grocery store   Two years later he became clerk for Louis Briggs, clothier, and was with this firm for twelve years, but desirous of establishing in this line of business he opened a small clothing store at No 308 State street, later moving to No 73 Smith street, then to No 109 Smith street, and in 1915 came to his present location, No 183 Smith street   It has been due exclusively to his own efforts that his business has grown to its present large proportions and he is looked upon by his associates and fellow-citizens as a most capable business man and substantial merchant   He is a member of the Independent Order of Odd Fellows, and in religion is a Lutheran

Mr Hansen married (first) July 4, 1888 Methea Madsen, a native of Esbjerg, Denmark   Mrs Hansen died in Perth Amboy, New Jersey, May 10, 1894   To Mr and Mrs Hansen were born three children Christina Tofte wife of Frank Van Pelt, of Tottenville, Johanna Tofte, wife of Olaf Neilsen, of Perth Amboy, Ellen Tofte wife of Carl Carlson, of Perth Amboy   Mr Hansen married (second) March 21, 1896, Anna Jensen, of Perth Amboy, who died June 20, 1918   Mr and Mrs Hansen were the parents of four children   Emmanuel, who during the World War was a member of the 29th Division of the 104th Supply Train, drove a truck for eleven months in France, and is now associated with his father in business, Peter, associated with his father, Mary, wife of Hugo Kahree, of Perth Amboy, Wesley Von Qualen an electrician of Perth Amboy

---

WILLIAM TESTA—When a lad of fifteen William Testa of Perth Amboy, but a native son of Italy, came to the United States and in course of time established a business in Perth Amboy   When the World War engulfed the United States in 1917, and the opportunity came for military service, he enlisted, virtually sacrificing the business he had built up so carefully and laboriously   But he served his adopted country overseas and returned in safety, and again began the work of building up a business of his own   He has succeeded very well, made many friends and "Billy's Tire Shop" is well known, well patronized and well liked by its many patrons   He is a son of Emidas Testa, born in Italy, now living in his native land a blacksmith by trade   Emidas Testa married Julia Grilli, yet living in Italy, and they were the parents of five children William, of further mention, Pasqualina, living in Italy, Menica, Sisto, a fine mechanic associated with his brother William, and Settineo, residing in Italy, the children are all unmarried save William

William Testa was born in Force, Italy, June 29, 1889, and there attended school until he was fifteen years of age, when he came to the United States finding a home and employment in New Castle, Pennsylvania where for a year he worked in a box factory going thence to Philadelphia Pennsylvania, where he spent two years with the Quaker City Rubber Company manufacturers and dealers in rubber, engine room supplies, hose, packings, tires etc   There he obtained his knowledge of the rubber business, and after two years in New Brunswick,

New Jersey, where he gained an expert knowledge of vulcanizing and other features of the rubber business, he opened a shop under his own name in Perth Amboy. That was in 1914, and until his entrance into the United States army in 1917 he diligently applied himself to the upbuilding of the business. When he enlisted, he turned it over to others, was sent overseas with the 87th Division, American Expeditionary Forces, and served until the armistice was signed. He returned home with an honorable discharge from the United States army, and at once resumed business at No. 148 New Brunswick avenue, Perth Amboy, his place known as "Billy's Tire Shop."

Mr. Testa is a member of the Raritan Yacht Club, and St. Peter's Roman Catholic Church. He married, August 6, 1919, in Perth Amboy, Lulu Ricci, born in Perth Amboy, daughter of Elesis Ricci, a famous sculptor of New York City, and his wife, Rosa (Lund) Ricci.

PHILLIP BORAK is among those of foreign birth who have become prominent business men in Perth Amboy, New Jersey, and he has always based his business principles and actions upon strict adherence to the rules that govern industry and strict integrity. His enterprise and progressive spirit have made him a typical American in every sense of the word, and he well deserves mention in a work treating of the business life and substantial development of this community.

Israel Borak, father of Phillip Borak, was born in Russia, came to this country when a young man and settled in Perth Amboy, where for a number of years previous to his death, which occurred November 24, 1919, he carried on a successful dry goods business. He married Ida Magaram, a Russian by birth, and they were the parents of the following children: 1. Annie, who is the wife of Hyman Weeden. 2. Jennie, who is the wife of Hyman Greenspan. 3. Monte, mentioned elsewhere in this work. 4. Phillip, of further mention. 5. Samuel, of further mention. 6. Bessie, unmarried, resides at home.

Phillip Borak, son of Israel and Ida (Magaram) Borak, was born in Russia, in 1883, and when he was twelve years old came to this country with his mother, his brother Samuel, and his sister Bessie. Upon landing in New York they came immediately to Perth Amboy, New Jersey, where they have ever since resided. Phillip Borak assisted in the support of the family, and for a time sold merchandise throughout Middlesex county. At the age of sixteen he secured work with A. Belafsky, with whom he remained for a time, but being a young man of serious ambition he was eager to establish himself in business, so with what little capital he had secured he started a wholesale and retail meat and produce business at the corner of Broad and Division streets, Perth Amboy, and in 1908 moved to his present location, No. 269 Smith street, where he carries on a successful enterprise at the present time, his genius for business manifesting itself unmistakably. Mr. Borak is also interested in the real estate business and much of his time is spent along this line, his brother Samuel being most concerned in the management of the meat market. Mr. Borak joined Raritan Lodge, No. 61, Free

and Accepted Masons, in 1914 Since then he has also become affiliated
with Chapter, No 41, Royal Arch Masons, Council, Royal and Select
Masters, Commandery, Knights Templar, Valley of Jersey City Consistory, Ancient Accepted Scottish Rite, and the Ancient Arabic Order
Nobles of the Mystic Shrine He is also a member of the Benevolent
and Protective Order of Elks and of the Independent Order of Brith
Abraham

Mr Borak married, February 6, 1910, Jennie Tierstein, a native of
Brooklyn, New York, and they have two children Sylvia, born January
14 1911, Regina, born August 21, 1917

With his aptness and adaptability, Phillip Borak has placed himself
among the representative business men of the community, and his reputation as a man of talent and integrity has already gone abroad, he being
considered a leader among the younger generation of business men
today in and around Perth Amboy

Samuel Borak, son of Israel and Ida (Magaram) Borak, was born in
Russia, December 11, 1889 He came to this country with his mother,
brother and sister, when he was but seven years of age After receiving
an education in the public schools in Perth Amboy, he became associated
with his brother Phillip in the wholesale and retail meat business He
is prominent in Masonic circles, having attained to the thirty-second
degree, is a member of the Benevolent and Protective Order of Elks, and
was one of the organizers of the Young Men's Hebrew Association of
Perth Amboy He married Molly Florence Roth, a native of Perth
Amboy, New Jersey, and they have one child, Helen Sarah, born March
23, 1918

LOUIS BRIEGS, at the age of fourteen, alone and without friends,
came from his home in Germany to seek his fortune in a strange land
among a strange people This was in 1866, and fourteen years later
(1880) he made Perth Amboy, New Jersey his home and business headquarters Eight years later he erected the building which he now occupies with his tailoring establishment, the largest in Middlesex county
Louis Briegs is a son of Karl Briegs, who lived and died in Germany,
a tailor, as was his father and grandfather for several generations Karl
Briegs married Theresa Ingber, who also lived and died in Germany
They were the parents of three children Bernhardt, who died during the
Franco-Prussian War of 1870, Louis, of further mention, Ida, now
widow of A Sutter, who resides in Brooklyn, with three children

Louis Briegs was born in Germany, November 29, 1848, now, at the
age of seventy-two, is an honored resident and merchant of Perth Amboy,
New Jersey He remained in his native land until 1862, then came to the
United States, finding a home in Brooklyn, New York, with his uncle,
Julius Briegs There he learned the tailor's trade and for six years
followed that occupation in Brooklyn, New York, prior to moving to
Keyport, New Jersey, where he was employed as cutter in a clothing
factory, and in 1874 he started in business for himself in partnership with
L Conover In 1880 he located in Perth Amboy and opened a tailoring

establishment, which has grown to vast proportions under his management during the forty years that the Briegs establishment has been a Perth Amboy institution His present residence, located at No 89 Market street, was erected by Louis Briegs in 1900 In political faith Mr. Briegs is a Republican, his religious belief Presbyterian He is a member of the New Jersey Club, the Independent Order of Odd Fellows, Free and Accepted Masons, a Knight Templar and Shriner, Knights of Pythias, and the Benevolent and Protective Order of Elks

Mr Briegs married, in Perth Amboy April 15, 1882, Rosa Hauser, born in Jersey City, daughter of Frederick and Rosina Hauser Mr and Mrs Briegs are the parents of two sons Fred A , and Harold, both born in Perth Amboy

---

JACOB ASTRIN, proprietor of the large wholesale tobacco and confectionery business at No 221 New Brunswick avenue, Perth Amboy, and a prominent citizen of the community, is a native of Russia, born in the town of Semiovonka, December 27, 1887, a son of Nathan and Rhoda (Yahudin) Astrin, old and esteemed residents of that place The elder Mr. Astrin passed his entire life in Russia, and was engaged in the grocery business in Semiovonka, his death occurring there when his son Jacob was a youth He and his wife became the parents of seven children, two of whom are deceased Of the five now living, three daughters, Fannie, Helen and Lena, reside in Russia, while the two sons, Jacob and an elder brother David, make their home in this country

After the father's death Jacob Astrin, then nineteen years of age, came with his mother and brother David to the United States, the latter taking up his abode in Bayonne New Jersey, where he is now engaged in the real estate business. Mrs. Astrin and Jacob, however, came to Perth Amboy, where the youth attended school for a time in order to complete his education begun in Russia, and then secured a position in the handkerchief factory of H Rosenthal & Company of Perth Amboy He worked for one year with this concern and learned the details of the industry, but being of a strongly independent and enterprising turn of mind, he then gave up his position, determined to engage in business on his own account Mr. Astrin was only twenty-one years of age when he established his present industrial enterprise, his place of business being located on Fayette street, but in spite of his youth he displayed marked ability as an organizer and business man and his venture prospered highly In 1917 Mr Astrin removed to his present establishment at No 221 New Brunswick avenue and there the business has continued to increase until it is now one of the important industrial enterprises of Perth Amboy and carries on a large trade in this locality Its success has been wholly due to the capable management of Mr Astrin who has devoted himself to its development with industry and zeal He is a man who is not afraid of work and well earns the respect and confidence he has won in the community, where he is justly known as a self-made man Taking a keen interest in the general welfare of the city, Mr Astrin prefers to remain independent in politics instead of affiliating himself with any political party, but is a member of four fraternal organizations, namely, the Order of Owls, Brith Abraham, Zionists and Independents He attends Shaary Tfilloh Synagogue, and is an active and respected member of the congregation

Jacob Astrin was united in marriage, February 4, 1912 in Perth Amboy, with Rebecca Treegoob, like himself a native of Russia born in 1889, a daughter of Wolf and Martha Flora (Mazer) Treegoob Mrs. Astrin came with her parents to the United States as a child and resided with them up to the time of her marriage in Philadelphia, Pennsylvania, in which city they still make their home

---

MAX ZUCKER, of Perth Amboy, New Jersey, was born in Austria, May 24, 1884 His father, Arthur E Zucker, was born in Austria, there lived and there died in 1904, aged fifty-eight years, a wholesale flour and feed dealer His mother, Pearl Zucker, died when her son Max was two years of age They were the parents of seven children. Rose, wife of N Lenz, of Passaic, New Jersey; Bessie, wife of I Landau, of Passaic, Morris, died in Newark, leaving a family, Isidore, residing in Passaic, Emil, residing in Newark, Samuel, residing in Pawtucket, Rhode Island, and Max, of further mention

Max Zucker spent the first fourteen years of his life in Austria He then came to the United States, unaccompanied by others of his family, and found a home in Newark, New Jersey For two years he was employed in a wholesale store in Newark and during that time he attended public night schools He then established in business in Perth Amboy, New Jersey, at the corner of State and Commerce streets, and in 1904 moved to No 223 Smith street In 1919 he moved to his present residence, No 125 Kearny avenue He is a member of the Benevolent and Protective Order of Elks, the Young Men's Christian Association, and of the congregation Beth Mordecai.

Max Zucker married, in Perth Amboy, May 26, 1906, Henrietta Spitzer, born in New York City, daughter of Mr and Mrs. David Spitzer, of Perth Amboy Mr and Mrs Zucker are the parents of a son, Arthur, born September 10, 1908

GUSTAVUS GUNTHER, when a boy of six years, was brought from Germany to the United States by his parents, Frederick and Pauline (Fischer) Gunther, and during the seventy years which have since intervened Middlesex county, New Jersey has been his home He was still a minor when in 1862 he enlisted in the Union army, and he has never since failed in loyalty to the land which received him as a child and gave him the opportunity to develop his manhood. When Frederick Gunther with his family came to the United States in 1850, he settled in Middlesex county, New Jersey, and became the owner of a farm near Metuchen, upon which he resided until his death That farm has never passed out of the family and is now owned by Henry Gunther, a son of Frederick Gunther, the original Gunther owner In Germany, Frederick Gunther was a cashier in the government postoffice

Gustavus Gunther was born in Germany, March 7, 1844, and there his first six years were passed. He attended the public schools in the vicinity of his father's farm near Metuchen. He early became his father's farm assistant, and when the time came to choose an occupation for himself he decided to continue a farmer. The outbreak of the Civil War in 1861 stirred his ardor, and in 1862, at the age of eighteen years, he enlisted in the Union army for one year. He served out his term of enlistment, was honorably discharged at its expiration, and returned to the farm. There he lived the quiet, contented life of a farmer, prospered, and reared a family. Finally the years grew heavy, and in 1920 he sold his farm and is residing with his son on Magnolia street, Highland Park. He is a member of the Grand Army of the Republic, an independent in politics, and a member of the Reformed church.

Mr. Gunther married, in Stelton, New Jersey, November 20, 1880, Sarah E. Langstaff, born August 28, 1846, daughter of Augustus A. and Rebecca (Fitz Randolph) Langstaff, her father a farmer. Mr. and Mrs. Gunther have three children: Laura, married William Christ; Charles R., married Tillie Everett, six children; Juliet, married Albert Lewis, two children.

LEONARD ZAREMBA—Coming to America, a stranger in a strange land, at the age of fourteen years, Leonard Zaremba has risen from the foot of the ladder and become one of the substantial citizens of Perth Amboy.

John Zaremba, father of Leonard Zaremba, was born in Slovakia, but now lives in Perth Amboy, having retired from active work. His mother, Mary (Stas) Zaremba, was also born in Slovakia, she died March 22, 1915, in Perth Amboy, at the advanced age of seventy-eight years. They were the parents of six children, of whom four are living: John who lives in Plainfield, New Jersey; Frank, a resident of Perth Amboy; Tessie, who is the wife of Steve Romanec, of Perth Amboy; and Leonard of whom further.

Leonard Zaremba, son of John and Mary (Stas) Zaremba, was born in Slovakia, February 6, 1878. He lived there until fourteen years of age, and attended school, then came to America with his father, mother, and sister Tessie. The family came direct to Perth Amboy, where the boy obtained work as a water boy with the Valentine Brick Company. He remained in their employ for eleven months, then for three years worked around at different shops in Perth Amboy, most of that time with the Staten Island Terra Cotta Company, then went to the American Smelting and Refining Company. He was first an ordinary workman for about two years, then was made weigher, and finally scale tester. He remained with this company until 1905, but since then has been in business for himself. Since 1905 his home has been at No. 362 Imslee street.

Mr. Zaremba has long been a citizen of his adopted country, and votes the Republican ticket. He is fond of all outdoor sports, and indulges in a fishing trip when occasional opportunity offers.

Mr. Zaremba married, on April 23, 1901, Anna Danielak, who was born in Slovakia, March 23, 1880 She came to New York City with two sisters when quite young, and lived there until 1901, when she came to Perth Amboy Both her parents died in Slovakia Mr and Mrs Zaremba are the parents of five children Leonard, Jr, born August 7, 1904, Joseph, born August 4, 1906, died November 15, 1907, Anna R, born November 1, 1908, Olga, born September 25, 1913, died April 2, 1917, and Albert John, born May 13, 1920 The family are devout members of the Roman Catholic church

---

SAMUEL HYMAN SIEGEL, D. D. S—Filled with ambitious ideas of the future and with a determination to make use of the many opportunities held out to the immigrant who desires to improve himself, Samuel Hyman Siegel arrived in the United States, May 20, 1904, a lonely lad who had left home and kindred to seek his fortune in the New World, so full of promise

Samuel H Siegel was born in Wilkowischky, Russia, now Lithuania, April 25, 1885 His parents, Kasriel and Mary Siegel, who are the parents of two other sons, one of whom, Maurice Siegel, is a practicing dentist in New Jersey, and three daughters, two of whom are living in Brooklyn, New York, and the oldest in South Africa, were occupied with gardening and farming in Wilkowischky The income from this not being sufficient for the upkeep of the family, Samuel H, the second in order of birth of the children (his sister Sara being the oldest), at the age of twelve, secured work after school hours in a girls' Hebrew school as assistant teacher, the money thus earned being spent partly to pay for his clothes, the remainder being contributed to the family purse He graduated from a Russian public and high school, and also received a thorough knowledge in Hebrew and Talmud, and a good knowledge of the German language and its literature, teaching both Hebrew and German in the school above mentioned After taking up his residence in this country, he became a naturalized citizen, and acquired the English language by attendance at the public evening school He then entered the Baron De Hirsch Trade School, for a two years' course in electricity, from which he graduated, and then worked as an electrician, preparing himself after working hours for matriculation in college After a short period of time he passed the Regents' examination, equivalent to a high school education, and entered the New York College of Dentistry, where he passed all three years with honor, and graduated in 1911 He at once applied for and obtained from the State Board of Dentistry licenses to enable him to practice his profession in both New York and New Jersey. At the time of his study at the New York College of Dentistry, he was assisting in the publication of a Jewish monthly called "The Future" He was also one of the organizers of the Hebrew Dramatic League in New York City, from which league developed many known Jewish actors on the Jewish and English stage, he was very active therein, and participated in performances during the first years of its existence

Dr. Siegel engaged actively in the practice of his profession in Brooklyn, New York, from the time of his graduation until September, 1917, when he removed to New Brunswick, New Jersey, where he opened an office at No. 119 Albany street, corner of George street, remaining there up to the present time (1920). He is a surgeon dentist, is thoroughly equipped in office appointments, progressive and up-to-date in everything pertaining to his profession, and is in receipt of a large and constantly increasing clientele. In addition to his professional duties, he is interested in financial affairs and is connected with the National Bank of New Brunswick and with the New Brunswick Trust Company. He has also contributed various articles on dental topics to dental magazines, namely "The Dental Digest" and "The Dental Outlook," which have been read with great interest, also the "Dental Cosmos." Dr. Siegel is a member of the Hebrew Synagogue, the Allied Dental Societies of New York, the Improved Order of Red Men and the Workmen Circle.

Dr. Siegel married in Brooklyn, New York, December 12, 1910, Yetta Abrams, born in Russia, and they are the parents of three children, Vivian, born August 3, 1914, Alma, born July 21, 1917, and Eleanor, born September 7, 1918. They reside at No. 113 First avenue, Highland Park, the property being purchased by Dr. Siegel in March, 1920.

JOSEPH GREINER, who owns and conducts the handsome barber shop at No. 183A Smith Street, Perth Amboy, is one of those solid practical Americans who are Americans by choice rather than by the accident of circumstance.

His aged father, now eighty years old, was born in Bavaria, and later removed to Alsace. He was a farmer all his life and several years ago retired to a well earned and much needed rest. During the recent war, however, he was compelled to work for two brothers. He still lives in Alsace. He married Katherine Thomann and they were the parents of fourteen children, of whom three now live in America, Peter, a barber, of Woodbridge, New Jersey; Joseph, of whom further mention follows, and Louise, who lives in Brooklyn, New York, and is the wife of William Wengatz. The mother is still living and in good health at the age of seventy-nine.

Joseph Greiner was born March 9, 1869, in Dornach, Alsace, now Dornach-Mulhouse. He remained at home until nineteen years of age, receiving a good education. Striking out for himself at that age, he went to France where he lived for two years following the trade of barber. The appeal of the New World struck him with great force, and others of the younger members of his family shared his enthusiasm. So with two brothers, Louis and Eugene, and a sister, Katherine, he came to America. At first they all located in Woodbridge, New Jersey, where Joseph remained for eighteen months working at his trade. On July 3, 1892, he removed to Perth Amboy and opened a barber shop at No. 200 Smith street. He remained at this location for seven years, win-

ning the confidence and respect of the members of the best families of
the city He next removed to No 175 Smith street, where he remained
for sixteen years In 1916 he removed to his present fine location at
No 185A Smith street, and now has a splendidly equipped shop, with six
chairs, which is conceded to be the best patronized barber shop in Middlesex county On the side he has charge of the building in which his place
of business is located, acting as agent Outside the business world Mr
Greiner has varied interests He is a member of the Royal Arcanum,
the Knights of the Golden Eagle, and the Improved Order of Red Men
He is a Republican in political affiliation

Mr Greiner married (first) Emma Josephine Hirner, who was born
in the famous old city of Stuttgart Germany, she died May 4, 1912, in
Perth Amboy, New Jersey Their children are Emma Josephine, born
October 20, 1893 wife of Ira L Crouse, Sophie Katherine, born August
13, 1895: Lillian Pauline, born August 17, 1897, now the wife of Harold
Gordon Lawton, of Morristown New Jersey, Joseph Nicholas, born
May 21 1902, and Sarah Catherine, born October 11, 1910 Mr Greiner
married (second) Mary Cremer who was born in Cologne

WILLIAM G PRILL—The Prills came to Middlesex county in
1886 and located in South River, where Frederick Prill, father of William
G Prill, was employed as a brickmaker until 1920, when he retired and
moved to Milltown, where he now resides His wife, Julia (Seaman)
Prill, died in Milltown, New Jersey, February 12, 1912

William G Prill was born in Germany, December 3, 1881, and there
spent his early childhood the family coming to South River, New Jersey,
in 1886 He attended public schools, and early learned the confectioner's trade with an expert candy maker of Plainfield, New Jersey He
opened his own candy store in South River in 1899, he then being but
eighteen years of age He operated that store successfully until 1910,
then moved to Milltown and there opened a confectionery store for the
sale of the candies and sweets which he manufactured in his own plant.
He is succeeding in his business undertaking and is one of the prosperous merchants of his town He has an expert knowledge of the manufacturing department of his business, also a fine business judgment
which never fails him His store is at No 452 Main street, Milltown,
New Jersey

SOL RUBENSTEIN—This branch of a well known family came to
the United States from Poland, Europe where both Isaac and Amelia
(Freyer) Rubenstein parents of Sol Rubenstein, of Perth Amboy, New
Jersey, were both born They were married in Poland and there lived
until 1866, when they came to the United States, landing in New York
City There Isaac Rubenstein conducted a dry goods business until
1891, when he moved to Perth Amboy, New Jersey, there continuing
in business until his retirement, when he returned to New York City,
his present home (1921) His wife died in New York, October 4, 1886,
aged forty-two, the mother of five children, as follows Samson, engaged

in the printing and stationery business in New York City, Hattie, wife of Emanuel Goldberg, of New York City, Jennie, wife of M Roseman, of New York City, Sol, of further mention, Flora, wife of M Seamon, of Elmira, New York

Sol Rubenstein was born in New York City, July 22, 1872, and until sixteen years of age attended the public schools In 1888 he became his father's assistant in the dry goods business, and for five years continued under his capable father's business training In 1892 they came to Perth Amboy, New Jersey, and established a store at No 99 Smith street for the sale of gentlemen's furnishing goods, trading under the firm name, Isaac Rubenstein In 1895 they moved the business to State street, where for seven years the business was successfully conducted under the same firm name In 1902 Isaac Rubenstein retired and returned to New York City, and Sol Rubenstein opened a store under his own name at No 77 Smith street In 1907 he moved his business to its present location No 135 Smith street, where he conducts a prosperous business in gentlemen's furnishing goods exclusively, his the largest store of its kind in the city He is a director of the Perth Amboy Building and Loan Association, member of the Masonic order, the Benevolent and Protective Order of Elks Young Men's Christian Association, Beth Mordecai Congregation, and is treasurer of the Progress Club He is a man well and favorably known among his townsmen and ranks with the efficient business men who are upholding the business integrity and fame of Perth Amboy

Mr Rubenstein married, in Perth Amboy, Adele Stricker, born in Bohemia Europe, daughter of Marcus and Barbara Stricker, her parents both deceased, and sister of Joseph E Stricker, prosecuting attorney of Middlesex county, New Jersey

---

ABRAHAM SISKIND, upon arriving at legal age, left his home and native Russia to come to the United States, the land of freedom and promise Sixteen years have since elapsed and he has so well improved the advantages offered that he is one of the prosperous merchants of Perth Amboy, New Jersey He is a son of Nathan Siskind, who died in Mackstowe, Russia, having there spent his entire seventy years of life, and there his widow yet lives aged sixty-eight He was engaged in the lumber business all his active years They were the parents of seven children, of whom Abraham and Rosa (Mrs J Samach, of New York City) are in the United States, Sarah (Mrs Gilbert), is in London, England, the others are living in Russia

Abraham Siskind was born in Mackstowe, Russia, July 25, 1873, and there grew to man's estate After his school years he began working with his father in the lumber business, continuing until 1904 when, having gained his majority, he came to the United States, making the long journey and voyage alone He came direct to Perth Amboy, New Jersey, but later went as far West as Chicago, Illinois, where for eight months he was in the employ of his uncle, a junk dealer The young man then returned to Perth Amboy and established an instalment business under his own name He dealt in wearing apparel and was quite successful, continuing until 1911 when he opened his present store at No 310 State street There he carries a full line of ladies' and children's wearing apparel, and caters to a large trade his business having steadily increased in volume from its opening in 1911 He is a member of Zionists Church and congregation, and of the Hebrew Progressive Association

Mr Siskind married, in New York City, April 25, 1906 Lena Siskind, also born in Mackstowe, Russia and of the same family. Her parents were land holders in Russia, and there both died Mr and Mrs Siskind are the parents of three children all born in Perth Amboy, New Jersey: Anna, born March 29, 1907, Eleanor, born February 27, 1911; Nathan, born February 17, 1914

FRANK BECZA —The oldest hotel in Milltown, is the Middlesex Hotel on Main street, its proprietor for the last six years having been Frank Becza, who purchased the place in 1914, running it very successfully assisted by his wife Mr Becza's death having occurred in the early part of 1920, his widow became the owner and proprietress and is carrying on the business equally well The parents of Frank Becza were George and Mary (Simon) Becza, both born in Austria The father was a farmer, and brought up his son to assist on the farm

Frank Becza was born in Austria, September 24, 1872, and died in Milltown April 13 1920 During his childhood in Austria he received the customary education given in the common schools there After coming to this country he entered into the hotel business and was engaged in it at the time of his death Lodges and clubs did not interest Mr Becza but he was an upholder of the principles of the Republican party, and was a member of the Roman Catholic church, as are also his wife and children Mr Becza was also connected with the Milltown National Bank

Frank Becza was married in South River, New Jersey, November 15, 1899, to Mary Sentill, born in Austria, August 18, 1878 Her parents were John and Teresa (Budnar) Sentill both being Austrians by birth Of this marriage five children, all natives of Milltown, were born. Marie, born October 27 1900, Emma, born April 15, 1904, Julius born, March 4 1906, Ella born August 8, 1911 Steven, born November 14 1913

MARTIN BARTOS was born in Bohemia August 15, 1867 He received his education in that country, remaining there until fifteen years of age

Martin Bartos father of our subject, was born in Bohemia, and died there when the boy was only nine years old His mother came to America leaving him with friends in his native land; he joined her later The elder Martin was a skillful tailor, and also acted as sexton for a Roman Catholic church for twenty-nine years He died at the age of forty-five He married Frances Parik who was born in Bohemia, December 24 1827, and died in Perth Amboy, New Jersey, August 6,

1915. They had seven children: Emily, who died in Brooklyn, New York, at the age of fifty years, Frances, the wife of Anton Jiranek, of Brooklyn. Antonia, a widow, who resides at Perth Amboy, Sophia, Emily, and Annie, all of whom died in infancy, and Martin, of further mention.

Martin Bartos learned the tailor's trade, which his father had followed, in Bohemia, but upon arriving in America he became a cigar-maker. This trade he followed for six years, then came to Perth Amboy and joined his brother-in-law in the liquor business, their location being at No. 299 New Brunswick avenue.

Mr. Bartos' favorite recreations are hunting and fishing, and he takes a three days' hunting trip every season. He is a member of the Benevolent and Protective Order of Elks, and of the Foresters of America, belonging to a New York City lodge.

Mr. Bartos married Mary Zatloukal, who was born in Moravia. Their son, Joseph, was born in Perth Amboy, and now conducts an express business in that city. He was with the American Expeditionary Forces in France during the recent World War.

ABRAHAM ONIKELSKY, one of the principal wholesale produce merchants in Perth Amboy, New Jersey, was born in Poland, November 14, 1870.

Jacob Onikelsky, father of Abraham Onikelsky, was born in Poland, and came to America when a very young man, coming direct to Trenton, New Jersey, where he remained during his lifetime. He was a jewelry merchant all his life and a highly-respected citizen. He died in 1903, at the age of fifty-two years. His wife, Ida, survives him, still living in Trenton, at the age of seventy years. They were the parents of six children, all of whom are living: Abraham, of further mention; Harry, Samuel Isaac, Morris, and Fannie. All are in business.

Abraham Onikelsky lived in Poland until he was thirteen years old, receiving his education there. Coming to America at that age, he at once went to Trenton, remaining there until 1906, and being engaged in the produce business. In 1906 he sold his store at Trenton, and coming to Perth Amboy, embarked in the wholesale produce business. Possessed of excellent judgment and good business ability, Mr. Onikelsky has made a marked success in his chosen line, and handles a large share of the wholesale produce business in this vicinity.

In political convictions, Mr. Onikelsky is a Democrat. He is a member of the Independent Order of Odd Fellows and of the Foresters of America. He is interested in all public affairs and does all in his power to forward any cause which advances the public good.

Mr. Onikelsky married, in November, 1891, in Trenton, Bessie Fishtel, who was born in Poland and came to America with her mother when very young to join her father who had just preceded them. Mrs. Onikelsky is a daughter of the late Max Fishtel, of Trenton, who became very wealthy before he died.

Mr. and Mrs. Onikelsky are the parents of seven children, all living: Solomon R., who is proprietor of the Madison Hotel in Perth Amboy, and is also the proprietor of two very successful motion picture theatres in South Amboy and South River. David, who is associated with his father in business Serena, the wife of Harry Robinson, of Trenton, Isadore, in the wholesale produce business in Perth Amboy, Ethel, living at home, Samuel, a graduate of the Perth Amboy High School, in the class of 1919, and Julia, living at home The family are devoted attendants of the Synagogue

---

JOHN RYMSHA —All honorable success is based upon a definite aim in life and the persistency of purpose which enables one to persevere in a given course regardless of difficulties, obstacles and discouragements There are many self-made men in America whose life record proves this fact, and among them is John Rymsha, president of Rymsha & Company, Incorporated, dealers in coal, wood and ice, with office and yard at No 989 State street, Perth Amboy, New Jersey

John Rymsha is a son of John and Louisa Rymsha, his father for many years a farmer in Poland To Mr and Mrs. Rymsha were born ten children, of which number only four are living Michael, still resides in Poland; Simon a resident of Poland Julia wife of Peter Cheraskawick, of Freeland, Pennsylvania, John, the youngest child, of further mention

John Rymsha was born in Poland, July, 1869, and attended the schools of his native place until he was twelve years of age, when he set sail for America, and upon landing in New York City went immediately to Hazelton, Pennsylvania, where he worked in the mines for a short time, subsequently becoming clerk in a grocery store in Freeland, Pennsylvania In May, 1897, he came to Perth Amboy, New Jersey, and secured employment in Goldberger Brothers' Grocery Store, remaining with this concern for three years, then holding different positions with different concerns In 1913 he established himself in the ice business in Woodbridge, but after a year and one-half he returned to Perth Amboy and transferred the business to its present location at No 989 State street, where he also deals in coal and wood under the firm name of Rymsha & Company, Incorporated Hand and hand with the development of this profitable business, Mr Rymsha is carrying along plans for its perpetuation, and two of his sons are being trained in its every detail The success which has come to him has been fairly earned and achieved through his own force of character, perseverance, indomitable will and business genius He affiliates with the Benevolent and Protective Order of Elks Independent Order of Foresters of America, and the Improved Order of Red Men His hobby for a number of years was fishing but it is now chicken raising

On May 6, 1896, Mr Rymsha was united in marriage with Johanna Spier a native of Eckley, Pennsylvania and the daughter of the late Vincent and Marcella (Turezin) Spier, the latter a resident of Freeland, Pennsylvania Mr and Mrs Rymsha are the parents of three children Alvin J, born March 29, 1897, now associated with his father in business, Leon born May 6, 1903, associated with his father Bernard Vincent, born June 22, 1905 a student in the public schools of Perth Amboy The family home is in Sewaren New Jersey

ANTON MASSOPUST.—There is always particular interest attaching to the life of a man who has turned the tide of success and has shown his ability to cope with others in the daily struggle to reach the coveted goal It is not necessary that the man who achieves this success be made of sterner material than his fellowmen, but there are certain indispensible characteristics that contribute to the prosperity of the individual, these are enterprise, determination, and the ability to recognize and improve opportunities These qualities are elements in the character of Anton Massopust, of the firm of Massopust Brothers & Company, real estate dealers, at No 692 State street, Perth Amboy, New Jersey

Joseph Massopust, father of Anton Massopust, was born in Austria, and died in Perth Amboy in 1906 at the age of sixty-nine years He came with his family to this country in 1885, from which time until his death he resided in Perth Amboy, engaged in the wine business He married Barbara Preissler, an Austrian by birth, and they were the parents of eleven children, of whom the following are residents of this city: Joseph, William; Anton, mentioned below, and Mary, now the wife of A Sieboth Mrs. Massopust passed away in 1892, aged fifty-five years.

Anton Massopust, son of Joseph and Barbara (Preissler) Massopust, was born in Austria, November 1, 1874, and when he was eleven years old he was brought by his parents to the United States Upon landing in this country they came to Perth Amboy, and the lad further pursued his studies in the public schools of the city until 1889, when at the age of fifteen he entered into active life, his first employment being in a brick factory His next position was as clerk in a grocery store, where he remained for two years Mr Massopust was a young man of great ambition and did not find himself content while employed by other men, continually desiring to embark on an enterprise of his own, and this he found possible in 1905, when he organized the real estate firm of Massopust Brothers & Company, at No 692 State street, Perth Amboy In manner quiet, but forceful, his close application to business has been his dominant trait, the result of the organization being largely due to his tenacity of purpose and rare energy Besides holding the office of president of the Massopust Realty Company, Mr Massopust is director of the Raritan Trust Company, and the North Amboy Building and Loan Association, his thorough business qualifications being recognized and in great demand on boards of directors

He ever manifests that lively interest in everything relating to the public welfare, and his adherence to principle is inflexible and unwavering, his readiness to take the initiative being strikingly shown when he came forward but a youth to begin his career in the business arena Mr Massopust is a member of St Mary's Catholic Church, and affiliates with the Benevolent and Protective Order of Elks He was united in marriage with Mary Wabersich, October 10, 1908

HERMAN ELLIS —Working his way up by indefatigable industry and genuine worth, Herman Ellis, of Perth Amboy New Jersey, has risen in the business world from a peddler's cart to a position of dignity, commanding the respect of all with whom he comes in contact

Herman Ellis was born in Russia, in 1865 His father, Daniel Ellis, was born in Russia, and there died, he was in the metal business His mother, Judith, was also a native of Russia They were the parents of twelve children, only two of whom are now living Herman, of further mention, and Rosie, wife of H Fingard, of Winnipeg, Manitoba

Mr Ellis came to this country at the age of twenty-eight years, and located in New York City He began at the foot of the ladder, starting with a peddler's cart But the young man was ambitious, his goal was nothing short of success He was handicapped at first with lack of familiarity with the language and customs of the people with whom he dealt, but with never-failing courtesy, and strict honesty, he won friends and a footing in the business world He worked for six years in New York City, then came to Perth Amboy Here he continued peddling, but not being content to stay down, he gradually handled more and more business, and by economy, industry and foresight, he accumulated considerable capital Then, nineteen years ago, he took up the wholesale iron and metal business and also real estate. Since that time he has forged rapidly forward to success, and now conducts the largest business in his line in Middlesex county.

But Mr Ellis is not wholly the business man Winning his own way, he has not forgotten to lend a hand to other men who are still struggling. He makes a special point of looking out for his countrymen when they come to our shores, and helping them, not only to financial independence, but to a true understanding of American principles and ideals He is a member of every Jewish society and lodge in the city, and is particularly active in the work of such societies as carry out his individual idea of helpfulness and charity He is also a member of the Benevolent and Protective Order of Elks, and of the Woodmen of the World He served one term as health commissioner, and is a director of the South Amboy Trust Company, and the Matawan Bank

Mr Ellis married Freida Kravitz, and they are the parents of three children all living. Sophia, wife of Leo Feldman, of Perth Amboy; Bessie, wife of Harry Marks of New Brunswick, New Jersey, and Sadie, who resides at home The family are devout attendants upon the rites of the synagogue

---

MONTE BORAK.—A man of merit, who owes his position in business circles and public life mainly to his own efforts and whose career is certainly worthy of biographic honors, is Monte Borak, owner and manager of a department store which is located at No 275 Smith street, Perth Amboy, New Jersey.

Monte Borak, son of Israel T and Ida (Magaram) Borak, was born in Russia, January 21, 1881, and attended the public schools of his native place until he was fourteen years of age, when he emigrated to this country and immediately commenced selling merchandise throughout Middlesex county, working in this capacity for three years He then entered a brass factory in New York City, and at the end of one year, opened a restaurant in Long Branch, later returning to Perth Amboy and accepting the position of manager of Wedeen's Department Store, where he remained for fifteen years On February 16, 1918, Mr Borak left this concern and started to supply factories with general merchandise, opening his present store at No 275 Smith street, May 21, 1919 Mr Borak is in the best sense of the term "a self-made man " Beginning when but a youth in a strange city, he has made his way up the ladder of success to the present position which he holds today, which is that of a substantial citizen of the community Mr Borak and his brothers are connected with the real estate business in Perth Amboy to a large extent He is also in the importing and exporting business with South American countries, and contemplates making a trip to South America to complete arrangements he will open an office in New York City at No 104 East Seventeenth street

Mr Borak is affiliated with the Benevolent and Protective Order of Elks, the Young Men's Hebrew Association, and a few other orders What time he can spare from his ever-increasing business demands he spends much of in the open, being particularly fond of fishing and automobiling

Monte Borak married, May 7 1901, Lizzie Charnes, a native of Russia, and daughter of the late Herman and Annie Charnes, of Lakewood, New Jersey Mr and Mrs Borak are the parents of two children: Hyman, born August 17, 1902, and Mollie, born January 6, 1909.

The years that Mr. Borak has spent in Perth Amboy have been years of arduous devotion to promoting his business interests, and as a man whose business capacity is of the highest order, he stands as a valued citizen using his talents and his opportunities to the utmost to promote the welfare of his adopted city

LOUIS PAVLOVSKY, one of the most successful merchants of Perth Amboy, New Jersey, where he is the proprietor of a very large and prosperous meat market and an influential citizen of the community, is a native of Russia, his birth occurring in that country in the village of Zmerinka in the year 1883

Louis Pavlovsky is a son of Peter R and Bessie (Flushman) Pavlovsky, also natives of Russia The elder Mr Pavlovsky came to the United States as a young man, and after residing at West Hoboken, New Jersey, for some time, came to Middlesex county and settled at Perth Amboy Here he established himself in the butcher business, opening a store at No 359 State street, but is now living retired from active life at the age of sixty years, contenting himself with caring for his personal holdings in real estate, which are considerable He and his wife are the parents of three children, as follows Louis, of further mention; Ida, who became the wife of Henry E Jacobs, of Brooklyn, New York, where he is engaged in the drug business, and to whom she has borne three children, and Abraham, who resides at Perth Amboy.

Louis Pavlovsky passed the years of his childhood in his native land, and it was there that he received the elementary portion of his education, attending for that purpose the local schools He was thirteen years of age when he accompanied his parents and the other children on their long journey from Russia to the United States and after arriving in this country, lived for a year at West Hoboken, New Jersey There he continued his education at the public schools, but when fourteen years old, he and the whole family removed to Perth Amboy, where they have continued to reside ever since When his father opened the old meat market, at No 359 State street, the lad began to work there, and served a sort of apprenticeship, in which he learned the details of the business The establishment was continued at its original location for twenty-three years and was then moved to its present location at No 316 State street, where it has remained ever since, a period of fifteen years After the retirement of the elder Mr Pavlovsky, Louis Pavlovsky took over the management of the concern and is still the active head of the business He possesses an unusual business ability, with good judgment and fore-sight, and under his capable direction it has grown to its present large proportions and come to be one of the largest establishments of its kind in the neighborhood Taking example from his father, Mr Pavlovsky has interested himself in local real estate, and has become the owner of much valuable property in and about Perth Amboy, realizing fully that in so flourishing a community, and with a steadily increasing population, the values are obliged to rise He is also active in social circles, and is a member of several fraternal orders, including the Royal Arcanum and the Sons of Zion He attends the synagogue of Shari Tafilo at Perth Amboy

Louis Pavlovsky was united in marriage, July 8, 1906, in New York City with Rose Abramson, like himself a native of Russia, her birth occurring in the city of Kovno and a daughter of Harry and Minnie Abramson Harry Abramson is a rabbi of the synagogue at West Hoboken where he and his family reside Mr and Mrs Pavlovsky are the parents of three children, as follows Mollie B, born April 26, 1907, Elias, born October 26, 1908, and David, born December 31 1909

KEVER MEYER —The enterprising spirit so characteristic of for-eign born men in this country is manifest in Kever Meyer, who has improved his opportunities and by indefatigable energy has worked his way upward to a position among the successful men of Raritan township, Middlesex county, where he is now engaged in agricultural pursuits and in conducting a house which is open during the summer season for the reception of those who seek pleasure and recreation in the country and at the sea shore His activity along these lines has brought to him richly merited prosperity, and he is justly regarded as one of the leading men of his community

Kever Meyer is a native of Austria, born October 8, 1866, son of Henry and Diana Meyer, the former of whom also devoted his attention to the tilling of the soil, the son following in his footsteps Kever Meyer emigrated to this country and located in the vicinity of Rahway, New Jersey, where he purchased a farm consisting of sixty-four acres in the year 1904, which he has since brought to a high state of perfection, the ground yielding bounteous return in the shape of crops of various kinds as the result of his wisely expended efforts. His produce, of high quality, is easily disposed of in the markets of the vicinity, and command good prices. Mr Meyer is Jewish in his religious faith, contributing of his time and means to the church which he attends, in politics the candidates of the Republican party receive from him his loyal support

Mr Meyer married, December 5, 1894, in Newark, New Jersey, Anna Greantall, daughter of Harry Greantall. Mr and Mrs Meyer became the parents of three children, as follows: 1 Celia, born October 21, 1896, became the wife of Morris Robinowitz, and they are the parents of one child, Sydney. 2 Jacob, born March 26, 1898. 3 Harry, born October 14, 1912

JENS PETER KNUDSON.—When Hans Knudson, with his wife, Carrie Sophia (Hansen) Knudson, came from their native Denmark to the United States in 1872, they settled on a farm in Raritan township, Middlesex county, New Jersey, and there their son, Jens Peter Knudson, was born, April 24, 1873. The lad grew up on the farm, was educated in the district school, and early became his father's farm assistant. He remained at the home farm until 1907, when he bought his present farm, which lies within a mile of Metuchen. In 1915 he established a retail milk business and has since conducted both farm and business. He has been successful both as a farmer and business man and is one of the substantial men of his community. He is a Republican in politics, is affiliated with Metuchen Lodge, Free and Accepted Masons, and with the Royal Arcanum

Mr Knudson married, November 26, 1903, in Raritan township, Lily Cook, born September 10, 1873, in New Brunswick, New Jersey, daughter of George T. and Anna E (Townley) Cook, of New Jersey birth. Mr and Mrs Knudson are the parents of four children: Lillian Marie, born November 2, 1904, Irving P, born August 29, 1906, George Theodore, born May 13, 1908, Richard Frank, born January 15, 1912

CHARLES BURGER, now a prosperous farmer of Piscataway township, Middlesex county, New Jersey, was born in Germany, October 17, 1883, son of Nicholas and Margaret (Webber) Burger. The first twenty-eight years of his life Mr Burger spent in his native land, there obtaining a good education and becoming a skilled painter and decorator. In 1911 he came to the United States, bought the Graham farm in Piscataway township, and there has spent the last ten years as a farmer. In politics he is an Independent, and in religious faith a Lutheran

Mr Burger married, in Germany, January 6, 1902, Elizabeth Steinmetz, born in Germany October 6, 1885, daughter of John and Dorothy (Deinan) Steinmetz. Mr and Mrs Burger are the parents of six children: 1 Elizabeth, born October 3, 1903. 2 Carl, born June 22, 1906. 3 Nicholas, born February 1, 1910. 4 John, born September 9, 1915. 5 Emma, born August 9, 1917. 6 Helen, born December 9, 1919

Mid—33

JOHN HENRY WITTNEBERT—The first of the Wittnebert family of whom there is definite information is Ernest Wittnebert, who lived in Germany, a farmer, and there was twice married. By his first marriage he had three children, John Henry, Bernard and Casper, and by his second marriage he had Louis, Andrew, Christian, Godleib, August, Amelia and Hannah. Ernest Wittnebert came to the United States at about the same time his sons and daughters did (about 1850), and bought land with them in Middlesex county, New Jersey, near Metuchen.

The first two sons of Ernest Wittnebert to come to the United States were Bernard and Casper, who arrived in New York City about 1848. In 1850 John Henry Wittnebert came with his half-brothers and sisters, children of Ernest Wittnebert by his second wife. He joined his brothers, Bernard and Casper, in New York City, and for a time worked there, but later, becoming dissatisfied with city life, they moved to New Jersey, locating in different small towns and on farms in Middlesex county, near Metuchen. Since that time that locality has been the principal seat of the Wittneberts who are now numbered among the large and substantial families of that section. Their principal occupation has been farming but whatever the occupation they prospered and are highly respected. Strong in their regard for the land that gave their father a home and opportunity, the members of the present generation have proved their citizenship in every way, and during the World War, 1917-18, several wore the khaki and all responded readily to the demands of the various campaigns and drives.

John Henry Wittnebert and his wife, Anna, were the parents of seven children, all born at the home farm near Metuchen, Middlesex county, New Jersey. 1 Henry F., a farmer at Metuchen, married Emma Smith, of Pennsylvania, and they have two children: Louis H and Florence. 2. Bernard, a butcher of Metuchen, married Ella C Gibson, of Rahway, New Jersey, and they have a daughter, Grace. 3 Otto, a farmer of Metuchen, living at the home of his brother, Henry F. 4 Jennie, married J F Simmons, a baker of Perth Amboy, and they are the parents of four children, Julius, Jeannette, Robert, and William Simmons. Charles, Everett, and Edward Wittnebert, the three other children of John Henry and Anna Wittnebert, died young.

HARRY GOLDBERG—The conservation of odds and ends of manufactured goods, the turning of what would otherwise be wasted into new channels of usefulness, is a worthy industry. Harry Goldberg, in the wholesale junk business which he conducts in Perth Amboy, New Jersey, exemplifies the thrift which the American people as a mass learned only through the exigencies of a great and bitter war.

Mr Goldberg came from Russia alone, with little more than his two hands and his undaunted courage, to make his way to success in the country of his choice. Both his parents were born and died in Russia. The young man came directly to Perth Amboy and immediately turned to the work that came to hand. He established a little business as huckster of vegetables, putting all his energy and business ability into this small beginning This was in 1905, and his first location was at No 406 Washington street. He removed to his present location in 1916 after he had won some measure of success Gradually he changed the nature of his business, taking up the handling of junk as opportunity offered, and for some time past has devoted all his time to this work of retrieving useful material from the discard He is advantageously situated at the intersection of New Brunswick avenue with the Lehigh Valley railway tracks

Mr Goldberg has become a thorough-going American citizen, never failing to exercise his franchise, and voting always for the best man, regardless of party. He is a member of the United Hebrew Lodge, No. 502, Independent Order Brith Abraham.

Mr Goldberg married in Perth Amboy, New Jersey, Jennie Daitz, also a native of Russia, who, like himself, came to this country alone to seek her livelihood They are the parents of three children, all living: Abraham Paul, born March 15, 1907, Fannie, born July 1, 1909, and Nathan, born in 1912 The family worship with the Congregation Sharai Tefiloh

---

MAX S BERNSTEIN—The business men of a village, town or city are the men to whom the residents of the place look to for supplying their daily needs, and therefore they are the men upon whom reliance must be placed, men of good judgment and reliable actions, progressive and enterprising, and among this number is to be found Max S Bernstein, proprietor of a general store in Lincoln, Middlesex county, New Jersey, the recipient of an excellent patronage

Max S Bernstein is a native of Russia, born in the year 1877, a son of Samuel and Sarah (Leviett) Bernstein, also natives of Russia The common schools of his native country furnished him with a practical education, and later, having decided that the opportunities for a business career were better in the New World than the Old, he emigrated to the United States and took up his residence in the State of New Jersey, town of Lincoln, where in 1903 he embarked in business on his own account, opening a general store, of which he has been the proprietor ever since and during the years that have intervened he has built it up largely, adding thereto as his means allowed, and by his courteous treatment of customers, his efforts to furnish them with the best merchandise at the lowest possible figure, he has retained his old trade and gained a considerable new one He is a member of the Jewish church, Jewish Society, and casts his vote for the candidates of the Republican party

Mr Bernstein married, in New York City, Mary Leff, born in Austria, who was brought by her parents, Samuel and Rosa (Waller) Leff, to this country when a child Mr and Mrs Bernstein are the parents of eight children, as follows Harry, Theodore, Nathan, Charles, Abraham, Esther, Anna, and Lillian.

ADDENDA—INDEX

ADDENDA

Madsen, pp 43, 44—Ingfred T Madsen is a director of the City National Bank

Sorensen, pp 206, 207—Jens M Sorensen is a charter member, and for several years has been the president, of the Perth Amboy Rifle Association, which is a branch of the National Rifle Association, and is also active in the shooting matches At the present time (1921) he is the holder for this section of the State of a record of sixteen successive bullseyes on 500 yards, no other Rifleshot has ever shot more than eleven successive bullseyes on 500 yards in Middlesex county

Wilson, pp 273, 274—Raymond P Wilson is also a member of Palestine Lodge No 111, Free and Accepted Masons

---

INDEX

BIOGRAPHICAL

BIOGRAPHICAL

CPSIA information can be obtained at www.ICGtesting.com
Printed in the USA
BVOW031241050212

282214BV00003B/70/P

9 781177 841832